The
Tailor's Daughter

The
Tailor's Daughter

Janice Graham

ST. MARTIN'S PRESS ❧ NEW YORK

THE TAILOR'S DAUGHTER. Copyright © 2006 by Janice Graham. All rights reserved. Printed in the United States of America. No part of this book may be used or reproduced in any manner whatsoever without written permission except in the case of brief quotations embodied in critical articles or reviews. For information, address St. Martin's Press, 175 Fifth Avenue, New York, N.Y. 10010.

www.stmartins.com

The following fashion plates have been reproduced with kind permission:

Pages 34 and 239 from *Victorian Fashions: A Pictorial Archive,* edited by Carol Belanger Grafton, courtesy of Dover Publications; pages 85, 118, and 332 from *English Women's Clothing in the Nineteenth Century,* edited by C. Willett Cunningham, courtesy of Dover Publications; pages 146 and 352 from *Victorian and Edwardian Fashions from "La Mode Illustree,"* edited by JoAnne Olian, courtesy of Dover Publications; pages iii and 304 courtesy of Barbara Williams; pages 204 and 261 *Civil War Gentlemen,* edited by R. L. Shep, courtesy of R. L. Shep Publications.

Book design by Irene Vallye

Library of Congress Cataloging-in-Publication Data

Graham, Janice.
    The tailor's daughter : a novel / Janice Graham.—1st ed.
       p. cm
    ISBN-13: 978-0-312-34913-4
    ISBN-10: 0-312-34913-0
       1. Deaf women—Fiction. 2. Women tailors—Fiction. 3. Single mothers—Fiction. 4. Social classes—Fiction. 5. London (England)—Fiction.
    6. Aristocracy (Social class)—Fiction. I. Title.

PS3557.R1988T35 2006
813'.54—dc22   2005051698

First Edition: October 2006

10 9 8 7 6 5 4 3 2 1

To my dear and faithful friend,

Karen Custer Holthaus

To the Reader

The idea for this story began with a visitation of sorts. Inspiration is a fickle guest; sometimes it pops in out of the blue, sometimes it makes a grudging appearance only after I have spent considerable time researching a topic. Always, I have been awake and conscious. This was different. The character waltzed into my head one night just as I fell asleep, when my mind was absolutely still. There she was, quite vivid and very much her own woman, fitting a coat on a gentleman client. I remember how she ran her hand over his shoulder and down the sleeve in a manner that led me to believe she had some extraordinary power of intuition to compensate for her lack of hearing. Now, I've never had any exposure to tailoring or deafness, and I didn't have the slightest idea who she was or from what mysterious depths she had emerged, but she claimed me, and so I wrote her story.

Although she is a work of fiction, I have attempted to authenticate the era in which she lived as accurately as possible, and I am deeply grateful to those persons who helped me in my task. Many of them have enriched my personal life as well as my story. I am particularly indebted to two distinguished Savile Row tailors, Angus Cundey of the legendary Henry Poole and Andrew Ramroop of Maurice Sedwell, both of whom were so very generous with their time and resources. Sharon Volk, at the Kansas School for the Deaf, introduced me to student Heather Meyer, whose graceful, eloquent signing revealed to me the beauty of the language. A sincere thank-you to David Westerman, my patient and good-humored ASL instructor, and to Roger Quick for fielding questions pertaining to Anglican clergy. Victoria List scholars from all over the world promptly responded to my inquiries: Sally Mitchell, Miranda Morris, Anne Whitfield, Sheldon Goldfarb, Ellen Jordan, and Jill Grey. A special thanks to Professor Nancy West. Barbara Daniel encouraged me in the early stages of researching, and Rhoderic Bannatyne, with his superlative command of the English language, made suggestions that greatly enhanced the text. My deep gratitude to Diane Reverand at St. Martin's Press for believing in this book, and to Loretta Barrett for her friendship and superb guidance.

Chapter One

WE ALL BELIEVED I HAD PASSED THROUGH THE WORST. IT WAS LATE in the summer, and I recall that the room was often stifling hot and the light lingered into the evening. Then the splitting headaches began. I could not tolerate sunlight. I could not bear even the faintest rays without excruciating pain.

People whispered things in my dreams. "It's Indian Oil, darling. I'll just rub a little on your forehead. There, that will help."

"Balsam of Myrrh. It has miraculous healing properties."

These were the last words I ever heard. Strange words that evoked faraway places with caravans of creatures I thought must be camels, taking me to those places where camels live. My godfather, Colonel von Sacher, was there, and I remember being overjoyed to see him again. I told him he mustn't pat me on the head the way he did when I was little, because my neck was very stiff and painful. The light always hurt my eyes, and I wanted it to be night. I asked him if we could travel by night.

Then, at some point, night fell, and it grew cool. I remember my first conscious moments and how it was so very quiet, so peacefully quiet. All that heat and turmoil had passed and I was in my bed and I could feel my body again. Everything was so still. I thought how kind they were, how considerate. No lumbering carts in the street, no hawking cries, no clopping hooves. They had quieted the world so I could rest and get well again.

In my exhausted state following the fever, with my sensibilities weakened, I was not alarmed by the silence around me. I felt hands ministering to me, pressing cool cloths to my forehead, coaxing me with a little broth in a bowl. They kept their voices low so as not to disturb me. At some point I awoke to find the headaches had subsided. My room was dark and very still, and I thought it must be the middle of the night. I felt well enough to attempt to get out of bed, and I managed to stand, although my legs were quite weak. As I drew aside the heavy curtains and stood at the window, I recall the eerie silence that accompanied all these familiar gestures, sounding a vague alarm somewhere in the back of my mind. The sky showed signs of first light, and I could barely distinguish the shapes of figures hurrying by on the pavement below. Then a cab passed by, and I realized I could not hear it. I raised the window—absent was the familiar rattle—and leaned against the railing. After a moment, a cart loaded with coal came down the street. The horses' hooves struck the cobblestones and wheels ground along without a sound.

As I lit a candle and opened the door, I could not immediately bring myself to admit the possibility that I had lost my hearing entirely. I was acutely alert to any sensation that might create noise—the match bursting into flame, my bare feet padding across the cold floor, the swishing of my nightdress as I moved down the hall. At the top of the stairs, a faint dizziness swept over me, but I leaned against the wall and waited for it to pass. I was determined to prove my fears unfounded.

We had taken the lease on our house in Savile Row when I was ten years old and still in the habit of stealing down to the workshop to play when I should have been in bed. I always had to avoid the third step from the bottom. Even the slightest weight caused a protracted and ear-grating squeak, which Mama inevitably heard as she sat at her desk in the drawing room. In six years, the step had never been repaired, and we had all grown quite accustomed to its lament. I set the candle on a table in the hall, lifted my nightdress, and cautiously descended on unsteady legs. I reached the third step and landed on it heavily. Nothing. I rocked back and forth. Not a shred of sound. I continued to the bottom, then turned and climbed back up again, stamping firmly on each step along the way while I steadied myself on the rail. At that moment our housemaid appeared at the top of the stairs in her nightcap and shawl, looking quite rattled and groggy and not knowing what to make of me.

"Oh, Lucy, I'm dreadfully sorry," I said. "I didn't mean to alarm you. It's the step. They repaired it, didn't they? It doesn't squeak anymore."

I didn't hear her reply; I was feeling quite faint all of a sudden. I had overexerted myself, and I could feel another headache coming on.

I caught only a glimpse of Lucy's expression—a raw, unabashed sadness—and then she had her arms around my waist, holding me up, helping me up the stairs. I didn't want to know why there were no sounds anymore. I wanted to crawl back into my bed and go to sleep and wake up and have everything the way it had been before.

WE ALL BELIEVED THE LOSS of my hearing was temporary, that it would return with time—or with the right remedy. I remember everything about the men who came to cure me. They came through my door one after the other, a parade of buffoonery and arrogance, of cold-heartedness and curiosity, of self-serving interest and—on occasion—compassion. Most of them loved their medicine more than they loved humankind. I say this because most of them sought to cure my deafness as though it were not part of me. I scrutinized their faces, hoping to find some sign of genius or of Providence, saying to myself with each new face, *Perhaps this is the one. This man has some special knowledge. This is the man who will cure me.*

I would ask them questions, but since I was so slow to understand their replies, they pushed me out of the conversations and directed their responses to Papa or Aunt Lavinia. I was never told beforehand what they intended to do to me. They expected me to submit to their ministrations like a dumb animal. They applied leeches to my ears and washed them out with foul-smelling liquids; they gave me herbal remedies to swallow, others to be applied in compresses all throughout the day and night. I was given ointments that made the skin crack and peel off, leaving my ears raw and throbbing. I drank concoctions that disgusted me. One doctor we visited clamped wires to my earlobes and shot electrical currents through them until the skin tingled, then burned. When I cried, he increased the current even more. When one outraged doctor failed to hypnotize me, he blamed my deafness on my unwillingness to hear.

As remedies failed, I waged a daily war with despair. I would walk around the house trying to find things that would make a sound that I could hear—tapping a spoon against a glass, clapping my hands, banging big metal ladles against pots and pans in the kitchen. They thought I'd gone quite mad. Papa would be in the sitting room hiding behind his newspaper, ignoring the noise and the tactful entreaties of our housekeeper, Mrs. Scholfield. Only much later did he confess to me that he was trying to conceal his tears.

It was a bleak and terrifying journey from the world of hearing to the world of silence, and I suppose it was only natural that, in my isolation, my attention was drawn to those things I already understood. Tailoring was our world. It was all I had ever known, and nothing else held any interest for me. I first experienced the magic of our trade toddling around Grenfell's dusty workroom, clutching precious scraps of velvet or silk in my tiny fists. They assigned me a little stool in a corner, and there I would occupy myself for long hours, diligently sorting and re-sorting remnants of trimmings and cloth. To the apprentices perched on the tables, it was mere child's play, but Old Crawley used to wink knowingly at me over his spectacles. He was fond of telling Papa how much I resembled him—the way I cocked my head and frowned as I studied my little scraps, debating the velveteen over a sea-green superfine, or perhaps a swatch of white satin and a smidgen of creamy lace. Old Crawley knew my mind.

Ever since I can remember, I have been in thrall to elegance and style. I observed things that slipped by unnoticed to everyone except my father, like a thread hanging from a buttonhole or clumsy shoulder padding. He and I had an eye for perfection, and we could easily be swept to rapture by the suppleness of a doe-skin glove. Even the language of our trade evoked visions of refined elegance. Before I knew what the words meant, I could recite descriptions of garments we were making—Viscount Dupplin's "blue Witney peacoat bound with braid and lined with check Gambroon," Lord Cairn's "Paisley vicuna dressing gown with embossed crow's-feet olivettes." In my young mind, tailors worked magic, and I longed to be one of them.

Ours was a proud tradition dating back to the early seventeen hundreds. I never tired of hearing Grandpa's story—embellished over the years—of how he had come to London from Somerset as a journeyman and set himself up at an inn, bribing noblemen's valets in exchange for their repairs and alterations. My grandfather was a clever and ambitious man, and before long he was able to take a lease on a shop in the City. When mobilized into a regiment during the Napoleonic Wars, he showed up for duty in a uniform he had made himself. His splendid figure amidst the tattered-coat volunteers so impressed the commanding officer that he pulled Grandpa from the ranks and sent him home with an order for twenty uniforms. By the time Napoleon was defeated, Grenfell & Son had a thriving business in the City.

In the beginning, our lives were no different from other prospering families. We had a comfortable place in the society of wealthy manufacturers and merchants whose lives, like our own, were guided by rules of order that assured us wealth on earth as well as in heaven. Our week consisted of six long days of sober work and Sundays of equally long and sober prayer. We were early to bed and early to rise; we looked forward to boiled beef on Wednesdays and roast mutton on Sundays. Papa's only excess was the fine brandy he drank in the office at the back of his shop every Sunday evening.

Then, when I was ten years old, our father decided to give up our shop in the City and take a lease on number 19 Savile Row. At last, we were to join the enclave of fashionable tailors clustered around the Burlington Estate in St. James. I shall never forget that day I first laid eyes on Savile Row, for it marked the passage to so many changes in our lives.

It was the start of the Season, a mild morning in April, and Regent Street was crammed with shoppers. We were stalled for the longest time until the driver maneuvered our barouche around a line of carriages parked outside a palatial emporium. We turned off Conduit Street into Savile Row, and I sat forward with my gloved fingers pressed to the windows.

"Which one is it?" I asked.

"It's at the end," Mama replied. "We're not there yet."

I turned to glance at my brother who sat in the corner with his head buried in a book. At twelve, he fancied himself quite the young man of letters.

"Goodness, Reggie, must you be reading now? Aren't you the least bit curious?"

"Why should I be? 'Nothing to see but streets, streets, streets. Nothing to breathe but streets, streets, streets. Nothing to change the brooding mind, or raise it up.'" He was forever quoting his books to me.

"That sounds like Mr. Dickens," I ventured.

"Right you are."

"Oh, he never has a nice thing to say about London. I don't like him at all."

Mama gestured with a nod. "We're coming up on it now."

Even Reggie closed his book and peered over our bonnets.

I scrutinized the long row of neat brick and stucco houses. Our lease at number nineteen had once belonged to a Dr. Erhardt, a surgeon who had retired to the country. There were other physicians and lawyers who lived nearby, but there were many fashionable tailors as well. Discreetly lettered signs hung over the front entrances, but there were no window displays. It was quite a change from our old street, a bustling thoroughfare fronted with gloviers, milliners, and drapers.

Just around the corner stood the Burlington Arcade, a sublime esplanade of tiny shops. I had never seen it, and Mama had promised we would make a stop. Reggie declined—preferring to stay in the carriage and finish his book, and our driver deposited my mother and me in the Burlington Gardens with the understanding that they would meet us at the other end in Piccadilly Street.

I was so awestruck that I stalled—my feet absolutely refused to carry me forward—and Mama had to pinch my arm to get me moving again. The Burlington Arcade is sheer heaven. It resembles a little covered village with high windows recessed into a vaulted sky. Nowhere will you see shop windows so dazzlingly clean—not a drop of rain or a mote of dust settles on the panes to dull the eye's pleasure. Above each glass-fronted shop is a mezzanine where the shopkeeper resides, and above this are very private and very luxurious accommodations for young gentlemen.

Mama was walking much too briskly, as if she were intent on reaching the other end of the arcade before I broke some rule and had us chased out by the menacing-looking beadle. I freed my hand from her tight grip and dashed over to a display window that had caught my fancy. There, spread out on a looking glass, were the most amazing wares I had ever seen. There were snaffle-chain puppy dog collars in rose gold, and silk-braided leads in a rainbow of colors; on the shelf above, a set of silver embossed brushes were displayed on a cambric and lace kitty bed finished with silk tassels. I was dangerously close to smudging the pane with my nose, but caught myself when I saw my breath cloud the glass and pulled back just in the nick of time.

"Veda," Mama hissed softly, grabbing me by the arm. "Do control yourself."

She fussed over me for a moment, making a pretense of retying my bonnet, and for some reason she seemed a little more relaxed after that. We took our time, pausing in front of Lord's where she admired some very fine gloves tinted the most delicate shade of pink I had ever seen, and a milliner's shop with hats of such extraordinary plumage I thought them better suited for a cock than a lady.

There were two gentlemen lounging outside Lord's as we paused to view the display. They were ever so courteous to Mama and me, stepping politely aside as we approached and tipping their hats. Both were superbly outfitted in blue-black cut silk velveteen morning coats and cream twill trousers. They were immediately joined by a dashing young captain who strode up with his helmet tucked under his arm and his cape thrown back over one shoulder, tapping a silver knobbed whip against the finest riding boots I had ever seen. I was awestruck, the pink gloves forgotten as I absorbed every tiny detail of their dress: the captain's tasseled sword knot, the subtle treatment of black braid trim on the morning coat. Papa says that these are the men who dictate fashion. Fashion is not made in the tailor's cutting room, regardless of what Grandpa likes to believe, but here in the streets of St. James.

My father would have been content to stay in Southampton Row, but Grandpa understood that the opportunity for expansion lay with the wealthy, and the wealthy had moved West. Then there was the prickly matter of Old Pauley, Grandpa's friend and nemesis, who had left the Old City of London years ago and settled in St. James. Old Pauley had become an institution by then; the back room of his shop had evolved over the years into a discreet club. Pauley's Palace it was affectionately called by the elite and titled who gathered there in the afternoon for hock and claret, lounging and smoking cigars in his leather chairs beneath a crystal chandelier he had imported from Venice.

We grew up under Old Pauley's cloud, and my father was always struggling to live up to his standard. Certainly, this is why he decided to transform Dr. Erhardt's surgery at the back of the shop into a private room for lounging, hoping to encourage our clients to casually drop by Grenfell's just as they did Old Pauley's. I liked the room very much. I liked the scent of cigar and leather, and the way Papa displayed a very nice crystal decanter and port glasses on a captain's table beneath a rather badly executed portrait of a race horse given to us by a sporting client in settlement of his bill. There was even a gaming table against the wall, but it was only for show, since Mama forbade cards. I had heard that Fife & Sons provided guest bedrooms on the top floor to accommodate customers visiting from their country estates—and the ladies who sometimes accompanied them. But Mama would never tolerate such impropriety. She felt Papa's little club room was more than adequate for the social whims of his clients.

Grandpa's old friend and client, Colonel von Sacher, was particularly delighted by our new situation and the opportunity to drop by without notice, which he did frequently. Whenever he settled his bulk into a chair following an afternoon riding up and down Rotten Row, he brought into our closed domestic world the swagger and glory of the Empire. Breathing heavily, he would stretch his mud-streaked legs before him, take out a pocket handkerchief to mop his flushed forehead, and proceed to disclose the horrendous sums of money he had lost on disappointing horseflesh. The Colonel loved his horses and his dogs and never had anything good to say about women, but since he was the one who gave me my name, I have always kept a soft spot in my heart for him.

He claimed to have spent his best years in India where he had been a student of the Vedas—the sacred Hindu scriptures in which true knowledge is revealed. I was christened Mary Ann, a good Christian name, but the Colonel was my godfather, and his overbearing insistence on calling me Veda was for many years a matter of serious contention in our family. It wasn't until I grew old enough to talk and emphatically expressed my preference for the name that the matter was settled of its own accord—although I cannot recall why, at the age of four, I was so disposed to like the name.

There was indeed some inexplicable bond between the two of us, and he favored me with privileges little girls rarely enjoy. Whenever he dropped by, he always asked to see me, but he had not the slightest idea how to talk to children. I would sit on the floor beside his chair like a pet, bored by the conversation yet thrilled at being admitted to this exalted masculine sanctum. Most of the time I was ignored. I know my father felt uncomfortable having me in the room, but the Colonel rambled on as if I were not there, and I listened like an invisible spy. He was prone to maudlin discontent, and there were times when he churned himself into a bilious sea of spite. Generally, it was about women.

I recall one particularly dull winter afternoon after we had settled into Savile Row, when the sooty drizzle had confined us indoors, depriving us of our habitual outing to the Burlington Gardens. Colonel von Sacher's arrival was ever so welcome, as I had been pent up in the sitting room since lunch with Aunt Lavinia, stitching letters of the alphabet into a horrid old sampler. Summoned by Papa's apprentice, I slipped into the club room and took my post beside the Colonel who sat with a cigar in his hand and a port on his knee. Papa was with a client; only Grandpa and the Colonel were present.

"I dare say, Edward, I admire a well-turned shoulder as much as the next man, indeed, I do," the Colonel was saying. He paused to allow a coil of grey smoke to roll off his tongue. "Deuce knows, the weaker sex parades itself wonderfully—wonderfully. But the mind—now, then, that's another thing altogether." He stared at the tip of his cigar in severe consternation and then briskly flicked an ash into the plate at his elbow.

"Indeed, sir, God intended man to have the superior mind, no doubt about it," Grandpa replied from his armchair. "Excessive knowledge in a woman is most unbecoming." He leaned forward, took up the decanter, and with a palsied hand began to refill the Colonel's glass.

"Unbecoming? Unbecoming, did you say?" the Colonel barked, causing Grandpa to spill the port.

"Ah, sir, it appears I have missed your meaning as well as your glass," Grandpa answered dryly.

"Confound it, Edward, you should know better," said the Colonel, blotting his damp knee with the handkerchief Grandpa offered.

"Indeed, my friend. I have never known your ideas along these lines to be conventional." Grandpa settled back into his chair, scratching his white mutton chop whiskers and glancing at me with an uncomfortable look.

"The mind is not made for prettiness. It's made for thought," the Colonel said. "And a woman's mind *can*—mark my words, I say *can*—be as trenchant as a man's, if she's given the proper instruments." He carefully circled his lips around the cigar and played with it a moment before he continued. "Oh, there are exceptions to our perfect little specimens of blond loveliness, you know. Although you won't find many here in England, Lord knows. In America, perhaps. Certainly there are in India, among the upper classes of course."

There was silence. Grandpa knew that these occasional swings into nostalgia were best left without comment.

"Veda," the Colonel said, turning to where I slumped with my head in my hands, staring at his rain-splattered boots. He always smelled of boot wax and horses.

"Yes?" I replied, sitting up straight. He rarely spoke to me directly.

"You will live up to your name, won't you, girl?" He threw a warning glance at Grandpa. "I say, Edward, you don't allow her those ladies magazines, do you? I should forbid it, if I were you. Damn sentimental slop. Weakens the mind. Histories are the best antidote for that. Give her histories to read." Then, turning his watery eyes back on me, "And read the newspapers, my dear. Read *The Times*. You may be a mere tailor's daughter, but don't let that taint your mind, child."

I have always wondered if it was perhaps my dark corkscrew curls that convinced him I was to be an exception to his rule of "perfect blond loveliness." Now, looking back with an outlook shaped by my own sorrows, I think he had been terribly disappointed in love, and that he still carried a smoldering passion for a foreign woman of great intelligence.

AFTER WE MOVED TO SAVILE ROW, we were always striving to distinguish ourselves as more than just tailors. From the first night we slept in the new house, it seemed that a division had been drawn between east and west, between past and present. Although I still had an attic room, it was all mine as I was now old enough to leave the nursery and sleep on my own, and Nanny Mulgrove found employment with another family. A new four-poster bed had been ordered for me and wedged under the eaves, along with a small writing desk and chair, a washstand and basin, and a new chest of drawers. I missed Nanny terribly, but I found my new independence to be exhilarating.

Mama decided we should have new servants to reflect our new status, and she replaced everyone except Cook with persons who had been in service to more fashionable West End families—although several maids she interviewed declined employment when they learned we were a tailoring family. Since livery had long been a Grenfell specialty, Papa designed splendid new bottle-green uniforms for our coachman and footman, and our new housekeeping staff were kitted out in fine black wool dresses with silk velvet collars and lace-trimmed white aprons and caps. The first time I saw them attired and assembled in the drawing room, they all looked so smart and proud that for a moment I almost believed us to be a family of rank.

At once, Mama began to discourage visits from our old friends from the City. At the same time, we were clearly not suitable company for our new patrician neighbors. We soon learned that the two briskly stepping young ladies residing at 14 Savile Row were Admiral Lord Seymour's great-nieces, and the old dowager with the ear horn was the author of a series of fashionable silver-spoon novels, which were very popular with the upper classes. Several times a week on our morning excursions to Piccadilly or Regent Street, we would pass the two nieces, one of whom appeared barely older than I, and neither of them ever so much as graced us with a nod. Sometimes from my window I would see them set off together at a rapid pace with quick, mincing steps, chattering away to each other beneath their bonnets, their brown taffeta billowing around them and their ribbons flapping in the autumn breeze, and I thought they looked very much like two smug little squirrels on a daily raid. Their great-uncle came to Papa to be outfitted for court, and Papa dressed him so sublimely that the Admiral sent his coachman to fetch a photographer. Papa graciously endured him for nearly an hour as he strutted around the shop resplendent in black silk velvet tailcoat and breeches with patent leather shoes and a cocked beaver hat while they waited for the photographer to arrive. Even after that, the nieces never once gave a hint of even the slightest association with us.

Chapter Two

OUR EDUCATION WAS A SUBJECT OF MUCH DISCUSSION DURING the first year in Savile Row. With more servants, I was freed from some of the domestic duties that had previously occupied my time. Now, in addition to the uninspiring lessons in composition and grammar and mathematics taught by a stout little Scots governess, I was tortured with German and French by a very unromantic old tutor with smudged spectacles and tufts of grey hair sprouting from his ears. Only my art instructor brought some excitement into the stultified air of our schoolroom. She was a young painter with bohemian sympathies that she cleverly hid from my parents. Every Tuesday and Thursday I watched her from the window of my room charging down Savile Row toward our door with her tartan shawl slipping carelessly from her shoulders and her sketchbooks tucked under her arm, drawing the unwanted attentions of gentlemen in the street—for she was eighteen and heartbreakingly beautiful. Her name was Esther Tigues. Esther possessed a flagrantly rebellious spirit, which I found to be a welcome relief from Mama's cowed reverence for public opinion— Mama who absolutely would not, *could not* do anything that the world pronounced unladylike. Esther was never punctual, and her nails were perpetually paint-stained, although she assured me she scrubbed them raw every evening.

As we grew more familiar, I would beg her to let me tidy her up a bit. We would climb the stairs to my room, and I would sit cross-legged on the floor beneath the window mending her torn petticoats and letting out the side seams of her bodices, for she had been wearing the same dresses for years. Esther, clothed in my dressing gown, would sketch me as I worked. We both enjoyed the arrangement, for watercolors bored me and she was constantly out of repair, which is the way with many people who find something outside themselves better worth studying than their own persons. According to Mama, no respectable Englishwoman would exercise her artistic talent beyond portraiture or landscape painting, but Esther had actually studied in Paris at the *École des Beaux Arts* and had even painted nudes.

It was in her sketchbooks that I saw for the first time the masculine anatomy unclothed, and she always spoke about the human form naturally and objectively, without the slightest hint of repulsion or shame. I was so eager to prove myself worthy of her tutelage that I plunged right in with resolve and quickly overcame my initial shock. My sentiments were confirmed when she informed me that every Christmas, Queen Victoria and Prince Albert offered each other Mulready's chalk drawings of nudes. After that, I was able to admire Esther's work without the slightest twinge of guilt. As my lessons in anatomy progressed, I began to see Grenfell's trade from a new light. Indeed, there were "secrets" to our trade I learned long before I ever cut into my first cloth—most notably the way the masculine bulge tends to lie naturally to one side or the other, and how certain adjustments must be made in a fly-seam according to which side a man "dressed."

It was Esther who introduced me to a system of human proportions that had been observed and studied by Renaissance artists, which led me to wonder why it had never been applied to our trade. Of course my primary interest was how clothing might enhance the human form, how it might hide or correct the faults of an imperfect body that is generally quite lumpy and lopsided, but the sketchbooks Esther brought me were full of the naked torsos of beautiful young men with perfect proportions. They were indeed admirable, but limited in their usefulness. I had always excelled at drawing, but I never aspired to the life of an artist. It was always the way fabric could be molded to the human form that intrigued me, the way a tailor could gently stretch and shape a superfine worsted under the weight of a hissing steam iron to restore a bit of youthful dignity to a slope-shouldered old man.

One evening at dinner I happened to mention the Female School of Design, a college for industrial and applied art at which women learned to design china and book decorations, and—of most interest to me—fashion plates.

"Who's putting these ideas in your head, Veda? Is it Miss Tigues?" Mama asked sharply.

Aunt Lavinia eyed me with alarm. She was Papa's sister, but she shared Mama's rigid sense of propriety.

"Why, I don't know what you mean, Mother," I fibbed, avoiding her gaze. I felt Mama was always looking for a reason to send Esther away.

"That place is a trade school. It's not for ladies." She laid down her fork and peered at me keenly. "Must I remind you, Veda, a woman who works for her bread is not fit for genteel society."

"Yes, ma'am," I said, but it seemed to me such a dishonest thing to say. There was no woman I admired more than Esther, and I knew how hard she worked for her bread. She was paid a miserly four shillings for my two-hour lessons, half what we paid that whisker-eared old French tutor.

Grandpa—who was to dine later at his club with friends—sat in the corner reading a newspaper, which he now rustled noisily before interjecting, "Why must you fret so over the girl's education, Harriet? She's quite accomplished, you know."

"Except for music," Mama pouted, not daring to look at Papa. "It's a shame, truly it is, that the child has never learned the piano." It was a reproach I had heard for years. We were not a musical family. My father was tone-deaf and music was nothing but irksome noise.

"She'll have an inheritance," Grandpa said. "That's all she needs to make a good marriage."

Mama bridled. "I beg your pardon, but she will need associations as well, and forgive my bluntness, Edward, but I shall fret. I shall fret until the day you lay me to rest. It's my moral duty as a mother." Her hand shook nervously as she tried to hoist a creamed onion onto her fork. "It's all about associations. She must meet the right kinds of people." She gave up on the onion and went for her napkin, which she pressed tightly to her lips for a moment—a mannerism she adopted when she needed to calm her nerves. It was one of those quiet little dramas that beleaguered every meal. Her opinions always seemed to annoy Grandpa, and he often did everything to discredit her.

Grandpa returned to his paper in stony silence, and Mama said quietly to Papa, "There's a seminary in Wiltshire I've heard good things about, George. I've been meaning to talk to you about it in private, but since the subject's come up—"

I thought surely I had misunderstood. "For me?"

"Yes, dear."

From across the table, Reggie gave me a searing look. He wanted nothing more than to be sent away to boarding school, but it had been decided long ago that he would be tutored at home. If he were to take over Grenfell's, Reggie would need to learn all levels of tailoring. Remaining at home would allow him to make an early start to his apprenticeship.

"It's a fine establishment—run by Octavia Hill," Mama said to me. "You'd be associating with young ladies of rank, which is very important."

"So I'd live away from home?"

"Yes, dear."

I remember how the news struck me. The roast mutton in my mouth tasted like a wad of shoe leather. I couldn't swallow for fear of choking to death, which I thought might not be so bad.

Aunt Lavinia dabbed at her mouth and turned her daft cow eyes on me as though seeing me in a new light. She rarely spoke out, not even to concur with the most inoffensive and commonplace statements, but she did emit a kind of soft hum when she approved of something, and now she nodded and hummed.

Mama continued, "Veda, I know you're fond of Miss Tigues, but I'd be horrified to think you might strike up friendships with young women of that type." I held my breath, terrified of what might follow.

"Now, now, Harriet," Papa cut in, "I've never heard one word to make me doubt Miss Tigues's reputation, and she is a fine artist, you know." It was he, after all, who had engaged her.

"Oh, I have no objections to her as a tutor, George, and she's very obliging."

Indeed, I thought ruefully, remembering all the time Esther spent on my mother's errands to the boot shop or the stationers, for which she was never paid.

"However," Mama continued, "I should certainly not wish to have Veda mix socially with young women like her."

I liked the idea of going to school, for my friendships in Southampton Row had been severed and I sorely missed the companionship of other girls, but I could not imagine living away from home and Grenfell's—returning only on an occasional weekend and holidays. Nor could I imagine making friends with girls like Lord Seymour's nieces—even if they should desire it.

"If you wish her to go to a boarding school, there's a good establishment up at Nottingham Place," Papa said, and I glanced up to see him throw me a look meant to calm my fears. "It's a day school. A very good institution, I'm told. Dr. Buchanan sends his daughters there." He laid down his napkin and sat back, leveling a warm smile on Mother. Then he rose from his chair and went around the table, leaned down and pressed a tender kiss on the top of her head. That kiss had a much-needed effect. She looked up at him with a half-smile breaking through the gravity of her countenance. She had grown stouter over the years, and her once fresh blond curls were now thinning and dulled with grey, but he loved her still.

"I'll leave the matter in your hands, dear," he said, patting her on the shoulder. "But I do believe that schooling Veda at home is every bit as acceptable as a boarding school. As for her associations, well, that depends a good deal on us. She'll make a good match, Harriet. Indeed she will."

My father, reading my heart that day, knew I had no wish to be sent away. I would have readily forsaken all hopes of girlhood friendships rather than live apart from Grenfell's, with its goose irons steaming on the coal stove and its bundles of garments waiting to be assembled. I had grown up among our cross-legged tailors who spent their days perched on a table like frogs on lily pads, whipping countless unseen stitches. I had hidden behind curtains watching noblemen strike poses before our tall mirrors while Papa chalked up their basted coats. In our streets, we would cross paths with woolen merchants carrying bolts of cloth, and trotters on their way to the buttonhole lady with a bundle of coats and the latest news and gossip. Down Cork Street, or Clifford Street, or Old Burlington Street, I could open a door and find more tailors and cloth merchants, trimmers and pressers. We were our own world, and I never had any desire to leave it.

Whenever an important client had an appointment at our showroom, I would make sure I was at my window at the appointed hour, peering down to get a look at the man as he stepped from his carriage. After all, any bodger could cut cloth from a pattern, but a good tailor had to develop a quick eye to seize at a glance the shape of a lapel or a particularly interesting trimming on a cuff. A tailor is a judicious thief, stealing a line here and a cut there in the time it takes a man to alight from his coach and disappear inside, and then he takes this memory back to the cutting bench and interprets what he has seen with his own particular mark.

I had the eye for this. I remember the first time I caught sight of Lord

Cooling—later appointed Lord Chancellor of the Exchequer—entering Grenfell's on the pavement below. I ran to my writing table and jotted down my impression of his shape, and that evening at dinner I waited patiently until there was a lull in the conversation, and then I asked about the fitting.

"He has very long arms," I commented. Papa's tired eyes lightened with amusement.

"Does he, now?" he replied.

"I'd guess thirty-three inches. Very unfortunate."

Very unfortunate was my father's standard phrase when there was a particularly difficult shape to dress.

"Indeed, thirty-three it is," he said, nodding with subdued pleasure. "So, then, Miss Grenfell, what kind of adjustments might you make?"

"Well, perhaps extend the shoulder," I replied confidently.

"But his shoulders are already very broad."

"Then we could lengthen the coat."

"But then it would make his legs appear short."

"Oh, he's a long-legged man. I think he could bear a little length on the coat."

I was such a pretentious little thing, but Papa always laughed heartily at my pretense. He made me feel ten feet tall.

In both showroom and workroom, my father exacted a neatness that befitted his personal style. There was never a cup of tea to be found sitting around, nor a tape measure misplaced; clutter on the cutting board was intolerable. He would glide by and scoop off anything he deemed unnecessary to the process at hand.

What I admired most about him was that he never allowed himself to be rushed or harried, not even by the most frantic and bullying client, nor did I ever see him strike a servile tone, although there were many men of wealth and rank who tried to exact as much from him. Nor would he accept failure even when faced with such challenging problems as old Lord Henley who had lost both his lower arms with Nelson at the Battle of Trafalgar, or August Greatbatch, a distinguished Member of Parliament with a back so deformed he could not raise his eyes above knee level, or Bishop Miege whose long body and short legs lent him a comical ape-like appearance. My father taught me that it was the most demanding, impossible clients who would push a tailor to his greatest successes. If he did not have the originality of some of his rivals, his clients never felt anything less than absolute confidence in his hands.

Tailors are repositories of delicate information, and the tailors of St. James are necessarily the most discreet of all. The relationship between a tailor and his client is as privileged and confidential as that between a parishioner and his priest, and Papa often said he heard things in the fitting room that one would never dare tell a priest. Stories only surfaced after the death of a client, and if we were still dressing the heir, then his secrets went to the grave with him. But we talked within our family. Whenever Papa mentioned a new client, I would steal down to the pattern room after dinner and find his brown paper template where an apprentice had noted every little detail of style and personal preference, as well as names of friends, their title and rank, family anecdotes or scandals, his habitual club, political tendencies, sporting habits, even his favorite port. I would memorize it all.

Chapter Three

I HAD INHERITED OUR FATHER'S TALENTS, BUT MY BROTHER REGGIE had been blessed with our mother's blond loveliness, which I so coveted. His fine, fair countenance seemed to bring the summer sky into a room with him. In the street, girls peeked at him from behind their bonnets and whispered and giggled when he passed. Even Esther confessed once that she found his looks to be absolutely princely. Yet he never showed the slightest interest in girls, and he took no pleasure in his appearance. I never once saw him voluntarily look at himself in the mirror. Whenever he was forced to do so—generally when Papa was fitting him for a new suit— Reggie would adopt an attitude of excruciating boredom and seek to entertain himself by whistling silly tunes or making faces at me. Until he started to shave, I think he groomed himself entirely without the aid of a looking glass.

Mr. Nicholls had come into our service when Reggie was nine. Just down from Oxford, a clergyman with no prospects for a living, he had wished to reside in London rather than pursue the post of curate in a distant provincial parish. He was an odd-looking young man with spectacles and bright red hair he wore long in the Romantic fashion, a fault Papa was willing to overlook as he had excellent recommendations from Oxford and came from an old and respectable lineage—his greatest misfortune being that he was the youngest child of a country squire with four sons. Mama was a little worried about his Methodist persuasion—Mama believing Methodists to be frenzied fanatics given to ranting about miracles and apparitions—but obtaining a young tutor as brilliant and well connected as Mr. Nicholls was a feather in her cap, and she was willing to overlook his zealous tendencies.

At the beginning, even Mr. Nicholls was unaware of my brother's mental gifts. In the workshop, Reggie had acquired a reputation as a serious, well-intentioned boy, but he had not the slightest gift for our trade. He took ever so long to finish a baste, and his stitches were always too loose or uneven. It was clear that his heart was not in his work, and he was often distracted—confusing customers' patterns and cutting into the wrong fabrics. Once he nearly blinded himself when he tried to cool down an overstoked iron by pouring water over the coals. The tailors and cutters were all truly fond of him, but they must have doubted his ability to take over the firm. Yet, not a word of misgiving was ever breathed to Papa who never doubted his son's promise. Reggie would be a master tailor. He was a Grenfell, and hard work would do the rest.

Several years after our move to Savile Row, Grandpa and Aunt Lavinia went to live in Kensington with my Aunt Mary, Papa's widowed elder sister. It was difficult for Grandpa to remove himself from the daily operations of the firm, but we all believed the retirement would benefit his health. Thus we found ourselves reduced to a family of four. The fact that there were fewer watchful eyes undoubtedly contributed to Reggie's downfall. Although at twelve I was still very much under my mother's thumb, Reggie, at fourteen, came and went as he pleased.

What I first noticed was the steady accrual of books in his room, beginning with Latin and Greek grammars, and the Bible and prayer books, followed by editions of Homer and Virgil—first in translation, but later in the original.

Once, very late at night, I peeked into his room and found him at his desk hunched over a much-used leather-bound volume, thumbing through a dictionary as he jotted words into a notebook. A candle sputtered only inches from his face, so close I feared his soft-falling blond curls might catch fire—but Reggie seemed oblivious to the danger.

"Ah, my dear Vevey," he sighed when he noticed me in the doorway in my nightdress. "What are you doing out of bed?"

"A cart woke me, and I couldn't sleep." I yawned wide. "I thought perhaps you were up."

I had heard Papa complain that Reggie was always falling asleep in the workroom. I knew why, but I wasn't about to tattle.

"Yes, indeed, I'm still awake," he said, rubbing his eyes with his knuckles.

"You'll ruin your eyes with all this reading, you know."

He straightened and stretched his legs, then laid down his pen. "The translations come quite easily now. Mr. Nicholls says I'm nearly fluent."

"What are you translating?"

"Homer's *Iliad*. From the Greek."

I padded barefoot across the rug and peered over his shoulder.

"What strange letters," I exclaimed. "But they're very pretty," I rushed to add. "Goodness gracious me, you don't mean to say you can read this—"

"Indeed, I can. Mr. Nicholls is an excellent tutor, no doubt about it. I used to want to go away to school, do you remember? But I'm quite pleased the way things have turned out."

"You're very happy in your books, aren't you?"

"Oh, yes. I'm in another world. I can almost forget my throbbing fingers."

"O, Redgepedge, let me see," I said, reaching for his hand and holding it up to the candlelight. "Are they all needle-pricked?" He winced as I touched a swollen fingertip.

"That brute Crawley tied back my finger." Crawley was Papa's senior tailor. He'd spent forty-three years with his back bowed over his folded knee.

"It helps you hold the position with the thimble," I explained.

"I know, but it's so sore it hurts to hold my pen."

"You'll get calluses," I said lightly, trying to be sympathetic. "Then it won't hurt."

"I'll end up with deformed hands just like Father's," he said with distaste.

"Don't you want to be a tailor?" I asked.

"I hate it. I hate what we do."

"You can't mean that," I said, a little stunned by his frank admission.

"Oh, but I do. I'm useless at it. You know it. Everybody knows it except Father. Or rather Father knows but he refuses to see."

"It takes time. It will come. You'll see."

"I have no talent for the craft. Not like you."

We were quiet for a moment. I gazed down at his ink-stained fingers and the Greek letters, thinking how different we were from each other.

He went on, "You used to slip down to the showroom and I'd hide on the stairs and watch you play. You'd prowl around a mannequin with a tape measure around your neck, slashing the air with your chalk. I could hear you muttering to yourself, and you sounded just like Father."

"Once you locked me in the pattern room."

"I was ever so sorry later."

"Yes, and you always made it up to me. You would copy lines from your poems and leave them on my bed."

"Ah, yes, but you didn't care much for my poems."

"Of course I did. But I liked the ribbons better. Once you gave me a pink one with tiny satin rosettes. That was my favorite."

We were thoughtful for a moment, both of us staring silently at the flickering candle.

"I was jealous, you know," he said.

"Jealous? You were jealous of me?"

"Father always gloated over you."

"I don't want him to love me more than you, but I can't help it, Reggie. I can't change the way I am."

"I wouldn't want you to change a hair on your head."

"What will become of Grenfell's?" I said, stifling a yawn.

"Oh, you can have it," he teased, the gravity lifting. "Dress yourself in a fine coat and silk cravat and take over the shop."

"How scandalous!" I giggled. "Can you imagine?"

"I can imagine anything from you."

"But truly, Reggie, you can't abandon Papa. You're not serious, are you?"

I gave a violent shiver, and he gave me a pat on the hand. "The only thing I'm serious about is sending you back to bed, little sister. Go now, before you turn into an icicle."

OVER THE YEARS THAT FOLLOWED, under the influence of Robert Burns and John Dryden, and Homer and Dante, I watched him emerge from his chrysalis of timidity. As silks and satins were the stuff from which my dreams were fashioned, so books were to him. Mr. Nicholls arranged for him to procure reading material from a lending library operated by a bookseller in Regent Street, and he so prized his young pupil that he used money from his own small stipend to buy newspapers and magazines for Reggie. Reggie treasured any book that was his own. Knowing this, at Christmas, after thoughtful consultation with Mr. Nicholls, I always gave Reggie a recommended translation or new edition, which pleased him ever so much. I felt Reggie was terribly unappreciated by Papa, who made no effort to understand him. Papa generally gave Reggie dressing table accessories, such as buttonhooks, stud dishes, or manicure sets—the kind of thing for which Reggie had no use whatsoever. They were gifts to the son Papa wished to have, not the son he had.

By the age of fifteen, Reggie had read all the works of Byron, Wordsworth, and Sir Walter Scott, and had a thorough grounding in ancient and modern history. By then his aptitude for serious studies was known to our family, although it was rarely discussed. I think Papa was frightened of Reggie's precocious brilliance, and he disregarded his accomplishments. As a result, Reggie was very shy around Papa. But what a different creature he was in the company of young scholars! He talked brilliantly with his tutor on a number of subjects absolutely foreign to Papa and the rest of us, and among Mr. Nicholls's friends he was known for his extraordinary imagination and subtle wit. When Reggie turned sixteen, Mr. Nicholls began entreating Papa to send him to Oxford, opining that Reggie showed the genius and promise of a young Byron. Our father found it all too much to believe, that our mild-mannered Reggie had a head full of historical panoramas writhing with grandiose heroes. Such entreaties only hardened Papa's heart, for it was his wish that Reggie continue in the trade. He would be a tailor.

More and more, Reggie resorted to deception to keep the peace, and out of love for Reggie, I came to be a party in the subterfuge. At night, when the rest of the family had retired, I would steal down to the workshop, light up a gas lantern, and finish whatever work he had left behind. Sometimes it was a baste he had not finished, or a shoulder that had to be carefully stretched and molded. If he left any poorly executed work, I would rip it out and start again. I never once viewed this arrangement as an injustice. I did it willingly, and I even delighted in showing off my skill at the more refined tasks that were executed by senior tailors, for I could never aspire to more than the menial drudgery performed by tailoresses. I generally finished the work in half the time it would have taken Reggie.

Finally, one evening over dinner, in a rare display of temper, Papa denounced Mr. Nicholls as a smug, meddling clergyman who fanned dangerous passions in his young charge and exaggerated the worth of a boy's self-conscious scribbling in order to obstruct the rightful wishes of a father. Whether Papa believed this or not, or was speaking out of frustration, it wounded Reggie to the core. That night, Papa declared an end to Reggie's lessons with Mr. Nicholls. In retaliation, Reggie refused to return to the shop. He shut himself in his room for three days with his head buried in his books. Only I was allowed admittance. Each night before retiring to bed, I brought him cold meat and whatever Cook had set aside for his dinner. He was growing more and more dejected by then, and he was keeping a flask of liquor under his mattress. We never argued, nor did we talk about the difficulties. His room was a sanctuary. He would sit me down, and with trembling hands and a quick, excited voice, he would read me page after page of his hero's exploits. The formidable worlds he created in his poems were nothing like the quiet life he led. I was young and in awe of my brother, but I suspected that behind all this wild beauty lay a mind anchored to reason by a badly frayed rope. He was only seventeen, and he frightened me because I didn't recognize him anymore. I would return each night to my room, drop on my knees, and plead with God until I shook with cold, and then I'd crawl into bed and cry myself to sleep. I wanted him to want what Papa wanted; I didn't want him to be a silly poet. But I knew how wrong we all were.

In the end a compromise was negotiated. The lessons were shortened, although not abandoned altogether, and Mr. Nicholls would tutor Reggie at his own lodging, reducing his fees even more. Papa had finally realized that Reggie would not be forced, but he knew the clergyman's financial difficulties and hoped to make the lessons so unprofitable for Mr. Nicholls that he would eventually give up. But Papa underestimated Mr. Nicholls's willingness to make personal sacrifices in order to encourage Reggie's talents. For another year the lessons continued.

We never knew about the music lessons until the day Esther and I were invited to tea at Mr. Nicholls's lodging. Mr. Nicholls had a piano in his small sitting room, and Reggie played for us. Right away, even with my modest understanding of fine music, I recognized Reggie's achievement. He played a little piece by Chopin that was simple to the ear but required great dexterity and was, according to Mr. Nicholls, quite advanced. He stumbled at places in the piece and grew impatient with one passage that was particularly difficult, but he played with a depth of feeling of which I never suspected him capable. He wrapped his heart around each note and chord, each phrase and pause, as though wooing a mistress.

That afternoon, I finally realized that my brother could no more sit in a workshop whipping stitches than I could play Chopin. Our world was prosaic to him; he would never see the poetry in what we did.

By then, Reggie realized that his dreams of Oxford were hopeless, and despair closed around him like a noose around his throat. I still helped when he found himself overburdened with work from the shop, but now he took the bundles of garments back up to his room. I would visit him after dinner and perch on the side of the bed, with sleeves and collars and back panels spread around me while I stitched away, ever so content to be in his presence. He had begun to drink heavily by then, and I was afraid for him, but I was even more afraid he'd send me away if I didn't hold my tongue, so I said nothing. Sometimes he was so drunk he would rise from his chair, stumble to bed, and collapse unconscious across the tangles of thread and pieces of garments waiting to be basted. I would remove his shoes and wrestle him under the blankets, then continue working at his side until I had finished.

Then, a miracle happened, and my prayers were answered in a most unexpected way. Mother and Father called us in to the breakfast room one morning and announced that Mother was in the family way, and that we could anticipate the arrival of a baby brother or sister in January. Mama had lost one baby not long after my birth, and we had given up hoping for another, so this was indeed joyous news.

"Do you realize that this just might be the little heir Grenfell's needs?" Reggie said to me that evening as he leaned out his window, scanning the soot-blackened rooftops along Savile Row. It was late in September when the air had the fresh feel of autumn and twilight fell early upon us. I was tidying up his room, something I had fallen into the habit of doing.

"It might be a girl," I said, stooping down to retrieve a very filthy stock. "Redgepedge, you must change your linen more often." His appearance, although it had never been tidy, was growing more and more ungentle-manly. "This is nasty." I winced. I slung the stock over my arm, which was already full of shirts and undergarments.

"But if it isn't? If it's a boy?"

"Well, it will be too late."

"Why?"

"Because Papa's getting old."

"Well, he can just totter along until this younger son is old enough to hold a bloody needle!"

"Reggie!"

"I can't do it anymore," he muttered dejectedly. He was sitting on the window ledge lighting up a cigarette, and his hand was trembling as he cupped his fingers around the flame. He exhaled and then plucked a flake of tobacco from his lower lip. "I'll be damned if I'll bury myself in that bloody workroom with a bunch of idiots!"

"Reggie!" I cried, and he turned to me. I was ready to be angry until I saw the look in his eyes. "You're not well," I said, dropping the linen on the floor, ready to take some kind of action, but not knowing what to do. I stood there, wringing my hands. "Shall I send for the doctor?"

"Don't be silly," he scoffed.

"You mustn't drink so much," I whispered. I was sixteen by then and dared to reprimand him.

He paused to watch the lamplighter make his way down the street, and then slowly, with a resolute turn of his head, he leveled me with an absolutely fiendish gaze. "I shall throw myself from this window before I return to that dungeon."

"You'd better not!" I cried. "Papa's right about Mr. Nicholls. He's taught you to be ashamed of us. That's wrong! Papa tailors for gentlemen and noblemen! He's the finest there is! How dare you speak like that of the Grenfell name!"

He seemed amused by my outburst. He flipped his cigarette out the window and stood. He was ever so handsome at that moment. Even unshaven and out of repair with his hair curling every which way and his shirt and trousers terribly wrinkled because he'd slept in them, I found him ever so charming.

"My dear little Vevey, why couldn't this have passed to you?"

"But it did not, and we mustn't question the hand of Providence."

The fiendish hero in him seemed to soften even more with these words. He closed the window, but he remained with his palms pressed against the glass, looking out as though from within a prison.

"You speak like a grown woman. You put me to shame."

"That's not my intent."

"You know I'm in love with him," he stated flatly, his breath fogging the windowpane.

"Yes, I know. I know you worship him. But it will pass. Young men outgrow these things."

He pulled himself to his full height and turned toward me. His eyes were very blue and liquid. "Do they?" He smiled. "How do you know?"

"Esther told me so."

"You're not shocked?"

"It's not unusual to have these kinds of attachments when you're young."

"Did Esther tell you that, too?"

I nodded.

"Well, I don't know if I agree with her, but I do applaud her bohemian spirit." He gave me a doting smile. "You'll make a good match, Veda, I'm sure. You are striking, you know, and you'll have a small fortune. With that, you should be able to marry well. He must be a good man. A wealthy and amiable man. I would have nothing less for such a dear sister."

I do not know what prompted his change of heart, but the next morning, a sober Reggie emerged from his room and appeared in the workshop all shaven and neat and took his place beside Mr. Crawley. That afternoon he wrote a letter to Mr. Nicholls informing him of his desire to discontinue their lessons, and he sent a check for all sums due, plus a sizable bonus.

Seeing such a pronounced and sudden change in his son, Papa was beside himself with relief and pride. I think from that moment on, he forgave Reggie his ineptitude and failures. Now, when our best and most distinguished clients visited the shop, Reggie assisted the fitting. When the Earl of Westmoreland summoned Papa to Whitcomb Hall in Dorset to make a dozen new hunt coats, Papa took Reggie along. Fitted out in Grenfell's best, Reggie looked every bit the young gentleman, and Papa intended to show him off. He was clearly grooming Reggie to follow in his steps.

Reggie no longer needed my help at the end of the day. On the few occasions I tiptoed to his door, the light was out, and he was sleeping.

One night in late October, I was awakened by the sound of a rock striking my window. I threw up the sash and leaned out. In the rain-darkened street below stood the bulk of a black cab. By the light of the lantern swinging from the coach, I watched one man struggling to help another descend. I knew immediately who they were. I lighted a candle, grabbed my shawl, and ran barefoot down to the front door to let them in.

Even in the dark drizzle, with his eyes hidden by his tall hat and his spectacles, I could read the fear on Mr. Nicholls's face. Reggie's hat was gone, and his face was dirty and bloodied and his coat torn.

I silenced my alarm and motioned him up the stairs, leading the way to Reggie's room with my candle.

Once Reggie was on the bed and the door behind us closed, the clergyman sank weak-kneed onto a chair with his hat in his hands. He was pale as a ghost, and I thought he might faint.

"What happened?" I asked while I poured water into a basin and soaked a cloth.

"He came to see me, and I turned him away. Oh, God, I turned him away. I thought I was doing the right thing—"

"Please, sir, tell me quickly, is he hurt badly? Do I need to send for a doctor?"

He sat dazed, gripping the rim of his hat, staring at me through his rain-fogged spectacles as though he had not understood a word I had said.

"Sir, do you know what happened to him?" I repeated sharply, feeling a little inclined to slap some sense into the man. I leaned over my brother and lightly sponged his face. "Does he need a doctor?"

"I think—I think he must have fallen—a riding accident—oh, Lord in heaven, I don't know—"

More than likely, he'd been assaulted—a drunken fight perhaps—but I kept my thoughts to myself.

I could smell the drink on Reggie, and he had been sick as well. His coat was wet, and I thought it was from the rain. I reached for the candle and brought it closer.

"What's this?" I cried. Suddenly it occurred to me the thick odor permeating his clothing was that of fresh blood.

"Here, sir, help me!" I commanded, and I shoved the candle into his hand and frantically unbuttoned Reggie's coat. The buttons were slippery with blood, and it was all over my hands, and his white undershirt was soaked in it.

There were huge great wounds in his stomach.

"I'll go for a doctor," Mr. Nicholls announced. He was still very white, but he was able to muster some degree of self-control.

"Is your cab still outside?"

"Yes—I believe so."

"Go for Dr. Lister. He's just down in Sackville Street. Number Twelve."

I was like a dog on his heels as he pounded down the stairs. I stopped at my parents' room to awaken them and then raced to the basement and informed Cook and our housekeeper, Mrs. Arbuthnot, what had happened. While they dressed, I dashed off to awaken the housemaid, then returned to find Mrs. Arbuthnot lighting a fire in the kitchen stove. She peppered me with questions, but I could tell her and Cook little except that Reggie was upstairs dying. She then hurried upstairs to Reggie's room while Cook sallied around me, grumbling and grousing as if I were in her way, clearly in no mood to indulge me with reassurances. When I heard a coach pull up, I ran to the kitchen window and peered up at the pavement. Dr. Lister had arrived with Mr. Nicholls, and after that there was nothing I could do.

I stood at the foot of the stairs for a few minutes and listened to Mama wailing and Papa shouting at Mr. Nicholls, but I found it all too much to bear. Finally, I crept down to the shop, to Papa's back room, and curled up in the chair where the Colonel always sat. I stayed there for a long while, praying for Reggie. I made bargains with God, the kind we make when we're afraid, offering myself up as a sacrifice to good works and charitable deeds, and promises of a life of purity and devotion. I prayed for fortitude and the courage to bear myself up to where the Almighty might reach me, for I despaired that the Almighty would stretch his hand so low as human hearts were wont to sink.

Under Dr. Lister's ministrations, Reggie fell in and out of consciousness, lingering painfully for nearly two weeks. From what Mr. Nicholls could tell us, and what we gleaned from Reggie's nearly incoherent ramblings, we were able to piece together the tragic tale of that night. Having been turned away from Mr. Nicholls's door, Reggie had gone off on a binge of drunken carousing worthy of one of his heroes. He drank and gambled his way around Piccadilly, first at the Bull and Mouth, then the Lemon Tree, and finally the White Bear, by which time he had accumulated enough winnings to enter a game with Lord Bentley and some young peers who fancied themselves sharper and more skillful at gaming than a tailor on the cob. But luck fell to Reggie that night, and he walked away from the table with even more winnings, including Lord Bentley's horse. Lord Bentley, who could barely stand upright himself, stumbled with

Reggie to the livery stable and turned over the fine beast in a most gentle-manly and honorable fashion. He warned Reggie that the horse was a hunter and high-strung, and not often ridden in town, but that he was worth ten times the wager that had been lost. Reggie trotted away into the cold misty air, intending to return to Mr. Nicholls's place to show off his prize. But he fell into a stupor and remembered nothing along the way ex-cept that it had begun to rain, and the horse had suddenly taken fright. Reggie lost control and was thrown into the air. He came down atop a spiked railing somewhere around Berkeley Square, his body impaled on the wrought-iron spearheads.

It was nothing short of miraculous that Reggie had managed to with-draw himself, slide to the sidewalk, and make his way back to Mr. Nicholls's door, and we hung our hopes on this miracle, thinking that God surely would not have allowed such a thing to happen only to fate him to die in the end.

Other physicians were brought in, and surgery was debated. Reggie was removed to hospital, only to return home the following week with a hope-less prognosis, the wounds having progressed to a severe and fatal inflam-mation of the stomach lining. He was given laudanum and then morphia to ease the pain in the latter days.

Even before his return from hospital, we had begun to worry a good deal about Mama. Her fragile condition and the health of her unborn child were so much in Papa's mind that he insisted she go to stay with Grandpa and my aunts. But after three days in Kensington, unable to bear the anguish of waiting daily for news, she hurried back to Savile Row. She was forbidden by her physician to keep vigil at Reggie's side, but the gloom of his impending death hung over us with all the heaviness of the velvet pall that was already being quietly produced in the workshop below. Mama could not help but be contaminated by that gloom; it was in every-thing we ate, in the air we breathed, in the clasp of a handshake or a kiss on the cheek

Two days after her return, Reggie fell into a coma, and that night it pleased God to release him, to the inexpressible grief of us all.

Nurse and Mrs. Arbuthnot tended to Reggie, washing him and dress-ing him. They cut off locks of his fine blond hair for Mama and Papa and me, and I went in to see him. At first I was afraid, but everything seemed to have changed in the room once his anguished spirit had been released, and I sat peacefully at his bedside for hours on end, embroidering a waistcoat I had begun for him just before his accident. I never really believed he could die, and so it was only at the end that I began thinking of how I might offer him something as a token of my love. Among Reggie's books, I found his Greek grammar, and I set about embroidering the Greek alphabet onto the waistcoat. It would be elegant and discreet—cream silk letters barely visible against the cream silk, but in my rush to finish it before he was lowered into the grave, I made a miserable mess of it all. I who lauded myself on my skill at every needlecraft could not even turn out a simple waistcoat in which to bury my brother. Mr. Nicholls, seeing how distraught I was, suggested the embroidered satin be sewn into a small quilt to fold over his legs, which I did, thus salvaging my gesture if not my pride.

Although we tried to keep the news from her, Mama surmised from the frequency of footsteps going to and from his room that Reggie was gone. Two days later she went into a tedious and prolonged labor. While she lay in her suffering, she could hear the sounds of the workmen carrying the coffin up to his room, and the sounds of their footsteps as they brought it back down with Reggie sealed within.

Reggie's coffin was carried downstairs to the dining room, sealed with wax, lowered into a large oak coffin, and then covered with the black velvet pall. It remained there for two days, beautiful and peaceful under the gas light, while friends and distant cousins and uncles and aunts who had not seen him in years now came to bid him good-bye.

As Mama grew weaker, even Reverend Weightman, who had visited daily since Reggie's accident, always bringing his good warmth and blowsy cheer into our somber household, began to show signs of despair. But no one was cursed with a heavier yoke than Papa, for when Mama's waters burst, he remained at the surgeon's side during his many efforts to get hold of the child which lay cross for the birth. Mama died forty-six hours from the time she took to her bed. The infant died with her.

I recall little of those days leading up to the funerals. Curtains were drawn, lamps were dimmed, and black clothes appeared. Mrs. Arbuthnot saw to it that everything was handled according to the strictest convention, for that was what Mama would have wanted. It was confusing having two coffins in the house at the same time and three deaths to mourn. I stayed in the house for two days until our seamstress, working day and night, got out a proper mourning dress for me. I didn't want to shame Mama. We received hundreds of written condolences from all ranks and positions, from tradesmen to aristocrats, and it fell to me to return thanks. Although the stationers sold printed cards that I could have used, I wanted my mother to be proud, and so I answered every one of them personally, by hand.

Chapter Four

WE NEVER SPOKE OF OUR GRIEF. WE NEVER TALKED OF OUR LOSS. Once we had been a family of four and then, suddenly, we were two. I thought we would never recover. We attended to the superficial, to our heavy symbols of mourning, and limped through the next months in silence—hobbled, vulnerable, and incomplete.

It was, by all accounts, a most dreadful winter, with months of fog and heavy snowfalls rendering the thoroughfares treacherous and the narrow streets impassable. For days Savile Row was completely unapproachable and cut off from the world. A single horse-driven hansom could not make it down our street nor any of the streets around us, and a four-wheeler needed at least a pair abreast. From my window, I watched many a passenger alight from a cab bogged down in a drift and stand shivering in the snow-blown street while the horse strained to pull the carriage free. At Grenfell's, work slowed to a standstill. Tailors and cutters huddled near the coal stoves sipping tea and trying to keep warm. My tutors—all except Esther, naturally—had no inclination to brave the streets, which pleased me ever so much, but left me with vacant hours that I filled threading black ribbon through my underclothes and looking through catalogs for mourning accessories. We were required to have black-edged writing paper and visiting cards, as well as black sealing wax, and the list went on and on. Although I was not yet seventeen, Papa insisted I wear black. Mourning dress is frightfully extravagant, and crape, I soon discovered, is impractical. It creases if you so much as touch it, and it is completely ruined by the slightest drop of moisture. I dared not go out in such weather dressed in proper mourning fashion, for I would have returned with sodden skirts utterly ruined by the snow, and every layer down to my petticoat soaked through.

That winter, to ease me through my bereavement, Esther decided to teach me to dance. Public dancing was out of the question while in deep mourning. Esther pointed out, however, that I would someday emerge from my black cocoon and would need to acquire some social skills. And besides, it seemed the most practical way to keep warm with the temperature in the sitting room in the fifties. Esther thought it best to begin with a quadrille as it is invariably the first dance on the program. We summoned Lucy to help us move back the tables and chairs, and then, with Esther singing and tapping out the rhythm in her stockinged feet while her boots dried in the kitchen, she taught me the series of figures—how to advance and retire, thread the needle, do-si-do, and return to my place.

Twice during those dull winter afternoons, dear Mr. Nicholls came to visit. Although his Methodism shunned dancing, as a child he had learned the quadrille, and out of kindness did consent to be my partner while Esther hummed a lively tune. In the spring, he invited us to tea at his lodgings, and he played Strauss for us on his piano. That's when I heard waltz music for the first time. I shall never forget the exhilaration of the moment, swirling around the room with Esther as my partner while Mr. Nicholls joyously pounded the keys, his red hair flying from side to side and his head working like a metronome gone wild. Esther and I laughed giddily as we spun round and round, knocking into lamps and chairs and caring for nothing but the moment of delirious abandon.

THOSE MONTHS OF DEEP MOURNING while the city lay buried in a bitter winter tested my spirits to their limits. Walks in the Park were out of the question, and we had few fixed social obligations beyond our regular excursions to Kensington to visit Grandpa and his sisters, and attending the eleven o'clock Sunday service at St. James in Piccadilly. Since Mama's death, there were fewer callers, and Papa rarely reciprocated, so that our visitors dwindled in number. The house was becalmed for days on end, and I played countless games of Commerce and Snip with Esther and sought amusement by watching at my window for chunks of snow to avalanche from the rooftops and flatten some poor pedestrian on the narrow pavement below. I thought my father oblivious to my grief and loneliness until one day Esther arrived out of breath with a bundle under her arm and dragged me upstairs to my room where she untied a number of sketches of medieval garb and spread them out across my bed.

"Do you think you might like to make some costumes?"

"Costumes?"

"For Frederick Watts. There's a baroness—she wants her portrait painted dressed as Guinevere, and it's been impossible to find a costume she likes. I overheard him moaning about it at Holland House and I thought of you."

By the time she had said this much I was already at the window holding the sketches up to the light.

"But I'd need a fitting. Several in truth."

"That can be arranged."

"But she can't come here."

"She has a London residence."

"Papa would never allow it."

I could tell she was just waiting for this moment. She clasped her hands and said, "He already has. I sought and obtained his approval."

"Is this true?"

"You can go with an assistant from Grenfell's. There's really nothing improper about it. After all, you'll be in the presence of a lady of the nobility."

Baroness or not, my mother never would have allowed such a thing. From the time we arrived in Savile Row, all her energies were spent making sure I had an education and upbringing that would lift me out of the rank of trade, with the hope of marrying me to a gentleman. Now I would be no better than a seamstress.

Esther said, "It's something to keep you busy. It's not as if you need the work."

I looked up and saw her tender, mournful eyes on me. She had understood my reservations.

"It will be a good distraction." I smiled. "I think I might enjoy it."

But before a fitting could be arranged, the Baroness changed her mind. Rather than Guinevere, she thought she might prefer an Elizabethan costume, and then she set her heart on dressing like Queen Philippa, with her husband in costume as Edward III. She could not make up her mind. After a while, hopes for the enterprise faded from our thoughts.

Then one evening at dinner, Papa brought it up.

"I'm much relieved, Veda, that this whole scheme never came to pass. I think I would have regretted putting you in such a position."

I had been sitting quietly staring at my soup. The broth was tasteless. "I hate to sound like Aunt Lavinia, but I do think Cook's soups are getting worse and worse." I picked up my spoon and fished around the pale liquid. "There's hardly a carrot or turnip to be found. I think you should have a talk with her."

"What I'd really like to talk to you about is having your portrait painted."

I calmly laid down my spoon and looked across the table at him. "Have my portrait painted?"

"It was something your mother always wanted to have done, and I deeply regret not having given her my permission."

All he had of my mother were several miniatures painted when she was much younger.

"Were you thinking of Esther?"

"Miss Tigues? Certainly not," he replied, mildly indignant. "I mean it to be an important portrait. A serious portrait."

"But Esther does serious portraits. She's a very good painter."

"No, no, my dear. The gentleman I have in mind is quite a favorite with society. Son of a Scottish laird. And—" he paused, lifting an index finger to make his point, "he's married to the niece of the Duke of Rutland. Did a portrait of the Queen years ago when she was young."

The Duke of Rutland was one of Grenfell's clients.

I was speechless. My first reaction had been one of indignation, that Esther's talents should be ignored, but then I saw what he was trying to do. He was trying to make amends for that earlier error in judgment. It had only been fate that had saved us from the kind of social bungling that used to plague Mama in her dreams at night.

"You may be a tailor's daughter, but you will not be a seamstress," he pronounced, looking over the rims of his spectacles to emphasize the point. "You shall have your portrait painted by a Lord."

Much to my astonishment, Sir Francis Lamb accepted the commission. That we had been recommended to him by his wife's uncle, the Duke of Rutland, surely had something to do with it. Sir Francis did not generally paint portraits of tailoring families.

If Esther was wounded, she gave no sign of it.

"He's very exclusive, Topsy. It's quite a thing to be painted by Sir Francis," she said. She wrinkled up her nose and added, "He's so accustomed to painting such ugly people and trying to make them look ten times more magnificent than they really look, I can imagine how delighted he'll be to have you as a subject."

"I was hoping it would be you."

"Your father came to me, you know, to ask for suggestions."

"He did?"

"This is to be something grand, by an eminent artist. The painting will be worth something."

I leaned forward and kissed her on the forehead. "Thank you," I whispered.

"I did suggest Rossetti, you know."

"Rossetti? You didn't!"

"Yes. He does occasionally do portraits." Esther had taken classes with Mr. Ford Madox Brown upon her return from Paris, and she knew everyone in the art world—Royal Academicians and Pre-Raphaelites, modern-life realists and madmen who painted fairies. She knew their scandals and muses as well, and she had entertained me with many stories over the years, so that I felt I knew them intimately. But I had never met any of them.

She added, "He's much struck with your appearance."

"Mine?" I started. "When did he see me?"

"Oh, on several occasions," she answered, very mysteriously. "Once, when you dropped me off at Holland House—I was to dine with Mr. Brown and you thought I looked so unkempt that you ran after me to give me your bonnet and shawl—"

"Oh, goodness, yes. I remember."

"Well, Mr. Rossetti was watching from the front hall. He thinks you're a real stunner."

"A stunner?"

"That's his word for a real beauty."

"Me?"

"You have a most extraordinary allure, Vevey."

"I'm a giant!"

"But you carry yourself with grace."

I blushed. "I got that from Papa," I conceded. "I have Papa's gait."

No one had ever before commented so favorably on my appearance. I was dumbstruck.

"He's taken with your hair."

"My hair?"

"He's hair-mad. He has quite singular tastes."

"Indeed!"

"You don't see it, do you, Vevey? How you're growing into a real beauty. And your complexion is exquisite. I'm really quite relieved that you won't be sitting for him. I'm afraid you'd give his poor Lizzie much to worry about."

SIR FRANCIS WAS IN THE country and did not return to London until March, but even then I was still in mourning. I was not at all happy about having my likeness painted in black. "New black is so harsh," I whined to Papa as we followed a butler up a wide central staircase to the studio.

We were led into a vast room that resembled the set of a costume drama. There were animal skins draped over stately chairs, wigs dangling from the tips of jousting spears, entire suits of armor stationed like guards in every corner, with odd bits of furniture and tapestries and old costumes lying about everywhere. The high walls were hung from floor to ceiling with paintings of hunting scenes and portraits of great ladies and fine noblemen.

Sir Francis received us graciously, but even in his smock, surrounded by his artistic clutter, he was very much the aristocrat. He was a slight man with an arrogant bearing—a slender nose and narrow face framed by a well-trimmed beard, and small, delicate hands. Briefly, they discussed my portrait. To my great relief, Papa had no fixed idea of the kind of painting he wanted, but preferred to leave it in the hands of the master.

As soon as my father left, Sir Francis set a pair of spectacles on his nose and then clasped his hands behind his back, striking a fine, gentlemanly pose in his black cut-velvet smock. I felt suddenly very young and shy under such intense scrutiny.

"How old are you, my dear?" he asked.

"I'm sixteen, sir," I replied.

"You're not yet out, are you?" He was staring hard at me.

"No, sir." I paused, and then muscled up the courage to add, "But I don't want to look childish."

"My dear, that would be impossible." He removed his glasses, cleaned the lenses with the edge of his smock, and settled them back on his nose again. "Were you afraid I'd paint you surrounded by toys?"

He did not seem to expect an answer, but indicated with an imperious flutter of his fine fingers that I was to follow him to one end of the studio where a raised platform stood surrounded by a clutter of benches, chairs, props, and easels. He lent me his hand to help me up the stair.

"Just stand there for a moment. Don't move."

While he stood squinting at me and stroking his beard, my eyes swept over the room. There were paintings hanging from the walls and exhibited on easels, and standing on the floor propped three to four deep. All of them without question were men and women of rank. My gaze fell upon one in particular, a very large canvas depicting a grand dark-haired lady in a Malachite-green riding habit, mounted on a silky bay. What on earth could he do with a tailor's daughter?

At that moment, we heard footsteps and voices in the hall. The door was thrown open by the footman, and into the room swept a lady.

"Ah, Lady Hambledon!" he shouted as he whirled around. "What a delightful surprise. Do come in."

Once relieved of her bonnet and gloves, she smoothed down her dark glossy hair, retrieved her cane from the footman, and advanced across the room toward us with a hobbled, uneven gait. The infirmity was the first thing you noticed, but her bearing was so grand and proud that she seemed to wear this defect as though it were an honor bestowed upon her by God. As she approached, I realized it was the very same lady whose portrait I had been gazing upon. I recognized the eyes, wide pools of grey set below a broad, manly forehead. She was not beautiful, but she was the type of woman one could not easily forget.

Sir Francis went forward to meet her, greeting her formally with a bow, but it was evident that theirs was an old and familiar friendship.

"Sir Francis."

"My dear Lady Alice."

She took his arm. "Do forgive the intrusion," she said as he led her to a seat. "I wanted to see how Harry's portrait was coming along."

"If Lord Ormelie would make time in his schedule to sit for it, it might be finished by now."

"Ha! I knew it! I knew he'd try to get out of it!"

He swept aside a scattering of peacock feathers and wilted flowers, and settled her onto a long velvet bench beside the stage where I stood.

"Your son has better things to do," he rejoined before disappearing behind a tall Japanese screen.

She called after him, "Believe me, Sir Francis, he can always find time for those things he enjoys."

Sir Francis emerged with a heavy cow bell in his hand and rang for his servant. "He told me he was designing some new lighthouses up near Whitby."

Lady Hambledon's brow furrowed deeply. "Indeed, yes, the lighthouses. You are quite right. I'd forgotten the lighthouses."

"And what was this about installing steam-heating in Lord Stamford's library?"

"Ah, yes! Which proved quite successful. Lord Stamford was quite happy with the results."

"He's entirely right to throw his energies into problems of domestic economy. Lord Ormelie is quite the modern man."

A smile broke over her face, and her voice modulated to a velvet tenderness. "Oh, yes, my Harry is very much indeed a modern man—but he has a purely medieval soul."

It was something you noticed within minutes of meeting her, the way she loved talking about Harry. When she was not fretting, when she was speaking of his qualities, which were many, her grey eyes seemed to lighten a shade, so that she seemed much younger, and more approachable.

Roberts, a grizzled old servant with a few tenacious wisps of white hair, appeared just then, and Sir Francis shouted, "The chaise, Roberts. The cane chaise. Where is it?"

Then he disappeared with the old man into a corner of the room concealed by high curtains.

Lady Hambledon had finally taken note of me up on the platform. With both hands folded over the silver knob of her cane, she said matter-of-factly, "My son is ever so difficult to track down, you see, and I sometimes find myself playing the spy. It's a most delicate situation for a mother, wouldn't you agree?"

Having been deemed too unimportant to be introduced, I merely curtsied and said, "Yes, ma'am."

"What is your name?"

"Veda Grenfell."

"Veda? That's not a Christian name."

"No, ma'am, it's a Hindu name. It was given me by my godfather. I liked it better than my Christian name."

"Is that so?"

"Yes, ma'am."

"And your parents approved?"

"Not at first, ma'am."

"Then I should think you an obstinate child."

"I have been called as much, ma'am."

This drew a smile of amusement over her face.

She allowed her gaze to drift around the room, assessing the paintings with a shrewd and critical eye. After a moment, she turned back to me, affecting a look of commiseration, and whispered loud enough for me to hear, "His work is rather boring, but you'll not find a better portrait painter." I caught the glint of humor in her eyes as she added, "But then, the fault may very well lie with the subject. I know many of them personally, and I can tell you this—they are not particularly inspiring specimens." She tilted her head, studying me. "You could prove a very interesting subject, however. I do hope he's not going to make you all soulful against some elaborate floral thing."

"I don't know, ma'am."

She glanced back around the room. "I don't see Harry's portrait." Then, raising her cane and jabbing it in my direction, she said, "Miss Grenfell, do come down from there and find that horrid bell of his and ring for Wacey. We must have some tea. We can't wait on Sir Francis. We'll expire for lack of refreshment."

I followed her bidding, lifted my skirts and cautiously descended the stairs, found the cow bell amidst a jumble of paint-stained cloths, and swung it mightily.

As I made to return to the stage, she patted the bench beside her and said, "Come, sit here. You must keep me company since I've been abandoned. That was most ungentlemanly of him, was it not?"

She wrestled her skirts around to make room for me, and I settled down next to her. I found myself again under the close scrutiny of her cool eyes, but at the same time I sensed that she was slowly warming to me. As for myself, I was simply observing, taking in everything about her, and finding her fascinating.

"Grenfell. There was an old archbishop, I recall. Are you a relation?"

"No, ma'am. We're a tailoring family." I added quickly, "In St. James."

Her eyebrows rose, registering a flicker of condescension, and I wondered if she might regret having asked me to share the bench with her, but she only said, "Well, I'm sure your mother doesn't have to go gallivanting around after you, now does she?"

My face collapsed. Her eyes darted down to my black dress and back, and I knew she had understood. I lowered my eyes to my hands folded in my lap, wishing Sir Francis would return. It was a very awkward moment. We are taught to ignore indiscretions of this sort and to avoid airing private troubles in public, so what she did at that moment struck me as remarkable and quite courageous. She reached out and took my hand in hers.

"My goodness." She frowned. "Your hands are like ice."

At that moment, the door opened and a grey-haired housekeeper entered.

"Bring us some tea, Wacey," she commanded, all the while rubbing my hand between hers. "And send up a foot warmer. This young lady's freezing."

As Wacey retreated, there was scuffling behind the curtains, and Sir Francis and Roberts appeared, dragging a gilded chaise into the light. They set it down, spent a moment in discussion, then dragged it back behind the curtain again.

She turned a bemused smile on me and said, "It takes him forever to make up his mind. And then he'll have to set the stage. We might as well make ourselves comfortable." Now she had taken my other hand and was rubbing it briskly. She leaned over and in a conspiratorial tone whispered, "He never lights a fire in here. You'd think for the prices he charges he'd throw in a few pieces of coal."

I laughed, and she said, "There we are! A little laughter!"

"You're very witty, ma'am."

She leaned down again, very dramatically, and said, "I'm only like this when I have a good audience, dear. When I have the right audience, I'm a regular Judy. But mind you, Punch would never have it over me. I'd crack his skull open with one blow of my cane here."

She finally stopped rubbing my hand, which was good because her hands were laden with heavy gold rings and she was inflicting pain along with warmth.

"There," she said, examining my now-flushed hands. "That's better."

"Thank you, ma'am. That was very kind of you."

"You've lost your mother?" she asked gently.

"And my brother," I added. I thought I could be calm about it—I had been laughing just seconds before, but to my absolute horror, tears rose in my eyes.

"Oh, my dear," she said in a grave voice. "Pray do forgive me. I've upset you."

I shook my head violently. "It's all right. Really, it is. You see, I'm never able to talk about it to anyone. Not even to Father."

"And that's quite wrong. Do you have other brothers and sisters?"

I shook my head.

"Just your father?"

I nodded. Then she did a most extraordinary thing. She took me in her arms. Much to my embarrassment, tears broke loose and flowed down my cheeks.

Her embrace was so warm and gentle. I don't recall ever having experienced such spontaneous affection—not from Mother, who had generally shown her approval by a stiff pat on the head, nor Father, whose gestures of love never exceeded a kiss on my forehead or cheek, nor even Esther who treated my grief like a canvas to be painted over.

I wept quietly, my face pressed against her warm bosom, heedless of who she was and where we were, and she held me through it all, until finally, feeling myself wept out, I raised my head and wiped at my eyes.

"Oh, goodness, look what I've done," she said lightly. "Sir Francis will be furious with me. I've ruined you."

I shook my head savagely. "No, no, you haven't."

She fished into her sleeve and withdrew a crisp cambric handkerchief and gave it to me.

"Will you be all right?" she asked.

I nodded, and blew my nose. "I've spoiled your handkerchief."

"My dear, I have hundreds. Please keep it. You can return it next you see me."

She smoothed back my hair, which seemed to have come totally disheveled during my outburst. My mother had never touched me like that. "I hate wearing black," I sobbed, then took a deep breath. "It makes me look like a big ink blot."

Her laughter was young and girlish, and I marveled at how such a strong face could be so softened by the spirit within.

"A big black ink blot." She grinned, fussing with my hair. "I hardly think so." She glanced over her shoulder to see Sir Francis returning with Roberts carrying a long Roman-style bench. At the same time, Wacey marched in followed by two maidservants laden with tea and a warming pan.

"And they all converge on us at once! We'll be warmed and refreshed, and you shall be painted!" She turned my face to her, took the handkerchief from me, and blotted my cheeks. "Don't worry, dear. He'll only do sketches today. You can be as splotchy as you wish. Even if you had measles it would make no difference."

While the servants laid out the tea service, Sir Francis and Roberts busied themselves hoisting backdrops onto the stage. I was in no rush to begin the portrait; I was content where I was, sitting next to Lady Hambledon, sipping tea and eating bread and butter. She had a way of slipping back and forth between grandness and familiarity that might have been disconcerting to others, but once I had been touched by her warmth, I no longer felt the chill of her noble airs.

"That's you, isn't it, ma'am?" I asked, nodding to the painting that stood on a large easel.

"Indeed. When I was young and fearless. Do butter me a piece of bread, dear." I reached for the butter knife and she continued. "That's Hermit. A splendid animal. Splendid. Lord Hambledon's favorite hunting stud. The portrait is really about him, not me. Do you ride, dear?"

"No, ma'am," I said, and passed her the buttered bread. "But my brother does. Or he did. That's how he died."

"How ghastly. I'm so sorry."

"The horse was supposedly some fine hunter. He had belonged to Lord Bentley."

"Lord Bentley? Might the horse have been Dante?"

"Yes, ma'am, it was."

"I knew that horse. He was sired by Hermit. That horse was evil. Absolutely evil. Lord Bentley had no business selling him." She turned to me, her grey eyes widening with sudden revelation. "That was your brother?"

she exclaimed. "That ghastly accident with Dante? That was your brother?"

"Yes, ma'am."

"Oh, my dear. My poor dear. I am so sorry."

"Thank you, ma'am. That's very kind of you to say so."

Our attention was diverted to the stage where Roberts was dusting off a backdrop painted to resemble the Italian countryside, with tall cypresses flowing over distant receding hills. A bench had been stationed between two plaster columns, and Sir Francis whirled around and motioned me to the stage.

"Come, Miss Grenfell. Let's try you out with this."

He reached down to help me up onto the stage and had me sit on the bench.

I looked down to find Lady Hambledon had risen to her feet.

"Sir Francis," she said, hobbling forward with her head angled to one side, "I do think there's something Aurelia-esque about Miss Grenfell. Wouldn't you agree?"

He looked up from the bench he was dusting, studied me for a moment, and said, "You're quite right, Lady Alice. I'd say it's the mouth."

"Yes. She has Aurelia's mouth."

"Who's Aurelia?" I asked.

"Aurelia's my daughter."

"Is she my age?"

"How old are you, dear?"

"Sixteen."

"Only sixteen? Goodness! I'd have given you eighteen or nineteen! Why are you in black?"

"My father wished it so."

"I understand. Yes, I understand perfectly." She nodded kindly. "No, Aurelia is twenty-three now. But I never see her anymore. She's married and lives in France."

I couldn't help but notice the troubled expression that passed over Sir Francis's countenance, for he was standing before me just then. He quickly averted his eyes and struck a pensive pose, with a hand on each hip and his smock gathered behind his back.

"I'll start with some sketches," he announced.

"And I'll be off," said Lady Hambledon. "No—" She waved off Sir

Francis. "I know my way out. You get on with this young lady." She pointed to the foot warmer. "Roberts," she commanded, "the pan is cold. Do make sure it's refilled and placed under her feet."

She approached the stage and said, "You must come to take tea with me at Ellesmere House."

"Thank you, yes." I nodded, and I found myself suddenly dropping to my knees and reaching down for her hand. There was not a second of hesitation. She offered me her own hand most willingly and comfortingly.

"So, the next time you come for a sitting, you'll call on me afterward. I'll send a carriage for you."

"Oh yes, I would like that very much."

"I'll send a note to your father, dear, so he won't think I've stolen you. I have a house very near. I'll be here for the Season. Well, most of it. When I'm not chasing Harry."

"So, Lady Alice, how shall I sit this young lady?" said Sir Francis, bounding nimbly from the platform to stand beside her.

She took a step back. Leaning on her cane thoughtfully, she said, "Whatever you do with her, make sure you paint her full of courage and promise."

Then she turned and crossed the room, her lopsided frame rocking back and forth with each step, and there traveled with her an aura of dignity even the Queen did not possess.

In my mind, I could see her goading that bay over hedgerows he had no inclination to jump.

Chapter Five

LADY HAMBLEDON WAS NOT ONE OF THOSE MANY PEOPLE WHO, acting in the zeal of the moment, promises great things and then delivers nothing once that charitable ardor has cooled. After my next sitting, I found a carriage waiting for me and was driven directly to Ellesmere House, the St. James residence of Lord and Lady Hambledon.

I was led through an entrance hall filled with rugs and darkish paintings of hunting scenes, past the daunting glare of a massive stag's head, up a winding staircase to Lady Hambledon's drawing room overlooking Green Park. She awaited me seated on a rather unusual chair, a high-backed ancient thing of carved black wood that might have been plundered from a monastery or a feudal hall, with her feet resting on a regal-looking footstool. Apart from this artifact, everything else about the room was quite simple. The walls were hung with watercolors of flowers and birds, garden scenes and interiors, and there were countless portraits and sketches of Harry and Aurelia. Even the furniture was designed for comfort and intimacy, and I could not imagine it as a reception room for grand ladies and noblemen. Certainly those rooms existed in Ellesmere House, but I never saw them.

"Miss Grenfell!" she cried with a childlike glee. I was tempted to run to her and throw my arms around her, but I restrained myself.

"Your Grace," I said, performing my most graceful curtsey.

"Oh, do come give me a little kiss. I'm sorely in need of kisses this afternoon."

I obliged and bent down, and kissed her gently on her soft cheek.

"You are a tall thing, aren't you?" She smiled, giving my hand a squeeze before I removed myself to a sofa.

"Yes, ma'am," and then I found myself blurting out, "And I have awfully big feet." Immediately I wanted to kick myself, it was such a vulgar thing to say, but she only laughed.

"That's to be expected, dear. Your feet must be in proportion to your height. According to Harry. He's very knowledgeable about those things. Besides, you carry yourself most proudly, dear. Yes, I've noticed. I've noticed a good deal about you. Mark my words, it's the bearing that matters. Not these little defects with which God in his wisdom has burdened us."

She was referring to herself, and it humbled me. "Yes, ma'am," I said.

There was a knock, and a footman entered carrying two tiny brown-and-white spaniels, one in each arm.

"There they are, my darlings! Did they have a good brisk walk, Johns? Oh, look how their eyes sparkle! Here, give me Waverly. Give Ivanhoe to Miss Grenfell. You don't mind, do you, dear? Surely you love dogs."

I didn't, but I supposed I could learn. "We've never had pets, ma'am," I said, taking the fluffy little thing in my arms.

"A dog is not a pet, dear. A dog is quite simply man's most precious companion. These are Harry's dogs."

I shall never forget how Ivanhoe turned his big, brown, soulful eyes up at me and then licked my hand. I cringed inwardly at the bristly tongue—what a queer sensation!—but then the animal curled down in my lap, settled his head on my arm, and heaved a great sigh of contentment. Gingerly, I laid my hand upon his back. He seemed so small and fragile, I feared hurting him, but I stroked him gently and found it to be undeniably pleasant.

"Ivanhoe," I said, half to myself, half to him. I looked up at Lady Hambledon, who was scratching Waverly behind his ear. "Lord Ormelie must be quite a fan of Walter Scott."

Lady Hambledon looked up with sudden interest. "You've read Scott?"

"My brother read all his works. And then after he died, I began to read them, too."

She gave me an encouraging smile. "That must please your brother."

It was an odd reply, and I asked, "Do you think he knows?"

"I'm sure of it, dear."

I looked down at Ivanhoe. "I don't think he made the right decision, do you?"

"Who's that, dear?"

"Ivanhoe. He should have married the Jewess, Rebecca. She had much more character than that insipid little Rowena."

"Ah, you have touched at the heart of the matter, Miss Grenfell."

"Please, ma'am, if you would, call me Veda," I said, hoping I was not exacting an intimacy she did not desire.

But she only smiled and nodded, and seemed quite pleased. "Veda. Yes, indeed, Rebecca had courage, but Rowena—" She gazed thoughtfully at Waverly, then continued, "Rowena is man's perfect woman, you see. Rowena has that air of timidity and dependence that a man finds so utterly charming. That's what distinguishes her from all the other fresh, round, dimpled young things."

"But is that not a weakness?"

"That is the best weakness in the world."

Her words had a troubling effect on me. I cast my eyes down at Ivanhoe and said, "I fear men won't find me so charming. I'm certainly not a Rowena. Not even close."

"Nor am I," she stated flatly.

I raised my eyes expectantly, and she leaned forward, making her point most emphatically with her persuasive grey eyes. "There are exceptions, my dear. There are men who have the courage to take on a courageous woman. There are men who love the Rebeccas."

"Not if they all read Scott," I exclaimed, intending it most earnestly, but she burst out with laughter that filled the room and startled both spaniels.

"Well, it's partly up to us, now, isn't it?" she said. "We must teach them, mustn't we?"

"Which does Lord Ormelie prefer?"

"Right now, Harry's in a Rowena state of mind. But I have confidence in him. He'll come around."

At that moment we were interrupted by the chambermaid's knock.

"It's Lady Wotton and her daughter, Miss Wotton, ma'am."

Lady Hambledon appeared momentarily perturbed, and then a shrewd look lit up her countenance. "Show them in. And you may bring us tea now, Mary."

When the door closed behind Mary, Lady Hambledon turned to me with an air of amusement. "Well, my dear, today you will meet a bit of society. This young lady is a magnificent Rowena in the making. She just came out last Season, and her mother is breathing down Harry's neck like a right old dragon. They know Harry's in town or they wouldn't be calling today."

I straightened and patted at my hair. As always, her observant gaze took note.

"Don't fret, dear. You're quite presentable." She smiled. "You are fond of fashion, are you not?"

I must have looked like one of the spaniels perking up. "Oh, yes, ma'am."

"Well, the conversation will undoubtedly spend a good deal of time in that rut."

"Actually, ma'am, I prefer men's fashions."

"Men's fashions?"

"Yes, ma'am. I find we're in a rather ugly phase right now. With women's fashions."

"And do you like French fashions?"

"Oh, yes, ma'am. I much prefer the French dressmakers."

We could hear footsteps in the hall, and she leaned forward and whispered hurriedly, "Then when you're out of mourning we shall go to Paris together, and you'll advise me on a new wardrobe. Would you like that?"

My mouth dropped open, but I checked myself, sat very upright, and turned my gaze to the door so as not to miss the entrance of Lady Wotton and her daughter. Regardless of the dubious social position I held, I had nothing to fear. I was in Lady Hambledon's camp, cradling Lord Ormelie's spaniel in my lap. And in the mind of a young girl with a head for fanciful thoughts, already succumbing to the charm of a man who was as yet only a myth, that gave me a definite advantage over anything plump, pretty, and spoiled.

FRANKLY, I WAS DISMAYED TO discover that a painting is not executed as quickly as a morning coat. Sir Francis's technique was laborious and thorough, involving initial sketches in pencil, followed by small studies in oil where he determined the color scheme before he began the large canvas. Having concluded that my exceptional height would produce a monotone study in black were he to paint my full figure, he chose to paint only my head and shoulders, posed with my back to the viewer, looking over my shoulder, with my hair flowing loose in masses of waves. Behind my head spread a fan of shimmering peacock feathers. I found it a little disappointing. I had hoped for something grander, more distinctive, but I trusted him and hoped for the best.

One afternoon I shared my doubts with Lady Hambledon, and to my astonishment she called on Sir Francis during my next sitting. He was deep at work that afternoon, and she made an unusually quiet entrance, declining to be announced, nor would she remove her bonnet and mantle. She hobbled slowly across the studio and came up behind Sir Francis.

He turned, looking a little put out by the interruption.

"Oh, don't scowl so," she chided. "I shan't stay. Go back to your muse."

He adjusted his spectacles and turned back to the easel. He had a habit of working with his face so close to the canvas that he appeared to be painting with his nose.

She stepped up and peered over his shoulder.

"Ah, my friend, this is one of your finest," she murmured.

"Indeed," he muttered.

"She has such a fine complexion."

"Quite," he grunted, scratching his mustache with the end of his paintbrush. "Unusual purity. Quite difficult to capture."

I blushed, but neither of them seemed to notice.

Lady Hambledon added casually, almost as an afterthought, "What a divine neck. Such a pity the tulle hides it." She leaned down and whispered in his ear. He laid down his palette and sat quietly stroking his beard. After a moment, he turned and said something to Lady Hambledon that I could not hear. She nodded and approached the platform.

"Veda, dear, that fichu you're wearing. Is it fixed to the dress?"

I looked down at the black tulle tied around my neck.

"No, ma'am. It's attached with the brooch."

"Would you remove it, dear?"

I glanced over her head toward Sir Francis who nodded approval, so I unfastened the brooch, laid it in my lap, and removed the tulle.

"Would you object to a portrait with your neck bare?" she asked. "You must tell him if you do."

I looked down at the front of my bodice, wishing I were older and could wear a low-necked evening dress rather than this black monstrosity.

Well, I thought, *I can't change the dress, but I can wear it with a little more audacity.* I unbuttoned the top three buttons and loosened the neck so that it hung more loosely, then draped the net tulle low over my shoulders. *There,* I thought. *Let's see how they'll take to that.*

When I glanced up, Sir Francis was barreling toward me, his eyes dancing with excitement. He struck a pensive pose while he wiped his hands clean on a rag, his mouth screwed up in concentration.

"Yes!" he shouted all of a sudden, then he threw down the rag and hurried up onto the platform with me. He laid his hands on my shoulders. "Here, turn yourself just slightly. Like so. Yes. A little more angle. Is that too uncomfortable to hold?"

"No, sir."

He played a little with the tulle, adjusting it so it hung from one shoulder.

"May I have the brooch, dear?"

He took it from me.

"Now, hold out your hand," he said. "Hold it like this, near your shoulder, with the palm slightly open." He laid the brooch in the palm of my hand and said, "Yes. Like so. As though you were offering it to someone. Yes. Splendid. Splendid!" The more he looked at me, the better pleased he seemed. "Roberts!" he cried at the top of his lungs. "Roberts!" He snatched the peacock feathers from the vase behind me and flung them to the floor.

I glanced around for Lady Hambledon. She was already on her way out. Roberts came hurrying through the door, and as he passed her, scurrying toward his master, she paused and smiled at me over her shoulder.

"Roberts!" cried Sir Francis who had his arms wrapped around a plaster column. "Help me dispose of this. Quickly, man. Quickly."

When I looked back, she had gone.

FROM THAT DAY ON, SIR Francis worked with an intensity I had not previously witnessed. The sittings became longer, and he seemed heedless of my comfort. Sometimes I felt I did not even exist, that he was painting something he saw in his imagination, not the flesh and blood that sat, cramped and shivering, before him. It was not unusual for friends to call. Lady Hambledon was not the only one on terms familiar enough to interrupt him at work, but now he tolerated those interruptions with less magnanimity. Some days he refused to receive anyone at all.

That was the case on the day I met Harry. If it had not been for Harry's good-natured impertinence, we never would have met at all.

Harry charged into the studio that day like a man who had never been refused entry to anyplace by anyone, flashing that winning smile of his and sweeping his hat from his head with a flourish. Roberts followed close on his heels, muttering objections. Of course, the first thing I noticed was the way he dressed. I was predisposed to judge him favorably, but nothing had prepared me for the man himself. He wore his clothes with the self-assurance common to most gentlemen of his rank—the impeccably cut coat, the well-blocked hat, the crisp, white linen—but he wore them with that indefinable essence called style.

"Sir Francis!" Harry cried. "Good afternoon! I've brought you a most unusual client to sit for a portrait."

Roberts, seeing the battle lost, stopped in his tracks, announced "Lord Ormelie" in a croaking voice, and shuffled out.

With his nose buried in the canvas, Sir Francis muttered, "A new client? I do not need a new client, my dear man. What I need is a session without interruption. Besides, I still have your own portrait to finish."

"But this is a most unusual subject."

"I certainly hope it's not as elusive as you are."

"Not at all! Not at all! He's chained to London on a short lead."

Sir Francis laid down his palette and turned to Harry with the air of a man expecting to be pleasantly entertained. "How are your lighthouses coming along?"

"Rather like my portrait, I'm afraid." Harry set his hat on a chair, dropped his gloves inside, and struck a pose with one hand resting on his furled umbrella. "In the absence of a distinct model, no one wishes to proceed." Then, in a brief but rapid discourse, he began articulating the difficulties of advancing new ideas among backward-thinking men. "They look to God for an explanation of everything. That is the stumbling block. I don't know how the deuce they expect to move forward until they admit that Nature is a governable process." This he stated as though anyone who thought the contrary had their head screwed on backward. "So, until their thinking is enlightened on that score, there will be no new lighthouses."

He paused long enough to step forward to the easel and look over Sir Francis's shoulder. His eyes swept from the portrait to me and back to the portrait, then to me again. I smiled, and Harry smiled back. I liked him instantly.

Sir Francis said, "Lord Ormelie, may I present Miss Grenfell," and Harry bowed.

I was under instructions not to move, but a curtsey was in order, and when Sir Francis saw me gather up my skirt and start to rise, he cautioned, "Please! Miss Grenfell. Hold your pose. We can dispense with formalities."

I don't know what Harry would have said to me at that moment, for he was about to speak when we were rudely interrupted by a disturbance at the door, and there entered a gentleman with a monkey on a lead.

"Good God," Sir Francis exclaimed, shooting to his feet as though faced with an elephant charge.

I laughed, and Harry shot me a bemused glance that could have been interpreted as "Quite right!"

Lord Stamford was a red-whiskered gentleman of the stiff and quaint sort, some years older than Harry. His monkey was dressed in a smart little scarlet waistcoat with gold embroidery.

Harry made introductions, which were fairly lost among a stream of exclamations by Sir Francis, mixed with reassurances by Lord Stamford that Galahad, as the monkey was named, was quite tame and inoffensive.

"This is your subject?" Sir Francis balked. "A monkey?"

"He's my wife's pet," Lord Stamford explained, "and I would very much like to indulge her on her birthday with a portrait of the creature."

"I don't do monkeys," exclaimed Sir Francis, looking insulted.

"Indeed," Harry said with solemnity. "In appearance quite unlike anything you've done before, but in behavior perhaps not all that dissimilar from your usual patrons." He paused and a grin broke over his face as he added, "Myself included."

"Lady Stamford holds your work in high esteem. A portrait of Galahad by yourself would be a most cherished possession," Lord Stamford said congenially, like a man who assumed others were set upon the earth for no reason other than to carry out his wishes. "She is so very fond of the little fellow."

Sir Francis frowned at Galahad and stroked his beard. He must have been torn between the creature's repulsiveness and a disinclination to refuse a personal request from a peer, particularly one as wealthy as Lord Stamford.

"Really, he's a very expressive little chap," Harry said, studying the creature who had jumped up into Lord Stamford's arms to glare at us defensively. "Look at him. Look at those eyes. Fascinating. Absolutely fascinating. Such intelligence."

Lord Stamford said, "I should like a modest portrait, something for her boudoir."

They went on like this for a while, Lord Stamford and Harry whittling down Sir Francis's objections, until they reached the understanding that the painting would remain in a private place and never be offered for public exhibit, thus protecting the artist's reputation from ridicule. One more stipulation—that one of Lord Stamford's servants remain throughout each sitting to handle the creature—and the deal was struck.

"Now," Lord Stamford declared, quite pleased with himself, "where can we find a costume for the little gent?"

"Costume?"

"Indeed. I should like him in a hat and coat. Formal dress."

Sir Francis was losing his patience. "My good sir, I cannot help you there. Generally, my clients furnish their own dress."

Lord Stamford looked to Harry, and Harry gave a little twirl to his umbrella, then swung it upward to direct our attention to the portrait of his mother on the wall. "Take him to Old Pauley's. Mother swears by them. They can turn out anything for anyone and do it better than any tailor in London."

The gesture, reminiscent perhaps of some beloved circus trick which had at one time brought such delight to the monkey, so tempted him that he leaped from Lord Stamford's shoulder to the extended umbrella and swung playfully from the object by one hand, startling Harry who flung his umbrella and the creature to the floor. The monkey screeched a most horrid reply and made a line straight for me, scrambling up the platform, up my skirt, and into my lap with such astonishing swiftness that I had no time to flee. I sat there on my stool with his wiry little arms clinging pathetically to my neck, a gasp frozen in my lungs, fearful of moving or breathing. Lord Stamford and Harry raced forward, both of them effusing apologies. When Harry reached for the lead to pull the monkey off

me, the little creature bared his teeth and chattered away at him with indignation, all the while clinging to me with pathetic resolve. Suddenly, it
was all too comic: I took a look at Harry's horrified face and burst into
laughter.

"Pray, leave him be," I cried, between upheavals of laughter. "I think
he means me no harm."

"Miss Grenfell," Harry answered, both embarrassed and flustered, "I
am mortified. Pray forgive me. I—I'm afraid I'm not accustomed to the
behavior of these animals. I never imagined—" Turning to his friend, he
bridled, "Really, this is unbearable. Good God, Nolly, he could have bitten her."

"I'm sure, no harm has been done, sir," I begged him, thinking how utterly charming he was when distraught. "He seems quite innocent." To be
honest, I was not half as calm as I pretended, for the jabbering creature
had nestled beneath my hair, and I could not summon the courage to dis-
engage his grotesque little hands from my neck.

Lord Stamford, besieged by an outraged Sir Francis, turned to Harry
with an unperturbed air and claimed, "Not at all! He adores ladies! Never
harmed a lady in his life! He's a regular little gentleman! Aren't you, now,
little fellow?" Then, still addressing the monkey, Lord Stamford stepped
forward and reached up to entreat him to return to his master, but he only
succeeded in provoking a fresh stream of distressed screeches.

"Good Lord," Lord Stamford barked, recoiling all of a sudden and
glaring at me as though I had bewitched the animal.

I was terribly aware of them all staring up at me, and this grotesque little thing trembling on my shoulder, and decided the solution rested with
me. I reached up and gently groped for the creature.

"Here, now, Galahad," I said gently, taking his hand in mine. "Do
come down and be presented like a gentleman."

He must have found my voice soothing, because he took my hand and
allowed me to lower him into my lap.

"I'm Miss Grenfell," I said, shaking his hand and praying he wouldn't
take a finger off with those ghastly little teeth of his. He had discovered
the brooch in my lap and seemed mesmerized by it. Seeing him momentarily distracted, Lord Stamford climbed up onto the platform and swept
him up into his arms. Galahad went willingly back to his master, but he

took my brooch with him; he stuffed it in his tunic pocket and refused to return it.

A few awkward minutes followed with Lord Stamford, who had earlier claimed the beast to be inoffensive, reluctant to force Galahad to give up my brooch for fear that he might be bitten, and Sir Francis arguing that the creature be coerced into compliance. While they proceeded to discuss the matter in a gentlemanly but strained manner, Harry retrieved his umbrella and returned to the platform where I sat.

"You know, Miss Grenfell, I'm not a creationist, and I must say the more I'm around this pet of Nolly's, the more intrigued I am by natural history. There are some astonishing theories out there, particularly one by a Mr. Darwin, but he's been too timid to publish his ideas, which is a pity, as we need good minds and courageous men attacking these problems, don't you agree?"

I couldn't have cared less about Darwin and natural history, for I was feeling suddenly very distraught. I had met Harry and been attacked by a monkey, all within five minutes. My nerves failed me. I broke into tears.

"Miss Grenfell?" he said. "Miss Grenfell, are you all right?"

"No, I'm not," I said, brushing a fat tear from my cheek.

He stepped closer and looked up at me with genuine concern in his eyes. "Good gracious me, you're in shock. Of course you are. How thoughtless of me." He pulled out a handkerchief. "Here."

"Thank you, sir." I sniffed.

"It was a ghastly piece of business, indeed. You braved the ordeal with such good humor. Truly, you did. It was very brave of you."

I sniffed again, and nodded, and dabbed demurely at my eyes.

"And I assure you, we shall retrieve your brooch."

I dismissed that with a flutter of the handkerchief. "Oh, I don't care about the brooch." Finally, giving up all pretense of civility, I blew my nose. "I am sorry for your handkerchief, sir," I mumbled through the cambric. "Goodness, how humiliating."

"What is so humiliating, Miss Grenfell?" he asked with such sweetness it made me want to cry all the harder.

"Crying."

"Why, crying is a natural human response to many situations. When the nerves are drained, it produces a psychic exhaustion, and any lady would be exhausted by such a trial as you have just endured. That must have been quite frightening."

I frowned down at him. "Are you always like this?"

"I beg your pardon?"

"What I mean, sir—"

"Ah! You mean, am I always so analytical?"

"Yes. I think that's what I mean."

"I'm afraid I am."

I let out a deep breath punctuated with sobs. I was thinking how soft the handkerchief was, and how much older he was, and how I must seem like such a baby to him.

Suddenly his eyes lit up with recognition.

"Oh, my goodness, of course! I should have realized who you were. The portrait—"

"I beg your pardon?"

"Mother has spoken to me about you."

"It was the crying. That gave me away."

He seemed warmed by my weak attempt at humor. "Ah, yes, she told me as much. She felt quite badly about it all."

"On the contrary, sir. She's been most comforting to me."

"She's taken a liking to you."

"It's been mutual, sir."

"You must understand, it's quite unusual for her. My mother doesn't collect people."

"I didn't think she did, sir. I'm very fond of your mother. It means a great deal to me that she desires my companionship."

He scrutinized me, and I saw his mother's shrewd gaze behind his grey-blue eyes. "I don't see a likeness," he said.

"A likeness?"

"To my sister."

"Sir Francis seemed to think there was."

"Oh, he just humors my mother." Harry studied me thoughtfully for a moment. "What has she told you about Aurelia?"

"That she's married, and lives in France."

He hesitated, and I know now that he was judging my character, and debating how much he should reveal.

"Miss Grenfell, that is true to an extent. But I feel I should warn you, in case you find yourself in the company of others who know the whole truth. My sister—my sister is indeed married." He paused and then went on in a reverential tone. "She is married to Christ. She converted to Catholicism and now lives in the south of France. In a convent."

A quiet shock ran through me, but I held his gaze and determined to be worthy of his confidence. "I shall keep this to myself, Lord Ormelie."

"It's common knowledge. Everyone knows."

"Perhaps, but if she had wished me to know, she would have told me, don't you think?"

"She pretends it isn't true."

"Then I shall pretend along with her, if she so wishes."

He smiled at me, and a kind of relaxed warmth came over his countenance. "My mother is a good judge of character, and she was right about you."

"All she talks about is you, sir."

"Oh dear, how frightfully boring for you."

"Come now, sir, you know better than that."

He grinned broadly, revealing that blistering bright confidence of his in a quick twinkle of the eye.

And then he was called away by Lord Stamford who had succeeded in retrieving my brooch, and it was a long while before we met again. By then both of us had been changed by events that were beyond our control, and I look back upon that meeting with awe and count it as one of my blessings. It was memorable not only in light of the events that followed, but because the encounter was unexpected and innocent. Harry later confessed to me that he had often thought of me and had inquired after me of his mother, but she had refused to indulge him on this matter, offering only the most general information about my station and person, that I was the daughter of a wealthy tradesman who enjoyed the respect and patronage of the landed gentry and nobility, and that he should not pursue my acquaintance. I thought surely she was discouraging him on account of my lower status, but Harry tended to believe it had more to do with my youth, and that her intention was to protect me from him.

Chapter Six

BY THE END OF MARCH, THE PORTRAIT WAS NEARING COMPLETION. I was too young to understand how the subtle suggestion of disrepair and the ambiguity of my gesture set an extraordinary tone to an ordinary portrait of a tailor's daughter in mourning, but Lady Hambledon attested to its brilliance. By all accounts the pose was unconventional, and I was a little concerned about Father's reaction, but since he had never come to see how the work was progressing, I made no objections. At the end of one sitting, Sir Francis announced to me that he had decided to show the painting at the Royal Academy's Summer Exhibition, an event that marked the opening of the London Season.

Needless to say, I was thrilled by such an honor and couldn't wait to share the news with Esther. I told her all about it one afternoon as I was on my knees putting up the hem of a new dress I had finished for her just in time for a musical *soirée* at Mr. Brown's.

"It's really all quite extraordinary, wouldn't you agree?" I said, sitting back on my heels and smoothing out a wrinkle in the mauve figured silk. "After all that's happened, Tiggy, I feel quite blessed, meeting Lady Hambledon, and now this—having my portrait entered in a competition. I can't wait for you to see it. Lady Hambledon seems to think it's quite good—although I can't tell. It is a good likeness—but he's done something to the mood—I can't describe it. I think I appear older than I am, which worries me a bit. I do hope Papa—"

Esther cut me off. "Oh, do hurry, Topsy. I'm getting tired." She shifted her weight with a heavy sigh.

"It's the silk. It's very difficult to work with," I answered. "And you're fidgeting."

"Oh, but must you take so long? It's only a hem."

Esther's behavior perplexed me. These days, any mention of my portrait soured her, and my growing intimacy with Lady Hambledon was a real bee in her bonnet. She took no pains to hide her disapproval of my carriage rides through Hyde Park with my new friend, although she knew how very much I enjoyed watching the parade of fashionable people during the fashionable hour. Esther had always detested the scene and had only scathing remarks for people "who had nothing better to do but see and be seen by each other while poor wretches like us look on." She always spoke disparagingly of the "idle rich" and had an annoying habit of debunking every good thing I had to say about the privileged class.

I could only attribute it to jealousy, although I was slow to acknowledge that she could resent the little bit of pleasure that had come my way during these sad months. When she grew cross and grumpy, it frightened me. She was slipping away from me, and I couldn't bear to lose her.

"Be patient just a little longer," I replied as I quickly whipped up the last few feet of skirt. "It will be worth it, I promise. You will be angelic in this dress. You'll be the most beautiful girl there."

"You will do something about the sleeves, won't you? They're much too tight. I can't move my arms," she complained.

"I'll take care of it. Don't fret. You'll be absolutely stunning, I promise, and you will catch the eye of someone very rich. He'll have a seat in Parliament, and fifteen thousand a year, and a pack of hounds, and he'll fall madly in love with you."

"How frightfully original," she quipped.

"Oh, come now, I can't believe that you wouldn't be enticed by the prospects of land and title."

"I am quite content with my station in life," she said. "You should be with yours."

"But I am content," I insisted. "What makes you think I'm not?"

"The way you go on about Lady Hambledon and her son."

"Well, would you advise me to refuse her generosity and her friendship when it has been so freely forthcoming? Goodness, you talk as if I'm some scheming little tart."

"You don't seem to understand, Vevey. If a man marries below his station, they're both reduced to a most wretched situation. Why, look at Lord Stamford. Look what's happened to him since he married that circus performer." Lady Stamford, I had since learned, had been born Flora

Stachelek and had once performed acrobatic stunts on horseback in her father's circus. Galahad had been part of her act.

"Whatever do you mean?"

"Why, he's disgusted everyone! The only society he keeps now is a terribly raffish bunch. Although he's still master of the Quorn Hunt. They
haven't taken that away from him—he's far too wealthy and breeds such
good hounds. He has a very grand estate, you know, but no one will visit
him anymore. At least no one respectable."

Esther knew very well that Lord Stamford was one of Harry's closest
friends. Her inference was so pointed that I couldn't help but take offense.

"Are you saying Lord Ormelie isn't respectable?"

"Oh, come now, Topsy, you must know he has a reputation."

"What kind of reputation?"

"Oh, he has quite a wild streak."

"How do you know this?"

"From Ned. Ned knows him quite well. They were at Oxford together.
Ned's been up to Yorkshire to visit him in that monstrosity of a castle of
theirs."

"Blackroak Hall?"

"They've got a spectacular collection of authentic armor. Ned went up
there to make sketches of it."

Our conversation was beginning to feel like a jousting contest, and I
felt obliged to foil her thrusts when all I really wanted was kindness and a
little complicity.

"You speak as if you're trying to discourage my good opinion of him."

"Indeed, I am."

"And why is that?"

"Because you seem to think he has shown a particular interest in you."

"That's poppycock. I think no such thing."

"I don't believe you."

"Well, what if he should show an interest in me—although I don't
mean to suggest he has. What then?"

"Then I would discourage that as well. I am your paid companion. And
I have certain responsibilities toward you, in much the same way as a governess would have."

"Well, whatever you've heard, I believe Lord Ormelie is completely
without malice."

"That's because you only hear about him from his mother. I hear he's jilted more than one lady."

"Oh, Tiggy, that is quite unkind!"

"But it's true!"

"Why do you assault his character so violently?" I snapped suddenly.

"Why do you defend him? You've only met him once."

"You haven't met him at all!"

My hands were trembling so that I couldn't finish basting her skirt, and I got to my feet and tore off my work smock. "There, that's good enough. I'll finish it tonight."

When she saw how she had vexed me, she laid a hand gently on my arm, but I shook her off.

"You judge him unfairly. Lord Ormelie may be a precocious young man, and perhaps he may appear irresponsible, but he is always a gentleman." I was fishing for combs in my hair, which had come loose, and my hands were working nervously as I spoke. "Do you know what I think? I think he's a genius. I do. And sometimes I think genius is wasted on respectable people. Quite honestly, I would take one talented man over a hundred respectable dullards any day."

Esther's face softened all of a sudden, and she stopped my fidgeting hands and quieted them in her own.

"I only repeat gossip to amuse and entertain you. What you and I think of Lord Ormelie or anyone else in that society is of no importance whatsoever."

"But it is," I pleaded softly. "Because when you slander Lord Ormelie, you slander his mother, and she's the closest thing to a mother I have."

"But you have Aunt Lavinia," she teased.

"Oh, please." I laughed. "The idea!" Aunt Lavinia had wanted to move back to Savile Row to keep house for us, but Papa had firmly refused her offer.

"Here," she said, sweeping aside her skirts and turning her back to me. "Help me out of this dress and let's go for a walk. I much prefer that to quarreling. Come with me to Regent Street. I have shopping to do there."

As my fingers worked their way down the row of buttons, I cautioned her quietly, "Pray don't harangue me so, Tiggy. I can't bear it. It makes me feel so alone."

"But you never want to hear ill spoken of anyone, and it is my duty to warn you of any associations that would reflect badly on you."

After a hesitation, I asked, "So your friend Ned has been to Blackroak?"

"Years ago."

"Did he meet Aurelia? Harry's sister?"

"I didn't know he had a sister."

"She ran away from home. To join a convent."

Esther cast an incredulous look over her shoulder. "A convent?"

I nodded.

"How shocking!"

"Lady Hambledon never sees her anymore."

There was a tense silence as I finished the last button and she peeled off the bodice.

"I know you have something to say," I said good-naturedly. "Go on. What is it?"

"You'll just say I'm being ungenerous," she mumbled as we tugged the dress over her head.

"I'm not as naïve as you think. Honestly, a young English girl who runs away to France to join a convent must be running away from something."

"Well, Ned says the Earl is a bit of an ogre. He said it's surprising Harry's as decent as he is, given the father's such a tyrant."

"Aha! A kind word about Harry has fallen from your lips!" I teased as I laid the dress across my bed. "Albeit quite inadvertently, I'm sure."

ALTHOUGH I WOULD NEVER HAVE confessed as much, I had indeed indulged in fancies of Harry—my favorite was the one in which I waltzed with him at a court ball beneath the approving gaze of his mother. However, it would be more truthful to say that I had been inspired by Harry—inspired by his charm and good looks and grand bearing. As Esther said many years later, with coarse but accurate wit, I dreamed of dressing Harry—not undressing Harry. He would be for me what the Prince of Wales had been for Old Pauley, a walking fashion plate of exquisite taste and elegance that only Grenfell's could offer.

Back then, all I knew was that I wanted desperately to impress him. I had to draw his attention. And I knew precisely how to do it.

The very day after our encounter, I had begun a suit for Galahad in the secrecy of my attic room. I knew Pauley's would accommodate Lord

Stamford with utmost efficiency and timeliness, so I had to act swiftly. To order the cloth, I bypassed Mr. Balducci, Papa's new Head Cutter, and wrote directly to the wool manufacturer myself. For the dress coat, he would need a superfine wool, something light that would be borne easily on his slight frame. For the waistcoat, I chose a cream silk that I embroidered in a white exotic motif of my own design, finishing both coat and waistcoat with a lining of regal blue silk to set off the mahogany sheen of his fur. Although Grenfell's did not make shirts, I had been making these items myself ever since I could thread a needle, and I quickly got up a shirt of fine light-weight linen with a tiny frill down the pleated fronted section and tiny bone buttons. For his collar, I went directly to Dent & Ravenscroft, knowing they could be trusted to produce just the right amount of stiffness and follow my specific instructions as to the turn-down of the collar, which was ever so important on a client with a neck as tiny as Galahad's. His silk hat would be from Dobbs & Sons. I paid for everything out of my own pocket money and had the orders delivered to our home rather than the workshop. Galahad would be my first real client, and I would dress him as though I were dressing a gentleman of the highest rank.

This whole scheme had been planted in my head as soon as Harry had mentioned Old Pauley's name. Even though I had been terrified of the monkey, I had handled him quite deliberately, mentally noting his weight, the length of his arms, the breadth of his chest and its peculiar shape, the slope of his shoulders. At night, as I sat at my worktable basting the pieces by candlelight, fitting them on an old doll of mine that I had mangled in an attempt to re-create Galahad's shape, there were times when I'd sit back and stretch, and look at my handiwork and break into hilarious laughter. If I were mad, I was happily so.

Several days after I had sent our trotter off with the package to be delivered directly to Lord and Lady Stamford's London address, Lucy interrupted my algebra lesson to say that Father needed to see me urgently, at once, without delay, in the shop—and that I was to comb my hair and remove my smock before presenting myself. In the back room, I found the tailors chattering away like magpies, but they all grew silent when I entered and cast their eyes back down at their work. In a moment, Papa came in. He had never once reprimanded me in front of the employees, but I could tell from the look on his face that he was not going to spare me that humiliation. He stopped in front of me with a jaw set like stone, tugging his waistcoat down over his stomach the way he did when trying to compose himself.

"Miss Grenfell," he began.

Hoping to spare him the effort of an inquisition, I simply said, "It's the monkey business, isn't it?"

An apprentice behind me sniggered. I heard a soft thump as if he had been walloped on the head, and then there was silence again.

Papa was taken off guard, and I whispered, "Might we discuss this in your club room?"

"The club room is for gentlemen, Veda," he hissed back.

"Pray tell me if they liked it," I pleaded in a low voice. "I'm dying to know. You can scold me later."

Papa took in a breath as though of one mind and let it out as though of another. "Yes, indeed, they did." He nodded.

"Truly?" I cried, clapping my hands together. "Did it fit?"

"Impeccably," he answered with grim resignation.

"Who has come?"

"Lady Stamford herself. Veda," and he took me by the arm and led me into the back hall, "this was most indiscreet. We do not advertise."

I started to interrupt, but he silenced me.

"And that's precisely what you were doing, child, is it not?"

I nodded. "Yes, Papa."

"If Lady Stamford wishes to have her monkey clothed by us, she will come to us. We do not go to them."

"So she was happy with it?"

"She wants to meet you."

"I didn't put my name on it," I said in defense of myself. "I sent it with the compliments of Grenfell's."

"My dear, it was not too difficult to surmise who was the guilty party. Now come." He took his handkerchief and cleaned a spot on my cheek, and I followed him into the showroom. Fortunately, there were no other clients, and only Mr. Balducci was present. Lady Stamford was quite what I had suspected, a very pretty young woman with tight blond curls springing from beneath a little hat perched forward on her head at such an angle I feared the feathered creature nesting there might tumble down her pertly sloped nose with the slightest movement of her head. She wore a magnificent mink-edged mantle that nearly took my breath away. To my disappointment, Galahad was not with her. I curtsied deeply and then stood with hands crossed over my skirt and demurely lowered eyes.

"My dear Miss Grenfell," she said, "why, Nolly had no idea who you were, and it turned out to be such a splendid stroke of luck. What a delightful suit of clothes you've made my little Galahad! And they fit him to a tee! Pray tell me how you did it? Without a fitting!"

I said in a quiet voice, "I have a good eye, Lady Stamford." Then I raised my gaze and asked, "Did he like his suit?"

Papa pinched me very hard on the arm, but I didn't even wince.

"Oh, my dear, he loves it! Why, I couldn't get it off him for days! I was terrified he might get into mischief and spoil everything before we had a chance to have his portrait made."

Once again I answered demurely, although I could feel a little smile tugging at my mouth. "Should he spoil them, madam, I'll be glad to make him a new set."

Papa squeezed my elbow tightly, and I curtsied and swept gracefully from the room. Back at home, I ran upstairs to the drawing room where I found my math tutor sleeping, and I dragged him to his shaky old legs and waltzed him around the room. It had been a long time since I had been so happy.

Chapter Seven

I WAS NEARLY SEVENTEEN, AND IN LITTLE LESS THAN A YEAR, MY lessons with my tutors would cease and I would "do nothing," as Aunt Lavinia put it, which meant that I would busy myself finding a husband. "Doing nothing" involved a whirlwind of activities. I would be permitted to belong to clubs and visit libraries, enjoy public assemblies, lectures, and private parties.

I was looking forward to coming out in society, but the thought of going through all this without Mama's guidance left me feeling quite uneasy. For all her nervous habits and tendency to worry about our place in society, she had been absolutely sure of herself within the walls of our home. I missed her in ways I never would have imagined; those very things that, as a child, I had most resented were the things I mourned most deeply. Mama had ordered my life and kept me firmly in hand. Mama had been capability itself. She and Father had shared a love of order, and her judicious management of domestic affairs was a virtue for which Father praised her highly. Whenever he complimented her on her prudent economy and well-regulated household, Mama would look pleased as Punch, and I often heard her affirm—quoting the Book of Common Prayer—that one of the express purposes of marriage was to "promote the mutual society, help, and comfort of the partners." In this regard, Mama was without equal.

Mama had come from a provincial manufacturing family of the lesser landed gentry, and she managed our house in London much the way her grandmother had managed their modest mansion. She kept the most orderly household records of anyone we knew—Aunt Lavinia and Grandpa both attested to this. Every morning she would be at her writing desk, recording in her memorandum books all manner of household business, all of which was annotated with printed tables and guides as well as her own candid observations. In these memorandum books could be found the exact wages she paid a certain Betty Briggs twelve years ago, from the first day of her employment as a housemaid to her last when "the impudent, saucy slut ran off in the middle of the night, leaving all the clothes to dry and iron!" She kept note of all furniture sent out to be repaired, new linens purchased for the home, when the chimneys were swept, when the pewter and copper had last been polished. Although in the city we had no need for ample provisions, Mama still kept a detailed inventory of cupboards and storage trunks, chests and boxes; she knew the location and condition of every piece of china, glass, and silver we owned, each bed sheet, counterpane, pillow, and quilt, and every phial of medicine. Mama chose our suppliers, and she knew precisely how much had been spent on commodities. It was Mama, not Cook, who monitored the amount of food in the larder.

Aunt Lavinia always faulted us for refusing her assistance after Mama's death. She had been ready, bags packed, to move back in, but neither Papa nor I had wanted her. What we had lost was a mother and a wife, and for all other things we had a housekeeper and cook, we had housemaids and menservants, we had my tutors and Esther. Aunt Lavinia was well meaning, but she was dim and terribly forgetful, and her meekness grated on Papa's nerves—not to mention her obsessive needlework, which she turned into countless doilies and antimacassars. She was more like a child than a woman, and Papa had no patience for her. He feared her incompetence would only aggravate a cook and housekeeper whom even Mama had professed difficult to manage.

Mama had believed that sound health was impossible without a stout moral constitution, that behind every epidemic lay a moral infection. She had always equated health with virtue, and virtue with respectability, and as we prospered and our station in life improved, she fully expected contagious illness in our family to decline. She tracked our winter colds and gastric illnesses in her memoranda just as she tracked all other occurrences. As Grenfell's grew, so did the invisible buffer between our bodies and disease. In St. James we breathed an atmosphere of gentrified air, purer by virtue of the elevated moral and social rank of those people with whom we came in contact.

Mama still sat like an eternal, never-to-be-silenced judge upon all my thoughts and actions, and whenever I ignored her voice rumbling in the back of my head, I was plagued by a sense of guilt and foreboding. Somewhere evil awaited me; somewhere there lurked retribution for my rebellious thoughts and deeds. I forced myself to believe that sitting week after week in Sir Francis's big drafty studio was not the least bit injurious to my health, although my nose was often red, and my fingertips and toes like ice, for he was much too engrossed in my portrait to notice until my teeth began to rattle so hard in my head that it caused my jaw to tremble. Then he would offer effusive apologies and order up a warming pan or pot of tea, but often my discomfort passed unnoticed, and I was too timid to interrupt his concentration.

Sir Francis's enthusiasm for my portrait spoke to my vanity, but it was often drowned out by Mama's voice in my head, condemning it as the first step willfully taken toward a world of questionable virtue. Had Mama been alive, she would have sat through every sitting with me, and I would have been painted soberly, respectably, my dress buttoned to the collar, my tulle fichu knotted around my neck and pinned in front with my brooch, my hands folded in my lap. The portrait would never have inspired the imagination of the artist, nor the viewer. It would have been unremarkable. And perhaps I would have been saved.

When my health began to decline, I refused to recognize the fact until I awoke one morning and sat up to find that my bed felt more like a ship in a tempest than something with four posters firmly planted on the ground. As I walked across the room, I found myself listing to one side, as though the world and I were no longer on the same plane. My attempt to pass through the doorway resulted in my running straight into the doorjamb. With my head spinning, I stumbled back to bed and lay clinging to the sides like a life raft. For the longest while I lay there with my eyes closed, wondering what dreadful thing was wrong with me. The slightest movement set off violent nausea and dizziness, and I dared not so much as turn my head. When I did not come down for breakfast, Papa sent Lucy up to my room.

"Pray don't fret," I mumbled when Lucy returned with him. I forced myself to roll over and open my eyes. He had not even bothered to remove the napkin tucked under his chin. I remember the dab of raspberry jam on his cheek, because it stood out so sharply against the alarming paleness of his face. He was terrified of losing me. "I'm sure it's nothing," I muttered, hoping to reassure him. "I'll be quite all right."

Mrs. Arbuthnot was summoned, and Grenfell's trotter went for Dr.

Lister. My blinds were opened and then drawn again as the morning light aggravated my dizziness. Pillows were plumped, and an herbal tea was sent up.

For two days all kinds of medical men came and went. Dr. Lister declared it a cold with complications of the ear and nose, but as my symptoms were few and accompanied by no fever at the onset, there was a growing suspicion that my ailment was not *physik* but mental.

Dr. Mosely was the first to give it a name.

"Vis nervosa," he pronounced, as though identifying something quite familiar and harmless, possibly even friendly. He was one of our new clients. I greatly preferred him to Dr. Lister, who had treated Reggie and Mama. Dr. Mosely was younger and had all his teeth, whereas Dr. Lister wheezed, and a sharp metallic smell always permeated his clothing and his skin.

"What is *vis nervosa?*" I said, opening my eyes to focus on him. He had only just arrived, and after consultation downstairs with Father had been sent up to my room. I liked that he seemed so sure of himself and this new diagnosis. I wanted very badly to know what was happening to me.

"My dear," he said, pulling a chair up to sit by my bed, "I hear you have endured great loss in your family recently."

"Yes," I whispered.

"Tell me, are you highly emotional? Does just the slightest agitation seem to unlock a floodgate of tears?"

"Well, yes," I whispered, sitting up in bed with sudden interest. He knew all about me without my uttering a word.

"Your vital powers have been depressed."

"Have they?"

"It's nervous depression, my dear." He seemed very cheerful and comforting.

"Will it go away?"

"Most certainly, but you must help yourself along. You must fight it off."

"How do I do that?" I asked, eager to please him.

"You must rest, and above all, you must avoid extreme states. Let nothing agitate you or excite you. You must think pleasant thoughts." He patted my hand. "Think of spring balls and handsome young suitors."

I spent the day in utter boredom. Aunt Lavinia arrived and took over the sickroom. She pulled a chair up to the darkened window and spent the day embroidering by the pale light that stole in around the curtains' edge, emitting intermittent melancholy sighs. She seemed quite content. She was so unobtrusive that at times I completely forgot she was there. When Esther called, as she did every afternoon, she was turned away with the excuse that her visit would only excite me.

That night a cough set in, and by morning I had a fever. Dr. Mosely could not be reached, so Dr. Lister was summoned.

"Nervous depression, indeed!" he muttered scornfully, shaking his head as he looked down my throat. He took the candle from Lucy and held it as close as he could to my mouth. "Open. Open wide. Wider." He seemed disgruntled by having his medical opinion challenged. I was afraid I might end up with candle wax on my tongue in retaliation. "You're far too young for nervous depression," he grumbled. His breath smelt strongly of ale and his eyes were bloodshot.

He passed the candle back to Lucy and turned to Aunt Lavinia.

"It's a cold, just as I thought. Just took a while for it to establish itself." He ordered Lucy to bring hot water and some small, clean cloths, then he turned back to me and with his fingers applied pressure to various points around my face—my forehead, along the sides of my nose, below my eyes—asking me if I felt discomfort in those areas. When I said yes, he nodded. Although he didn't seem to show the same cheerful assurance that Dr. Mosely had done, I felt he knew what he was doing. When Lucy returned, he moistened the cloths with hot water to which he had added a few drops of a liquid from a phial taken from his bag. The odor was strong and stimulating but not unpleasant. He laid the warm wet cloths across the bridge of my nose. The effect was immediate. I sighed with relief and closed my eyes.

"Is that better?"

"Oh, much." I smiled. Tears swelled in my eyes, as often happened at a kindly gesture toward me. I fought to remain calm, thinking about my *vis nervosa* and Dr. Moseley's admonition to fight against it.

Dr. Lister instructed Lucy and Aunt Lavinia to bathe my face several times a day in this manner, and said he would be back to check on me in several days.

With this firm diagnosis, Aunt Lavinia sent Lucy out for a bottle of Swift's Miracle, an elixir she swore by. It was a ghastly tasting concoction, and I made a bargain with her: I would dutifully swallow my daily dosage if Esther were allowed to visit. The only drawback was that Swift's Miracle produced such drowsiness that I cared very little for what was going on around me. As soon as I awoke, Aunt Lavinia would spring to her feet and carefully measure out a spoonful of the spirits, then pour me a large glass of milk.

"It's the milk that does the trick, dear," she claimed. "It goes down so much more easily with milk and honey. There, dear. Yes, drink it all down."

So I washed down the remedy with copious quantities of sweetened milk. Within minutes I had returned to the blissful state of sleep.

When I was alert enough, Esther read to me or we played tame card games. Papa made frequent but brief visits. Esther and Aunt Lavinia constantly fought over the window. Esther would come in and open it, and when she left Aunt Lavinia would rush in and batten it down with the moral fury of a saint closing the gates of paradise against a mob of unclean spirits.

For two weeks I consumed large quantities of Swift's Miracle and warm milk and Cook's watery soup, but just when my dizziness had nearly disappeared, and my head no longer felt as though a balloon had been inflated inside it, I was struck down with violent gastric pains.

I remember Dr. Lister, still wheezing from the climb up to my room, inclining his bearded face over me. "Good Lord," he exclaimed to Aunt Lavinia who hovered at the foot of my bed. "Have you been feeding this child anything nourishing at all? She's thin as a rail."

"Why, she takes a little broth, doctor. But I've found that, generally, Swift's Miracle provides all the nourishment she—"

He cut her off. "Is this it?" He had found a bottle of the infamous Swift's on my bedside table.

"Indeed, sir. Are you familiar with the remedy?"

He opened the bottle and sniffed it. "Ecod. Pure laudanum."

Upon learning I had consumed large quantities of milk along with it, he called for Mrs. Arbuthnot and interrogated her as to the supplier.

"Jenners, sir," our housekeeper replied, but I caught a hesitation in her voice. I noticed it at the time, and I remembered it later. "It's good milk, sir."

"You've never been supplied by the Regulated Dairy Company?"

"No, sir," she answered. Then she took a look at me and started. What she saw must have struck some obscure nerve of remorse in her unscrupulous heart, for she recanted in a troubled voice. "Well, at least not to my knowledge, sir."

"What do you mean? Whose responsibility is it?"

"It's Cook does the ordering, sir."

"Send her to me."

"She's not in, sir. She has her afternoon, sir."

He picked up the pitcher on my bedside table and peered into it. "Bring me a fresh pitcher of milk. And a clean glass."

He waited at my bedside, gazing down at me with a deeply furrowed brow while he smoothed his beard with his red knuckles. He seemed terribly concerned. Aunt Lavinia, timid and wide-eyed with worry, hovered over his shoulder.

"Am I very sick?" I asked him.

He patted my hand. "We will see," was his only reply.

When Mrs. Arbuthnot returned, he poured some milk into a glass and waited a few moments before holding it up to the light. Then he moistened the tip of his tongue with the milk and tasted it hesitantly. When he had finished, he took out his pocket handkerchief and wiped off his tongue.

"You say Jenners is your supplier?" he asked Mrs. Arbuthnot.

"Always has been, sir," she answered stiffly. "My late mistress, God rest her soul, she always claimed they were the best."

"This milk has been diluted with chalk and water."

Aunt Lavinia gasped.

He turned back to Mrs. Arbuthnot who seemed to me much paler than she had been when she first came in. "I must question the veracity of your reply," he charged in a low, steady voice, drawing out each word. "There have been no cases of typhoid reported from families supplied by Jenner's. And I believe what we have here is typhoid."

Aunt Lavinia took a step backward, and then a chilly silence filled the room. No one dared take another breath.

Indeed, Mrs. Arbuthnot's next reaction was to remove her own pocket handkerchief and cover her mouth with it. Even in my weak condition, my eyes caught the smallest detail, and I noticed she was clutching one of Mama's nice cambric handkerchiefs embroidered with her initials in blue.

"I'll ask Cook when she returns, sir," she mumbled from behind the handkerchief, avoiding my gaze. "I'll ask her about the milk, I will, sir."

She quickly curtsied and hurried from the room. I remember listening to her flight down the hall, her heavy keys jangling at her waist.

There was so much confusion from that point on, with people coming and going, arguments in the hallway, Aunt Lavinia sobbing and Papa shouting, which frightened me because Papa never raised his voice. I recall being left alone for a long while, and suffering violent cramps, and there was no one to hear and no one to help me from my bed. Later that afternoon Esther found me on the floor in a terrible state. It must have been ghastly, so repulsive, to deal with me, but she cleaned me up and changed my gown and helped me back into my bed. Esther told me that Mrs. Arbuthnot had absconded that very afternoon, which was evidence enough of her guilt, and Cook had returned to find a constable sitting at the kitchen table interrogating Lucy and the scullery maid.

Lucy declared she knew nothing about what was going on, but attested to the fact that Jenners had not delivered our milk for months and that we now took our milk from the Regulated Dairy Company.

"It's cheaper, sir," she had said quite bluntly. "I know it for a fact. Heard Mrs. A talk about it."

Then Father came downstairs with Mother's memorandum books, which had remained locked away in her writing desk. The precision with which she had inventoried the contents of our house made quite an impression on the constable who claimed that his job would be much easier if there were more ladies who managed their homes with such economy. Of course that was no longer the case, as there was terrible disarray in the kitchen and pantries. The stolen items numbered in the hundreds—silver plate, silver tea service, silver dishes and heirlooms and candlesticks and wine goblets, fine china serving dishes, porcelain vases and silver bowls.

It was a frightful scene, Esther said, with Papa at the kitchen table with his head in his hands, Aunt Lavinia guilt-stricken, Lucy in tears, and Cook hotly denying any wrongdoing, pointing the finger of blame at Mrs. Arbuthnot who had been in complete control of our household expenses since Mama's death. Cook had claimed, "Mrs. A told me the master wanted to rid himself of all those things. Said they were sold. Master's instructions. That's what she said, 'n' I believed her. Didn't have no reason to doubt her."

Nevertheless, Father dismissed Cook. She sent up a cold meal that evening and was gone the next morning.

The next day they went through the house and discovered that in addition to the silver and china, we were missing costly French bed linens, delicately embroidered tea towels and bath towels. Even some of our gold embroidered footmen's uniforms that had been stored in trunks were now gone with all the rest. We had paid for services never performed and commodities never received. Mrs. Arbuthnot and Cook had thinned down our soups, our milk, and even our household belongings, and made themselves quite a little profit in the end. In all, Papa totaled our losses to be more than £400.

I have only flashes of memory of those months that followed. I recall Esther's tender care and Papa sitting beside my bed, stroking my face and holding my hand. Aunt Lavinia found her courage in platitudes and scripture, which she read to me in her thin, wistful voice. I think they were more for her own benefit than mine. A character as timid and sensitive as hers surely felt herself partially to blame. She could not bring herself to touch me—Lucy and Esther had to clean me and feed me—but she never left my sick room except to eat and sleep. With her eyes cast down on a piece of embroidery or knitting, she would prattle away about how to manage a house and servants, implying that I would live to one day marry and run a house of my own. It was her way of offering hope and cheer.

"It quite appalls me to see my brother's home so deplorably nasty! It's just as well that she was found out,"—*she* being Mrs. Arbuthnot, whose name was no longer uttered aloud—"and although you had to pay such a terrible price, I know it will all turn out for the better. We have a new cook now, dear, she's been loaned to us by one of your father's clients. She'll do until we find a permanent one. And Mrs. Samson's daughter comes to do the laundry and clean, since we need Lucy to care for you. Oh! but you mustn't worry your head about that, dear, we'll manage. We'll manage better than before. I don't blame your dear father, of course I don't, but he knows better now. He thought she could be trusted, but he knows better now." She put down her needlework to wag a finger at me. "Servants and housekeepers are not to be trusted."

She sat by the window and read to me from pamphlets on the management of domestic affairs. As the days dragged on, she thought it might be helpful to turn out needlepoint pillows emblazoned with her nuggets of wisdom.

"I'm working this one in lilac and blue. Robin's egg blue. Don't you think it's lovely, dear? This one says, 'Once an upper hand is lost, it's not easily regained.' Now, isn't that true? Did I tell you about my cousin Charlotte? When her husband began to lose his reason—he was eighty then—why, she was afraid to visit me because she knew when she returned there would be mutiny in the household. Poor Charlotte."

At some point, I didn't notice her anymore.

Chapter Eight

I SURVIVED THE TYPHOID, BUT IT SEEMED THE COLD I HAD SUF-
fered earlier had infected my ears, leading eventually to a fever that affected my brain. The doctor said I was fortunate to have survived it at all.
At first, I was convinced the loss of my hearing was temporary and would
pass in a few days. But as I recovered my strength and the deafness continued, an atmosphere of quiet crisis fell over our house.

The world around me lost its reality and receded into a misty distance.
I had awakened to a world in which people appeared and disappeared
ghostlike with no warning, and mouths moved and made no sound. Each
day brought a new shock. The simple, physical details of living no longer
came to me through my ears. The nub of my pen no longer scratched the
paper; my cup met my saucer without a clink; the hands of the grandfather clock on the landing advanced the time in a silent world. Sometimes I
was not quite sure if I had performed an action or not, because it made no
sound.

We used pen and paper at first, and then slates and chalk, but as my
headaches lessened and I could tolerate light, I tried to read lips. Aunt
Lavinia showed infinite patience. She would repeat herself five or six times
if necessary, without so much as a hint of annoyance. If, after several attempts, I failed to understand her, she figured out that a slight change of
vocabulary might unlock the meaning for me. Still, I could generally make
out only a few words, and I surmised the rest.

Papa, I realized with great disappointment, was very difficult to understand. He hardly moved his mouth at all when he spoke, and his mustache
interfered with what little lip movement there was. He almost always communicated on a slate. He would ask short questions about my health, but
this was not what I needed from him. I wanted to know about Grenfell's
and his clients, about our new housekeeper, Mrs. Scholfield, and how

Aunt Lavinia was managing, but his simple, terse replies written carefully on the slate were like dry bones tossed to a starving man.

Esther tried very hard to maintain the spontaneity of our chatter. She would sprawl at the foot of my bed with ink pot and paper, scribbling out her thoughts, then wait impatiently while I read what she had written. Conversation with Esther was an exuberant hodgepodge of mime and written and spoken words. She poured her heart into the tiresome task, but often it was only meaningless gibberish played out in utter silence. Try as I might, I could make no sense out of it. Had we been children playing games, I would have found her wildly entertaining, but this was not a game.

I recall the first day I dressed and came downstairs for dinner, hoping to leave behind in my stifling room the shroud of depression that now darkened my thoughts. I was still very weak, and the brain fever had affected my balance so that I stumbled a little when I walked. I wore a new dress of pale mauve since I was no longer in deep mourning, and I recall how much this small thing lifted my spirits. Then I sat down at the table with Aunt Lavinia and Papa. Papa stood and raised his wineglass and said something to me that I assumed to be words of welcome and encouragement. He noted my new dress with a nod of approval.

"Do you like the color?" I asked.

He said something I was not quite sure I understood, but his eyes shone with approval.

Then he sat down and turned to Aunt Lavinia. While Lucy served us, they conversed together for a while in a normal manner. With a sudden chill of apprehension, it occurred to me that I was unable to follow even a trace of their conversation. I understood not one word of it. I was shut out; I wasn't there. Somehow, all those weeks confined to my room had sheltered me from the full realization that I was excluded, absolutely, from the world in which sound existed.

As Lucy silently arranged a portion of roast beef on my plate, I felt the most awful sensation come over me. An intense heat raged inside my head. At the same time, there settled over my heart a gloom of such substance, such weight, that I thought for a moment I would not be able to breathe.

I must have made an audible sound, for when I lifted my eyes, they were watching me.

"Pray forgive me," I muttered, and I rose from the table and hurried from the room.

I WANTED DESPERATELY TO UNDERSTAND what was going on around me, and I believed the failure was my fault. I thought I should be able to understand the words on their lips, but I was stupidly mistaken. I understood practically nothing. And writing everything down was cumbersome. Yet, I felt the greatest loss was not that of fundamental meaning—it was the quick wit and meaningless words casually interjected into a conversation which make verbal exchange so pleasant. It was like the difference between clothing the human form in a rudimentary and shapeless garment, and clothing it in something of substance that reflects individual taste as well as the dictates of our society. Our voice and the way we use language is every bit as personal as our style. I had not realized how much my father's voice, and the way he used it, played such an important role in the impression he left on others and had a good deal to do with his success as a tailor. There was so much self-assured style in his mellifluous voice that even the most critical and cynical of clients would relinquish their notions and give themselves up to Papa's vision. It was the same way with Esther and her laugh; Esther had a vibrant, voluble laugh that drew you into her merriment. Although I eventually grew accustomed to it, at the first, watching their lips move at me in silence, watching them laugh and yet make not a sound, all this made them seem almost unreal to me. Separate from their voice, the whole person was no longer the same.

All my normal activities ceased. Even my old tutors had gone from my life. They were not prepared to educate a deaf girl.

At times my loss drove me to despair, so impenetrable was the barrier it dropped between me and the world I once knew. Only the written word connected me to all that I had left behind. I began to read a good deal. I camped in Reggie's room, buried in his books, feeling more connected to him than to the living world that bustled by outside my window. Since I could no longer hear that world, it didn't even exist until I drew back the curtains and looked down upon the teeming street. Horses and carriages drifted eerily by; ragged boys stood at the corner waving newspapers and flapping their mouths in soundless fury. It had always made such a racket before, and I knew it still did, but I was cut off from it now.

I picked up a pen and began to record my thoughts in a journal. I was not a diarist as a young girl—my hands were too busy with needle and thread, but as I gradually grew aware of what I had lost, written words helped to ease my anguish. It is through these writings, and of course my Talking Book, that I have been able to reconstruct my life. If I have added a touch of invention or portrayed my understanding of the hearing world to be greater than it often is, I beg indulgence. I should not wish to burden the reader with the very difficulties with which I struggle moment by moment. For one who, on occasion, may be unintelligible in spoken conversation, it is greatly comforting to know that in these pages I have a clear and distinct voice.

I spent many hours in the sunny drawing room, with Aunt Lavinia seated opposite me, embroidering little bits of nonsense. I think she was fonder of me now. I think she felt my deafness would have a much-needed taming influence on me. She had been deeply wounded when Papa had rejected her offer to run our house following Mama's death, but we had seen our folly and repented our ways. Grandpa was left to the care of Aunt Mary, and Aunt Lavinia returned to take her rightful place in her brother's home. Together, we were the picture of perfect domestic serenity. There I sat, with a basket of colored yarns at my feet, my hands working steadily to the rhythm of contentment, and all the while my thoughts were swimming in unfathomable depths of depression. My entire world had been diminished. I was condemned to eternal uselessness.

My thoughts often drifted back to the last months before my illness. The last days I lived as a normal girl—the last days in which every moment was played out against a backdrop of sound—I was able to recall with a heightened sense of clarity. Perhaps this is why Lady Hambledon's few pieces of correspondence were so precious to me. I received many letters of encouragement and solace from family and friends, but hers I kept with me all the time, in my pocket, folded neatly and tied with blue ribbon. I took them out and read them so many times during the day that I began to fret that I might wear out the paper, and so I would force myself to abstain, convincing myself that by foregoing the pleasure, I would make it that much greater. It was the last thing I did as I snuggled down in my bed. I'd untie them and read them, and hold them to my heart. They helped me to sleep.

She wrote:

My dear, I am greatly relieved to hear of your steady recovery, and I look forward to receiving you again as soon as your health permits. Your cheerful countenance is sorely missed.

I myself have had the misfortune to suffer several riding accidents and found myself laid up for months on end while bones healed. It is indeed taxing on the spirit, but you must put your faith in God and keep looking toward the light. And there *is* light, my dear. He promises it to us. He will keep His promise.

You have come to mean a great deal to me. I should never pretend that mothers and daughters can be replaced, but special friendships can fill up the emptiness created by their loss.

As you now know, my precious Aurelia is all but dead to me. I have not seen her in eight years, and I am told I shall never see her again; the rules of the convent forbid it. Yet, with every breath I take, my heart utters a prayer that I might see her once more.

But for now, it is you who are foremost in my prayers, my dear Veda.

May the Lord Bless you and Keep you,

May He make His Face to shine upon you, and be gracious unto you.

May the Lord lift up His Countenance upon you

And give you peace.

Her faith not only consoled me, it took me by surprise. I had not imagined this to be a prominent feature of her character. Virtue can exist outside of faith, but it walks on shaky legs, and despite the example set by Prince Albert and our Queen, I know that privilege, rank, and wealth sleep fitfully in the same bed with honesty, humility, and faith.

There was a second letter:

My dearest Veda,

I have seen your finished portrait and it is beyond a doubt one of Sir Francis's most exciting works. He is indeed an accomplished artist and comfortable with his talents, but you inspired him to attempt something outside that place of comfort. He worked steadily on it all throughout your illness and asked about you whenever I stopped by his studio. He continued to see you as vividly as if you were sitting there in the chair, your offering clutched in your hand. When we learned of the complications in your situation, he was deeply moved.

"I shall bring that girl to life, Lady Alice," he announced to me. "Every stroke of my brush, I shall do it. Indeed, I shall. She'll not fail."

Now, dear Veda, I have never known Sir Francis to be sentimental, but he was touched by your plight, and I do think he believed your life hung on the completion of that portrait.

Perhaps he was right. Because you are well and will soon be coming to visit again.

The portrait hangs in a place of honor in his studio. He eagerly looks forward to the day you are well enough to view it.

With my deepest affection, I remain sincerely yours,

Alice Breadalbane,
Countess of Hambledon

OUT OF DISCRETION, LADY HAMBLEDON never referred to my deafness, but she did send a physician to me. He came once, briefly, with the hurried arrogance of a great man of science unaccustomed to ministering to a patient of my lowly rank. He addressed Aunt Lavinia, explaining that the tiny bones inside my ears were stiff and needed to be softened to allow sound to pass through. He prescribed camphor oil, to be heated and poured into the ear—a remedy we had already tried without success. He also suggested a change of air. A warmer climate would be advisable, a place like Italy where I could sit outdoors without my bonnet and allow the sun's heating properties to loosen my ear bones and restore my hearing.

Of all the physicians who came to treat me, he was the only one who departed without taking the small packet of banknotes Papa had discreetly placed on the hall table. Papa was greatly offended.

The last letter, which came several weeks later, broke my heart:

My dear Veda,

I write in haste, as I must leave London tomorrow at dawn and have all my affairs to put in order before my departure. A difficult situation has arisen, and my husband urgently requires my presence at Blackroak Hall.

It is doubtful that I will return before next year, but I will receive you then with all the familiarity and affection that has been reserved for you during your illness, and will accrue with interest in my heart until we meet again. In the meantime we shall correspond, and you will keep me informed as to

your progress. You are young and full of promise. Do not let this obstacle—
daunting though it be—deter you. Life does not always yield its fruit easily,
and when we cannot get to the top branches where the best and juiciest
pieces cling, we must shake the tree. Shake it hard, dear Veda. Shake it with
all the strength of your heart and soul. There is still much for you to harvest.

I must go. I keenly regret that I will not be in London to attend the RA's
Summer Exhibition and see your portrait hung there.

I remain your eternal friend,
Alice

I wrote several letters to her after that but received no reply.

IT WAS THE PROSPECT OF attending the Royal Academy's Summer Exhibition that kept my spirits alive. Ever since I could remember, Mama had
dragged me off each summer to the Academy's public opening. This time,
Father, Aunt Lavinia, Esther, and I had been invited to a Private View—
an afternoon when the academy was open to an exclusive few, when the
humble masses would be shut out and the great and glorious would mingle and pronounce their opinions on art. I had heard that Mr. Gladstone
would attend, perhaps even Mr. Disraeli. D. G. Rossetti would be there as
well as Mr. Millais and Esther's onetime teacher, Mr. Madox Brown,
along with the famous critic Mr. Ruskin who had his wife stolen by Mr.
Millais. The most distinguished names from the worlds of letters, music,
and theater, even the Church, would be in attendance. But accomplishment was not the only way to get one's foot in the door; rank, wealth, and
the right acquaintance would do. Countesses and duchesses secured invitations along with models and pretty ladies, and they pressed together in the
gallery, standing skirt-to-skirt and gazing upward in unfeigned admiration
at the works of art hung on the hallowed walls. It was an occasion when
one dressed his absolute very best. It was an occasion for stylish hats and
bonnets tied under the chin in perfect bows, for well-blocked and well-
brushed hats. It was the best of occasions in which to shine.

The event meant so much to me. Not only did it mark my return to social normalcy, but my portrait—one of only three exhibited by Sir
Francis—would be the subject of scrutiny by men and women of power
and prestige. I had nothing to do with the success of the portrait, but I was
terribly anxious all the same. Besides, Papa had not yet seen it. He admit-

ted that he had felt disinclined, out of superstition, to lay his eyes upon it until I was out of death's way.

"I'm a ball of nerves," I confessed to Esther that morning while Lucy was doing my hair. "What if it's dreadful?"

"I'm quite sure it's not dreadful."

Lucy raked the comb through a knotted tangle of curls, jerking back my neck. She disliked doing my hair.

"Pray use the brush, Lucy," I pleaded. I suppose she grumbled, because Esther gave her a look of mild rebuke. Esther often did my hair, but now I needed her in my line of sight to see her mouth.

"What if Papa doesn't like it?" I continued.

She scribbled her thoughts on the slate and handed it to me.

Your P's a dear, but appalling taste in painting—very boring—quiet little tea-table tragedies.

She was making an effort at humor, but I could never hold up a smile for long. The strain of reading lips took the smiles out of me.

"I'm afraid," I said.

"Afraid of what?"

"All these people will be talking to me, and I won't understand a word."

"I'll be there."

"We can't use our signs," I said.

Esther and I had invented some simple signs—for the family and servants, and common daily activities.

"Why not?" she gestured.

"We would call attention to ourselves. Everyone would stare. Then they would know I'm deaf."

"Then I shall write it out," she gestured.

"But it's so slow and tedious."

She took the slate and added, *There will be programs. Everyone always takes notes. It will look natural.*

It was my first carriage ride since my recovery, and Papa had the coachman lower the top so I could see around me. We left the house early enough to take a leisurely route down to Piccadilly and along to the Academy. I drank in all the familiar sights of the city—the fresh new window displays, the wonderful tender green of the trees in first leaf and the sprawling deep green of the grassy lawns, the crush of carriages and cabs with an occasional phaeton bouncing along behind a sleek bay. A dense throng of humanity pressed along the pavement, tumbling into the streets and across the corners. Odors assailed us as we passed from one street to the next—some less pleasant than others, but all of them distinctly London. It had not changed one bit, and yet to me it was completely altered from the city where I had lived before. I wondered if I would ever be comfortable in this strange new world.

We obtained our programs and decided to view Mr. Frith's *Derby Day* before moving on to the gallery in which Sir Francis's works were hung. Billed as a "great panorama of modern life," the work had sparked a good deal of attention, and there was a vast crowd pressing around the massive canvas so that we had to wait quite a while to get close enough to view the painting. It was one of those marvelous narrative scenes that Esther finds so tedious and I thoroughly adore—an expansive, exuberant tableau of people gathered at the edge of the racetrack doing what people do. There were tricksters tricking, Reformists ranting, a hungry little acrobat eyeing the picnic laid out by the footman of a haughty lady who waited in her carriage, expressing on her milk-white countenance the deepest ennui while a tired old fortune-teller whispered in her ear. Here we were, depicted with all our foibles and follies, a society divided by short-sighted, iron-clad notions of rank, composed into a brilliantly harmonious whole. I thought Mr. Frith had painted us as God might see us—connected to one another in ways we are too small to understand.

It was the only painting in the exhibit that really drew me in. It told its story without words, through individual narrative incidents that melted into one another, and I regretted when Aunt Lavinia linked my arm through hers and herded me away. After that, as we strolled through the gallery, I found little interest in the dried and static countenances amassed on the walls. I turned my attention instead to the animated expressions of the people around me. It was overwhelming, all this movement with no sound, all these mouths jabbering with Lord-knows-what going on around me that others understood because they could hear. I think it was here in the Academy that I understood for the first time the hugeness of my loss. We encountered many people Papa knew. Many of them acknowledged us with a nod or a brief greeting, or a hand to the hat; only a few snubbed us entirely, as did Lord Conyers, an MP with a porcine figure and fleshy little grommets for eyes. Many paused to speak to us most pleasantly, and it impressed upon me the respect with which my father was viewed by men of rank and prestige. I also encountered for the first time the dilemma that would haunt me for the rest of my life: how to reconcile a lady's demure demeanor with the necessity of scrutinizing expressions in order to understand what was being said.

By the time we found Sir Francis's space, I was feeling the strain of trying to follow conversations, and my head was aching. Esther found it first. When she tugged on my sleeve, I followed her gaze to the wall. There it was—my portrait. It took my breath away. I had never found myself beautiful, but—as Esther had predicted—he had made me ten times more magnificent than I appeared in real life. The painting was not as large as many of the others, some of which were life-sized portraits of noblemen and ladies of high rank, but it must have had a certain appeal, because there was a considerable crowd gathered to admire it.

I turned to look at Papa's face. "Do you like it?" I asked anxiously.

I need not have worried. Whatever reservations he may have had about the unconventional way in which I was posed, his pride got the better of him. He was positively beaming.

"Brilliant," he said. Papa always had a distinguished bearing, but just then I thought he might burst a waistcoat button or two. "By Jove, it's brilliant."

Aunt Lavinia looked as pleased as Punch. I could tell she was trying very hard to maintain her restraint.

I turned to Esther. She had scribbled on her program, "Glorious!"

"Is it, truly?"

Just at that moment, I caught sight of Sir Francis approaching me. He had been the center of that crowd of admirers huddled below my portrait. There were two young ladies, a naval officer, and a balding gentleman with spectacles and a neatly trimmed grey beard watching me curiously. Clearly, they recognized me as the girl in the portrait. Sir Francis appeared terribly pleased, and I was aching to converse with him, but I stood there, waiting quietly while he and Father exchanged greetings. I could not follow their conversation, but I gathered there was considerable excitement about the portrait. Finally, Esther slipped me her program on which she had scrawled, "He's already had offers for the engraving rights."

I looked up at Sir Francis. "You mean the picture will be published?"

He smiled and said something to Papa, and I gathered that there was an agreement in the making.

I wondered why on earth anyone would want to buy engravings of my portrait, but it was not the type of question to ask even if I could hear the answer.

Meanwhile, Sir Francis had turned to his friends and introduced them to us. Fortunately, the bearded gentleman seemed to recognize Esther, and I could withdraw from the conversation. I looked back up at my portrait. It was certainly very flattering, but it was more than that; he had indeed achieved an ambiguity of meaning that, as Lady Hambledon had explained, was at the core of its appeal. I regretted that she was not here to see it. It was, after all, her small touch that had sparked the inspiration.

After a moment, Sir Francis was ready to take his leave. He knew of my deafness and had dealt with a very awkward situation with great discretion. He took my hand to bid me farewell, and I inclined my head to speak to him, trying to keep my voice low, praying that my words would come out quietly.

"Has Lady Hambledon been informed of this good news?"

My question prompted such a complete collapse of his countenance that I thought I had misspoken.

"About the engraving rights, I mean. I thought I might write her, unless, of course, you have already done so."

A look of vexation spread through the small group. The women whispered to one another behind their bonnets; the officer seemed flustered. I wondered what I had said to cause so much consternation.

Sir Francis was speaking to me. I suppose I should have ignored him and turned to Esther for an explanation, but I thought, surely, this much I could comprehend. I fastened my eyes on his moving lips, sifting through all the possibilities of words he might be saying, trying to fit them together into something sensible. When he saw I was not understanding him, a perplexed look crossed his face. It was a look that would plague me the rest of my life, the look of total bewilderment when people crashed into that invisible, impenetrable barrier of my deafness.

"Pray, could you speak more slowly," I begged him.

He paused and glared at me in indignant horror. Then, provoked by my failure to understand, he raised his voice, perhaps more loudly than he had intended, for there passed through the crowd one great collective look of stunned embarrassment. I realized, too late, that everyone around us had ceased speaking, so that his words must have resounded like a cannon in the frozen silence around us.

I was humiliated, and near tears. "I'm not hard of hearing. I'm deaf," I said. "It does no good to shout."

Sir Francis blushed deeply, and he muttered something, and then quickly took his leave.

Then, Esther thrust her program under my nose. On it she had scribbled, *Lady Hambledon is gone.*

"I know she's gone," I said. "But has something happened?"

Esther impatiently flipped a page of her program where she had continued. *She died.*

I stared at the writing, refusing to believe it.

"What do you mean?" My voice felt so pinched, I wasn't sure if I had spoken or not.

Esther mouthed one word: "Dead."

Surely, I thought, this much I have misunderstood. "Dead? Are you saying dead?"

People had begun to move away from us. I was making an abominable scene. Papa was dreadfully vexed. He took my elbow, but I pulled free.

"What has happened? What did he tell you?" I demanded.

I whirled around to search for Sir Francis. He had escaped to the other side of the gallery and was engaged in conversation with an elderly lady seated on a circular bench. I picked up my skirts and hurried up to him. With quiet determination and complete disregard for manners, I took my program and my pencil and thrust them at him. He started, and the old woman muttered some exclamation of alarm or another, but I stood my ground. My lip was trembling, and I thought I might fall into a most distressful state if he didn't oblige me with a full explanation. I spoke not a word, but he took one look at me and his stony face softened, then he took the program from my hand and wrote at some length. Aunt Lavinia appeared at my side and must have offered an apology, but he dismissed her with a wave of his hand and finished his note to me.

His hand trembled as he wrote.

She fell into a coma & passed away just last week.

I read it and looked up into his eyes. They had taken on a watery, stricken look. He made a gesture to his head and muttered something.

"What's that?" I asked.

He wrote, *A head injury. From a riding fall.*

I closed the program on those dreadful words. My hands, too, were trembling. The silence around me was formidable.

I didn't dare look into his eyes. I feared we might both lose our composure. He graciously took my hand and squeezed it. I cast one last glance at him from beneath my bonnet, curtsied, and then, concealing the crisis in my heart, made my way out of the gallery.

I KEPT MY LOSS TO myself. I hoarded my grief. When Esther tried to offer words of comfort, I turned my eyes away. The only person with whom I might have shared my sentiments was Harry. I wrote him a letter but then talked myself out of sending it. Somehow, I felt insignificant in the scheme of things. I knew my friendship had meant something to Lady Hambledon, but I was only a passing acquaintance to Harry. There was little chance we would ever meet again.

Out of courtesy, I sent a short note of condolence to Blackroak Hall. I received only a printed acknowledgment in reply.

Chapter Nine

Of all the tutors we interviewed to teach me lip reading, why was it that only Mrs. Crabtree wanted the position? She had the stubbornness of a mastiff and jowls to match. They hung like soft swags below each jaw, connected in the center by a chin that tumbled down her neck. When she turned her head sharply, it took a long time for all that flesh to settle down again. It was terribly distracting for me, and visual distractions were not what I needed when I was trying to read lips. She smelled strongly of cooking oil, and whenever she settled her wide skirts into a chair, she gave off a cloud of most unpleasant vapors. She wore a dingy lace morning cap over a head of thinning grey hair, which she scratched repeatedly with the point of a knitting needle, for she often knitted during our lessons. The entire creature needed a thorough brushing and airing. Papa wouldn't have lasted five minutes in the same room with her. I think she took me on because she knew she had little chance of employment elsewhere. We were stuck with each other.

To begin with, she had no method. She just sat there, talking at me, often with her face cast down at her work, repeating herself over and over with the stubborn belief that I would eventually understand what she was saying.

"You must try harder, Miss Grenfell," she would mouth at me. That much I understood; it was her standard response to my failure. Or, "You must pay close attention, Miss Grenfell."

"I am paying close attention, but it would help if you would look at me," I replied one day.

With the air of one who has suffered great injury, she laid down her knitting, took up her slate, and wrote, *You must learn to understand in all situations. You cannot always expect people to make allowances for you.*

I replied, "And is it your desire that I learn to read lips through the backs of heads as well?"

To this she made no reply at all. Whenever I was sharp with her, she would sit in miffed silence for the rest of the hour, head buried in her knitting, making no effort whatsoever. So I would pick up a book and read, or sit at Mama's secretary writing in the journal I had begun to keep, until it was time for her to leave.

She was infinitely useless. I was making no progress.

The only person able to offer any assistance was Mr. Nicholls, Reggie's tutor. The winter following Reggie's death, Esther and I had been invited to his lodgings to take tea on several occasions. He had always shown himself most solicitous and kind, and after my illness, he had shown me great compassion. If he had rarely called on us, it was out of respect for my father—he understood all too well the heavy sense of guilt and accountability that we all bore for Reggie's death—but he wrote me letters of encouragement and sent me some of his precious books. It was he who suggested that we should pursue pedagogical solutions rather than simply muddle through.

Then one day I received a most extraordinary letter from him:

My dear Miss Grenfell,

You have written to me of your dissatisfaction with your new governess, and being of the opinion that there must exist better-trained ladies than the one whom you now employ, I have taken the liberty of calling on an institution here in London dedicated to teaching deaf children. It is modeled after an institution in Edinburgh which has had great success.

I pray you will not take offense at this gesture, thinking perhaps that I have acted too rashly on your behalf, but I feel strongly that this calamity that has befallen you must not crush you. In the absence of influences that are necessary to maintain the faculties of intellect, self-culture and active exertion are of the utmost importance; without them, those faculties will wither and grow dim. The mind is God's gift and must be nurtured with as much diligence as the soul. You have written to me that you feel yourself diminished in the eyes of everyone you meet, that your clumsiness in social situations is humiliating, and your slowness to comprehend has marked you as an inferior person. When I read this, I felt it my duty to respond.

I write this perhaps prematurely, for I am not yet completely satisfied with my inquiries. I have met with the director of the school, but I shall return this

week and observe a class in session. I should not propose the formal setting
for yourself, of course, as these children have all been born deaf. But I am
certain I shall be able to obtain some valuable insight as to the pedagogy that
is used, and I will pass this information along to you in hopes that it might be
implemented by your governess—or by another of more worth.

> Your devoted friend and servant,
> Mr. Edgar Nicholls

On Monday, there was the following:

My dear Miss Grenfell,
I am grateful for the vote of confidence implied by your brief note, but I fear
I may have spoken too soon, for upon closer examination I have found the
school to be greatly inadequate to the needs of a young woman endowed
with gifts as great as yours. I am heartily ashamed at having raised your
hopes, but only prematurely, if I may say, because I do not intend to allow
this to rest.

On my second visit to the school, I was given the opportunity to examine
several of the model students. To my astonishment, I found them no better at
reading lips than am I. Their knowledge of the written language is equally
lacking. Although they were able to read passages from the Bible, when I
wrote down a simple question, they had tremendous difficulty deciphering it,
and their responses struck me as a hodgepodge of scripture and passages
they may have memorized from primers; they seem to have little ability to
translate original thought into language. The only mode of true communication of which they seem capable is that of finger-play or finger-language,
which all the students use, even though it is strictly prohibited in class and in
the presence of teachers. Indeed, their faces light up when they communicate in this mode, and they grow exceedingly animated. But this last technique is not a desirable substitute, as you would not wish to attract the
attention and curiosity of others, although it would be most useful in the
home, as you and Miss Tigues have already established.

I was greatly disturbed by my findings and left the school feeling more
despondent than I care to admit. Thus, I have taken it upon myself to devise
a system of instruction that I believe might help you progress toward normalcy. If I may be permitted to call upon you next week, I would like to present my ideas to you and your governess.

I intentionally planned his visit on the day Aunt Lavinia routinely called on Grandpa and her sister in Kensington, for I knew from experience that the more hearing people there were in the room, the more difficult it was for me to follow a conversation. I was surprised to find Mr. Nicholls considerably changed since last winter; his beard had been neatly trimmed, and his copper curls were shorn close to his head. Were it not for the uncouth make of his tobacco-colored coat, and the shabby hat, I would have taken him for a gentleman of rank. He had gained a little weight in the chest, which lent him a more robust, manly figure, and I wondered if he had been getting his meals on a more regular basis. I was a little mystified by my feelings, for I found his appearance quite pleasing.

Mrs. Crabtree seemed very impressed by Mr. Nicholls. To my astonishment, I saw the dull complacency which she reserved for me get itself up into something appallingly flirtatious. She became all bounce and vigor and coy sweetness, making a horrid spectacle of herself. From the moment he walked into the sitting room, she behaved as if she were the mistress of the house and I were a brainless child. She presided over the tea table with false airs, chiding Lucy for being so stingy with the biscuits and demanding that a fire be lit even though it was a mild September day. Whenever I tried to speak to Mr. Nicholls, she would silence me with a sharp, reprimanding look, and then engage his attention with questions. Mr. Nicholls listened and responded most courteously, but it soon became evident to him, as well as to me, that she was cruelly and intentionally excluding me from the conversation. I followed very little of what was said, but I did gather that she was begging him to explain his new ideas for teaching as if she had her ward's best interests in mind, which Mr. Nicholls and I both knew to be false. As the minutes passed by, I could see he was becoming more and more perplexed, because each time he attempted to address me, she would intervene. If he turned to speak directly to me, mouthing his words slowly and clearly in hopes that I might understand, she would interfere and respond in my place. If he moved to pick up the slate to write on it, she would distract him with more questions, or more tea, or another biscuit. Eventually, with a pretext of wiping it clean, she removed the slate from his reach and kept it—seemingly absentmindedly—in her own lap, so that he was left with just the chalk in his hand.

Finally, realizing I had to foil her rudeness with rudeness of my own, I set down my tea cup and rose from my chair.

"May I have the slate please, Mrs. Crabtree?" I said, quite politely but firmly. I towered over the stout old woman, all five foot, nine inches of me, with my hand outstretched and that look I can get on my face when I am not to be denied. Her mouth quit moving for a moment, and her great jowls quivered in astonishment.

I repeated, "Pray pass the slate to me so Mr. Nicholls can explain his teaching methods."

Then, a most amazing look crossed her countenance, as though she had momentarily mistaken me for someone with intelligence, and now, re-membering I was but an idiot, she should address me as such.

She picked up the slate and wrote on it, *I will sort this out. These things are beyond your understanding.*

There it was, in black and white. I don't know if it was nervousness or simply the absurdity of it all that caused me to laugh, but I did.

"Pray do forgive me," I said with a glance to Mr. Nicholls, but I saw that my laughter had brought a twinkle to his eyes, and he reached for the slate just as I offered it to him. When he read the words she had written there, I think I'd never seen an expression alter so quickly from mirth to horrified indignation.

As he rose to his feet to speak in my defense, I quickly surmised that Mr. Nicholls, whom I already knew to be a man of extreme emotion, had a temperament to match that red hair of his. I laid a hand on his arm to quiet him and entreated him with a gaze that had not lost its humor.

He tugged on his waistcoat, then clasped his hands behind his back and waited stiffly, with the pugnacious demeanor of a boxer anticipating his moment in the ring.

I turned to the governess and said in what I hoped was a voice modu-lated with kindness, "My dear Mrs. Crabtree, may I remind you once again that the absence of one sense does not imply an absence of sense in general. I am not a child without judgment and education, and I wish to be treated with the same deference you would accord a ward with perfect hearing. But you seem unwilling to do this." I paused, scrutinizing her face for some indication of repentance, but there seemed to be only that same look of stubborn denial. So I made up my mind then and there. I continued, "Therefore, I am taking it upon myself to give you notice. As of this moment, your services are no longer desired."

I stepped back, allowing her room to stand, for at the moment she was hedged in by Mr. Nicholls, myself, and the tea table.

She swung her head around to Mr. Nicholls and made some short entreaty, but I knew, without glancing at him, that he was holding as fast as I.

I said gently, "Pray, take your knitting and go. Leave this house at once. You may return tomorrow for whatever sum is owed to you."

And so she did. There was no fury, only numb bewilderment. While she packed her needlework into her bag, I rang for Lucy. Mr. Nicholls had regained his composure, but—just in case she might make one last stand—he remained on his feet, lending his authority to my own.

When she left, I was just so full of joy, so relieved at having banned her from my sight forever, that I danced around the sitting room like a savage for the longest time while Mr. Nicholls looked on, grinning broadly. Finally, when I had vented my relief, I came twirling up to stand beside him, quite out of breath.

"Oh, my dear Mr. Nicholls. You have saved me from the dragon," I said, hand over heart in a most dramatic fashion.

He scrawled on the slate in his elegant handwriting, *Perhaps I should return when your Aunt is home?* I realized then that we were in a most delicate situation, without a chaperone. That problem had not occurred to me.

"Oh, but that would be such an inconvenience to you, and I feel like so much time has been wasted already. Would you teach me? Could you teach me?"

I think my lack of restraint took him off guard, for he blushed to the roots of his red hair.

"I would be honored," he said, mouthing the words clearly and adding a stiff little bow.

He seemed as eager to begin as I was. After removing some papers from a small document case he had deposited beside his chair, with a glance around the room, he indicated Mama's secretary.

"May I?"

Pulling up a second chair, we settled down, side by side, and he laid his notes before me. I saw that he had already taken great pains to make a thorough presentation of his theories and the methods he hoped to put into practice. Beneath my quiet composure, while I read, I felt my heart swell. His compassion and caring had touched me deeply. I could see why Reggie had grown so fond of him.

It was most uncanny, as though he had read my thoughts. While I was engaged in reading his paper, he was busy writing something which, at one point, he slid across the desk under my eyes.

Miss Grenfell, there is something I want you to know before we proceed. It is most important. It concerns your brother. May I speak of it?

I recoiled inwardly as I read the words, but I nodded.

I was devoted to your brother as a tutor, he wrote. *But only as a tutor. I never encouraged his peculiar sentiments for me. When he made them known, I assured him that my affection for him—which was great—was of the proper kind, & that he must not hope for a friendship that went beyond the boundaries of propriety.*

I was much too affected to meet his gaze, so I only said, "I understand, Mr. Nicholls."

He scribbled at the bottom of the paper, *I do hope I have not offended you by speaking so bluntly.*

"Not at all." I paused, then added, "I'm most relieved." Then, gathering my shawl about my shoulders, I closed my thoughts to those dreadful memories and said, "Now, let us begin."

THAT EVENING, I WAITED UNTIL we had finished dinner, knowing what I had to say would distress my father to no end and hoping that a good meal would put him in better humor to digest bad news.

"Papa, today I took it upon myself to dismiss Mrs. Crabtree."

I wasn't sure if I had been understood, because Aunt Lavinia turned to me with a bland smile and Papa, who was pouring himself a glass of port from the sideboard, set down the decanter, removed his spectacles, and rubbed his eyes.

"Papa?"

He turned to me, his spectacles dangling from his fingers. I could tell he was very tired.

"You dismissed Mrs. Crabtree?" he repeated, quite distinctly.

"She was worthless and a waste of your money. In her place I have engaged Mr. Nicholls."

From the gravity of his face, I knew that I would have had an ear full, had I been able to hear all he had to say on the matter. But by virtue of my deafness, he was obliged to let his feelings simmer in silence, the only alternative being to pick up a slate and write them down, but he looked too tired for all this. I felt very sorry for him, but I was quickly learning that it was in my interest to use my deficiencies to my advantage when at all possible.

In the absence of an immediate reprimand, I went on presenting my case.

"He has taken a charitable interest in my plight and has proposed a plan for teaching me to read lips. I think with him I shall make some progress. And you know him, Papa. He is devoted and earnest. I have learned this afternoon that he has abandoned his Methodist persuasion and accepted a position as rector at St. Albans. A very prestigious position, I might add." I kept watching Papa's face, hoping to read there some softening of his heart. "Clearly, he's an honorable man. He's proposed to give me an hour each day, and two hours on Tuesday, which is very generous for a man with so many parish duties." I don't know how my voice sounded, but I found my stomach was twisting itself in knots in an effort to plead my case.

He shook his head. I couldn't tell if it was a gesture of denial or resigned despair.

I rose from the table and approached him.

"I would never have learned a thing with her. And without learning to read lips, my life is on a path to total isolation. You know how difficult it has been to find someone to even attempt the task, and it is daunting, you have no idea—even with Mr. Nicholls—" He seemed to flinch as I spoke the name, and I instinctively reached out and laid a soothing hand on his arm. "Even were I to have the best teacher in the world, I think I know how impossible it will be. I believe I am in the best situation to understand what will produce the desired results. I'm almost seventeen now. And the calamities of this past year have made me become much more sensible and womanly than I would have been otherwise. In a month, I shall be out. Whatever that means. It certainly doesn't mean the same thing for me as it does for other girls. There will surely be no garden parties and no court balls and no suitors knocking on our door. I only want—I just want—"

He did not let me finish. He took me by the shoulders, leaned forward, and kissed me on the forehead. Papa rarely showed his affection, and it was all it took to break down my reserve. Much to my chagrin, I found tears streaming down my face. Papa pulled out his handkerchief and passed it to me, and I blotted at my wet cheeks. Then he took a step back, adjusted his spectacles on his face, and took up the slate that always lay beside his plate at dinner. He wrote, *I believe Mr. Nicholls was unjustly discredited.*

That was all. Then he strode proudly from the room.

I HAD SUCH GREAT EXPECTATIONS for Mr. Nicholls. I waited for him each day with the hopes that he would unlock the world for me. I watched from my window, and when I saw him coming down the street, I would dash down to the sitting room and shake Aunt Lavinia from her afternoon stupor, tug ten times on the bell rope to summon Lucy for tea, and finally position myself in a chair with my hands folded across my smock and my eyes fixed on the door, waiting for it to open.

He began by taking passages of scripture I knew by heart and reading these to me, believing that preknowledge of the discourse would assist me in recognizing the shape of words on the lips. After repeating this opening exercise, he would break down the passage, excerpting short phrases and words, repeating them until I could recognize them. Then he would arbitrarily mix everything up, and then I was hopelessly lost. To his credit, he never lost hope, although I was often close to despair.

Believing I might be more inspired by secular works, we turned to poetry, and he would depart each day having left a new poem for me to memorize. Then, the following lesson, he would proceed as before, reading parts of the poem back to me while I watched his lips, later breaking it down to phrases and then words. Lip reading is immensely difficult, and the exercises were fatiguing business. A half-hour intensive session was enough to strain my eyes and tax my concentration. To read lips, the mind must learn to register lip patterns while working to select the correct meaning from a vast number of possibilities. Consonants and vowels are formed by tongue movements of which many are scarcely visible, and certain groups of consonants like *p,b,m,* or *sh, ch,* and *j* are indistinguishable. I despaired of ever understanding moving lips.

Every day before departing, he would turn to me with a firm handshake and a bow, and sober words of encouragement.

"Well done, Miss Grenfell. You have made progress today."

"I haven't."

"But you have."

"I'm so slow."

"Bit by bit, Miss Grenfell."

"I shall never understand what people say."

"I shall return tomorrow."

And he would take his leave.

My pleasures were small, and I took great delight in a successful exchange with Lucy or Mrs. Scholfield or Aunt Lavinia. Callers were even less welcome than before, because they tired me so. Although my world was diminishing, as I had feared, at least the smaller, closely circumscribed world within the walls of 19 Savile Row was no longer incomprehensible. With our signs and gestures and my determination to read lips, our domestic life became less strained.

In the evening, the drawing room would be ablaze with candles and a roaring coal fire, for I needed the light to see the slight distinctions of shapes formed by the lips. Candles are costly, but it was an indulgence Papa willingly permitted. With the flickering glow of candlelight, our evenings were merrier than they had been since Mama's and Reggie's deaths. Before my deafness, Papa generally left me alone and retired to his study to read, but now he would sit with Aunt Lavinia and me in the sitting room, and it was Papa who would read to me. As a way of preparation for these evening lessons, each morning I would read articles he had selected from *The Times,* as well as such trade journals as the *Tailor and Cutter,* on occasions going so far as to commit parts to memory. In the evening he would read them back to me, and I would try to associate the lip movements with the words. I was even permitted to read material that ladies are generally forbidden to read until after they are married. I particularly enjoyed *The Gentleman's Magazine of Fashions, Fancy Costume and the Regimentals of the Army.* It carried excellent color plates of uniformed officers and, most useful to me, detailed descriptions of seasonable fashions. The best part was the society gossip and the advice column for married ladies and gentlemen. My favorite magazine by far was *Punch,* which I had to hide from Aunt Lavinia.

In this way my education and awareness of political and social events became much greater than it would have had I pursued my very narrow interests. Knowledge was thrust upon me, and, according to Mr. Nicholls, knowledge was power. I often thought of Colonel Von Sacher, my godfather, and his admonitions. It seemed I was indeed living up to my name.

One evening when I became frustrated by my inability to understand what Papa was reading to me, I rose and said, "Please, waste no more of your time with me tonight. It's hopeless." My eyes ached from the strain and I could not bear to make one more ounce of effort. Adjusting my shawl, I set off slowly pacing the drawing room. This was the limit of my world—the blue and cream figured wallpaper, the mirrored mantle reflecting a regiment of flickering candles set in silver and bronze candlesticks, wall sconces supporting small bronze figurines, a few portraits of ancestors from Mama's side of the family, and tastefully framed landscapes of green leafy woodlands. Over the past year we had added numerous pencil sketches by Esther, along with her magnificent oil of a half-clothed Andromeda chained to a rock that Papa, knowing how much I admired it, had courageously offered me for my seventeenth birthday over the objections of Aunt Lavinia. She would not set foot in the drawing room for days after it was hung and still averted her eyes from the thing. My other favorites were two watercolor portraits of Arab potentates and a panoramic scene of a village in Ceylon, works bequeathed to me by the Colonel. Conspicuous by its absence was my portrait, which had been carefully stored in one of Grenfell's workrooms downstairs, for I could not bear to look at it without thinking of Lady Hambledon. The furniture was in the exact same arrangement it had been for years. The only change to our domestic landscape in recent memory had been introduced by Aunt Lavinia. Not one chair had escaped her crocheted antimacassars, nor were our tables free from her clutter—everywhere were little pieces of crochet or yarn or needles she had put down and forgotten. Papa never complained about it, although a year ago her untidiness and forgetfulness would have elicited sharp criticism. Now he never complained about anything.

I strolled past Aunt Lavinia, who looked up from her needlepoint and smiled kindly and said something I did not grasp.

Dear God, I thought, how can I make my way in the world without understanding the world around me? Am I doomed to live the rest of my life within these walls?

Then I was startled by a nudge at my elbow. I turned to find Papa standing behind me, holding out a slate on which he had written, *My dear, your sight is excellent & your observation acute. If you can take the measurement of a monkey's arm at a glance—you will learn to read the words on the lips of another.*

His confidence brought a smile to my face.

"Thank you, Papa."

He patted my hand. "Good night, dear."

"Good night."

I watched him shuffle from the room, elegant as always in his cut velvet dressing gown and tartan wool slippers. He never talked about his loss, but I could see it on his countenance, more so now since I watched him so closely all the time. He seemed to have aged decades within the past year, and his hair was now nearly white. Often when he glanced at me, I read fear in his eyes, for he was haunted by the thought of losing me as well. I think sometimes it was this that kept me from the pit of despair and kept me returning to the work at hand, to the studies or the reading, or the text to be memorized before my next lesson with Mr. Nicholls.

The bells were Mr. Nicholls's suggestion. Only a man of his sensitivity would have thought of such a thing. He made the proposition in writing and addressed it to Papa, which was ever so honorable.

Mr. Nicholls knew how profoundly deaf the fever had left me, how only certain percussive sounds could be detected by my physical being. One afternoon, at the end of our session, I expressed my regret that I could no longer hear the church bells toll the call to worship.

"You will hear the bells of St. Albans," he said to me at our next lesson.

"Mr. Nicholls," I said, "that is quite impossible."

He smiled mysteriously. "I have a plan."

The little experiment, as he called it, took place on a Wednesday at evensong. Papa accompanied me, and the three of us climbed the winding stairs up the church tower to the belfry. They had to leave me alone, which Papa was reluctant to do, but the sound would have deafened them. They passed a stool up the ladder, and I stationed myself with my back pressed against a solid oak post that supported the cross beams from which the bell was suspended, for I was told I would better experience the sound in this manner. I perched there, quite dainty and genteel in my peach silk and cream bonnet with my gloved hands folded in my lap, watching the pigeons bob along on the ledge, and then suddenly the big bell began to move. It took some time before she swung high enough for me to feel the percussion, but as the massive cast-iron bell tilted higher with each tug of the rope below, the clapper struck with increasing power, and I felt my body begin to resonate with each dull thud, as if I were part of the sound itself. I stood, untied my bonnet, removed my gloves and laid them on the chair. Then I turned and wrapped my arms around the old oak pillar, and with my eyes closed I embraced the sound that was passing through it.

That day, with my cheek pressed against the cool, weathered oak and my arms embracing it, there was an onslaught of sound the likes of which I have never known as a hearing person. I can only liken it to a multitude of languages speaking at once, the result of which is not cacophony but pure symmetry, and which leaves one with the absolute assurance that— without understanding a thing—one has understood everything.

THE FIRST ANNIVERSARY OF MAMA'S and Reggie's deaths had yet to be confronted. We limped through, mostly in silence, and marked the day with visits to their graves. Christmas was equally difficult, but before I knew it we had passed through the worst. Then the grey chill gave way to a softness in the air, the harbinger of spring.

My lessons with Mr. Nicholls continued. He was the rock in my life. Never once did he miss a session, even when he had taken ill with a cold and seemed so feverish that Aunt Lavinia forced her Swift's Miracle on him, which put him right to sleep. He spent the afternoon snoring on the sofa, or so I was told, covered with one of Aunt Lavinia's quilts.

Religion was never discussed in our household, and yet I cannot remember a time when our family did not attend services faithfully. After Mama's death, Papa found immense solace in the company of Reverend Weightman, and we adopted the habit of returning Sunday evening to hear him preach again. After my deafness, I could not be expected to sit through hours of meaningless moving lips each Sunday, and since it was the only day my father and I spent together, we established a ritual of rising late and taking breakfast at the fashionable Langley Hotel before enjoying a leisurely ride through the Park to Grandpa's house in Kensington where we spent the remainder of the day. I know Papa missed the community of believers, as did I, but it was just another way we were forced to adapt to the changed circumstances of our lives.

Then, one day, Mr. Nicholls arrived at the house with a lengthy handwritten document in his case.

"Here. This is for you."

"What is it?"

With his slender, pale hand he flattened out the sheets for me.

"This is a sermon," I stated.

"Yes. The sermon for next Sunday at St. Alban's."

"Is this your sermon?"

"Yes. But this is a copy I made for you."

"For me?"

"You may keep it."

"You wrote it all down for me?"

"So that you might follow the sermon. If you and your family should decide to attend, I shall reserve the front pew. That way you will be close enough to see my lips move."

"Mr. Nicholls! How very thoughtful of you." I turned over a few pages. There must have been thirty in all. "My goodness, the time it must have taken you to copy this—"

He seemed embarrassed. "It's nothing," he replied with a toss of the head. "I assure you. It's nothing compared to your efforts, Miss Grenfell. Your determination—" This word he wrote on the slate I handed him—he always caught the look of bafflement when I failed to understand. "Your determination to overcome your affliction—" He paused and, showing an unusual lack of restraint, placed his hand over his heart. "—is an inspiration to me."

His kindness overwhelmed me, but I feared Papa's resistance.

"I must speak to my father about this. You know how very fond he is of Reverend Weightman's services. Even though we never attend anymore, he abstains on my behalf so as not to leave me alone on Sundays. I fear he would see it as a betrayal."

He replied slowly. "I understand. You must do as your father wishes, but at least speak to him of my invitation."

"Yes, by all means. I shall speak to him."

"You cannot confine yourself within these walls, Miss Grenfell. You must refresh your spirit and your mind."

"I beg your pardon?"

He reached for the slate, wrote down his sentence, and handed it to me.

I read his words and looked up as he repeated, "You must refresh your spirit and your mind." There was a fiery intensity in his attention that awakened uncomfortable feelings inside me. For the first time, I began to wonder if his interest in me went beyond that of Christian charity and goodwill.

I looked back at the slate, but even with my eyes averted, I felt his acute and penetrating gaze.

The rest of our session proceeded as usual, but my awareness of this new sentiment added a tension that had not been there before. I was not sure how I felt about it. All I knew was that it unsettled me.

That afternoon, Esther arrived to find me in the attic bent over a cutting table, laying out a pattern on a few yards of sumptuous midnight blue satin I was making into a waistcoat for my father, who had not had time to sew anything for himself in more than a year. After my brain fever, I had moved into Reggie's room and converted the attic into my own workshop. It was the brightest room in the house, and whenever I was not required in the drawing room, I was up here, working on one project or another.

She burst into the room in her bonnet and shawl, her face all flushed and her eyes sparkling, crying something about "horrid creatures"—I suspect she had been followed again in the street.

"Poor dear," I teased, waving my cutting shears toward the street. "Have those wretched men been annoying you? How dare they!"

She said something about the spring weather bringing them out.

"Well, they should know better, shouldn't they?" I teased. "They should all stay at home—or at the very least dash over to the other side of the street when they see you coming." It went against Esther's nature to see romance in real life; she put it all into her paintings.

"Come." She took the menacing shears from my hand and laid them down. "Let's go out. It's a terrible case of the soots, but it is warm. And you spend too many hours up here."

"We must talk," I said, reaching behind me to untie my smock.

"Vevey, I warn you, I'll be quite miserable if I have to spend the afternoon cooped up here. Let's walk. We can talk along the way."

"That's not possible. Not for important things. Please, sit."

Our intimate conversations necessarily took place in the house, for our dialogue was an animated, odd exchange, with hands flying and mouths working wide in a most ungenteel manner. My strangely pitched voice inevitably attracted stares on the street, and any prolonged conversation while walking required me to watch Esther closely, which denied me the visual pleasure of my surroundings. Our outings had to be undertaken in mute complicity, with our arms linked as closely as our confounded crinolines would allow.

"Come, sit," I said as I located a slate and pulled a chair up to the window.

"What's so important?" she asked.

"It's about Mr. Nicholls." I wagged my head. It was the "sign name" we had devised for him, recalling the afternoon he had sat at the piano flinging his head from side to side while we waltzed around the room.

I had caught her attention. "Mr. Nicholls?"

With the look of a woman baited by the promise of good gossip, she untied her bonnet, tossed it onto my bed, and pulled up a chair opposite mine.

"What about Mr. Nicholls? Has something happened?"

I explained about the sermon.

As she listened, she took the slate and wrote, *What audacity! To think you would want to read his boring old sermons!*

"But he meant it kindly," I said. And then I added, "Esther, please, must you always paint people as false? Must I always defend the character of a person whom I admittedly see through the prism of my own muddled mind? I need some clearheaded advice. Help me to see him clearly."

It took her a moment to put aside her habitual air of cynicism, but finally she smiled, and reached out and squeezed my hand, and in a calm hand, she wrote, *Do you think he has intentions?*

"Oh, I don't know."

"Any signs?" She nudged my foot suggestively, and I laughed.

"Heavens no. He's taken no liberties with me."

Then she took my hand and mimicked a prolonged, lingering handshake.

I laughed again. "No. Nor that. He's ever so proper. It's just that he's so intense. So very passionate about helping me. It frightens me."

She appraised me with a long, quiet look, and then, with gestures, asked, "How do you feel about him?"

"I don't know."

Then I averted my eyes, but she waved her hand before my face and drew my attention back to herself again.

"Are you sure you don't know?"

I threw up my hands in despair. "Oh, Esther, what hope do I have of attracting a suitor? Where's the flood of invitations to the opera and plays and dinner parties? The only indication of my new status is that I now have my own calling cards. But on whom am I to call? Anyone who has the misfortune of finding himself face-to-face with me can do nothing but stand there and fidget most awkwardly until they have a chance to slip back into the crowd like a shamed mongrel. That's why we avoid our old favorite spots in the Park, isn't it? So we won't meet any of your acquaintances. I'm a stumbling block to any companion, man or woman."

Suddenly, a pitiful look crossed her face.

"Oh, Vevey." It seemed like a whisper.

"What is it, Esther? Is there something I should know about him?"

Her response was slow in coming, and her eyes bore the expression of one confessing.

"I'm engaged, Vevey."

"You're engaged? Is that what you said?"

She nodded.

I was stunned into momentary silence, then let loose a volley of breathless questions. "Who? When? When did this happen? How long ago? How is it I didn't know?"

She drew the slate from my hands and wrote, *How could I speak of my happiness when you were in such despair?*

"How could you not tell me?"

"I am. Now."

"Who is he?"

"Ned."

"Ned Jones?"

There was a time, I remembered, when she had spoken often of him. But that was when I could hear.

She erased the slate with the edge of her petticoat.

"Oh, Esther, for heaven's sake, don't use your petticoat." I jumped up to find a rag cloth, but she caught my hand.

"No, stay," she pleaded. She finished writing and passed me the slate. *We postponed our wedding until I felt you were well enough for me to leave you.*

"Leave me?"

"I can't continue as your companion, Topsy."

I understood every word of that awful sentence. It resonated so loudly in my mind that it seemed I had heard every syllable.

"You can't leave me," I whimpered. I don't even know if I voiced the words loudly enough for her to hear. It was a weak protest. Of course she had to leave me. Esther was twenty-six. I wanted her to be happy. How often had we schemed and dreamed of this very event, planned it down to the dress she would wear and where she would marry?

But the reality took the breath from my lungs.

THAT AFTERNOON, IN THE COURSE of our long and silent promenade through the noisy, sooty streets toward a bright little corner of Green Park, my thoughts turned to Mr. Nicholls. They wrapped themselves around him like a shipwrecked sailor wraps his arms around the only thing left floating from the splintered wreckage of his life. I examined him thoroughly, and each time he came bobbing to the surface of my dismal sea. He was not what I wanted, but he was what I needed. The fact of the matter was that I did not know what I wanted, for my desires were all muddled by the awareness of my limitations.

Chapter Ten

DESPITE OUR FAMILY'S PRIVATE SETBACKS, GRENFELL'S STAR CONtinued to rise. A tide of distinguished new customers swept through our doors that spring, and *The Town*'s review of the best tailoring establishments ranked us among the most celebrated "colleges of fashion." At about this time, we abandoned the tradesman's habit of living over our workplace and took the lease on the spacious house next door, allowing Grenfell's our old living quarters for expansion. Father put me in charge of redecorating and gave me the liberty to purchase whatever I should like for our new home. It kept me quite busy measuring windows, choosing color schemes, and going through pattern books. I even obtained his permission to hire Esther as a "consultant," thus putting a few extra pounds in her pocket. Dear Aunt Lavinia was ever so accommodating and went blithely along with whatever took my fancy. It was her idea to tear down the dining room wall and expand into the small sitting room beyond—"for all the elegant dinner parties you will throw, my dear."

Only Aunt Lavinia still entertained hopes of my attracting a suitor. Meek and retiring as she was, she took it upon herself to snatch the slightest opportunity to introduce me into circles beyond my narrowly circumscribed world of Esther, Mr. Nicholls, and Savile Row. Occasionally there was a dinner party or garden party hosted by her elderly friends or one of Father's associates which I agreed to attend just to please her, as she apparently took such trouble to secure an invitation for me. Inevitably there would be a few errant bachelors among the party, a draper's son or a woolen manufacturer, and Aunt Lavinia would take it upon herself to facilitate any limping dialogue between myself and the gentleman, but goodness, how tiring it all was.

THE END OF THE SEASON was the only time of year that Father allowed himself a long holiday. After our move to Savile Row, to please my mother, we took holidays in more fashionable places—Swiss spa towns were her favorite, although one summer was spent at Biarritz, which greatly improved my French. Papa had never been fond of travel, and after my deafness, we purchased the Thames-side cottage in Mortlake, and that was where we spent our holidays. The cottage was spacious and accommodating; Grandpa and Aunt Mary closed down the house in Kensington and came for August, as did Aunt Mary's daughter, Grace, and her husband, and their children. Mortlake was cooler than London and marvelously free of soot, so that I could wear white without worrying about overworking the poor laundry maids. There was little to do that first summer but take long walks through the fruit orchards and along the river, and play with cousin Grace's new baby. I was often delegated to push Grandpa in his wheelchair as I was oblivious to his grumbling.

One afternoon as I wheeled him along the gravel path outside the house toward the table set for tea on the lawn, I thought I had heard something. It was distant and vague, but I was stone deaf, and I thought perhaps it was coming from inside my own head. I had been told that these inner-head sounds did occur. Yet, when I stopped in my tracks, the sound ceased. Grandpa shifted in his chair and glanced over his shoulder at me.

"Yes, Grandpa. Just a moment," I said.

I cocked my head, but there was nothing, so I leaned into the wheelchair and pushed again. There it was. The same sound. It seemed that my motion was the source. I looked down at the gravel and the wheels, and it occurred to me that they must be making a crunching noise. Once again, I pulled the chair to a stop. Once again, the sound ceased. This time, Grandpa screwed himself around and glowered at me.

"Yes, Grandpa," I said, but I was trembling inside.

So, I put all my weight into the chair, and we lit off along the gravel path with me at a trot. There it was, still distant and vague, but very real— a kind of crackling resonance that coincided with the movement of the wheelchair. I must have shaken Grandpa terribly, because he grabbed hold of his armrests, losing his cane along the path, and I looked across the lawn to see Aunt Lavinia and Aunt Mary and my cousins look our way and freeze in a most amusing tableau of astonishment.

It was there! Sound!

"Grandpa! I can hear something!" I cried breathlessly.

To test my theory, I changed direction all of a sudden, wheeling the chair around onto the green grassy lawn. The sound ceased.

"Yes!" I cried.

The chair at a standstill, I ran back to the path, pulled up my skirts, and shuffled my feet hard against the gravel. There it was again, a little fainter than what I had heard before, but there was sound. I paused, then spun around, doing a kind of jig. There it was again. It was confirmed. A tiny bit of my hearing had returned. I ran back to check on Grandpa. He was red-faced and clearly perturbed, and greatly bewildered, but he had suffered no trauma.

"Grandpa," I said, pausing to catch my breath, "I think I heard a sound. I *know* I heard a sound."

But he only glowered at me.

"Please, Grandpa, shout or something!"

"That was most reckless!" he sputtered.

There were only fuzzy wisps of sound, but it was enough to help me read his lips.

"Again," I said, leaning over him.

"Child, halt these shenanigans at once. I am in need of refreshment."

"Shenanigans?"

"Yes!"

"Is that what you said?"

"Indeed!"

I threw my arms around his neck and hugged him, which I believe shocked him even more than his wheelchair derby.

The news that a slight bit of my hearing had returned was met with more skepticism than jubilation. Even Papa seemed reluctant to attribute too much significance to the fact. I was, after all, still deaf.

I think this was the defining moment in my sentiment for Mr. Nicholls, for I felt he was the one person who would most appreciate the enormous difference this made to me. I wrote him about it, but he was in the Trossachs and it was not until we returned to Savile Row in September that I had his response.

I had expected a letter, but instead he hurried over—arriving with a small bouquet of creamy pink roses. I met him in the outer hallway.

"Miss Grenfell," he said, as Lucy took his hat. "This is fine news! News for celebration!"

Rising from a bow, he offered me the bouquet.

I felt my face grow quite warm. No one had ever offered me flowers.

"How very kind," I mumbled. I dipped my nose into them. They were deliciously fragrant. "Please, Lucy, arrange these in a vase. And tell Aunt Lavinia that Mr. Nicholls has called."

We passed into the drawing room and found our habitual chairs at the table near the window.

"Have you seen your physician?" he asked.

"Yes, and he says this is not unusual. And I may continue to see slight improvement over the years, but nothing is sure."

"You say this helps you read lips?"

"Oh, yes. Very much so."

I explained to him how I could hear vowels but not consonants, and low pitched sounds better than high ones. How loud sounds resembled low rumblings or fuzzy wah-wahs.

"But this is enough to make a difference?"

"I no longer strain so hard to understand. Following a conversation is not so hard on me. It once seemed nearly impossible. Now, understanding is difficult, but not impossible."

"I always believed you would succeed, Miss Grenfell. You have made such improvement over the past year."

"But I always understand you, Mr. Nicholls. You make every effort to speak clearly and not too quickly."

"Can you hear any part of my voice now?"

"Oh, yes. It's deep enough. I can't hear anything when Aunt Lavinia speaks, but you, yes, I hear certain sounds."

"Then we must modify our pedagogy," he announced, suddenly very much the tutor. He reflected for a moment, his long pale fingers drumming against the armrests of his chair while he gazed out the window.

"So, you think there is still need for lessons?" I asked shyly.

He turned a look on me that was part surprise, part eagerness.

"But of course. Even more so," he replied. Then, with restraint, "If you so wish it."

At that moment, Mr. Nicholls glanced away, for I had not heard the drawing room door open. Lucy had entered with the vase of flowers, which she set on a side table before approaching me.

"Excuse me, miss, but your aunt's not well." Lucy clutched her head— our sign for one of Aunt Lavinia's frightful headaches. "She prays you'll forgive her, sir."

I tried to conceal my delight. "That's quite all right, Lucy. Please tell her that I'll be up shortly to see how she's feeling."

As Lucy closed the door behind her, Mr. Nicholls rose to his feet. "In that case, I must take my leave. It would be most incorrect for me to stay."

The proper attitude for me just then would have been to demurely avert my eyes, but I could not. Thus, I read in Mr. Nicholls's eyes an ardor he surely believed to be concealing from me.

I rose to my feet, straightened my skirts, and accompanied him to the door where I held out my hand. "Then we shall resume our lessons as usual?"

"Not as usual," he answered firmly, prolonging the handshake. "Our lessons will be quite different from now on."

FROM AUGUST THROUGH OCTOBER, OUR business slowed to half what it was in the spring, and we retained only a fraction of our workers, many of whom were journeymen in our Soho workshops or outworkers paid by the piece. Papa chose this period to make the move into our newly deco-rated home next door and expand the workshop. At my request, he al-lowed me to keep my old attic room for my own use.

It was here, one day early in October, that he and I finally had our discussion about my future. I was fitting a new coat I had nearly finished for him.

"Perhaps it was not a good idea to do this after lunch," I teased, as I made some markings at the waist. "There. That will do nicely. You can take it off now."

"Splendid work, Veda." He turned and struck an elegant pose, scruti-nizing his image in the tall looking glass. "Yes, splendid."

"Thank you, Papa, but you would expect as much from your daughter, would you not?" I draped the measuring tape around my neck and helped him out of the coat.

"You'll turn eighteen this month."

I paused, the jacket folded over my arm. My heart fluttered faintly in my chest. Could it be, at last, he was acknowledging my eligibility? Could Aunt Lavinia's gentle pleas and subtle remarks have pressed the point that more attention needed to be given to my situation? That finding me a husband was his concern as well as hers and mine?

"Yes, Papa. I'll be eighteen."

He appraised me thoughtfully for a moment, then asked for a slate and chalk, upon which he wrote: *I've given much thought to this, dear child, & I understand that it is highly unusual & will not be simple to implement, but I think it might be a fine solution to our predicament.*

"What's that?"

He answered that I had made great strides in learning to understand and that this was going to make me all that more successful.

"Successful? How?"

"I'd like you to come to work for me."

"Work for you?"

"Yes."

I faltered. "Forgive me, but this was not what I was expecting."

"Does the idea not appeal to you?"

"Oh, indeed it does, but—" I hesitated, then plunged. "Have you given any thought at all to my prospects of marriage?"

He seemed caught off guard.

"Marriage? Why—my dear child—good gracious, yes, of course I have."

"May I ask what your thoughts are on the matter?"

"My thoughts? Well, now—"

I passed the slate back to him, forcing a reply.

Reluctantly, he took up the chalk and wrote, *I should rather keep you here with me than marry you to a man unworthy of you.*

Clearly, I thought to myself, Mr. Nicholls falls in that category.

"Is such a man so difficult to find?" I asked.

A painful expression clouded his face, and after a deliberate hesitation, he wrote, *I have made queries on your behalf. I have met with no success.*

The words hit me like a blow to the chest.

"I see."

With a feeble attempt at levity, I said, "Well, if you mean to stick me in the back room with all the tailoresses, no thank you. I'd rather just stay up here in my attic and clothe my friends and family."

I looked down at the jacket draped over my arm and ran my hand over the soft wool. I had chosen the fabric myself and he was very pleased with it. On the worktable near the window lay bolts of creamy grosgrain and Honiton lace for the wedding dress I was to make for Esther. I had plenty of work to keep me busy, if that was his intent.

I glanced back up to see him writing in an agitated hand: *Never! You are my daughter & only heir. Most privileged position! Your station in the work-room directly behind the showroom. Next to Balducci.*

Then, drawing my eyes back to his countenance, he said slowly, so that I might comprehend every word, "It is my wish that you become familiar with all departments of our firm, dear child. It is to your advantage. One day, Grenfell's will be yours."

"Mine?"

He assented with a firm nod of the head.

"You mean for me to take over the shop?"

He wrote, *You could not appear in the front. We would need a gentleman to be the face of Grenfell's. A Head Cutter or a manager. Someone like Mr. Bal-ducci. But the business would be yours & you can cut & tailor to your heart's con-tent. You will be my deputy & heir & carry on the Grenfell name in tailoring.*

Oh, the dreams that swelled in my heart that night as I imagined laying my hands on the Earl of Ormesby's next hunting coat, or the Maharajah of Beawar's gold-braided military dress, or the new livery for the Duke of Aosta. I would take my place alongside the best craftsmen in the trade who dressed some of the most influential and stylish gentlemen in England—in the world. Somehow, domesticity and marriage paled beside the prospects of taking on Grenfell's.

Some of our tailors had been with Grandpa and had known me as a child, which facilitated my introduction to the firm as a bona fide em-ployee. Despite their familiarity with the Guv'nor's daughter, they must have found the arrival of a woman in their midst an amusing situation at best. I had the foresight to take certain precautions. To Lucy's shock and horror, I left off my crinoline—it would have been impossible to pass be-tween the workbenches with it.

"In some situations," I said as she helped me into my dress that first morning, "a lady has to put practicality before gentility."

"Yes, ma'am," she mouthed, her eyes brimming over with misgiving.

I also requested a workstation at the back in order to facilitate my comprehension of what was going on around me. This, I discovered later, was what prompted one churlish old trouser-maker to spread the ludicrous rumor that the Guv'nor had introduced his deaf daughter into the workplace as a spy. There were a few who believed this nonsense and kept me at a wary distance, but most were sensitive to my youth and deafness and knew my love of tailoring to be sincere, and accepted me—with limitations—into their circle.

So it was that instead of balls and musical *soirées* with their flirtatious encounters, their quadrilles and waltzes followed by sumptuous midnight suppers with roast capon and gooseberry ices at which I might engage in witty repartee with gentlemen of the marrying kind, I came out in society in the back room of a Savile Row tailoring firm, in the close company of cross-legged men who had eyes only for their stitches.

I COULD TELL MR. NICHOLLS did not approve of this new situation. It showed on his countenance—a certain anxiousness flickering in his eyes when I arrived, generally out of breath, in the drawing room each morning for our lessons. I regret that I often made him wait, for I had been at my workstation since dawn, and time passed quickly for me down there. Lucy often had to send a trotter to alert me that he had arrived. I was always very apologetic and promised I would pay closer attention to the hour, and he was very kind and never grumpy about it. Yet, a tension hung in the air whenever I spoke of my work. He must have weighed his concerns and concluded that it would not be to his advantage to voice them, for he could see how my life had turned around that year—first with our fashionable new home, then the return of a tiny fraction of my hearing, and finally, the intense satisfaction I derived from an activity he may have presumed beneath me, but which certainly gave meaning to a life I once believed doomed to inertia.

Esther, on the other hand, made no effort to conceal her opinions. I heard them in great detail one November afternoon as we were on our way to deliver one of Ned's paintings to a patron in Bayswater.

"How can you tolerate it," she said as she untied the ribbon beneath her chin, "down in that crypt all day long? Surrounded by all those uncouth men?" She removed her bonnet and laid it in her lap so as not to cast a shadow over her face.

"You know, Tiggy, the men in our workroom in Savile Row are really quite respectable."

"But it's so outrageous! To expose a young woman to all that."

"To what? I don't have an inkling as to what they say unless I look up and focus on reading lips, and I'm far too busy working to put any effort into that."

"I don't understand your father. It's savage."

"Savage? Pray how are they any more savage than some of your painter friends?"

We hit a pothole and the carriage lurched violently, and Esther reached to steady the painting propped in the seat next to her.

"I paint because I must," she replied. "I cannot live without it. I could have stayed at home and sought a husband with means, as my sisters have done, and painted meek little paintings of interiors or pheasants' wings, but that would have been like cutting out my heart and hanging it on a limb to dry."

"And what makes you think my heart has no voice in all this? Do you think you love your painting more than I love tailoring?"

She looked at me quite soberly then, as though this had never occurred to her before.

"But it's different," she stressed. And then, rather delicately, she added, "Tailoring for men, there's a certain amount of contact, Vevey, is there not? With the client?"

"I'm not in the fitting room. The client doesn't see me. But that's not your real objection. You're afraid that by associating with tailors, I'll make myself undesirable. That no gentleman would have me. Well who's going to have a deaf girl anyway?" I looked away and then added, under my breath, "Except poor Mr. Nicholls."

She tugged on my skirt, and I reluctantly looked back at her.

"You will not even consider that."

"Why?"

"Because he's dull."

"He's not dull. And he's ever so kind."

"And he's poor."

"And Ned?"

Ned's common origins were a sore spot with Esther, I had learned, but she defended him with fiery devotion.

"Ned is brilliant and has brilliant prospects. There is not a man of wealth and rank in all of England that I would choose over my Ned. Not one."

Ned, I had since learned, came from a humble and intensely pious family and had once considered the church as a vocation. At Oxford he had fallen under the spell of Byron, Scott, and Keats, and most significantly Malory's *Morte d'Arthur,* the very same books which had so inspired Reggie. Then one summer, he had been generously invited by Harry, a fellow student at Oxford, to accompany him on a tour of the continent. Ned had been greatly affected by his visits to medieval cathedrals in northern France, and upon his return had devoted himself to art with a near mystical passion. Rossetti had then taken him on as a pupil and had championed him in the art world. From the moment he first glimpsed Esther in the lobby of the National Gallery four years ago, his fate was sealed—or at least this is my romantic version. Esther's account is much more prosaic. He did hold her in sufficiently high esteem to keep his distance and his silence until the day he felt his achievements had made him a worthy suitor. All this Esther explained in a long letter written the day after she had revealed her engagement to me. I had not yet met Mr. Jones—he was on yet another extended tour of Italy under the aegis of Lord Ormelie. Esther talked more about his painting than the man himself, but I could tell she was mad about him, and his pecuniary difficulties were not held against him.

There was a commotion of sorts in the street, and we came to a sudden halt. Esther leaned out the window to see what had happened, and I fell back into my corner of the carriage. I could only take so much conversation without draining my energy, and I disliked exerting all that effort quarreling with Esther. I could not help recall that day well over a year ago when we had argued about Harry's respectability and she had seemed to think it necessary to dissuade me from aspiring to a society to which I was, by birth, excluded. Now she took umbrage with my decision to enter my father's firm for fear that I would be dropping to the lower rungs of the ladder. Everyone wanted me to stay in my place—whatever that was.

JUST BEFORE CHRISTMAS, I HOSTED my first dinner party. Ned had returned from Italy, and it would be a fine occasion to celebrate Esther's upcoming wedding and to show off our new home.

"Rather absurd, isn't it?" I said to Esther that morning as she admired the exquisite mahogany table and chairs I had ordered for our new dining room. "I mean, how many dinner parties will a deaf girl give anyway?"

"Many, I expect. Once she's properly married."

"You are an outrageous dreamer," I said, but not without pleasure. "And do you like the new curtains?"

"The room is splendid, Vevey. The entire house is ravishing. Truly."

"Oh, but it's far from finished."

"You have exquisite taste."

"You can do a lot with Papa's bank account," I smiled. I took her by the arm and guided her back to the drawing room. "It's going to be a very fine evening to celebrate a wonderful event."

"Are you sure you want to do this?"

"And why should I not? Really, Tiggy, it will be closer to a family dinner than a real dinner party, with Mr. Jones as a special guest."

"Please, call him Ned."

"I shall do so after we have been introduced."

HAD I BEEN GIVEN A room full of gentlemen from which to choose, Ned would have been the last man I would pick for Esther. I imagined her with someone bold who might tame her, for she had grown set in peculiar ways that were not always conducive to domestic harmony. Little did I dream she would be so thoroughly tamed by such an odd little man. Yet, I liked him, and I think I even would have liked him had he not been engaged to Esther. He was of medium height and figure, and of self-conscious bearing. Although I knew him to be Esther's age, he seemed much older. His dull brown hair was thinning on top, and he sported an unfashionably long beard and a mustache that curled down over his mouth. I realized with a pang of apprehension that I would not be able to read one single word that issued from those lips, buried as they were behind a thicket of whiskers. His gaunt face was full of tension, but when the conversation turned to art, a kind of missionary fervor lit up his eyes. I recalled that he had grown disillusioned with religion while at Oxford and had transmuted his zeal from religion to art. I thought there was much of Mr. Nicholls in him. I already knew him to be a man of high-minded principles, and as I watched him with Esther that evening in the drawing room receiving Papa's congratulations, I judged him to be an earnest man as well.

It was certainly a small dinner party as dinner parties go, but I had made a thorough study of Mama's etiquette books and consulted a new publication that Aunt Lavinia had spied in the window of Lever's Books in Oxford Street, and I had consulted with Mrs. Scholfield to ensure an impeccable service. I felt our servants were up to standard, and we would not be humiliated in that regard. As none of our guests were titled, we could dispense with the intricate rules of rank and seat dinner partners according to affinity.

"Mr. Jones," I said as Ned offered me his arm to take me down, "please do not feel solicitous on my behalf. You are our guest of honor, and it is you who must feel comfortable. For your convenience, I have provided you with a slate beside your plate so that you might scratch down anything you would like to say to me."

He said something quite incomprehensible, and I laughed and said, "Oh, Mr. Jones, I shall need telepathy with you, or else send you off to a good barber."

He paused at the door and turned to gesture to Sir Francis's painting that now hung on one side of our new drawing room. Then, with a knuckle he smoothed back each side of his mustache, and making every effort to speak clearly, he said, "I have heard a good deal about this portrait."

"My portrait?"

"From Lord Ormelie. He is a loyal patron of mine."

With a slight pressure to his arm, I pulled him aside, letting the others descend to the dining room, and then I turned and said, "Mr. Jones, if you speak a little more loudly, and face the light—yes, like that—I think I should understand better. Please, continue."

I must have impressed him with my earnestness, because he obliged me without any consideration for the others, and went on to explain how Lord Ormelie had not been able to attend the opening due to the death of his mother, but he had heard about the portrait's success with both critics and the public.

"You know him well, do you not?" I asked.

"Yes, quite."

"Did you know his mother, Lady Hambledon?"

"I did. Her death was most tragic."

In the silence that followed, he did not avert his eyes from mine, and a most sympathetic and mutual sentiment passed between us. Directing his attention to the portrait, I said, "For a year I could not hang it. It reminded me of her. Perhaps you know, it was while sitting for the portrait that I met her."

"Yes. Harry told me as much."

"I met him only once."

Ned shook his head, as though to shake off the remorse that clouded his eyes. "He's been awfully affected by it."

"Yes, I am sure."

He mumbled something I didn't quite catch.

"It's done what?"

"He has changed," he said gloomily, and then Lucy appeared at the door, quite flustered, and I realized they were all waiting, so I took his arm and we went down together.

I found great pleasure in watching over my family and friends that evening. The dining room was glorious. I had chosen a soft dusty rose paint for the walls and arranged a dark green palm near the window and lighter green ferns on columns; the candle stands stationed in each corner and the crystal chandelier above with its thirty-odd wax candles reflected back on us a gentle pinkish light, which was particularly flattering to the ladies. There were menu cards next to each place and fresh flowers down the center of the table set with new silver service. Mr. Tibbs's service was flawless. Everyone raved about Cook's paté, and our '41 Bordeaux drew accolades throughout the evening.

When I grew tired of trying to follow the conversation, I would withdraw into my little world, watching and thinking, and every time my thoughts had a moment to themselves, they turned to Harry. There was something about the way our lives had intersected and continued to intersect that intrigued me.

Several times during dinner, I caught Mr. Nicholls glancing eagerly my way—I have become quite an expert at noting behavior without giving that impression. This evening there was something strangely dejected about his attitude, a hang-dog look about him that was out of character, and I thought perhaps he was disappointed at having been denied the pleasure of sitting next to me. I would see him come Monday, at the usual hour, which he continued to sandwich in between his parish duties, and I made a mental note to be particularly attentive to him.

After dinner, while Papa plied his Madeira and cigars to Messrs. Nicholls and Jones in the dining room, Esther and I did duty with Aunt Lavinia in the drawing room. She had taken far too much claret and was struggling hard to keep her head up during a little game of Ombre. When the gentlemen returned, Mr. Nicholls seated himself at our new piano and performed a piece by Chopin. Not long after that, our guests took their leave.

I thought it all a grand success.

Chapter Eleven

WITH NED BACK IN TOWN THAT WINTER, ESTHER COULD TALK OF little else but him, and I began to understand more fully the implications of Harry's patronage. Although Ned followed his own star in matters of his art, his moods were greatly affected by his friend's opinions. Esther found this quite irksome, and as she could not grumble to Ned, she did so to me.

"Oh, you mustn't think that Ned submits meekly to Lord Ormelie's artistic whimsy," she hurried to say.

"Submits to what?"

She repeated it several times before I understood.

I knew this would be one of those discussions where I would be misreading half what she said, so we sat down at the writing desk and she took up a slate.

L.O.'s criticism infects Ned with an awful case of the glums, then Ned can't work & we squabble, & I pay the price.

"Really it's quite unfair to me." She pouted as she drew a heavy line beneath the "I."

"What does he criticize?" I asked, for by all accounts, Ned's technical mastery could not be faulted.

Subject matter, she wrote, *medieval civilization.*

"I gather Lord Ormelie is not particularly fond of melancholy knights and distressed ladies, is that it?"

With a miffed air, she scrawled, *Lost & totally useless culture, according to L.O.*

Ned painted small watercolors of medieval subjects, but his intense romanticism was offset by what I considered to be a very modern style. I knew that Rossetti, his old teacher, had encouraged him to be altogether himself, to have no shame of his own ideas, and above all to not chase after popular acclaim.

Impatiently, Esther wiped clean the slate and added, *Ned disregards whatever good I might say of his work—my favorable opinion blown away by one hint of criticism from L.O.*

"And has Lord Ormelie suggested a different subject matter?" I asked.

Suggested Ned station himself in a dog cart in Threadneedle Street & paint Bank and Royal Exchange! L.O. fond of French realists. Courbet. Ned finds them intolerably ugly.

"Well, from what I've heard about Lord Ormelie, he is very much a modern man. I believe he sees much good in progress and industry."

Let him paint progress himself! she scrawled.

"And yet, look at all the patronage he gives Ned," I said soothingly.

She looked up at me and said, "I do not see how Ned puts up with him. I could never think kindly of a person who spoke ill of my art. Even less call him my friend!"

"But he eagerly financed Ned's visit to Italy, you said so yourself."

She snatched up the slate again. *Because he thinks Ned's a good fellow & deserves recognition & thinks he's grand, & Ned won't send him off, because Harry's such a big bankroll.*

"So, Lord Ormelie likes Ned for the wrong reason."

"Yes."

"Look, Tiggy, what does it matter if he's opposed to his choice of subject? It seems to me he does nothing more than offer his opinion. Goodness, he doesn't go in for medievalism, but all the same he invites Ned up to Blackroak Hall to sketch their armor. I say that's very generous of Lord Ormelie—not to say open-minded, wouldn't you agree?"

"Ned doesn't go there anymore. No one wants to go there."

"To Blackroak?"

"Not since Lady Hambledon's death. A positively gloomy place, I hear." She paused, and her eyes softened. "Really, he is a good deal changed. It's quite sad."

She went on talking after that, but I looked away. Our conversation ended there.

NED AND ESTHER'S WEDDING WAS postponed once again, and rather than face the prospect of an August apart, they decided to spend it with us at Mortlake where they would be properly chaperoned by a coterie of elderly folk and little children.

Ned was delighted with the Thames setting of our cottage in Mortlake, an unpretentious house set on a large property with a small wood and several miles of river frontage with its own landing. He was outdoors every day, rain or shine, making sketches of a particularly scenic section of the riverbank and a small ivy-infested pavilion with steps running down to the water, with the idea of using it as a backdrop for his next painting. He had decided to portray the heartbroken princess Elaine from Malory's *Morte d'Arthur* as she floats down the river on her funeral barge toward Arthur's palace. According to legend, Elaine was the last descendant of Joseph of Arimathea. Abandoned by Lancelot, she would give birth to an illegitimate son, Galahad, the purest and noblest knight of the Round Table. I was intrigued by the subject, so much so that I sent to Savile Row for Reggie's copy of Malory's masterpiece as well as Tennyson's *Idylls of the King* so that I might spend my afternoons sitting under a shade tree with a book in hand, sinking into the same romantic state of mind as my friends while they painted and sketched. They were delighted to have me along. My presence satisfied the exigencies of propriety, but I made only small demands on their attention and was oblivious to their intimate exchanges.

One particularly warm afternoon, I fell asleep over my book and awoke to the sensation of a wet tongue licking my face. I was startled out of my wits and bolted upright only to see the little dog turn tail and run off into the woods. I barely had time to catch a glimpse of the creature, but it looked for all the world like one of Harry's spaniels. I stumbled to my feet and wiped my face, then shook out my skirt and looked around, but there was no one in sight. Ned's easel and stool were still in place, and Esther's sketchbooks were on the tartan blanket along with the boxes of paints and brushes. I called out, but no one appeared. Then I noticed a rowing boat moored to the landing, and I marched out on the dock and peered down into it. Whoever it was had arrived in a festive mood, for the bottom of the boat was strewn with empty ale bottles. Turning, I caught sight of the party emerging from the woods—Harry and two friends, and behind them a rather disheveled Esther without her bonnet and Ned without his coat. Harry's companions seemed quite amused by the stunt. The pair of them straggled out of the woods together, red-faced and drunk, attempting to support one another, until the heavyset man tripped over a dead branch and disappeared into a tangle of brush. The other stumbled forward and made a dive onto the blanket, rolled over onto his back, arms spread-eagle, and seemed to lose consciousness. Ned stopped on the bank and turned to face Harry, clearly giving him a piece of his mind, while Esther, eyes fastened demurely on the ground, tried rather unsuccessfully to tidy up her hair, which hung loose around her shoulders.

Of course, I could not have heard Harry's little surprise party creep up on us. Finding me asleep, they had gone off in search of the truant lovers and found them in a most compromising situation. It was a perfectly horrid trick they had played on us, and neither Ned nor Esther was amused. Nor was I. I was unhappy with my friends for having abandoned me in my defenseless state, but I was mortified to think I had been gazed upon most rudely by drunken men without my knowledge. As I was watching this soundless spectacle, Ivanhoe appeared again, racing down the bank and onto the landing. I don't know if the creature was only frightened and looking for a safe retreat, or if he remembered me, but he tore down the landing straight for me, and I bent down and scooped him up into my arms.

"You poor thing," I muttered. "What have these wretches been up to?"

When I looked back up, Harry had advanced down the bank toward me and was now standing stock-still with me in his sights. I wondered if he was too drunk to remember me. The carelessness of his dress only confirmed my suspicions. He was attired for the country in riding breeches and boots, but he wore neither hat nor coat, and his waistcoat was unbuttoned, and his cravat dangled from his neck.

I thought I should curtsey, but I was not inclined to subject myself to a man who had behaved so coarsely. Seeing him stalled there, I thought I should at least return his poor dog to him, and so I went forward. As I drew closer, I read the look on his countenance, and my indignation instantly melted away. His eyes, once lively and shining, were dull with a misery that I recognized all too well. He was as disheveled as his drunken friends, but I think the drink had no affect on him; he seemed pathetically sober.

He bowed, deeply and respectfully, and then brushed his damp hair back off his face.

Ivanhoe wiggled in excitement. "Here, sir. I believe he took fright."

He thanked me and tucked the spaniel under his arm.

Knowing of my deafness, he was clearly at a loss as to how to address me, and yet he made no attempt to rush away. He stood there, petting Ivanhoe, his eyes locked on mine. I sensed he would have wished to engage me in conversation had I been able to hear it.

He followed me with his gaze as I walked past him and up the bank. Ned was busy wrestling Harry's drunken friend off the tartan, and Esther was packing up their paints. I turned away from them, gathered up my books, and set off through the woods for home.

That evening Esther subjected me to a slate full of Harry's crimes—his ungentlemanly behavior, his crude manners, his debauchery. She and Ned had argued and she was in a foul mood. They saw little of each other the next few days. He went off to paint on his own and Esther sulked around the house, reading and sleeping. I joined the children in a tea party and made a costume for their grumpy old pussycat.

Several days later, I was in the breakfast room with Grandpa having my toast and coffee when Smithy, our Mortlake housemaid, announced a caller. I went back to the morning newspaper, presuming it to be a neighbor or friend of Grandpa's, but when I felt the table shake under his pounding fist, I looked up to see him waving in the direction of the door.

"Is it for me?" I asked Smithy, and when she nodded, I laid down my napkin and rose from the breakfast table.

In the hallway, she turned to me with eyes wide and said something I couldn't catch.

"What do they want?" I asked.

She only shook her head and motioned me to follow her to the door.

In the drive waited a carriage and two very fine horses, and on the steps stood a young man in livery. He bowed and—apparently forewarned of my deafness—turned to ask Smithy if I was indeed Miss Veda Grenfell. Once assured of my identity, he returned to the carriage, opened the door, took out a large basket, and set it at my feet. It was a plush little dog's bed filled with toys. He bowed and then produced a letter.

Without opening it, I said, "Have you come from Lord Ormelie?"

He nodded.

"Let me guess. You've brought me Ivanhoe."

He nodded and tried his best to conceal a bemused smile.

I couldn't help but smile myself as I broke the seal and read.

My dear Miss Grenfell,

There are no words to convey the depth of my remorse for my behavior. As for my friends, they go where I wish and exercise no judgment on my actions, which is precisely why I tolerate them and prefer them to more prudent society, and therefore I beg you exonerate them. I deserve no such indulgence.

Ivanhoe is yours should you wish to keep him. It was not until I saw you on the landing that the idea occurred to me that you of all people should be the keeper of my mother's treasure. Waverly disappeared from the estate at Blackroak and Ivanhoe is now quite despondent and all alone. Although he is actually my ward, I am not fit to care for the fellow.

Ivanhoe is the gentlest, most well-mannered, and most reasonable animal of his kind. I do not send him to you in the spirit of obligation, nor with an appeal to your charity, but as a gift in memory of one who held you in high esteem. If you find this gift to be a burden, please feel free to return him with the servant. He deserves a good and loving home and should not suffer from my want of judgment.

> I remain, your friend,
> Harry Breadalbane, Lord Ormelie

p.s. He would be most gratified for an occasional walk and a tidbit at mealtime (but not too many).

The groom had returned to the carriage and fetched the little spaniel who now stared up at me with big brown eyes as if I were his last hope in the world.

"Oh goodness," I declared, half to the creature and half to the servants who stood there waiting for my response. "We've never had pets. They shed, you see, and my father's so fussy about those things." But I couldn't resist those eyes. All the more so since Ivanhoe was a gift from Harry, and in a way, his mother. I slipped the letter into the pocket of my dress and reached for the spaniel. He was a timid little thing and weighed not more than a few pounds. "I suppose we'll manage, won't we?" I said to him. I thanked the groom and asked if he would wait for a reply, and I then ordered Smithy to take the dog's paraphernalia up to my room.

"Oh, do try to hide all the clutter, Smithy, until I sort this out with my father."

From my writing desk, with Ivanhoe curled in my lap, I wrote:

My dear Lord Ormelie,
You flatter me with such a precious gift. I am indeed acquainted with Ivanhoe. He was the inspiration for a lengthy conversation I had with your mother on the merits of Rowenas and Rebeccas. Ivanhoe was privy to that conversation, as was his brother, Waverly. I am sorry to hear they have been separated. I assure you I will do my utmost to see he does not languish from the loss of those who were his entire world.

   I pray you will not think it unseemly for me to speak of your mother, but I, too, want for a kindred heart with whom I can share memories of her. My friendship with Lady Hambledon was a thing apart—we had no society in common—and I grieved for her most profoundly in a lonely place in my heart. That you have provided me with a link to her memory means more to me than I can say.

   I am, my dear Sir,

Yours sincerely,
Veda Grenfell

p.s. I shall make sure Ivanhoe is not overindulged at the table.

That short letter took me nigh upon twenty-five minutes to write, and only after countless drafts and aborted starts did I finally seal it and send it down to the waiting groom.

Later that morning, upon returning from the village, I met Esther racing toward me along the lane. She seemed so distraught, stumbling and tripping as she ran, that I feared something dreadful had happened, but as I rushed to meet her, I saw that she was laughing and giddy with joy. She stopped, terribly out of breath, took me by the shoulders, and danced me around until we both tripped and fell to the ground. The lane was still muddy from an overnight rain shower, and I scolded her most sternly, and picked up the basket I had dropped, retrieving the little package of scraps I had got from the butcher. But I could not be angry with her, for I don't think I had ever seen Esther so deliriously happy. She rose to her feet and dusted off my skirt as well as her own, all the while babbling apologies, and then produced a letter from her pocket and showed it to me. I recognized Lord Ormelie's stationery at once; it bore the crest of the Earls of Hambledon. The letter was addressed to Ned.

My dear friend,

I repent, dear Ned, most deeply, for the shameful way in which I conducted myself the other day—I am quite adept at botching my own hopes for marital bliss, I have no need to botch the hopes of others at well. It was not until our little dispute that I became aware of the discord I have caused between you and your fiancée. I am referring to your upcoming tour of the continent and how your marriage had to be postponed because of it. You must think me a most perverse patron, but I assure you I am not—I am only a distracted, self-indulgent wretch and rather ignorant of everyone's desires but my own. I offered to sponsor you on another continental tour only because I saw a most positive influence in your work upon your return from Italy, and I was hoping to give you an opportunity to expand upon those experiences. I do not think in terms of wives and fiancées and appendages of that sort, and although I am for betrothal in theory, I feel the practice should be avoided whenever possible, and I assume as much for all gentlemen, which is clearly not an opinion shared by you, my dear friend. I mean to say by this, that the idea of a marriage followed immediately by a separation of many months is inhuman and brutal to both parties, an opinion which you do surely share, for you would not have postponed your wedding otherwise. So, in order to remedy this unfortunate circumstance of which I am the author, with the hopes of transforming myself once again into the benevolent patron loved by all, I hereby propose to provide you with an additional sum—to be worked out by my accountant—which would enable you to take along a bride. It will be my wedding present to you. Paris is certainly a pleasant enough place for a honeymoon.

I remain yours sincerely,

Harry

I confess to feeling gloriously vindicated when I folded the letter and handed it back to her.

"There," I said, linking my arm through hers as we walked back to the house together. "I hope you see him in a new light now."

She paused and turned to me with a dreamy smile. "I don't care if Ned ever paints another one of his silly knights as long as he lives," she said.

It was amazing to see how a face could be so transformed by happiness. By love.

THE WEDDING DATE WAS SET for the end of September, and I had only a few weeks in which to finish her dress. Esther had thought she was too old to wear white and wanted grey silk, but she had changed her mind after she had seen my sketches and envisioned the *tout ensemble* in a rich creamy grosgrain I had found at a draper's in Knightsbridge. As the prevailing ladies' fashion tended toward shapeless creations better suited to lumpy matrons than pretty brides, we turned to the French for inspiration. We also agreed that the costume should be simple. Esther had never been one to care much about dress, and an elaborate gown that impeded her movements or thoughts would have ruined the day for her. The final creation was heavenly—a gored skirt of creamy white silk bordered by two rows of wide satin ribbon with a purled edge, a trim-waisted jacket body to set off her fine figure, and slightly flared pagoda sleeves revealing undersleeves of the same rose-patterned French lace as her veil. The skirt was caught up at one side by a delicate wreath of fresh jasmine, orange blossoms, and true-lovers' knots of white satin, an arrangement repeated in the wreath that held her veil.

Those final days of September, as I sat by my attic window hunched over a sea of white silk and lace, my thoughts turned often to Harry. He was all muddled up in the stitches and flounces and rolled satin, along with Esther and Ned, and Reggie and my mother, and Harry's mother—rather like one long, quiet meditation on loss, hope and love, and impossible dreams come true. Earlier that summer at Mortlake, during my morning walks in our fragrant little rose garden, with the dew still heavy on the grass, I had derived immense pleasure in the observation of each new bud as it blossomed into a full-blown flower. Holding Harry in my imagination seemed to have the same effect on me. All it took was a remembered smile or gesture, and my tightly closed heart seemed to warm instantly, a little like those roses, throwing off a long, unseasonable chill, one petal at a time.

ESTHER AND NED'S WEDDING ASSEMBLED an extraordinary array of guests—I could not possibly imagine such an odd mix of society tolerating one another's company under any other circumstances. Mad-looking artists with wives in strange embroidered garments or loose-fitting tunic-like dresses outnumbered by far the more ordinary guests and wealthy patrons—the merchants, bankers, and industrialists and their fashionable wives who had begun to collect Ned's work, and Esther's as well. Esther arrived at the church with her father in a carriage drawn by four horses and postilions decked out with large white favors, an extravagance I later learned had been paid for by Harry. Ned was fitted out by Father in an elegant dress coat of impeccable cut and a grey silk figured waistcoat, and a freshly trimmed beard. I thought he looked very handsome—and very nervous.

Harry was there with one of his boating friends from that afternoon in Mortlake. I caught a glimpse of him at the reception after the ceremony, but his attention was engaged for a long while by the vicar, and later by Mr. Madox Brown and his wife. I was sure that he had seen me, and I wished terribly that he might make his way toward me, for it would be brazen for me to approach him. I was torn between appearing too eager to meet his gaze and the heartbreaking realization that I might not have a chance to see him again for a very long time. Then, the carriage rolled up to the church to drive the newlyweds to the coast. Amidst the crush of well-wishers and the excitement of the bridesmaids preparing to throw their old satin shoes for good luck, I lost sight of him.

After Esther's departure on her honeymoon, I was engulfed by a profound sentiment of loss. I found our family weekends at Mortlake particularly difficult to bear. I found solace only in my work.

I THINK THESE EVENTS HAD a good deal to do with all that followed, particularly with the way in which I began to take note of Mr. Balducci, our Head Cutter. Balducci had come to us from Pauley's on the tail of a quarrel with that firm, and Father considered himself most fortunate, for the Italian brought with him some of the most aristocratic names in all the kingdom. Grenfell's had always had a smattering of lords, but most of our clients fell into the category of professional men and landed gentry. The military business, which had brought Grandpa his fame, had been taken over by the firm of Gieves, and Pauley had warrants from the British crown and much of Europe's royalty. Grenfell's had seized a good portion of the sporting gentry custom when this became the fashionable mode of dress, and although we were certainly not short of clients, those clients ordered considerably less than a man of rank and privilege whose sole purpose was to enjoy those privileges to which his rank entitled him—privileges which required very specific garments for specific activities at appointed times of the day. In the course of one such gentleman's day, he might require a morning coat, lounging coat, dress coat, and evening coat—all with their assorted waistcoats, trousers, and accessories, as well as garments for walking, riding, fishing, and hunting. Then there were the many civilian or military titles associated with aristocratic privilege, each requiring its own uniform—if he were a knight of the Teutonic Crusaders or St. John of Jerusalem, he had his uniform. He might belong to the yeomanry or the Royal Horse Guards, or hold the office of Lord Warden of the Cinque Ports. To tap into that elite core of privilege would open up a flood of custom of the most enviable kind, and Balducci had promised to do as much. Indeed, the turning of the tides was already well underway. After only two years, our order book was already beginning to read like Burke's Peerage.

Balducci's influence was not limited to our business affairs; it spread to our personal situation as well. The expansion of Grenfell's Savile Row with its splendid new showroom, along with the leasehold and total renovation on the neighboring house where we now resided, had been his idea. Balducci operated under the principle that implied prosperity attracts business, which then generates real prosperity. This was Grandpa's philosophy in a nutshell, and it goes without saying that Balducci found a champion in Grandpa, whose declining health did not prevent him from making clear his sentiment on matters of concern. Grenfell's already offered the highest standards and quality of work. All that was lacking was a new image to attract the titled nobility. If Father had been reluctant to go this route before, he found the path much more inviting with Balducci blazing the way.

In October, Father invited Mr. Balducci to dinner—an unusual move as he had always maintained a certain social distance between himself and his employees. Mr. Samson, the Head Cutter whom Balducci had replaced two years before, had been with Grenfell's since Grandpa's time, and he had never once been invited to dine with us. Balducci was an elegant, clean-shaven man with wavy black hair he wore parted on one side. Although small of stature, he possessed a naturally powerful physique, which seemed not to have suffered from all the hours spent at his cutting board. In the workshop, he shed his jacket and rolled up his sleeves like all the cutters and tailors, but while the others sank into a posture that betrayed the tedium and hard labor required of us, Balducci retained an air of pride and dignity, as if he instinctively knew he was made for greater things than this. His profile was pure Medici—a sharply angled nose and chiseled mouth overshadowed by large dark eyes. He was not handsome by our English standards; indeed, his features were so emphatic as to seem theatrical. Once in the workshop I had watched him hold up for inspection an evening cloak we were making for the Earl of Claremont. He shook it out and twirled it around his shoulders with the air of a great stage actor, and I suddenly envisioned him at a Venetian ball in full evening costume, his face concealed by a mask both stunningly beautiful and yet grotesque. Indeed, I thought him an older, exotic version of our own elegant Bertie, Prince of Wales.

During my year in the workroom, I had seen little of him. His place was in the cutting room or showroom. My impression of him was formed by observation, for I could not overhear the gossip around me, and my limited exchange with the tailors nearly always turned around our work. It seemed to me that he favored other foreign-born employees, the Italians and Germans, but I found this understandable. I did notice arguments from time to time, but they were conducted out of my sight, and if a trouser cutter or vest cutter stormed back to his work station all churlish and sullen, it generally became clear that Mr. Balducci had expressed dissatisfaction with his work. If the Italian's temper flared on occasion, it was for good cause. Like us, he demanded nothing short of excellence.

That evening at dinner, with his characteristic Mediterranean zeal, he gave voice to our deepest ambitions. When he hailed Father as the greatest Master Tailor in the city of London and expressed his conviction that Grenfell's could, and would, rise above all our competition, he was only saying what we believed in the bottom of our hearts to be true. Such demeanor in an Englishman would have seemed ingratiatingly obsequious, but Mr. Balducci flattered us with panache. His mannerisms may have seemed too Italian for Aunt Lavinia's taste, and his skin perhaps a shade too olive-toned for her comfort, but I had always found his expressive hands and face a relief from English reserve. Although his accent made for difficult lip reading—he formed the letters quite differently from native English speakers—I often found it easy to follow the general flow of his conversation. When, during the course of dinner, I grew tired of making an effort and ceased trying to read lips, his mannerisms were entertainment in themselves. He was operatic in his style, and shamelessly continental. I had never made the acquaintance of anyone quite like him, and I was positively intrigued.

That evening—which I later learned had been orchestrated for my benefit—he laid out a startling proposal: Having noticed my talent and enthusiasm, he wished to open a department for ladies' riding habits, with me as its head. Moreover, by opening a ladies' division and bringing in two seamstresses under my supervision, I would no longer be seen as an oddity—the sole lady among dozens of working men. Now, I wasn't all that fond of ladies' garments, but riding habits were another thing altogether, and I knew it was a challenge I could meet. It didn't take much for me to join the Italian's crusade to remake our stodgy image to attract the best society in London. The fact that Balducci saw me as an integral part of our new image was most flattering to a deaf girl who only several years before had viewed herself as doomed to a life of futile longing and uselessness.

Chapter Twelve

ONE OF THE FIRST THINGS I NOTICED ABOUT BALDUCCI AS WE BE-gan to plan for our Ladies' Riding Department was his instinct for the feminine—a quality that served him well. I began to recognize that one of the keys to his success as a tailor was that he sought to dress a gentleman with a view to impressing the ladies. Although I was treated with respect by the other tailors, no one appreciated my opinions as much as Mr. Balducci. He engaged me at every step, soliciting my ideas on the decor of the new department, scheduling me to meet with the woolen manufacturers and the suppliers of trimmings, whisking me away from my sewing to ask my opinion of some fashion plates just arrived by post. He even approved of my suggestion that we install a mechanical riding horse—essential in order to fit a riding habit properly—which I promptly dubbed Marengo after Napoleon's charger. Most important, however, he reassured me that I would be perfectly capable of handling clients when the time came, despite my affliction. When I expressed my anxiety about meeting the public—for I was still very reluctant to engage in conversation with any-one outside my close circle of friends or our workplace—he left me the following note:

Do not trouble yourself, Cara. We will practice many times together. You will teach your assistant those little signs you use with your friends, and she will make sure you have understood correctly. I work often with foreign clients, and it is no different from translating from a foreign language. The important thing is to give your client confidence—and you can do this if you have confidence in yourself. Your gift is your ability to see your client in the habit that is not yet sewn, and your ability to manipulate the fabric. You know you have these gifts, but your client does not, therefore you must express this confidence in the way you greet your client and the way you attend to her. I think you will attend to your clients in a manner that is most flattering to them because of your affliction. I have come to know you well, Cara, and you are the most attentive and rapt of listeners. I have seen how you watch by turns the mouth of the speaker and the changing expression of his countenance, how you glance quickly out of the corner of your eye at others who are listening. There is no compliment to a client, nor to any person, so great as that fixed attention you give so perfectly. Your client will quickly note your attentiveness and forget your affliction. You will make her believe that because your hearing is faulty, your sight is faultless. Do not fret, Cara. I understand these things.

Mr. Nicholls had never approved of my involvement in Grenfell's. Although he could be cold and disapproving when he disagreed with my choices, he was nevertheless constant in his attentions and faithful in his pedagogical duties. As our time together was now limited and our lessons reduced to twice a week, I insisted we dismiss with the biblical and literary material and turn our focus on the language that would be most useful to me in attending to clients. I supplied him with vocabulary from that most peculiar and specific jargon that tailors speak, and even took him on a tour of the workrooms and cutting rooms and pattern rooms, so as to familiarize him with the instruments and tools of our trade. That was the only time he met Mr. Balducci, and I sensed that his dislike for our new director was immediate and visceral.

Mr. Nicholls remained silent on the matter until the day before Christmas Eve. He had solicited my suggestions on the decoration of his church—believing my taste in fashion somehow conferred a certain aptitude for the aesthetics of interiors—and I was pleased to offer my advice. It involved little more than the judicious hanging of sprigs of holly and laurel and garlands of evergreen, which was accomplished with a tall, sturdy ladder and the help of several volunteer ladies and two boys from the parish. Despite my preference for dramatic hangings from difficult-to-reach corners, no lives were endangered, and Mr. Nicholls was more than satisfied. We sat on the steps beneath the pulpit as the light faded from the stained-glass windows of St. Albans, and the boys were sweeping up fallen branches and twigs. I watched his face while he looked about at our accomplishments.

"Indeed, St. Albans has never looked so beautiful."

I could lip read Mr. Nicholls with considerable accuracy. Over the years his manner of speaking to me had become habit. Whenever we were together, he made sure there was light on his face—he had placed a candle on the pulpit and held another in his hand. Rarely did I have to ask him to repeat himself. Perhaps this was due to more than just accommodation; perhaps I could read his thoughts as well.

"It's nothing," I said. "It's much as it was last year."

"Oh, no. Not at all. You've paid attention to the lines of the arches and columns. It's quite beautiful. I'm grateful for your time." He paused. "I know you are very occupied these days."

"I am. And it is a good occupation."

He nodded, but I was unconvinced.

"Now that I shall be working with other ladies, are you more inclined to approve of my occupation?"

He turned ardent eyes on me. "Approve? Is my approbation of any concern to you?"

"Indeed it is. You are my friend."

He averted his eyes, and I was forced to speak boldly.

"You do not like Mr. Balducci, do you?"

"I should not like you working under his supervision." He spoke very clearly to me, so that there was no chance that I might misunderstand.

"Why?"

"I sense he is not to be trusted."

"It's because he's a foreigner. You judge him with prejudice."

"Your ambition blinds you to his true nature," he said, and I was so astounded that I asked him to speak up and repeat himself.

"My ambition?" I said, taken aback.

"I fear that you desire too much—you expect too much."

"Mr. Nicholls, it is my natural bent to be ambitious, and may I remind you that after my fever, when I confessed to you my despair and my sense of uselessness, and how I felt myself diminished in the eyes of the world, it was you who came forth with a banner of hope. And not only words of hope and encouragement, but action. You took action, Mr. Nicholls. You alone have worked to give me the only tool I have to make my way in a hearing world. Without your devotion to learning—your absolute belief that I could learn to read lips—I would not have one fraction of the pleasure I now take in the world. And now, I have an offer to be involved even more so in the hearing world, and in my father's world, which is the world I love most. I love tailoring, Mr. Nicholls. The destiny which God in His goodness has offered me goes far beyond what I had once hoped it would be. Pray do not turn your disapproving eye on me, for I would not want to have to choose between a friend such as you and a promise of an active and fulfilling life."

His gaze was sustained and so intense that I had to lower my eyes, and he had to touch my hand to draw my attention to his reply.

"If I am such a friend, then may I speak candidly?"

"It seems to me you already have."

"Has he asked for your hand in marriage?"

"Mr. Nicholls!"

"Has he?"

"That is far from his intention."

"That is precisely his intention."

I looked away, blushing hotly, and not wanting to understand further. My heart was racing in my chest, and I was too agitated to speak. I rose to go, but he stopped me, and I was forced to look at his face.

"You must not trust your happiness to such a man."

"And what if I should? He is my father's deputy and his managing director, and he has Grenfell's interest in mind."

"He has his own interests in mind."

"You slander him without justification. You have nothing, absolutely nothing, upon which to base these outrageous accusations."

"Is it an outrage to seek your hand in marriage?" he said then, all of a sudden so dejected and morose that my heart twisted in my chest.

I did not know what to reply. It seemed that any answer might condemn me—either as presuming too much or too little.

"I prefer not to talk of such things," I said, looking away.

He stepped around before me, the flickering candle next to his face, so that against my will my eyes were drawn to his moving lips.

"Next year, you will be twenty-one, and there is a certain independence that comes with age."

"Are you implying I would marry against the will of my father?"

"You would never do as much. I know you too well, and understand— no, *approve* most fervently of the filial duties you feel toward your father.

But I believe a young woman will feel more inclined to seek the truth in her heart when she is older and wiser."

"Mr. Nicholls," I pleaded, interrupting him, but he only drew closer, so that his face was very near mine and I could not ignore the ardor on his countenance.

"I assure you, I shall continue to resist the temptation to declare sentiments that have long resided in my heart. I have remained silent for lack of a heart willing and prepared to receive them. I only speak of them now, because I fear you may be turning your young life in a direction that would make it all the more difficult for one to express these sentiments in the future."

"Why is that, sir?"

"You must know, my dear friend, that modesty is a necessary virtue in the wife of a clergyman."

"Mr. Nicholls, I do not know if I am being flattered or if I stand accused of some indecency. And quite frankly, I don't wish to pursue this subject anymore."

I turned then, picked up my bonnet from the front pew, and tied it on my head as I hurried along the aisle to the door. I knew he would follow, for he was to accompany me home, but I had no desire to endure a carriage ride with him. Outside it was cold and the steps were icy, but I hurried down to the street and to my relief found a cab disposing of a passenger beneath the street lamp. I quickly climbed in, and as we drove off he came rushing down the steps of St. Albans, hat in hand, flagging the driver. Just then, he slipped and fell on his back on the steps. I called out to the driver to stop, and without waiting for the steps to be lowered, I jumped from the hansom and ran back to where he lay on the church steps. I kneeled beside him.

"Mr. Nicholls," I cried. "Oh, Mr. Nicholls, are you hurt?"

He sat up and brushed the dirt and ice from his shoulder, and I surmised from his countenance that he was in considerable pain and deeply humiliated. Several passersby had stopped and had asked if he needed assistance, but he motioned them away.

"Pray forgive me," I pleaded, afraid to touch him, yet anxious to alleviate his suffering any way I could. "I behaved impetuously, and now look what's happened. Can you forgive me?"

He only shook his head, seemingly disgusted with himself, and then rose to his feet.

He drove me home, and not a word was spoken all the way back to St. James. My heart was so full of things I wanted to say to him; I wanted him to know how his constancy was a source of strength to me, and how I knew him to be conscientious and pure in heart. But I knew any such declaration on my part would be viewed as encouragement, and I was not ready to take this step.

I CANNOT SAY WITH ALL honesty that I had never entertained the idea of marriage to Mr. Balducci. He was nearly forty, and by his own admission had never married because he found his work too consuming to allow him to accommodate a wife and family. The appeal, apart from his charm, and the fact that he had a way of making me feel quite special, was that his situation would be ideal for me. To marry a man who could take over Grenfell's, a man who shared my passion for the trade, who shared our family's devotion to quality and high standards of craftsmanship, this was a dream come true. We would make a formidable team; even Esther agreed with me here. From Paris, she wrote to me:

Dearest Vevey,

Yes, there is nothing so fulfilling as seeing the world through the same prism as your husband. Our passion for art is our world, and we are both in it with both feet. We may agree or disagree on little things, but on the big things we are wholly united. Should this Mr. Balducci situation evolve into something with prospects for marriage, you must absolutely pursue it! Pay no heed to Mr. Nicholls—he is too dull for you. Imagine! To carry on your Papa's work and keep the firm in the family, to maintain all your old interests and passions, to engage in an enterprise of mutual concern—and then, when there are children and you withdraw to the domestic domain, to offer him the support of one who is acquainted with his difficulties and can listen to him in perfect understanding, this is the ideal in matrimony.

I speak not of more intimate things—you and only you can be a judge of that. I have so much to share with you when I return—things I dare not write in a letter. Do be prepared to "hear" me out, for there is no one to whom I can open my heart as I can open it to you, dear Vevey. I have been so tetchy this past year, and much of it was because of the long engagement, but now we are sailing on open waters, and it is so much better than I ever imagined. You really must not listen to all those silly things those doctors say, where women and their pleasure are concerned. Returning to Paris with Ned as my husband has been bliss, and I see that we both share an openness about certain intimate things and are of the same mind—and we have both been favorably affected by this city, which is so marvelous for artists and for people with an open mind. We don't feel the same constraints and scruples we feel in London, are much freer in our thoughts and attitudes, and happier because of it.

Pray burn this letter after you have read it. It would not do either of us much good if it fell into your aunt's hands.

Your loving Tiggy

That winter, Mr. Balducci became a familiar face in our home. He was no longer merely an employee; he had assumed the status of family friend. He was not quite avuncular with me, but neither did he show the kind of interest in me one would expect of a potential suitor. He treated me no differently than Aunt Lavinia, teasing us both in a flirtatious and charming manner that was neither coarse nor vulgar. He was a consummate entertainer. Although I could not appreciate his verbal wit, he was so expressive in his gestures and facial mannerisms that he never bored me.

Mr. Balducci loved opera and had invited us as his guests on several occasions, but as Papa personally had little appreciation of opera and knew I could derive no pleasure from such entertainment, he had always declined. Balducci seemed to think that my deafness was not sufficient reason to avoid a spectacle which was as pleasing to the eye as to the ear.

"Cara, I have my own private box," he said one evening when he had been invited to dinner and had stayed a little too long, so that Papa was yawning and Aunt Lavinia's chin was resting peacefully on her breast.

"Yes. You have told me so," I reminded him with a smile.

He picked up the slate beside his chair and wrote, *The Duke of Aosta—my guest for Otello.*

"Yes," I nodded, "I believe you mentioned that you had entertained him."

"Magnificent performance!" he gestured. "And with opera glasses—" He whipped out imaginary opera glasses and pretended to spy on Aunt Lavinia on the other side of the room. "—you can see every action on the stage."

I could not help laughing. He sat back, beaming, clearly pleased with himself at having amused me. He reminded me of a little rooster in very nice plumage.

"You must all be my guests," he insisted with a sweep of the arm around the room.

"Mr. Balducci," I said, "opera is music. I'm almost totally deaf. Your generosity would be wasted."

Papa was watching us from his armchair—his legs crossed and hands folded over his chest in the manner of a man suddenly alert and keenly attuned to the actions of those around him. Balducci rose from his chair and spoke a few words I could not catch. Papa replied with an approving nod, and Balducci then picked up the slate and took a seat beside me on the settee, with his back to Papa. He had never taken such a liberty before, and I thought he must have requested Papa's permission.

He wrote, *Opera is more than music—it is color and movement—it is spectacle.*

I nodded, more amused than convinced.

I was waiting for him to write something more, and when he did not, I glanced up. His countenance had undergone a most deliberate transformation, like that of an actor taking on the persona of a character he wishes to portray, and doing so with such astuteness that the features themselves are altered by some subtle yet very real change. No man had ever dared look at me in that manner before. I was struck by a queer, disturbing sensation in my stomach, the likes of which I had never known. I think I may have quit breathing for a second or two.

Then, drawing my gaze back to the slate, he wrote: *Opera is passion. You will feel this passion. I promise you.*

No sooner had I read the words than he erased them, quite thoroughly. I was trembling inside. I stared at the dusty grey slate and tried to subdue the excitement rising in me.

"I suppose, perhaps, if I could read the libretto beforehand," I said, my eyes fixed on the blank slate, wondering if my agitation could be heard in my voice.

He had my response, and with that he rose, sought my hand to kiss it, as was his habit, and took his leave.

That winter, I attended four operas as Mr. Balducci's guest. After two performances, Papa declined further invitations, but dear Aunt Lavinia willingly accompanied me, although she was generally asleep before the second act. The box on the first balcony had belonged to the Duke of Burlington, one of Balducci's clients, and how he had acquired it I did not ask, but it was clearly now his own, and had been so for some time. I never saw him so much in his element as he was at the opera. When I grew bored watching the stage or scanning the faces in the audience with my opera glasses in hope of finding Harry, I would watch my little Italian friend. He empathized so completely with the drama that I found him quite comic. If he caught me watching him with an amused look on my face, he would break into a smile. Once, he scribbled a note to me, *Cara, you mock me, but I am not offended. I take my opera quite seriously, but I am not so serious with myself. Laugh at me if it makes you happy.*

The last performance of the season was *La Traviata,* and Balducci had invited the Duke of Genoa and his cousin to share our box. I was astounded at the familiarity between them, and I wondered if perhaps Italian society was not bound by such a rigid hierarchy as was ours.

The next morning, I went down to breakfast early, hoping to arrive before Aunt Lavinia so I might speak to Papa alone. When I told him the Duke of Genoa had joined our party, he seemed impressed but not surprised.

"Mr. Balducci enjoys an unusual familiarity with his clients, Veda. Even a few English lords invite him to their estates."

He brushed a toast crumb from his mustache and then sat back in his chair and turned an intense gaze on me.

"Veda, it is my opinion that Mr. Balducci is much taken with you."

"It's possible," I answered—a little coyly, I confess.

"I believe he may be contemplating a serious step with regards to you. Do you have any objections to the gentleman?"

I was not prepared to answer. There had been a time when I believed marriage was beyond my grasp. Now, my father was asking if I had any particular objections to a suitor.

"Do you think he would make a good husband?" I asked.

Papa suddenly became very moved, and through watery eyes he said, "To see you happily married—" He could not finish.

"I am not sure of my feelings for him. But there would be many advantages to the marriage. We both know that."

He asked me if I objected to his being a foreigner.

I answered, "I suppose I should, but I do not. He is very different from

Englishmen." Papa conceded as much with a deep nod. "But some of these differences put him at an advantage, from my point of view. Of course we are both aware of his talents and what he could do for Grenfell's. As for his person—" I paused, wondering how I might clarify feelings I myself found confusing, and give a sensible and womanly reply. "Well, he is an energetic and clever man, and I think I should never be bored with him."

"Indeed, and talented. Very talented. Turned out a first-class bit of work for Marlborough. Did you see it, my dear?"

"The full dress uniform? Yes, I did. It was excellent work."

Papa seemed to momentarily forget exactly which of the gentleman's merits we were reviewing. After a moment's reverie, he took note of the expectant look on my face.

"Ah, yes. Marriage. Now, what of his moral virtues, Veda? What is your opinion?" he asked.

I hesitated. Here, I felt a little less sure of my judgment.

"He is ambitious," I offered.

"And good-natured."

"Quite." I paused. "At least he is with me and you. I don't think he's quite the same with our employees."

"You speak of his temperament?"

I nodded.

"I have rarely seen signs of it, although I understand it has flared on occasion."

I knew Papa was ignorant of much that went on in Grenfell's. He was often out of the shop fitting clients, and when he was on the premises, he was in the showroom and worked with only a handful of the very best tailors and cutters. In all there were now over sixty employees spread out over the four floors of what used to be our private home. There were coat hands and vest hands, trouser makers and breeches makers; we had a counting house with counting clerks at the back of the showroom, and seven packers and porters whose sole job it was to expedite the garments. We were no longer a small, cozy little enterprise.

"I think some of them grumble quite a bit about him," I added uneasily, not wishing to cast an unflattering light on a man of merit.

"Quite normal, my dear. They are jealous of his talents."

"And because he is a foreigner."

"He does favor the foreign tailors, indeed. Hired another Italian just last week."

"Why would he do that when some of our older tailors are sitting around without any work?"

"He believes the foreigners turn out better quality."

"What is your opinion, Papa?"

"If they work better with their own countrymen—" He shrugged. "—why should I object?"

Papa pulled his watch from his pocket and glanced at it, then tucked it away. He had the sudden lighthearted manner of a man who has just swept his conscience clean.

"Well, my dear," he said, dropping his napkin beside his plate and rising from the table, "I am pleased. Yes, quite pleased." He tugged on his waistcoat. "We might all come through this quite well after all. Deuce knows, I had not expected as much."

The subtlety of that remark was not lost on me, despite my deafness. Papa had no desire to be rid of me; on the contrary, his resolute refusal to consider Mr. Nicholls as a suitor had more to do with his fear of losing me than any real objections to the clergyman. My marriage to Balducci would insure that he would never be abandoned.

Mr. Balducci was my champion, and I was little inclined to find fault with him. For that very reason, I had hoped my father might be more critical of his character, perhaps give voice to some of my own feeble doubts. If I had expected prudence from my father, I had just been sorely disappointed.

———

IN MR. BALDUCCI I DISCOVERED someone who derived as much pleasure as I did from carriage rides at the fashionable hour on Rotten Row. It was part of my apprenticeship, he declared, that I should turn a studious eye to the noble ladies who took their daily exercise in Hyde Park, sidesaddle on pretty ponies. I should know who they were, how they were seated, their own skills as *equestriennes*. I should be familiar with the breed, color, size, and allure of their mount, if the horse's tail and mane were braided or left to flow freely, the rider's taste in bridle and saddle, the color of the leather and its fabrication. Each of these things would influence my ability to sell my own talents and make my client appear at her very best.

That spring, Mr. Balducci and I became a part of the elegant and stylish show that performed daily along the pathways of the Park. Those outings with my friend at the reins of Father's phaeton with me perched beside him in a frothy dress of a pastel figured silk, shaded from the noonday sun by a parasol of some delicate, gauzy confection, gave me a new sense of belonging in a world I could only know through my eyes and my heart. I had never felt so at ease, so much suited to a time and place. I felt I was born to this, to stylish elegance and the show of wealth. We did it well, he and I. Although he was always very correct with me and never attempted even a subtle advance, we both knew we were setting the stage for an event which would eventually come, and which neither of us wished to rush.

During our rides, I was repeatedly made aware of the fact that Mr. Balducci had achieved a recognition that is rarely bestowed upon a man of trade. Lords and ladies acknowledged him with a nod or a smile, and although a few might cut him, he took the snubs with unimpaired good humor, foiling the thrust of their social daggers. On occasion, an acquaintance might pull his carriage up to a stop alongside ours, and Mr. Balducci would tip his hat and a brief conversation would ensue. I would be introduced, and I would smile prettily from beneath my rosettes and ribbons, all the while noting the cut of the baronet's coat and the weave of the cloth.

Returning to Grenfell's after our rides, with my head full of ideas, I would quickly dash off notes to Mr. Balducci.

I think Lady Ashelford would be much more suited to a single-breasted jacket with less elaborate braiding—she is top heavy! I would then sketch my proposed design, annotated with references or swatches of the fabrics and trimmings I envisioned.

He would always return my memoranda with a casual note penned at the bottom: *Cara, you are brilliant! Magnificent!*

Others might have been uncomfortable with his hyperbole, but I recognized it to be merely a part of his nature. Even without this flattery, I would have known his sentiment. He told me as much in a glance.

As promised, we brought in two experienced seamstresses as my assistants, and we spent many weeks training them in a system of communication—using subtle signs of the hands and fingers and face to facilitate my understanding during a fitting. Mr. Balducci himself would assume the initial contact with the lady and take responsibility for selling the garment, but I would be there beside him, reading as much as I could from the exchange, offering my suggestions and ideas when asked. Then, with my assistant, I would take the lady's measurements, and from that point on the confection of the garment and subsequent fittings were up to me.

Even with these precautions, success was not always assured. When I stepped up to greet Lady Dentworth with a curtsey, having been introduced by Balducci himself, she was so shocked at being attended by a deaf girl—staring at me in the wide-eyed, slack-jawed manner of one who has just suffered a blow to the head—that she threw on her cloak, called to her ladies maid, and dashed out the door without so much as a look back. Now, Lady Dentworth had a sister-in-law, Lady Cummings, who was much prettier and reputed for her skill as a horsewoman, and whom the prickly Lady Dentworth considered a keen social rival. When Lady Cummings heard of the incident, she decided to take a risk and come to me for her new riding habit. It was just as well since Lady Cummings had a far superior figure and dressed beautifully. When she appeared on Rotten Row that spring kitted out by Grenfell's in her snug-fitted habit, drawing much admiration from the crowd, and eliciting the simpering envy of her sister-in-law, I felt myself amply vindicated.

Merely observing the riders was not enough for Balducci.

Cara, he wrote on a slate one day, *you must take riding lessons. You must know how it feels to sit sidesaddle on a magnificent pony and prance along with all eyes on you.*

"That's out of the question," I replied.

"Why?"

"Papa would never permit it." I reminded him of Reggie's accident and tragic death.

But Cara, I would never permit you to ride anything but the best-trained horses under the tutelage of the finest instructor the cavalry offers.

Balducci won out over my father's fears and my own anxieties, and my lessons began in earnest that spring. We went through three instructors before we found one who was willing to adapt his instruction to a deaf girl; most of them merely shouted at me, which was useless and which caused them to become quite ill-tempered. We finally abandoned the idea of employing a horseman of the cavalry and turned to a retired horse trainer from North Yorks, a cantankerous old man whose reputation hinged on the fact that he had once worked with the famous trainer John Scott of Malton and was now employed by Tattersalls, the London horse auctioneers. William Goodburne was his name, a man as crooked in spirit as he was in body, which I suppose was the outcome of a life lived among the racing crowd.

Burnes, as he was called, was himself hard of hearing, and as a result of years of experience with horses, he had come to the conclusion that humans were the lesser intelligent of the two species, which manner of thinking came heavily to bear on his manner of behaving, so that few outside the society of jockeys and trainers could suffer his company. Cursed with longevity as well as a sour temperament, he had been reduced to overseeing the stables at Tattersalls. Mr. Balducci was against the idea of subjecting me to such an uncouth man, but I was too discouraged to reject anyone willing to give me a try, and so I appeared that morning in the stables, dressed in my most beguiling habit with my veiled hat perched on my head and a riding crop in my hand. Papa had wanted to come with me that morning, but I had refused. I would take Lucy, and if I was not pleased with Mr. Goodburne for whatever reason, we would return immediately. Burnes limped toward me across the arena, dusting a bit of straw from the sleeve of a coat that had seen much wear at the cuffs and collar, in boots so accustomed to his feet that corns and bunions had long ago ceased to complain. To my relief, he had no mustache, only side whiskers, wherein lodged a few crumbs from his breakfast. His bloodshot eyes had a hint of jaundice, and he smelled strongly of tobacco smoke. There was all about him the air of a man whom life had failed bitterly. He greeted me with a curt welcome and then paused, scratching his whiskers and silently noting my size. Clearly he had not been expecting a girl of my height. After a few minutes' consultation with the groom, they led in a grey gelding with a bobbed tail, and hoisted me into the saddle. Since my previous instructors had attempted to conduct their lessons from the side of the ring, as it is normally done, I was astonished—and relieved—when he mounted a bay hunter and trotted alongside me.

Burnes was not a patient man, but he soon found that he could throw his tantrums with impunity since I was deaf to his foul-mouthed tirades and could always turn my back on him—a situation which suited us both well. Nonetheless, his temper cooled quickly, and he was not beyond appearing foolish in his efforts to correct me by using gestures. What another young lady would have found unseemly, I found helpful. He even responded favorably when I asked him to draw up a compendium of terms and their meanings unique to equestrians and horse training, with the assumption that once I knew the language and could attempt to read it on his lips, I could then begin to try to make the correction he desired. I was terribly frustrated at first, but he seemed to think that I had a natural ability and that once I understood what was expected of me, I would make quick progress. Soon, I began to feel the horse respond to the pressure of my legs and the position of my hands and arms, and then I quickly became enamored with the sport. I did not need my ears to understand the animal; I had found a friend who minded not that I was deaf.

Had I been raised in the country, I would have grown up riding, but my experience with horses was that of a city girl. When we were not driving them, we generally tried to steer clear of them. Indeed, Mama had always found horses dangerous and had discouraged Reggie from the sport. Only women of rank and wealth rode for pleasure or rode to the hounds, and my lessons with Burnes always seemed to revive memories of Lady Hambledon. I recalled how I had admired her portrait mounted on the infamous Hermit, and I wondered about the tragic accident that had taken her life. Despite the dangers—which were even greater for a deaf woman—I felt she would have approved of my tenacity and spirit. Always, memories of Harry trailed not far behind.

I even sacrificed one of my two weekly lessons with Mr. Nicholls in order to make more time to ride, and my enthusiasm for my new sport momentarily eclipsed my love of tailoring. Perhaps I had taken on this sport in the service of my profession, but now the sport had overtaken me. I longed for the day when I would progress out of the arena and join the sea of bobbing heads in Hyde Park, but the congested streets and riding paths were a dangerous place for inexperienced riders, even more so for a deaf one.

Burnes was delighted when I told him I wished to learn to jump.

"In case I should ever be invited on a hunting party," I said, with a facetious tilt of the chin, but he took me in all seriousness, and that very day started me over low crossbars.

This proved even more of a challenge and required utmost patience on both our parts, for he was accustomed to shouting directions to the rider even within a few strides of the jump—at times asking the rider to abandon the jump altogether. I was forced to learn after the fact, and although he sometimes seethed with frustration, he admired my physical courage. By then I had suffered my fair share of refusals and falls, but we hid these little incidents from Papa. Lucy was sworn to secrecy, and even when I returned home bruised and in severe pain, I bluffed my way through the day, determined not to give them reason to stop my lessons, which Papa surely would have done had he known the risks I was taking. I would have withered and died inside had he done so. Riding gave me my first taste of freedom outside the familiar world of Grenfell's. More than anything else, it made me feel nearly normal again.

ONE WEEKEND IN JULY WHILE we were at Mortlake, I was in the breakfast room dipping my toast in my tea when Smithy soundlessly appeared at my side and slipped a note under my nose. It read:

Dearest daughter,
You will be twenty-one in October. But I see no harm in celebrating a little early. Come outside to claim him.
                    Your loving Papa

I squealed—and then I jumped up from the table, hoisted up my skirts, and raced out of the room. Outside on the gravel drive, Papa was conversing with a man on horseback; behind them, on a lead, stood a very pretty chestnut Arab.

I named him First.

I learned later that Mr. Balducci had been instrumental in acquiring him—just as he had urged Papa to acquire much of the property that now made up our estate.

You are a dear, dear friend, I wrote him that summer. First is perfect for me. He is the gentlest and most well trained of any horse I have ridden. Even Burnes likes him, and Burnes is a very critical judge of horses.

Balducci replied by post from his summer retreat in Menaggio on Lake Como.

You will be magnificent on him, Cara. I can see you now, trotting down Rotten Row this fall, fitted out in one of Grenfell's habits, causing the ladies much alarm and the gentlemen much delight. Such a commotion!

The only person who did not share my enthusiasm for First was Mr. Nicholls. He did not at all approve of my riding and thought it rash of my father to encourage the sport. I had urged Papa to invite him to Mortlake that summer—a courtesy that was long overdue—but when I received the clergyman's discouraging reply to the good news I had dashed off to him, I decided I could very well do without such a spoilsport for a companion.

I wrote to Esther:

Imagine! My own little chestnut Arab! You should have been there when I took Ivanhoe into the stable and held him up for First to sniff—Ivanhoe was trembling so violently I thought he might have a fit! I am having my most blissful summer ever, but there is no one here to share it with me. Cousin Grace and children are in Wales, you and Ned away, Balducci in Italy, and I was hoping to have Mr. Nicholls's company for the latter part of August, but I find him so terribly oppressive—so goody-goody and stern and disapproving, and absolutely without humor! He throws cold water on everything that gives me pleasure. I shall not invite him to Mortlake after all. I feel bad, because I think Papa was finally ready to entertain him under our roof, which is a big step for Papa. But this is only because Papa no longer scents danger.

I know he is in love with me, and in the past he concealed it well. Now he always appears so forlorn and dejected. My heart twists in my chest, for he would be a kind and devoted husband and is clever in a bookish and scholarly way, but these things appeal less to me than the excitement of creating, and should I marry him, I fear I should lose that spark, or rather it would be hidden beneath a bushel and flicker forever in darkness.

You wonder why I even still entertain the idea of marriage to him. But you see, I cannot be entirely sure of Mr. Balducci's intentions. Although we share a mutual sympathy and work together in a most harmonious manner, I have yet to see any definite sign of an interest in matrimony. As for Mr. Nicholls, on that score I have not the slightest doubt. Sometimes I think I might marry him for no other reason than to relieve his suffering.

And I'm not sure I could love either of them, and I would so much feel that to marry and never know passion like that which you and Ned share would leave me unfulfilled and forever restless.

I saw little of Esther that first year of her marriage to Ned, but we exchanged frequent letters. After their return from Italy, they spent three months in Oxford working on a mural. At first I feared we would lose that precious intimacy we had always shared, for now that she was married, she would defer to her husband in all things; he would be her helpmate, her counselor, her authority on all matters. Those thoughts she once shared with me would now be reserved for her husband, and if he wished to read my letters to her, and hers to me, he would be entitled to do so. But Ned was an uncommon husband, and theirs was an uncommon marriage, and Ned had no desire to interfere with our friendship. She even wrote me once that Ned's one true union was with his art, and that she was only his mistress, but since it was an affair sanctified by God and in the eyes of man, she had no objections, and rather liked it that way.

Now that she was a married lady, she knew secrets I longed to know. Just as she had initiated me into the secrets of the masculine anatomy, she initiated me into the anatomy of love. Ned and Esther often exchanged drawings in lieu of love letters, and Esther shared several of their sketches with me one afternoon. They were both children of Evangelical clergymen, and their drawings were infused with Evangelical meaning: There were self-portraits of the couple entwined together on a cross, others portrayed them as Adam and Eve in the Garden of Eden with the Evil Tempter nowhere to be found. Despite the biblical influence, there was never any intimation of guilt or sin, as if they had cut themselves free from those heavy chains. What I saw depicted was no morality tale, but only a portrayal of love perfumed with the most delicious kind of mysteries. I found them pleasantly disturbing, in much the same way Mr. Balducci's look had disturbed me.

Chapter Thirteen

ALTHOUGH THERE WERE EARLY SIGNS, IT WAS SOME TIME AFTER our expansion that we became aware of the tensions building in certain parts of the workshop. The cutters knew that Mr. Balducci could be extremely difficult to work with, but the counting clerks did not. With their territory marked off by massive marble counters and pillars, stationed behind gleaming mahogany panels, the counting-house remained a distinct and separate entity from garment-making. Rather like a small, prestigious bank, it was a little world of custom unto itself. Young Mr. Kirkwood, the clerk in question, was only doing his job the way it had been done by the clerks before him. When an account went twelve months without payment, it started carrying interest, and very delicately worded letters were sent out to the client as a reminder of the balance still sitting on the books. What troubled Mr. Kirkwood was the startling increase in unpaid accounts—most specifically, Mr. Balducci's clients' accounts. Our practice had always been to cut off future orders when there was any outstanding debt more than eighteen months on the books. Father's clients knew this, and although we had our fair share of bad debt, we refused to throw good money after bad. A client who could not pay for the coat and trousers he had already been wearing for several years should not expect us to make him a new one until the old bill was satisfactorily settled.

Balducci's clients had been accustomed to more generous terms, so when our counting-house sent out its steady stream of letters to the Grand-Duke-of-This and the Crown-Prince-of-That, those letters were viewed with horror by some and not a little fear by others, and all considered the wheedling and needling as an unseemly aggression. Letters from counting-house clerks to the secretaries of crowned heads of state are never considered urgent, until the time comes to order a new set of livery or official dress coat, and the order request is refused. Therefore, when the

Duke of Montrose ordered new livery for his coachman and received in reply a letter telling him he could not be accommodated until his outstanding debt was paid, the Duke's secretary wrote a letter of complaint to Mr. Balducci himself, a letter with very strong words, which letter was then read, word for word, to Mr. Kirkwood by Mr. Balducci—not in the counting-house, but on the showroom floor, before cutters and tailors and all the counting-house employees who had been assembled together that afternoon to make a public spectacle out of the event and humiliate Mr. Kirkwood in the extreme. Mr. Balducci held his public execution after hours, having sent word to all senior staff members that their presence was required that evening on a most urgent matter. Papa was out of town fitting Lord Montesquieu for his wedding at his country estate, and Lucy and I were returning home from the stationer's when I passed in front of Grenfell's and noted with curiosity that the showroom was still brightly lit. I could see from the street that there was a group of men assembled.

As we stepped up to the entrance of our house next door, I stopped and turned to Lucy.

"Lucy," I said, "go and find out what's happening."

It was November, and already the streets were dark and the gas lamps flickered bravely against the monotonous gloom of the city, so that when she stood on the street and peered into the window, she took no risk of being seen. Clutching her shawl against the mean wind, she came hurrying back to me.

"Is there some staff meeting going on?" But she only shrugged, and indicated she could not make any sense of it. She did, however, indicate that Mr. Balducci was there.

"He's making a speech?" I said, interpreting her gesture.

She nodded.

"Who is there? Is Mr. Crawley there?"

She nodded.

I certainly did not want to be seen spying through the window of my family's firm, but I found it most odd that our staff was being assembled in my father's absence, and I had not been informed. I could always go inside and go up to the shop through the back, but I was very bad at creeping up on people—I never knew if I was making a sound or not—doors and floorboards squeaked and I never was the wiser, so I dragged Lucy back with me onto the street. I confess I felt a little silly standing in the cold, huddled in the shadow of a waiting hansom, but I could not dismiss the sentiment that I needed to know what was happening, that it was important.

When I look back at the situation, I find it remarkable that I grasped as much as I did. The circumstances were favorable to me: The showroom was brightly lit, and the faces of the men appeared in such clarity that I could not fail to understand what was happening.

"He's berating Mr. Kirkwood," I whispered to Lucy. "My goodness. Such harsh words. He's reading a letter. What is he saying? . . . Oh, yes, a client has been . . . oh bother—what *is* he saying? My goodness, the look on old Mr. Crawley's face. And there's Mr. Blodgett, Head of the counting-house. He looks beside himself. Oh, there, Balducci's turned back this way again—" I quit my commentary then, because I did not want Lucy to know what I was witnessing. Although I could not make out every word, I was rather glad for it. They were horrific words. I had witnessed Balducci's outbursts in the past, but I had never seen his temper unleashed in such a savage manner. Even without reading his lips, it was clear that he was berating Mr. Kirkwood in the foulest language possible.

The entire scene—Balducci's beastly behavior, the mortified faces of the tailors and clerks, the blanched cheeks of the trembling Mr. Kirkwood—all of these appearing to me in my silent world—struck me perhaps more forcefully than they would have had I been a hearing participant. The scene was rendered with such vivid intensity that I felt sickened by the pain I saw on the faces of those men, our employees, and I wondered how this man who had been so kind and generous to me could harbor such a dark side.

"Come," I said to Lucy, clutching my cloak around my shoulders. "Let's go inside. It's too cold to bother."

I said nothing the next day, but the tension in the workroom was as thick as soot-blackened fog, and the atmosphere was every bit as dark. No one talked, and when I stopped by the counting-house on the pretext of checking the ledger for Lady Cartwright's riding habit, I noticed that Mr. Kirkwood's desk was bare.

When Papa returned, I asked him what it was all about, and I was merely told that Mr. Kirkwood had exhibited very poor form when he wrote letters to one of Balducci's clients demanding payment in a way the client found so offensive that we lost that client's business. He did not seem to be taking the matter lightly, but neither did he wish to say more.

Then, several days later, Grandpa came for dinner, which was quite unusual as he was now confined to his wheelchair, and traveling was a terrible inconvenience for him. I understood that there was to be a meeting after dinner with Mr. Blodgett, Head Clerk in the counting-house, for a financial review.

"May I stay?" I asked Papa in the hallway after dinner. "I know it's about Grenfell's, and I would so like to be present. I won't ask you to write things down or repeat things. I don't expect you to attend to me at all."

He consented, and that evening the four of us sat in the drawing room, and I looked on while they discussed Grenfell's finances.

Some of the language was incomprehensible to me, as it concerned our financial situation, and the vocabulary was not familiar. I understood "drop in profits," an expression repeatedly emphasized throughout the evening by Mr. Blodgett. He had arrived with heavy ledgers and opened them to show us precisely how many prominent clients had placed extravagant orders that were filled in a timely fashion and never paid. The problem was this: Balducci insisted we continue to give credit even when there was small chance of redeeming it.

"He has given us very clear instructions to leave his clients alone, that we are not to pursue them for payment," said Mr. Blodgett, and I had the distinct impression that he was afraid of revealing these things to Papa for fear of retaliation by Balducci. As he turned the pages of the ledger and indicated entries with an ink-stained and trembling finger, I detected on his countenance the timorous and apprehensive manner of a traitor rather than the placid and meticulous mannerisms of a counting clerk whose job it was to report on sales and gross profits.

"Of course, we do not want to lose influential clients," said Grandpa, but I could tell by his expression that things had progressed far beyond what we had once considered reasonable business practices.

They began to speak of things outside the firm, of property and leases, mortgages and expenses. They discussed the Mortlake property, and the Kensington property where Grandpa lived with Aunt Mary.

It was very tiring for me. My eyes were severely strained and my head ached from trying to follow a long conversation where exchanges flew constantly back and forth, but I was determined to understand as much as possible without interfering. Papa glanced at me from time to time, and I responded with a reassuring smile, but he did not even have the courage to muster up a smile in return. Even with my limited understanding, I knew this much: Papa had been neglectful, and he alone was to blame for our difficulties. We now lived quite extravagantly, and if Grenfell's gave the appearance of a prosperity that could not be sustained on the books, it was the result of Papa's imprudent management. If Balducci had been tyrannizing our employees and disregarding our policies in the pursuit of his own glorious reputation, it was Papa's duty to restrain him. I knew by the look on his face that he understood this as well as I.

By the end of the evening, one thing had been made alarmingly clear: We had accumulated massive debt, and profits had dwindled significantly. If action were not taken, our holdings would collapse like a house of cards, taking Grenfell's with it.

That Sunday afternoon, much to my surprise, Mr. Balducci called and closed himself in the library with my father. I learned of his arrival only when I came down to the drawing room where Aunt Lavinia was sitting at the table sifting through a jumble of tiny balls of silk threads in her lap. She looked up at me over the rim of her glasses and a curiously coy smile came over her face, and she said something I didn't quite understand, but I thought I caught Balducci's name on her lips. She put the threads back in her sewing basket, got up, and came over to me and started fussing with my hair.

"What *are* you doing, Aunt Lavinia," I cried, side-stepping just as she stabbed at my head with a hairpin.

Papa entered and closed the door behind him. He spoke to Aunt Lavinia and she closed up her sewing basket and left the room.

The clock must have sounded, because Papa glanced at it, pulled out his watch and checked it against the clock, then thrust it back into his pocket. With his face averted, I was struggling to interpret the situation. All I knew was that he was tense and anxious.

"Is Mr. Balducci here?" I asked. He raised his head, and with the air of a man determined to conceal his thoughts, he nodded and stated carefully that Mr. Balducci had come with a proposal of marriage.

I thought surely I had misunderstood, and I said as much, but he slowly shook his head, repeating himself clearly and distinctly so that I could not misinterpret.

Here it was, come at last, and to my astonishment I was totally unprepared.

"Oh, my," I muttered. I noticed my palms were suddenly sweating, and my heart raced in my chest. "Oh, my," I said again. "What did you tell him?" I asked, wiping my damp palms on my skirt.

"My dear," he said, with a thin smile, "I shall not dictate to you in matters of the heart."

It was a terrible moment, and I suddenly realized that it was no longer a matter of idle dreaming and playacting: I was being required to make a decision that would determine my future happiness, and I was weak-kneed with trepidation.

"But this is what you want, isn't it?"

He replied, "It would make me happy, indeed." But I was not convinced.

"Papa," I said, "you are worried," and as I said it his resolve melted, and he reached for my hand and patted it nervously.

"Perhaps, a little more time—for your sake," he answered.

"Did you give your permission?"

He nodded, but his eyes seemed dull and flat; he had the look of a man who had just offered his daughter as a sacrifice.

"Papa," I whispered, drawing close, as though we were conspirators in the enemy's camp, "I am not quite sure how I feel about him. I am not sure I really know him."

As I said this, my doubts seemed to find their reflection in his eyes.

"Then you must ask for time," he said, pressing my hand firmly. Drawing my gaze to the door, he indicated that Balducci was waiting. "Go," he said.

I FOUND HIM GAZING UP at my portrait above the fireplace, and I noted that a fire had been lit in the grate.

"Good evening," I said.

He set his glass of port on the mantle and turned to face me.

Since that evening last winter in the drawing room when he had persuaded me to attend the opera, not once, despite countless opportunities, had he dared gaze at me in the same unsettling manner—until now. I felt that same thrill—a feeling that worked its way all throughout my body in a way I had never experienced before. All of a sudden, I wondered if he had been intimate with other women, and I felt certain that he had. The thought of such a thing made me tingle, and my face flushed hot.

He had written me a letter, and he slowly reached inside his coat pocket and withdrew it, and held it out to me with thumb and forefinger; there was an awful, seductive air about the gesture that I found quite compelling. His dark eyes seemed to bulge with anticipation, and his lips, moistened by the sherry, glistened in the candlelight. As I took the letter from him, he lowered his head, just slightly, and the way he gazed up at me from beneath the rim of heavy black brows brought an uneasy feeling over me. How could a man attract me and repulse me at the same time?

I did not wish to sit down, despite his urging; I did not want to have him standing over me as I read the letter. My hands were unsteady, and the tumultuous feelings in my stomach left me light-headed and weak at the knees. I removed the candle from the mantle and crossed the rug to the settee, then took a seat at the end, leaning toward the side table where I had set the candle and arranging my skirts over the velvet bench, so as to discourage him from sitting down beside me.

I unfolded the heavy paper and was astonished to find he had written to me on Grenfell's stationery, which had been recently redesigned to reflect the new warrants bestowed on us. At the top, flanking our name, were the crests of the royal families whose official warrants we now enjoyed—thanks to Balducci.

Carissima,

If you have this letter in your hands, you may be assured that all other obstacles that might have prevented me from speaking to you on this matter have already been removed. Therefore, Carissima, only your heart and its inclinations stand between me and my most ardent desire, which is to make you my wife.

I am sure you have asked yourself why a gentleman of thirty-eight years has not yet married, and you have every right to know the answer. I am not a man of leisure, but neither would I wish to be one. My work is my passion, and I could not marry a woman who was a stranger to our world. In you, Cara, I have found a perfect partner. Do you not share the same view? Do you not feel that we are cut from the same cloth?

Since you have been working at my side (yes, Cara, I esteem you my Equal) I have had an opportunity to judge your character in situations where my future wife would be required to play an important role, and I have seen all I need to see in order to make my decision. I know that your character is irreproachable and you are of a good and agreeable disposition. Our workers see you as fair and approachable, and your authority rests on your merit as well as your name. You are the ideal woman for me.

I am quite impatient, Carissima. Do not ask me to wait long for your answer.

> Your devoted servant,
> Antonio Balducci

I closed the letter and folded my hands over it. I knew I would have to compose an answer in my head before I raised my eyes, and I did not know what to say. Nowhere in the letter was there a mention of love, or even attachment; there was flattery of the type I might appreciate from my father, but not the kind one expected from a lover. I was stunned and terribly disappointed, and I knew instinctively that I could never marry this man. The thought of becoming his wife, of living with him intimately, of subjecting myself to his person, both body and mind, sent a chill of terror through me.

I composed a demure and innocent smile and turned it up on him.

"My dear Mr. Balducci—"

"Antonio," he corrected, stepping up and seizing my hand and pressing it so tightly to his wet lips that it made me flinch.

I forced myself to linger in that pose, allowing him the pleasure of my touch, all the while fighting back my repulsion, then I withdrew my hand.

"I am deeply honored by your attentions, but—" I lowered my gaze. The look in his eyes frightened me; it was intense and quite savage, and I felt I had to remove myself quickly from the room.

"You must forgive my emotions," I went on, honestly flustered, "but this is quite unexpected. I must have time to consider your—"

Before I could finish my thought, he had taken the seat beside me— what little space I had left to him beyond the mass of flounces—and placed his arm along the carved wooden back of the settee, his fingers just above my shoulder. There was a most unsavory air about the gesture, matched by the way his eyes followed the line of my neck and bosom rather than meeting my gaze. That attitude, both unctuous and lustful, struck fear into my heart.

"Please, sir," I replied, hoping that my tone of voice conveyed the conviction I felt, "you must not pressure me."

I rose and withdrew hastily from the room, closing the door behind me. In the hallway, I found myself overcome by a powerful repulsion, and I picked up my skirts and ran up the stairs. Papa had appeared in the hallway below me, and he was speaking up at me, but I did not want to hear. Once in my room I grabbed my shawl from the back of the chair, removed my shoes, and climbed up on the bed next to Ivanhoe, who turned his startled eyes on me. I wrapped myself in the shawl, drew the animal into my lap, and sat there stroking his soft fur and trying to calm my rattled nerves. I did not know what had happened and why I had suddenly seen the man in such a strange and disturbing light. All I knew was that never again did I wish to be left alone in the same room with him.

For a year my happiness had thrived on the excitement of a possible marriage to Balducci, and the knowledge that I could not face the reality left me feeling empty and confused. What would be left to me if not Balducci as my spouse and Grenfell's as our shared inheritance? What other choice did I have? What kind of picture could I paint in my head without him?

TAKING MY PLACE IN THE workroom each morning became a new kind of trial for me in the days that followed. Balducci was not always present, but when he was, there was a swagger and a self-assurance in his manner toward me that led me to believe he thought my hesitation was only a matter of prudery, the normal behavior for a respectable young woman, and that beneath my facade of temerity lay a ready and willing heart. I managed to avoid meeting his gaze, but even then, even though I was not subjected to the sound of his voice or his passing steps, I could feel his presence. Indeed, deafness exacerbated my nervousness, for I feared his sudden touch, his unannounced appearance at my side at any moment. I had long ago recognized his scent, marked by an eau de cologne peculiar to him, which I imagined even more powerful in those days following his proposal, as if he believed an extra dab of perfume might secure my affections more quickly. I was reduced to an animal-like state, sifting through the familiar odors in the workroom to detect his approach. I grew distracted in those days, like a prey on constant alert to danger, and I was greatly relieved when he was called to the Duke of Marlborough's estate to attend a visiting Belgian prince in urgent need of official dress.

Only then, after my opinions of Balducci had been tainted by a nameless and troubling sentiment, did I realize to what extent the atmosphere in the workroom was affected by his absence. Balducci traveled very little, much less than my father, and the tailors were rarely released from his shadow. When he had gone, a sense of lightness and cheer swept through the workrooms, invading every level of operations. During his absence, our employees toiled with lighter hearts. There was a bounce in their steps, and smiles came easily to their faces. I watched them laugh and joke with one another during their breaks, and yet they worked every bit as efficiently.

Finally, I took it upon myself to query the men directly as to their opinions of Balducci. I knew they were reluctant to air their grievances to my father, for they knew he would only back Balducci, but I hoped they might find me more approachable, and, despite my deafness, more willing to hear them out. Not only that, but many of our cutters, and the tailors who owed their jobs to those cutters, had been hired by Balducci himself and would be reluctant to speak their minds.

It was difficult finding a suitable place to interview old Mr. Crawley without eliciting suspicion, but I finally arranged for him to be called out on an errand, and I met him in the carriage in front of the Red Bull Tavern in Regent Street. From there we drove to the Park. I had come prepared with a slate and chalk, although Crawley had picked up some of the signs I used with Lucy and Esther and was not above gesturing to make himself understood.

That afternoon, stationed at the side of a light and airy path, I learned of the strife that now permeated every aspect of our business. I discovered that our staff was deeply divided into Balducci's camp and those tailors who had once worked for Mr. Samson; the latter were out of favor and dwindling in number, and they all feared for their jobs, knowing that any complaint would be seen as a sign of insubordination.

To my dismay, I learned that there had been numerous complaints from clients about delays in delivery—letters written which my father had never seen, even a visit from Lord Roeberry one evening which Balducci had covered up. I knew that Balducci, who had promoted himself as an *artiste,* would recall work if not done to his liking. Although I agreed that Grenfell's standards should never be compromised, I learned from Mr. Crawley that afternoon that Balducci's standards were not the same throughout the firm—that he used this as an excuse for discrediting and discouraging tailors who had earned his disfavor. He would berate the tailor, calling his work sloppy and third-rate, requiring him to toil late into the night to redo the garment, and then blame him for the delay.

"But the work is good, Miss Grenfell," Crawley said, emphasizing this with a vigorous nod of the head. "It's good work. There's nothin' wrong with the work. I've seen it with my own eyes."

He went on to explain how the delays were creating strife between the various departments which had to coordinate their schedules to turn out a garment in a timely manner. All the operations were affected by Balducci's tactics, from the buttonhole maker to the packing and delivery department.

"I tell you, Miss, it's not right," he said, looking down at the hat on his knees, turning the frayed rim in his hands. I had to tug on his sleeve to remind him to look up at me so I could read his lips. He was in his eighties, and still had his eyesight, but he was a frail man with only a few sparse hairs on his head, and his body had taken on the shape of his trade, the hunched shoulders and twisted fingers.

"What can I do?" I said, when he raised his eyes to mine.

He shook his head forlornly. "He's got the Guv'nor like a fox in the hole," he said, jerking his fist with a gesture much like the one Smithy used to wring a chicken's neck in the farmyard at Mortlake.

"You mean to say, because we're so dependent on Balducci's clients?"

He nodded.

Little did he realize that Balducci's clients contributed only to our show of prosperity and not to our bank account.

Despite our precautions, Mr. Crawley feared the news of our secret meeting would make its way back to the workroom and Balducci's ears. After our interview, he took to the bottle and disappeared "on the cod" for three days. By that time I had confronted Papa with what I had learned.

I stood behind Lucy as she knocked on the door of his study, and when he had answered her knock, I swept into the room, gripping a candelabra in my hand, which was a sign that I wished to engage in a serious conversation. Seated at his desk in his dressing gown, a ledger opened before him, he turned his tired eyes up at me. Before this year I had rarely seen him reviewing financial matters at home; now it was a nightly chore.

"We must be rid of him," I said, setting the candelabra on the mantle and pulling a box of matches from my pocket. "Either we find a way to take back control, or we dismiss him."

When I had finished lighting the candles, I turned to find him writing furiously on a slate.

He passed it to me. *We must not act hastily. Things will work out.*

"There's a great deal of internal strife, but they hide it from you."

Then let them speak to me about it!

"They won't. They're afraid you'll take Balducci's side. You always have in the past. Which is why I took it upon myself to interview Mr. Crawley. I assure you it was done very discreetly. He spoke quite openly to me on a number of very serious matters."

Crawley? How dare he speak to you of these matters!

"And why not? Grenfell's is my heart and my home, and they understand this. You should be proud of the fact that they see me as fair and approachable. Even Balducci says this about me."

Insubordination!

"Who? Me?"

Crawley!

"Old Crawley? Sixty years with us and you call him insubordinate? You never used that word before Balducci. When I could hear, I never heard it on your lips."

You were too young to remember.

"He's turned your head."

He was trying to say something to me but I would not listen.

"Did you know Balducci bribes the packers to give his garments priority? And that Lord Roeberry himself came to the back door—absolutely furious, you can imagine—because his coachman's uniform was three weeks overdue—and that his secretary had written a letter of complaint, which Balducci intercepted and destroyed? He's greedy and dishonest, and he has a dark and vile side to his nature that I am just beginning to see. Is this the way you want Grenfell's run? Is this the man you want me to marry?"

As I cannot hear my own voice, I am never quite sure if I am making myself understood. When I concluded my tirade and came to that final question, I knew I had made my point, because my father went quite pale. He turned back to his desk and lowered his head into trembling hands, and my soul grieved for him.

"Oh, Papa," I cried, and I stepped up and knelt before him, imploring him to look at me. "I don't say these things to wound you. I say these things to you because I'm afraid. This is all we have, you and I, we have each other and Grenfell's. I can't sit by and watch him destroy the only thing I have to live for." I tugged his hands away from his face. "Look at me. I can't see your face. I can't understand you when I can't see your face."

I had grown so apt at reading the nuances of his expressions that it was almost impossible for him to conceal his thoughts, and he knew this.

Finally, he lifted his eyes to mine.

"Oh, no," I said, and my heart dropped in my chest. "Tell me I'm wrong. Tell me I've misunderstood you."

He bent over the slate, rubbed it clean with a cloth, then wrote: *You must marry him. We have no choice.*

"No choice? But you yourself said you could not decide my heart for me."

"If you refuse him, he will leave the firm."

I rose so rapidly to my feet that I stumbled on my skirt and reached for his desk to steady myself.

"You don't know him," I stated firmly. "He's not what you think he is. We'll be better off without him."

"Please, child. I beg of you. Consider his proposal."

"I have—and I shall never consent to be his wife, and I am sickened to think that *you,* Papa, would encourage me to marry a man we have discovered to be deceitful and cruel and—and whom I find reprehensible and repulsive."

I stormed across the room and turned back only when I reached the door.

"You do as you wish with matters that concern Grenfell's. But I shall not be your pawn."

He had risen to his feet and was watching me with a saddened look in his eyes, his hands thrust deep in the pockets of his dressing gown.

"Please, Veda, if you must refuse him—"

"I shall, have no fear. I shall refuse him."

"But just wait. Wait until I've decided what to do. Please, child. Give me time."

"I will give you as much time as he gives me. If he presses his suit, I shall reject him."

I left the room and hurried down the hall, passing Aunt Lavinia, who had been eavesdropping. There she stood, good-hearted and selfless in her lace cap, wringing her hands and smelling of lavender, watching me with forlorn and sympathetic eyes. I was suddenly struck by her powerlessness. I stopped and pulled her into my arms, a gesture which took her completely by surprise, as she certainly thought I must be the one who needed consoling.

"We shall be all right," I said in her ear, and she appeared quite relieved.

Chapter Fourteen

I DREADED ENTERING GRENFELL'S EACH DAY, ALL BECAUSE OF BAL-ducci. He had alienated me from my one true sanctuary, and I grew increasingly resentful of his presence and his attentions to me. He was far too self-admiring and presumptuous ever to dream that I might reject him, and my snubs had little effect on him. His manner of encouraging me, taking an interest in my development and persuading my father to permit me all sorts of cherished privileges, had quite naturally led me to see him in a favorable light, but the man I had once viewed as a generous champion had turned a starkly different face on me as our familiarity had grown. I had recently learned from Ernestine, one of my seamstresses, that he spoke of me with a kind of pride of ownership, claiming that he had taken an awkward and timid girl and turned her into a living advertisement for the ladies division of our firm. He gloated openly in his achievement, referring to me as his "finest production yet."

Since our Ladies Riding Department was still quite small—I had but seven clients—and as I worked quickly, and my two seamstresses were highly competent, I rarely returned after lunch. Instead, I dressed in my habit and took a hansom to the stables where I spent the afternoon riding First. It was the only activity that kept my mind off that horrid little man. His presence infected the very air in Grenfell's, and I much preferred the dangerous streets of London to the stifling, close atmosphere of the workroom. The fact that he was oblivious to this radical change in sentiment spoke volumes about the man. I had been chased from my Garden of Eden, and I despised him for making me flee.

One chilly October afternoon, I arrived at the stables almost in tears. I had spent the morning working at Balducci's side. He had asked for my suggestions on a new design he was to submit for formal dress at court, and he had taken advantage of the opportunity to repeatedly stroke my hand

and press his body against my shoulder. As he maneuvered most cunningly so that the others would not see, there was nothing I could do except squirm in my chair and attempt to withdraw my hand. It was a game to him, and even though I beseeched him with my eyes and whispered words of discouragement, and my muscles tensed like steel at his touch, he remained relentless in his advances. There was something oppressively sordid about his nearness, something I could not escape, nor understand. Back in the house, I rushed up to my room shouting for Lucy to help me change into my riding habit. Within minutes I was down the steps, my hat in my hand, and hurrying to our carriage waiting in the street.

We had been fortunate to find a stall for First at a stable in Bayswater where Burnes liked to conduct his lessons. It was not a fashionable place, but I could go there on my own without subjecting myself to the sharp scrutiny of those very ladies whose custom I solicited at Grenfell's. The grooms and stable boys knew how to attend to me and knew not to address me as they would a hearing person.

That afternoon, while waiting for First to be saddled, as I stood there in my smart habit and my feathered hat, I could not get thoughts of Balducci's advances out of my head. I could still feel his fleshy thumb stroking the tender part of my palm where the senses are finest. The memory was so overwhelming that I began to feel ill. Finally, I rushed into an empty stall, ripped off my gloves, squatted in the straw, and plunged my hands into a bucket of icy water. I washed and washed them in the water until they were red and painfully cold, and then I took a handful of straw and rubbed them until they were raw. All the while I was imagining what it would be like to have his hands on me, to allow him a husband's freedom over my body. I started to weep, and the more I scrubbed my hands, the more I wept.

Suddenly, there was a hand on my shoulder. The unexpected touch of a stranger when I imagined myself to be quite alone in a straw-bedded stall, startled me out of my wits. As I was already squatting on my heels and quite unsteady, I lost my balance as I rose. The look on Harry's countenance—so full of tenderness—and the way he rushed to catch me by the waist, caused me to fall, quite literally, into his arms. His lips were moving—although I could not make much sense of it. He was most animated and clearly anxious as to the reason for my distress, thinking some real physical harm had been done to me. I threw my arms around his neck, buried my face in his shoulder, and abandoned myself to my emotions. He was not shocked at such a liberty—only deeply concerned. He held me gently and warmly, and paid no heed to the tears I was shedding all over his starched collar. Whatever unsavory gossip I had heard about Harry could not hold up in the face of this sweet moment of rescue.

Finally, my tears subsided, and he waved under my nose a handkerchief of which I made good use. I was still sobbing, those long, jerking sobs that rise and fall in the wake of a moment of great distress, and he held me most gently while I tended to my blotched and tear-stained face. After a moment, he took one of my raw and reddened hands in his and examined it with a pained expression on his countenance.

Why?

I shook my head, in the manner of one who does not wish to discuss a painful situation. He studied me closely, and then, with the look of a man who is satisfied that the worst is past, he released my waist, bent down, and retrieved my gloves from the straw. With a gesture, he indicated I was to hold out my hands, and one after the other, he gently slipped on the gloves. Then, turning over my wrists, he carefully closed the buttons for me.

Through all of this, I watched his face.

Perhaps it was my boldness, the way I had to observe a face to interpret the nuances and mannerisms, perhaps it was this that sparked the intimacy that crept into our hearts at that moment, but when he had finished closing my gloves he did not release my hands, and I did not draw them away from him.

"Can you understand me?" he asked.

"Yes," I said, a smile breaking through the tears. "When you speak like this, and stand close to me."

"Ned—"

"Yes. Ned—"

"Ned says that you can read lips."

"Reading lips is not an exact science, sir, and I remember you are a man of science. So do not expect my understanding to be perfect."

"There is never perfect understanding. Even when we can hear."

"No, sir, that is very true."

His brow furrowed, and he cast a doleful look at my hands resting in his.

"I am sorry," he said, and there was more consolation conveyed in his eyes than in those words.

"I'm glad you were here," I said.

"I beg your pardon?"

He had not understood me, and I blushed. "Forgive me. I know my speech is odd. At least, I am told it's queer. It's been greatly affected by my deafness."

"It's a lovely voice," he said.

"Lovely?" I asked, a little amused.

"Yes," he smiled. "Lovely."

"I am told it's like the sound of a gull. But I don't recall the sound of a gull anymore."

"Perhaps, if you were to visit the coast—" He said more, but I did not understand, for I was lost in his eyes.

"I'm sorry, sir, will you repeat that?"

"—it might return to you. The memory of the sound of gulls."

"I have no memory for sound."

My speech was rattled by one final sob that surged quite unexpectedly from the depths of my bosom, and a look of perfect tenderness swept across his face once again.

"But I do recall what I have seen in great detail," I continued. "If the moment is important enough."

"Indeed! That is quite interesting."

"Yes. Rather like a photographic image."

"And this moment? Will you remember this moment?" he teased.

I took a long breath, and then replied, "I will recall this moment and everything about it so perfectly that, were I a painter, I could paint your visage, sir, long after you had gone."

I think he was startled by the frank response to his flirtatious query, but he did not toss it away, like so much superficial banter, but seemed to give it serious consideration.

A sound must have drawn his attention to the front of the stable.

"They are looking for you," he said.

"Then you must release my hands, sir, and allow me to leave."

If my voice was queer, I know there was a coyness in my eyes, and he saw it and smiled.

"I will release these hands," he said, quite clearly, "only if you treat them with great gentleness."

"Treat them—" I was not sure I had understood.

"Like this," he said, and he raised my palm to his lips and planted a kiss in the cup of my hand.

I could not allow that generous kiss to fade, and so I cupped my hand around his jaw, and cradled his dear face in my hand. I could read every line on his countenance. The gesture had taken him by surprise, but the surprise was a welcome one. He placed his hand over mine, and held it trapped against his cheek. I wished that he might never release it, that he might hold my hand captive forever.

"You are very kind, sir, to take care of me."

"I do so most willingly," he replied.

I withdrew my hand, reluctantly, but my eyes, always locked on his lips, surely betrayed my sentiments.

"I am quite composed now," I said, with a tweak of concealed irony, for I was anything but composed, "and I am most grateful for your solicitude."

I offered him the handkerchief, but he pressed it back into my hand.

"I have a collection of these," I said, glancing down at the Hambledon crest embroidered in one corner of the cambric. I looked back up at him. "I am not being facetious, sir. It was your mother's, and I still keep it folded in my drawer. In memory of her."

Prompted by this mention of a keepsake, he said with a rueful smile, "Ah! My little Ivanhoe!" and went on to say something I could not quite comprehend.

"If you are enquiring as to his health, he is in good health, and has adapted quite well to his adopted family." I smiled, feeling more and more at ease with him, despite the butterflies flitting around in my stomach. "He's a fat little fellow, now."

"Ah! I warned you!" He wagged a gloved finger at me.

"I confess, he is not walked as much as he should be. He's all too content to sit in my lap—when he's not sleeping at the foot of my bed."

Despite the limitations of our dialogue, there was no mistaking Harry's response to me. I could almost see his mind working behind those moody grey eyes, wondering how he might get through to me. Even at that point, when it was all beginning, all new and wonderful and fresh, when he came up against my wall of silence, Harry felt disarmed.

Having regained my composure, I brushed the straw from my skirt, favored him with a curtsey, then turned to leave the stall.

I overcame the urge to look back at him, but went directly to the arena where First was being held by an impatient groom. As I handed the groom my crop and prepared to mount, I noticed Harry had followed me, and my heart leaped with joy.

He called out to the groom and strode quickly toward me across the dusty flat.

"Say, Miss Grenfell, are you riding alone?" he asked.

"I ride only in the arena, sir."

He asked me a question, but I had caught sight of Burnes approaching, and to my astonishment, Harry turned and greeted him in a manner that suggested an old friendship between the two. I was terribly frustrated not to be able to follow their exchange, but I saw there was warmth and joviality, and they seemed to be acknowledging their mutual acquaintance with me.

Flushed with the kind of pleasure that comes from an unexpected surprise, Harry turned to me and said something about a horse, and after much gesturing and patience on Harry's part, I understood that Burnes was training Harry's new hunter.

"He is training me as well," I quipped, with a sly smile at Burnes, who seemed to hold me in higher esteem now that he knew me to be an acquaintance of Lord Ormelie's. "But I imagine I am much more of a challenge than any horse will ever be."

Burnes cocked a bushy eyebrow and conceded this was true. After another brief exchange between the two men, Harry turned back to me. "He says your father will not give his permission for you to ride in the Park."

"My father worries about my safety."

"And if you—"

"I beg your pardon?"

"If you had a companion? Someone to ride with?"

"I have no companions who ride, sir," I said, feeling the sharp sting of my isolation as well as my social station. Had I been a lady of rank, I might have had any number of friends to accompany me.

"You do now, Miss Grenfell," he affirmed. With a gesture for me to wait, and another quick command to the groom, Harry turned on his heels and strode from the arena. Burnes called after him; there was disagreement, it seemed. Burnes was not in favor of this arrangement, and af-

ter a warning directed at me—and which I made a pretense of ignoring—
he hurried off after Harry.

It was not an ideal day for a ride. The sun was lost behind a chalk grey
sky. Side by side, we passed down the cobbled road, then dodged our way
through the cross-current of wagons and carts and carriages into the Park.
I glanced behind me as the tree-lined path closed in behind us and wondered if it were as peaceful and serene as it appeared. There were few riders out. The more fashionable society confined themselves to Rotten Row
at the other end of the Park, but for once I was thankful to be away from
that crowded scene.

Burnes had cautioned Harry that I was a novice horsewoman and that
Harry would be held accountable for my safety. Burnes was particularly
worried that First, finding himself in the open park, would be difficult for
me to control. He was right, for I could sense the horse's excitement as
soon as we left the city streets.

But Burnes knew Harry well, and he was right to trust him. Since my
own instruction had been entirely by sight, I had learned to pay close attention to every minute command and position of the rider, every slight
change in angle of the torso or pressure of the leg or calf, and I saw that
Harry was an expert horseman, graceful and refined in his attitude. He
rode a splendid Arabian named Fellow who seemed to melt First's huge
heart.

Braving a dialogue, I pointed this out to Harry. "I can tell. By his
ears," I said, glancing over at Harry with an amused smile. Harry's eyes
were on me.

"You know horses this well?" he mouthed slowly.

"I am beginning to know this one."

He seemed quite eager to talk to me, but when I failed to understand
his next comment, I drew a bewildered and embarrassed expression.

"We need not talk," I said, trying to conceal my own embarrassment.
"We can merely enjoy the pleasure of the ride."

"But I am inclined to speak my thoughts to you, Miss Grenfell," he
said, leaning toward me in the saddle so that I could more easily read his
lips. I could see he was making a great effort to speak slowly, and this was
clearly a strain on him as well as me.

"You'll say nothing but charming things to melt my heart," I countered,
hoping to reward his patience with flattery, "just like your good Fellow is

doing to my little First, in their secret horse language, so perhaps my limitations work in my favor for once." I gave him a sideways glance. "A natural immunity to your charm, so to speak."

I caught the scrutinizing glance he cast at my figure. "You ride well," he said.

"See? Already, false flattery."

"Burnes said you had a good seat. He's right."

"Ah, but a lady's riding habit covers a multitude of sins."

"My mother rode often—" I did not understand the rest of his sentence. I was struck by the change in his countenance; a pained reverence crossed his face when he spoke her name.

I pulled First to a stop. "Please sir, would you be so kind as to repeat that. I confess, I often follow only the drift of the conversation, and I pretend to understand much more than I do. If you are speaking of your mother, I should wish to comprehend."

Stopping beside me, he repeated, "My mother said the same thing." He gestured to my skirt flowing down the side of the horse. "She did not like the Amazon saddle. She felt it was—"

"Restricting?" I repeated, hoping I had guessed right.

He nodded. "Yes, quite. On the estate, in Blackroak, she always rode astride the horse."

I smiled. "That sounds like just the thing she'd do."

He fell into a gloomy mood then, and I rather wished I had not spoken of that whole business of riding. He kept glancing at me as though he might want to renew our conversation but was at a loss as to how to converse with me. Like others of his rank, he showed no inclination to use gestures to facilitate our communication. He was also an impatient man and quite used to speaking quickly, with that brilliance that so charmed his listeners—a brilliance lost on me.

"Sir," I said finally, "do not worry yourself with conversation. I am dependent on my sight not only for understanding but also for life's pleasures, and beautiful things gratify me more now than ever before. Pray let us enjoy this ride together. I do so love the Park, even on grey days such as this."

I urged First to a trot, and Harry followed pace.

The morose and smoke-blackened sky was for me the only reminder of the city surrounding us. I could not hear the heavy carts laden with goods rumbling down the stone streets, the thudding of the horses' hooves on the macadam thoroughfares, the drays and cabs and crowded omnibuses, all the hue and cry and bustle of the masses, the shouts to buy, to sell, the cries of warning or greetings, or just the vague and muffled roar of thousands of figures pressing against one another, each on his way to his destination. I saw only the beauty of what lay before me—broad green vistas of wide paths laid out among small scattered groves of trees. Autumn had brought on a subtle change of hue in the woodlands, yet only the chestnuts and the elms had dropped their leaves, and these lay in yellow and brown beds massed at the trunks, giving off a sharp but not unpleasant odor of decay as we passed by.

Harry guided us that afternoon. At first he had intended to ride across the Park to Rotten Row, but when I expressed my reservations, he agreed that we would be better off in a more remote corner of the Park. We cantered for a while, and when I noticed a fallen tree along the side of the *allée*, I took advantage of Harry's expertise to coach me in a few jumps. Only then did he appreciate all that Burnes had achieved.

"How the deuce did he do it?" he said when I came trotting up to stop beside him, quite breathless and flushed.

"I beg your pardon, sir?"

"Burnes taught you to ride?"

"Indeed."

"Why, Miss Grenfell, I don't know how you managed. Burnes is brilliant with horses, but he is a brute with people."

"It was not easy," I said, dropping my reins over my knee while I removed my hat pin and adjusted my hat. "He's not a patient man."

"Quite nice," Harry said.

"Quite right?"

"Nice," he repeated. "Lovely."

I jabbed the pin back into my hat and blotted at my neck with Harry's handkerchief that I had tucked up my sleeve. "I'm not sure I understand, sir."

"You have changed a great deal."

"I have changed?"

"You are quite breathtaking, Miss Grenfell."

As he spoke I observed the action of his mouth and the play of muscles when he spoke, and I tried to imagine his voice.

"Did you understand me?" he asked, wondering at the blankness of my stare.

"I believe I caught the drift of your discourse, sir."

"I should like you to understand perfectly."

"Even if I did, my modesty would prohibit me from acknowledging it."

At that moment, his attention was drawn to a point over my shoulder. At first I thought he had recognized an acquaintance, but the quizzical frown that creased his brow and the way in which his eyes swung back to me indicated otherwise.

He leaned toward me and said, "There is a gentleman who seems unusually attentive to you—he has pulled up just behind you, in a phaeton."

"In a phaeton?"

Harry nodded.

"Is he driving a grey pair?"

Another nod.

Balducci! I thought. It had to be him. On occasions he came to the stables to watch me ride. It gave him great pleasure, he said, although he had little time for it these days.

"Is he short and dark—and staring at me obsessively?" I asked Harry.

"He is short and dark, but his gaze is directed at me—and it is not a friendly gaze. Do you know this gentleman?"

How I wished I could have replied to the contrary, then I might have set Harry on him like a hawk on a rodent.

"He is—" I paused, and smiled faintly, "—a family friend."

"So I need not defend your honor."

"You can defend me if you wish, sir," I replied with a coy lift of the brow.

"He is gesturing to you—and calling your name."

"I cannot know that, sir, since my attention is turned on you."

"But *I* can hear him."

"You can choose to ignore him."

"Do you wish me to ignore him?"

"I do."

"Then I shall," he said with gleeful and boyish humor. "I shall do just that." Settling his hat firmly on his head, with a discreet sign that I could not fail to interpret, he pressed his legs into Fellow's flanks, and within two strides both our horses had broken into a canter. With the rush of wind against my face and the tremendous surge of power beneath me, I felt as though I might break free of all the earthly constraints, that this horse and the man beside me might lift me up like winged angels and carry me off to a carefree place where communication was untroubled by faulty senses, and hearts were set free in a land unmarked by human pride.

I PAID DEARLY FOR THAT moment. Balducci avoided me all the next day. When my father finally returned to London and we met for dinner, I could tell by Aunt Lavinia's lack of composure—her fretful darting glances and the way she kept picking up her fork and laying it down without taking a bite, and her nervous habit of dabbing each corner of her mouth with her napkin when there was not a crumb in sight—that there was trouble brewing over my head.

After dinner, Papa sent Lucy to tell me he wished to see me in his study. When I arrived, I found him at his desk, penning a note to me. Although paper was dear, he preferred it to a slate whenever there was something substantial to be discussed. I saw he had already emptied his glass of port, and I picked up the decanter and refilled it for him, then took a second glass from the side table and poured another for myself.

I felt the floor tremble slightly; he had stamped on it to get my attention—undoubtedly to signal his disapproval—but I ignored him.

"If I am to be condemned," I announced as I whirled around to face him, "then I shall go to my execution giddy and in good spirits."

He shook his head, perturbed, but intent on finishing his thoughts before engaging in that tiresome act of reprimanding me.

His writing was interrupted when Lucy appeared at the door, announcing a caller.

"Who is it?" I asked when Lucy had gone, for I had read the tenseness on his face.

He rose to his feet and motioned me out of the room, taking a moment to check his appearance—retying his dressing gown and smoothing back his hair. By these actions, I knew our caller was someone of rank. I took my good time, sauntering deliberately back to the side board to set down my glass, so that I was just crossing the carpet when Lord Roeberry swept into the room with all the arrogance of an earl who deems it his right to call on a tradesman whenever it suits him. He was dressed for the theater in a jet black cape and spotless white gloves and carried with him the damp chill of the outdoors. My presence surprised him, and he stopped stiffly and swept off his hat with a slight bow. I acknowledged him with a quick curtsey and then left the room.

After I had found Lucy and signaled for her to eavesdrop at the door, I sat on the stairs at the end of the hall with a candle on the step beside me, reading Papa's letter. I had confiscated it from his desk while his back was turned, quickly folded it, and stuffed it up my sleeve. The ink had smeared, but it was still legible.

Balducci claims you snubbed him most violently yesterday, when he had driven out to the Park searching for you. He was quite concerned for your safety—knowing I did not want you riding outdoors—and his intentions were honorable. He said he found you in a "suspicious" tête-à-tête with Lord Ormelie whom he characterized as a "licentious cad." (I know you will disagree but it is Balducci's feelings we must consider for the present.) He now demands some show of remorse on your part or will assume he has been jilted—an impression I would not wish to give him as there could be serious consequences. He also insists we set a date for the wedding.

My dear, I shall be blunt with you. You have led him along, and he is now expecting you to agree to the marriage. You have waited too long to refuse him now.

What nonsense! I stared at the letter with a white hot glare, hoping to burn holes in the paper where Balducci's name appeared. Lord Ormelie a "licentious cad"? Me "leading Balducci along"? I could not believe I had misunderstood when we had last discussed this matter. Clearly, he had been forced to take this stance for a reason. I had been trapped by Balducci and sacrificed by my father.

I looked up to see Lucy tugging on my skirt to get my attention. Lord Roeberry was departing, and I dashed up the stairs and waited in the hall outside my room until Lucy had seen him out. After a moment, she reappeared at the bottom of the stairs, and I motioned for her to come up and tell me what she had heard. Lord Roeberry had complained bitterly about an order that had not been delivered as promised. This was the second such incident. I did not need to catch Lucy's every word to imagine his dissatisfaction. Gentlemen of rank—particularly those as snobbish as Lord Roeberry—did not go rushing around to their tailors at the eleventh hour to pick up delinquent orders.

There was one thing I made her repeat until it was very clear—she kept saying something about Balducci's involvement, but I couldn't quite understand. Finally, I dragged her off to my room and handed her a slate and chalk. I learned that Papa had asked Lord Roeberry why he had not come to him directly with his previous complaint. Lord Roeberry replied that he had been given to believe that Balducci was now a partner with the firm and that all complaints should go to him.

I knew precisely what Balducci was trying to do. He had discredited our employees in order to conceal the increasing strife in the workshop, and he had tried to cover up complaints from clients that would have thrown a bad light on his own character. That he had falsely represented his station in the firm, promoting himself as my father's equal, would prove to be a fatal error.

I waited for Papa to summon me back to his study, but he never did. Before I went to bed, I tore up his letter and dropped it on the cold grate where it would be burned in the morning when Lucy came to start the fire in my room.

There was one final abominable scene. My twenty-first birthday was the following Sunday, and a large family gathering had been planned. My cousin Grace and her husband and children arrived on Friday from Bath, and Grandpa and Aunt Mary drove over on Sunday from Kensington. Esther and Ned came down from Oxford, which pleased me enormously. Balducci had already been invited.

I believed Papa still had not made up his mind what to do, for he treated Balducci quite warmly, and Balducci was his typical unctuous self around our family. Grandpa plied him with our best claret, which he sipped while eyeing me over the rim of his glass, his little finger curled delicately in an attitude that drew attention to his gold ring and groomed nails. As it was my birthday party and I was the center of attention, I was somewhat protected from his simpering advances by the fortress of friends and family.

After cake had been served and eaten and the guests had fallen into conversation with one another, and the children were roaming freely about the room, and Grandpa had settled into an armchair by the window to read his paper, I whispered to Papa that I was quite tired from my exertion and would retire to my room for a while. I asked him to send Esther up when it pleased her, and then I slipped quietly from the room. As I passed down the hallway, I was startled by a hand on my elbow. I knew at the very touch it was Balducci, and I whirled around so abruptly that he seemed momentarily stunned.

"Cara—"

"You startled me," I said. "I cannot hear you approach."

"I wish to speak to you alone."

"Please, sir, I am quite tired from my exertion, if you would—"

But he stepped into my path, blocking my retreat, and stood with his hands clasped behind his back, imploring me from beneath lowered eyes in a manner I found most pathetic. I thought I might as well have it out and over with, and so I asked him to follow me into the drawing room. I remained at the door as he passed through and I lodged it open with a door stop—an action greeted with a flicker of disappointment from his dark eyes.

He began by talking about the incident at the Park. I did give him the satisfaction of a demure and attentive attitude, but I was also giving the appearance of understanding more than I did. Finally, he pressed for a response to his tiresome monologue, and I could do no more than smile. With that he grabbed me most clumsily around the waist and forced a long, wet kiss on my mouth that made my stomach turn over. I was far too stunned to react, giving him sufficient time to grope greedily under my arm with his hand, but before he could reach his mark I shoved him away, raising my arm to my face to shield myself from his advances. This was not enough to deter him; he grabbed my arm and pinned it to my back while bearing down on me with his terrible eyes. The muscles on his face were tensed with a savage determination, and his mouth was moistened and open as though roused for another attack. I freed my arm from his grasp and slapped him hard across the face, a blow which knocked some sense into his queer little head and sent him reeling back several steps. Suddenly, he quit nursing his red cheek and drew himself up proudly, and I realized we were no longer alone. I spun around to find Esther and Ned watching in astonishment from the hallway. Without a second's hesitation, Ned marched into the room and I rushed out to Esther, and when I glanced back, Ned was closing the door behind him.

FATHER ENGAGED A SOLICITOR TO negotiate Balducci's final salary. As there were numerous claims and accusations on both sides, it was not an amiable parting. A settlement was reached in which he would have his commission to date and salary until the end of the year. Within a month he had taken a lease on premises in Regent Street and was opening his own firm. Only a handful of tailors eventually went over to him, most of whom were Italian. Every other employee remained faithful to us, and the difference in the atmosphere around the shop after he had gone almost made up for the disaster that followed.

Balducci did his best to sow discord and disrespect before he left. He spread false stories in an attempt to discredit me, voicing his doubts about my virtue, my beauty, and my talent. I only found this out from Ernestine who was easily tricked into revealing what she had overheard. None of the tailors would have dared repeat his ugly accusations.

I had learned a valuable lesson: A man with two faces can only conceal his dark side for so long. Even if we have been singled out as favorites, the time will come when he will turn his head and the dark side appears. What was once visible only to others now appears to us, and we are baffled by its unsightliness. I had believed I was beyond the pale of his mistreatment, that he would never turn his dark side on me. I was terribly wrong.

If the tailors despised him, his clients did not. We lost nearly every client he had brought with him. Balducci may have made our workers' lives miserable, but none of us could deny his excellent production. Of course, the fact that he offered interminable credit was another drawing point. Papa and I wondered how he would ever manage, but that was not our concern. Our concern was how *we* would manage.

We kept the showroom in Savile Row and our house next door, but we sold the Kensington property, and Grandpa and Aunt Mary were forced to keep Mortlake as their year-round residence. Grandpa minded terribly as Mortlake was damp in the winter and the fireplaces smoked dreadfully, but the lease was only a fraction of that of the Kensington house. We cut expenses wherever we could. Papa sold all our carriages except the barouche and kept only a pair, greatly reducing our stable costs, although I was allowed to keep First. We sold the collection of paintings and expensive French furnishings that Balducci had urged us to buy for the showroom to impress our clients, as well as our piano. Ironically, only Mr. Nicholls had ever played it. Our home furnishings and trappings were pared down to the bare essentials; everything else went to the auctioneer's block. Although we were offered an important sum for my portrait by Sir Francis, Papa would not hear of selling it.

The decrease in orders meant that we had to close down our workshop in Soho, and we retained only a fraction of our regular staff. The Ladies Riding Department ceased to exist, and I returned to the back of the shop to work on gentlemen's garments. If Papa had any doubt as to who would be replacing Balducci as his Deputy, the tailors and cutters certainly had none. Despite my sex and my deafness, I had earned their confidence. Seeing me sweep through the workshop with my skirts bundled around my knees, trailing threads from my hems, flashing strange signs with my hands back and forth with Crawley, conversing on slates—none of this unconventional behavior shocked anymore. I knew every aspect of the custom now, every department and operation. I could pack a suit for delivery and cut into a bolt of cashmere for the Duke of Montrose with equal assurance. All we needed now was time to recover from this blow to our pride and prestige. That we would do with perseverance and toil. We were no strangers to that.

Chapter Fifteen

It was perhaps to my benefit that Esther was in Oxford-
shire during all this mishap and mayhem, for our correspondence helped
me clarify my sentiments.

How do I feel about it all, you ask? A Great Relief—like Prometheus Un-
bound scrambling down from his rocky cliff, and yet I am vaguely dispirited
by the incident. Incident. Was it more? Was it truly an engagement? And if
so, who jilted whom? Quite honestly, Tiggy, I am no more disappointed in
Balducci than I am in myself. What an atrocious error in judgment. I know
you place the blame on Aunt Lavinia, but I find this most unfair. Aunt Lavinia
may have exerted her influence when it came to nursing me back to health,
but she would never challenge Papa when it comes to approving a suitor.
Besides, given the disastrous outcome of her nursing, we should be thankful
she didn't intervene! Quite frankly, I don't know if she liked him or not. I
don't think she knows her own mind on the subject. And if she's unclear,
how could she give me guidance? Poor dear woman. She is a presence but
has never been a force in my life.

If there is one thing I have discovered about myself from this debacle it is
that I do hope to be married. I know you find this silly, that I should ever
doubt my inclination, but you must understand that after my fever, I feared to
dream as I had once done. My hopes and aspirations having been cruelly
obliterated, I had begun to hum the tune of spinsterhood. Balducci made me
believe that a man with exciting prospects could see me in the role of his wife
and the mother of his children, and the mistress of his household, and even
the partner in his enterprise. How ironic that he proved to be so dishonorable when he gave me faith in myself.

No, Papa and I must share the blame for the fiasco, although I believe poor Papa was blinded by Balducci's excellence and his charm. Balducci was really quite brilliant in his own way. God save us from brilliant, charming men.

Esther replied:

My dearest Topsy, you torture yourself needlessly. Of course you will marry and have children. Why do you fret so? You poor thing, I do wish I could be there to soothe you through these difficult times. I find it distressing that you take responsibility for a situation which was not of your own making. No, Topsy, the blame falls squarely on your father and aunt. It is their duty to shelter you from these nasty situations. Your father never should have allowed such familiarity to develop between you and that horrid little man until he had thoroughly scrutinized his character. I shudder when I recall the incident Ned and I witnessed—thank goodness Ned was there—I might have turned quite savage on the monster. You have no experience in these things, and you must not blame yourself.

We are all prone to change our opinions of people when we see them under a new light. I have found my opinions of Ned's friends—Lord Ormelie in particular—have changed a good deal since our marriage. I was rather possessive of my new husband at first and resented any intrusion from the outside, but I admit that Lord Ormelie has been ever so helpful to us since Ned has entered into a new phase of his work. Although he was perhaps a tad heavy-handed in his patronage in the past, his association with us now is strictly on terms of friendship, and Ned no longer feels the same obligations he felt before.

Indeed, I have news I have been bursting to tell. We are leaving Oxford and renting a little house in Burford, a charming village not far from here where several artist friends of Ned's have settled. He has decided to pursue a partnership with them to design functional wares—tiles, tapestries, ceramics, even illustrations for books. The design work appears to be very profitable. It's all been terribly rushed, as the house has just fallen vacant and we move at the end of next week. Now, Burford is in close proximity to Longmeade, Lord Stamford's estate, and Ned had already been commissioned to design a stained-glass window for the chapel they are restoring. As stained glass is all the rage and there are many grand houses in this area, other commissions may come of it. Ned creates the most stunning designs. I am quite impatient for you to see them. Lady Stamford has also asked him to paint a fresco of Cupid and Psyche in her bedchamber!

I am told that Lord Ormelie is often at Longmeade, which is only three miles from the village. You can see the castle (it is rather a mishmash but the tenants call it a castle) from the path that runs along the hill behind our new house. There is quite a lot of building going on up there. You did meet Lady Stamford, did you not? over the monkey business? We are told she is renovating the kitchen and building a new servants' wing to provide separate quarters for women and men—rather a moral necessity these days. Of course we all know how keen Lady Stamford is on proving herself acceptable to polite society. The older nobility continue to snub her—ever since the Queen refused to receive her at court. But things are changing in that regard. Look at the company the Prince keeps. Lord Ormelie says his dinner parties are full of actresses and Americans and Jews. As long as you're wealthy and dress beautifully, our dear Prince Bertie will have you to dinner.

Ned will be pleased having L.O. in the country from time to time. He is quite congenial and relaxed when he comes to visit—he was here twice last year, you'll recall. He never stays long anywhere. He is very much in demand, especially among the sporting set, and I have heard that society hostesses fall all over themselves to nab him for a weekend or a ball. But he does have his faults. He is wild. Ned says he's quite a gambler these days. He spent the entire summer at Newmarket with the racing crowd and lost a good deal of money on the horses—some of which were his own, but then he sold them and bought fresh ones, and took the new ones to London to train—to that man who gives you riding lessons, which was how you happened to meet him at the stables. But even when the Season is over, he spends very little time at Blackroak. His relationship with his father is more strained than ever before. Ned suspects he is quite miserable up there now. In September he goes off to Scotland to hunt grouse on his cousins' ancestral estates and then works his way back through the noble houses and the best hunts. He is always invited to Quorn Hall in Leicestershire, and I think this, and Lord Stamford's estate where he remains until the Christmas holidays, are the only places you can be sure to find him.

Goodness, all this writing devoted to the escapades of Lord Ormelie. I'm turning into a horrid old gossip. But I know you will find news of him entertaining. I know you are very much taken with him, although you would never admit to it.

You must come for a visit as soon as we are moved in. It will do you good. Despite your efforts at humor, I know you have been indeed wounded by this nasty little Italian.

In November, I went for a long stay in Burford.

The house had previously been owned by an artist who had transformed the upper level into a pleasantly sunny studio large enough for Esther and Ned to share. It was situated on the main road near the entrance to the town, not a stone's throw from the market and just down the street from the coaching inn. It was not an ideal location, particularly on market days when the streets were impassable and wooly sheep overran the village. The strays wandered about eating the heads off any flowers in bloom, and village wives went after them flapping their aprons. Within a day of my arrival, everyone knew of my affliction, and whenever I left the house I had to suffer disheartening stares and a good deal of stupidity from some rascally children who attempted to test my hearing by following me up the street shouting or clapping blocks of wood together or ringing a cowbell. Esther would hear the commotion and come out to chase them away, and eventually Ned had to pay a call on the father of one particularly cruel child before the persecution ceased. It made me realize how London often protected me from humiliation by offering me anonymity; in London I had become adept at concealing my deafness, but in a village such as this, there was no hiding.

The countryside beyond the village offered me a pleasant refuge. Nature was only just now withdrawing into its scant winter attire, and the glades still offered sufficient protection for all kinds of wild creatures, so that I inevitably flushed out a covey of pheasants or partridge, and one morning before breakfast I caught sight of a doe grazing in a sunny glen. The change of scenery did indeed put my mind to rest, and for the first time since I could remember, I was not thinking about Grenfell's. The only time I took up a needle was in the evening when I set about mending tablecloths and shirts and petticoats for Esther. She had never been a tidy woman, and marriage had not changed that.

As each day passed, I ventured farther from the village. First I followed the River Windrush, but later I took paths through the fields and meadows behind the village. I enjoyed walking with a destination in mind, and that soon became Longmeade, Lord Stamford's estate. I never pretended to call on that aloof nobleman and his pretty circus wife, but it was impossible to ignore the stately pile. As soon as I climbed through a stile in a stone wall and mounted a swell, or emerged from a grove of beeches, there it sat in the distance, its gables and turrets rising out of the morning haze in the manner of old baronial privilege asserting its lawful place upon the land. On sunny days, if Esther had time to accompany me, we would pack a picnic of cold meats and cheese and ale, but generally I took only a book and a small square oilcloth upon which to sit, and perhaps an umbrella. The only time I took Ivanhoe along, he trembled so violently that I concluded it was a torture rather than a pleasure for him, and thereafter I left him at home. Nothing short of driving rain or a freezing wind would keep me from my morning excursions. They became my balm, and the beauty of earth, sky, and wind that greeted me on those hills washed every troublesome thought from my mind.

Then, one day well into the first week in December, a very dignified dark-skinned gentleman dressed in a gauzy white tunic beneath his topcoat and thin little slippers alighted from a carriage with Lord Stamford's cook in the market square. Together they swooped down on the market, and within an hour there was not a knuckle bone or turnip to be found. Gossip was the only thing exchanged that day, and we soon learned that a maharajah, while on a state visit, had expressed to the Prince of Wales his desire to join a shooting party, and a specific wish to shoot at Longmeade because of his long-standing friendship with Lord Stamford.

The next day dawned cold but cloudless and calm, and with the prospects of a delightful morning before me, I wrapped a bun and some cheese and stuffed it in my pocket, and set off early for the woods. I had found I was quite an adventuress, facilitated by my keen faculties of observation and a good dose of common sense, and I was perhaps a little too sure of myself, for I had never yet failed to find my way back home. On this morning, I decided to explore a low rise of hills beyond Longmeade Castle, and after two hours winding along paths across grazing pastures and through small woods, I paused at the edge of a glen to rest. I laid down my oilcloth behind a high hedge of deep brush and, thus sheltered from the wind, took my refreshment. Feeling no urge to rush on, I removed my bonnet, spread out my cloak, and laid back in the spongy grass, letting the wind and sun dance over my face.

I must have fallen asleep, for I next remember being jolted awake by the sensation of something warm and wet hitting my cheek. Touching my skin, I found it was blood. I thought perhaps I had scratched myself on a bramble, but this was not blood from a mere scratch. I cleaned my hand on the grass and then rose to my feet, and as I looked down I discovered my skirt was stained with drops of blood. Suddenly, a shadow overhead drew my attention upward, and at just that moment a bird plummeted from the sky, followed by a second, and a third. I realized with a jolt that I was in the middle of a shooting field, and I grabbed my bonnet and my oilcloth and lit off across the glen.

As I ran, I flushed out a covey of pheasants; three long-tailed birds rose from the brush with their wings flailing madly. No sooner had they climbed into the blue than they were shot down. One of them disappeared into the brush, but another fell to the ground near my feet. It was not dead but lay there in its magnificently colored plumage twitching a blood-splattered wing. I was horrified, not only by the shock of witnessing the sad creature's death, but with the realization that I was in every bit as much danger as this bird. I had heard nothing; the gunfire was too distant and my shred of hearing too faint, and even should I hear the slightest rumble I would not be able to distinguish the direction from whence it came.

As I stood there, paralyzed by fear, not knowing which way to run, yet another flock of birds darkened the sky, and this time the shots brought dozens down on my head. These birds were smaller, I guessed partridge, but there were others, females of a species I did not recognize. They lay in brown masses of agony, some of them dragging themselves across the field before collapsing in a shattered heap. I began to call for help. I had no way to gauge how loudly I was shouting or if I would be heard, but I continued my frantic cry, and all the while the birds rained from the sky, spattering drops of blood onto my arms and my head.

I don't know how long I carried on. I think my voice must have been quite faint by the time they came across me, and judging from the looks on the faces of the two beaters who found me, I must have resembled something from a torture chamber, collapsed on my knees, with tears and blood smeared over my face and hands. They thought I had been shot.

Fortunately, the beaters were an old man and his grandson from the village, and they recognized me and remembered that I was deaf.

Within a few moments, a hunting party descended on me, at the head of which was the maharajah himself dressed in hunting tweeds and a spotless white turban that set off his walnut skin and jet black beard. I think I was every bit as startled by his appearance as he was by mine. I made no attempt to explain myself, as others were already doing so for me. I sat there in my puddle of bloodstained skirts with feathers stuck to my hands, trying to gain a little composure, and feeling terribly humiliated for having blundered onto the estate and provoking such a scandalous scene. Once they had concluded I was not injured, they hurried the maharajah away. Within a few moments a groom appeared on horseback trailing a second horse behind him. I was unceremoniously hoisted up onto the saddle and escorted off Lord Stamford's domain.

Once Esther recovered from my shocking appearance, she called for bathwater to be drawn, and I washed the blood and feathers from my hair and sent my gown down to be sponged clean. By the time I'd been settled in front of the fire with a pot of strong tea, we were both beginning to find the incident decidedly comical. When Ned came home, we opened up a bottle of brandy. I had more than my fair share, and by the time we sat down to dinner, we had all had a ripping good laugh over it.

Of course, the next day when the brandy had worn off, I was so shamefaced I didn't dare go outside. I sat in the shadows of the drawing room watching the passing villagers stop and stare through the bay window, pointing and whispering in amusement or horror. On the second day of incarceration late in the afternoon, I was upstairs in my room when the housemaid opened my door and announced a caller. Neither Ned nor Esther were home, and I was rather nervous at confronting a stranger alone, but rather than press the maid for more information, I tried to pin up some of my loose curls, adjusted my shawl and smoothed down my skirt, and went down to the drawing room.

He stood at the doorway, his face and figure in shadow, and not until he stepped forward did I recognize him.

"Harry!" I cried, clapping my hands together.

He held out his hands, took mine and pressed them warmly, planting a firm kiss on each of them.

He waited while I lighted a candle and set it on the table. Then I produced a slate from a side table, and some chalk, and we sat down side by side to converse.

He had heard about the incident upon his arrival the night before and had wanted to make sure I had not suffered any injury. I assured him that the only injury had been to my pride, and that I was most humiliated by the whole incident. He seemed to think Lord Stamford had been so keen on impressing the maharajah that he failed in his obligations to me, and that he should have sent someone over yesterday to inquire about my health. But I was glad, because it gave Harry an excuse to call, a duty which he seemed more than happy to perform.

Lord Stamford agrees, he wrote, *that we must make amends for our laxness.*

"He cannot always be on the lookout for deaf girls wandering through his woods, Harry," I said with a wry grin.

As long as you're not a poacher, he's really quite obliging. And he agreed that you should all be invited to the hunt ball on Saturday, he wrote.

I glanced up from the slate into his face, scrutinizing it for some sign of mirth.

"A ball? We're invited to a ball?"

"All of you," he said. "Ned and Esther, too."

"At Longmeade?"

He could see my astonishment and sought to allay my concerns by writing on the slate, *Lord Stamford's set is mixed. You'll find them very entertaining.*

"I'm honored, truly, that's very kind," I said, trying to be gracious, "and I'm sure Ned and Esther will be delighted to attend, but—" I hesitated, once again thrown off my concentration by the nearness of him and his eager attentiveness. There was a brief flicker of intensity behind his grey-blue eyes, and I wondered if he might be feeling the same stirring of emotion that I was feeling.

"But I cannot accept your invitation," I said.

"And why not?" he said with disbelief. "Even if you do not dance, there is much to enjoy," he said slowly.

"Oh, indeed, I would enjoy it ever so much, but it would be very thoughtless of me to put your hostess in such a difficult situation, for she will find it necessary to make sure that someone attends to me."

Harry wrote an energetic reply and thrust the slate under my nose with the impatience I had come to regard as part of his nature.

But I shall attend to you. He had chalked the *I* boldly. *There is no one in my circle of friends whose conversation is so fresh and stimulating that I would feel disappointed were I to ignore it.* Once I had read this, he retrieved the slate to erase it and, gesturing that I was to wait, he continued writing. Then he paused briefly to move his chair closer to mine as Mr. Nicholls and I had so often done, so that I might read as he wrote. *My friends,* he continued, *speak only of where they hunted that day, where they shall hunt to-morrow, whose hunt party they attended the previous week & where they shall be the following week. They pride themselves on their boredom & insolence.* Seeing I had followed this much, he wiped clean the slate and went on. *When I find someone who can speak on a topic in a truly knowledgeable fashion and with an independent turn of mind, and a spark of earnestness, then I will listen.* I gently tapped his hand, and with a smile I said, "Harry, talk to me slowly. I'll try to read your lips."

I could see the enormous relief wash over his face, and I thought that he must be truly fond of me to persist in this limping and slow exchange.

"Goodburnes is a fair example. He never fails to engage my attention when he speaks of horses."

"And what could I say that would hold your attention, sir? My talk is of bastes and trimmings and cuts of cloth."

"I have never heard you speak of those things."

"We have spoken very little."

This seemed to startle him, and after a pause, he took up the slate again and wrote, *Indeed, when I reflect upon it, I see you are quite right. But I have for some time had the illusion that we have on occasions spoken at length, although I see now I have been mistaken. I wonder, whence does this illusion come?*

When I had finished reading, I replied, "I cannot tell you, sir, as I have not been living in the same dream. I have the confirmed sentiment that I know much about you, but do not know you at all."

"Ah, yes, perhaps it is that." He paused, put down the chalk, and addressed me clearly. "I am not an easy fellow to know, Miss Grenfell. Although many believe they do so." Then, with an earnest gaze, he said, "I should like *you* to know me."

If my face betrayed the rush of sentiment I experienced at that moment, at least my wits maintained a firm grip on my tongue, and I said, "I don't know if you possess the necessary measure of patience for it."

"So you do know me," he answered with a broad smile. "Perhaps you will teach me patience."

"I can do no more than inspire it."

"You do well understanding me when I raise my voice and speak slowly."

"But deliberate and plodding speech is not in your nature, is it? You are a man of considerable spontaneity."

A puzzled expression clouded his eyes, and I knew I had pronounced the word badly.

I took the slate from his hands and wrote it down.

"Spontaneity," he repeated, when I passed him the slate. "Yes."

"And wit," I added.

He conceded with a bow of the head.

"And those qualities are lost on my senses."

"I must have other qualities that are easily perceived by you, do I not?"

At this I could not look him in the eye. My gaze dropped, and he drew the slate from my hands and wrote, *I beg your pardon—I was too forward.*

I read his writing and attempted a composed smile.

"Why is it you provoke me to behave in such a curious manner, Miss Grenfell?"

"What is so curious about your manner?"

He only smiled.

"Enough, sir," I said, a little flustered. "I shall not press you for an answer. We have both been sufficiently taxed for the day. Perhaps next we meet, we might enjoy together some of the country. I find it quite pleasant."

"This is not a good time of year for an excursion. The roads are muddy and dangerous."

"That may be, but I cannot spend the rest of my visit sitting indoors reading all day long, and I certainly don't dare any more excursions on foot." Then I demurred with a smile, "But of course, I would not wish to impose my company on you, sir."

He seemed most anxious to contradict me, and wiped clean the slate and wrote, *I spoke of muddy roads only out of concern for your safety and enjoyment. I would be delighted to accompany you wherever you wish to go. I assume Mrs. Jones will join us?*

"Most certainly. She has not seen as much of the region as she would like."

"I shall make arrangements."

He sprang to his feet and bowed deeply, and wished me good day.

I wandered around in a daze for several minutes after his departure, brimming over with excitement with no one to tell. Nor did I dare go out for a walk as night was quickly falling. As I was pacing the room, I felt the maid stamp on the floor to draw my attention, and she motioned me downstairs to the kitchen.

When the cook saw me, she broke into a toothless smile and pointed to where two fat pheasants sprawled on the chopping block. "From Longmeade," she said. As she stood there beaming with her hands on her broad hips, her delight reminded me of the faces of cutters handed a bolt of rich cloth for a duke.

HARRY AND I NEVER HAD our drive. The next day I received a hastily written letter explaining that his father had urgently requested his presence at Blackroak, and by the time I received it, he was already on his way to Yorkshire. I was positively crushed, but I felt sure I would hear from him before long.

Chapter Sixteen

CHRISTMAS AT MORTLAKE WAS A COMFORTABLE BUT DULL AFFAIR. Grandpa grumbled a good deal about remaining there through the winter, and there was the usual unpleasantness with the fireplaces. Early in January, a large parcel arrived for me from Harry. I took it upstairs and opened it in the privacy of my room. There was a beautiful little silver-studded collar for Ivanhoe, and a gold-tooled journal in red Morocco for me. On the first page he had written:

My dear Miss Grenfell,

I have given much thought to the manner in which we are obliged to communicate, and therefore I am presenting you with this Talking Book in which we can record our conversations. We can record them in their entirety, or just my part, or both parts, as comprehension proves necessary. It is offered to you in humble appreciation of the liveliness of your mind and my eagerness to understand the thoughts that fill it, believing as I do that these exchanges are worth recalling. Very little in my recent experience has been worth recalling, yet I find I recall with great pleasure the moments we spend together. Know that your smallest exertion is met with my deepest regard.

You will find in the same parcel a system I have designed and given to our senior carpenter here at Blackroak to implement. It is composed of a traveling bag sewn from an old but fine tapestry, with a small portable writing stand crafted of light cedar on which to rest the Talking Book should we find ourselves outside the realm of domestic comfort. You will notice there is an inkpot built into the stand, with small leather restraining straps, and phials of sand, and squares of blotting paper, whichever you would prefer.

I make only one request in return, which is that you share the Talking Book with no one but me.

In anticipation of that day, I remain
Your devoted friend,
Harry
p.s. I pray the collar meets with Ivanhoe's approval.

THAT WINTER SEEMED TO ME excruciatingly monotonous. We were beginning to feel the impact of Balducci's defection, and it was worrisome to
see the tailors sitting at their benches with little or no work to keep them
busy and a nervous and pathetic fear in their eyes whenever Father entered
the room. Their anxieties were justified as he eventually had to reduce
even our permanent staff, and we kept only one workshop off the premises. My only pleasures were my riding lessons with Burnes and my
sewing, and the frequent letters from Harry. I waited for them as one
holds one's breath underwater, with the days piling up until I thought I
might burst. When the morning post brought a letter, opening it was like
exhaling the entire monotony of a boring and useless existence and gulp-
ing in fresh, new life. Every word on every page of his letters would be
read and re-read until I knew them by heart. Entire worlds were created
around his letters as I envisioned him writing them: I imagined that he
would remove his coat and strip off the cravat, then, settling behind his
desk, he would loosen his collar and roll up his sleeves. I imagined the
room in which he wrote, the flickering candlelight or dull winter's sun that
illuminated his hand as it rose to dip the nub of his pen in a pot of jet
black ink.

They were thoughtful letters, revealing the workings of his mind.
There was little narrative of his day-to-day life, and sometimes I was surprised to find he was writing from Longmeade or Leicestershire or Newmarket when all along I believed him to be at Blackroak Hall. Harry the
reckless gambler, the horse racer, the dissolute womanizer, was not in
those letters, although I knew they all existed. He revealed to me the man
beneath those things and hinted at the troubled soul that had brought the
foolhardy man into existence.

When Harry wrote of his family's turbulent past, I sensed the restlessness of a man confined in spirit by an ancient and ponderous ancestry. He
wrote to me of Aurelia and the religious zeal that had consumed her at
such a young age, and how little he had understood her. He rarely mentioned his father, the Earl of Hambledon, yet every mention of Blackroak

unwittingly evoked his father's presence, as if the son lived eternally within the architecture of the father. Sometimes he spoke of his childhood at Blackroak and his years at Oxford as if that young man no longer lived. Sometimes he wrote to me of some youthful experiment he had conducted, or an interest he had once pursued with passion, as if describing these things in great detail might resuscitate that enthusiasm, or any enthusiasm for something good and industrious. I sensed by the end of each letter that he had momentarily rekindled his spirit, and he credited me with this, rightly or wrongly.

This is not to say that his letters lacked the dash and wit, the boisterous charm or precocious fluency that had made him such a favorite in privileged and intellectual society, but he seemed disinterested in revealing that side to me. I believe he was tired of that attitude and saw it as a hardened and arrogant response of his rank to the many problems facing our times. He seemed more interested in probing his own situation as a means of understanding the complexities of the world and had chosen me as his confidante, an outsider whose opinions might be solicited without risking the scorn of his own kind.

He wrote:

Even my education has been a departure in fashion from that of other young men of my rank. Ned will confirm to you my despair at finding Oxford under the spell of Mr. Newman's religious movement, which led me to leave that fine institution and turn to Edinburgh, which has long been one of the most distinguished intellectual cities in all of Europe. There were in that sober and illustrious university astronomers and architects, engineers and physicians who carried their standards into battle not against fanciful dragons, but the dark demons of disease and disaster, ineptitude and inefficiency. With these men, I found a passionate meeting of the minds; for me, there was more romance in the chemistry of clays and glazes and the science of climate and weather, than all the books of Mallory and Tennyson combined.

Yet, to pursue any of these things in any manner that might actually prove useful to myself or my country and thereby contribute to our mutual prosperity, would be viewed badly by society; instead, I must hunt, ride, and gamble my days away in a manner befitting my rank. I am a totem, a figurehead for our nation's virility, and I must stand up here, the decorous capital on the column of industry, a pretty thing, all pomp and show, deprived of any real function. You wrote, with great insight on my private conundrum, that you found me "ambitious by nature" and "painfully shackled by an honor-bound duty to leisure."

When I read this I believed you had seen me as clearly as if you had viewed me through a magnifying glass.

And yet, as fervently as I resist its pull, I cannot imagine myself in this life without Blackroak. Even as I grow older, I continue to delight in every rugged bank, every moss-grown nook, every scant and sturdy little flower that survives its blustering winters. I might wish for it to leave me, but I could never leave it.

Occasionally he wrote of his struggles with religion, his falling away from the church, his intense distrust of Evangelicalism, and his search for a "broken and tarnished grail." He wrote:

I believe that morality is not the exclusive privilege of the religious zealot; that a missionary fervor can animate even a fallen soul such as mine; that I can be of some good in this world even if my steed is hobbled and my lance is blunt, and my armor is nothing more than my tattered and trampled honor.

Although there are some who delight in my sins.

He later told me that it was sometime during the process of that exchange, through those long months, those plodding days, those hours spent bent over his pen, that he fell tenderly in love with me. His letters evoked that sentiment without acknowledging its existence, ignoring it and yet unable to pull away.

If he ignored it, I did not. I felt it like a pulse growing ever stronger with each letter. Sometimes I grew faint at the mere idea of seeing him again. When spring arrived and there was a possibility that he might reappear as he had once done, impromptu and without warning, I would go off to my riding lesson with Burnes, nearly faint with the prospect of a chance encounter. When it seemed he would not appear, I was both saddened and relieved. For what could become of such attachment? What could be done with it? Should it be allowed to burn itself out? Should it be stifled? I was certain of only one thing: It was hopeless.

In my efforts to understand Harry, I turned once again to Mr.

Nicholls. He was surprised to find me professing a renewed interest in Mallory and Tennyson, and a wish to read Digby's *The Broad Stone of Honor* and Carlyle's *Past and Present*. When I expressed curiosity about certain ancestral homes and old titled families of Scottish origin, he assumed the families were clients about whom we wished to inform ourselves, and I said nothing to discourage this assumption.

DURING THOSE MONTHS, I WAS growing more and more discontent at being confined to the back room. Having tasted a bit of the dignity and elegance of the showroom and the excitement of tending to some of society's most distinguished luminaries, I felt I had taken a giant step backward, that I had failed at more than just courtship. With Harry always in my thoughts, it was only natural that I began to dream of dressing him. I began to notice whenever a particularly fine bolt of cloth came through the workshop, thinking how nicely it would suit him. I even had a mannequin made according to his measurements, which I believed I had estimated well enough, and kept it in my room. I began experimenting with different coat designs, thinking how I might show his fine figure at its best. I looked through our supplier catalogs for the finest studs and buttons and tried to imagine the blue-grey tint of his eye and the soft warm brown of his hair set against a certain hue of figured silk for a waistcoat. My room became my own secret workshop, as it had once been when I worked for Reggie, and I would forgo my evenings in the drawing room to sew for Harry by candlelight.

One warm and humid night as I lay in bed, unable to sleep in the stuffy room, I rose to open a window. There was no breeze, and the outdoors seemed as close and stifling as my room. The moon hung bright and full above the city, throwing a pale ghostly light onto the dark ribbon of a street below. A wisp of thin black smoke rose from a chimney somewhere in the distance, and mist-thin clouds inched slowly over the face of the sky. I stood by the window behind my own curtain of silence waiting for a cart to roll by, or a cab, anything to animate the city, for there was nothing that left me so forlorn as darkness and stillness. At night, the world ceased to exist for me.

Determined to drive away the despair, I lit a candle, and as I turned to set it beside my bed, the flickering light illuminated the mannequin. I had produced some of my very best work for Harry, and it suddenly seemed pathetic to be making such fine and elegant clothes for a man who would never wear them. I stood fingering the fine cut velvet lapel and perfectly corded edge of the Venetian blue silk lounging jacket I had just finished, and I was seized by a sudden urge to try it on myself. Piece by piece, I undressed the mannequin and laid all the apparel on my bed. As I did so, it gradually began to make such beautiful sense to me. I could see myself in those clothes of my crafting, a trim, shapely figure with a style and elegance that men would envy. I knew only too well the powerful influence clothes exerted in the perception of the individual, perhaps more so than character or even manners; if that were indeed true, then with the right clothes, I would be perceived however I wished.

I stripped off my nightgown and began to put on the garments. In the stillness of my own world, in the darkness of night, I initiated myself into the long tradition of our family. As I dressed, I thought about this manly ritual ingrained in the lives of gentlemen, a ritual that my own father ranked above nearly all rituals. Papa had always been keenly attentive to his appearance. I remembered how Mama used to rise very early to allow him the absolute concentration he required to dress each morning. The disposition of his room had changed little since those days. A corner of the bedroom was furnished with a large wardrobe, a freestanding looking glass, a toilet table with wash basin and wings for his personal items, and a tall dresser with silk-lined drawers where he kept his accessories and the brushes, cloths, and sponges necessary for the upkeep of his garments. After Mama and Reggie had died, he allowed me into his dressing room one morning to witness the ritual.

He had stood before me in his dressing gown while Lucy cleared away the wash basin and towel. He had just finished trimming his beard and was examining his nails.

"Clean linen is the mark of a gentleman, daughter," he had instructed me. "The shirt and cravat must be changed daily."

This much I already knew; this was Beau Brummel's legacy. Grandpa often told tales of the dandy's legendary taste, his "exquisite refinement" and "perfection of line." It was said he even polished the soles of his boots.

Papa had flung open the doors of his wardrobe as though they were the gates of heaven and stood contemplating the coats that hung there. I never knew how many coats he had in all; he was always working on a new one for himself and restyling the older ones. He rotated them in and out of Grenfell's storeroom according to the season.

I shall always recall the pose he took, taking one step back while he stroked his mustache and narrowed his eyes, and when it seemed like all eternity had gone by, with the precision and speed of a serpent striking his prey, his hand darted into the wardrobe and withdrew a coat of midnight blue and flung it onto the bed. Then came the trousers, a fine buff colored pair which he laid beside the coat. Next came the waistcoat. One after another he studied them beside the blue superfine wool—a soft-hued buttery brocade, a cream satin, a sherry colored silk. Then followed the selection of his collar and cravat. Still deep in contemplation, he swung open a cabinet door, removed a tooled leather box and set it on the bed. As the accessories grew finer, there were more and more choices—a watch and albert to which he might add a pencil or sovereign case or vesta for his matches. He had an entire case full of alberts: silver single-fine chains, silk- and gold-braided chains, and the ones he wore after Mama's death, all of black vulcanite. Then there were fasteners and buttons, tie pins with heads of gold or mother-of-pearl, and studs of enamel and imitation jewels.

His selection made, he carefully returned everything to its precise place, and I waited in the hall while he dressed. Then he opened the door and ushered me back in to witness the final stages of the ritual, the waistcoat, the cravat, the tiepin, the studs and chains, and then the coat. Only then did he speak again.

"Cleanliness and simplicity are signs of moral virtue, my dear. That is the fundamental principle underlying how we dress. A gentleman must never wear a suit more than two days in a row. After that time, the dirt will be embedded in the fabric. Everything needs a good brushing. The softer brush for satins and velvets, the stiffer bristles for wool. If it is soiled, the fabric should be sponged gently with water and a damp cloth. And the coats must not hang too closely together. The fibers need to breathe. Of course, the gentleman's valet will tend to these things, but a gentleman must know what must be done in order to supervise that it is done properly."

Now I stood there, a gentleman, in front of my looking glass. The trousers felt rather odd and the shoulders were too wide, but the waistcoat was none too long, for I was nearly as tall as Harry. For all the imperfections of fit, I was beginning to like what I saw. I went to my dresser and came back with my hairbrush and coiled my hair into a tight knot at the nape of my neck. Striking a pose, with my hands clasped behind my back, all I lacked were the hat and gloves to complete the transformation. It was astounding. I knew without a doubt that I could carry it off. At that moment, I was absolutely convinced that I could serve Grenfell's like this, in a capacity that utilized my talents. I could not only enter the showroom, but I could ride First on Rotten Row as Old Pauley's son had once done, a living showcase for Grenfell's originality, elegance, and exquisite taste.

Of course, when I awoke in the crude light of morning, I sat up, took one look at the headless wooden form and thought I'd gone quite mad or had suffered a shocking nightmare. However, as the day wore on, I began to adjust to the wildness of my vision and reflect upon the difficulties ahead of me. Discussing my scheme with my father beforehand would be a recipe for failure. Instead, I proceeded to make myself an entire wardrobe to prove to him the earnestness of my plan. I had already established an account in the name of a Mr. Goodfellow to produce Harry's garments and paid for the orders out of my pocket money. Now I required assistance from our other departments, and I chose to bring my apprentice, Thomas, and my old seamstress, Ernestine, into my confidence. Ernestine assisted in the final fittings, and Thomas made my trousers. One evening I dressed in a black fine wool coat and an Oxford grey figured silk waistcoat, the most conservative and elegant of all my new apparel, styled my hair in a tight chignon, and went downstairs to dinner.

When Papa entered the drawing room and saw me standing before the fireplace, my hands clasped behind my back, I observed a quick hardening of the mouth and tensing of the jaw. He immediately saw my intent, that this was no impromptu entertainment, but a forceful statement of my demand that he see me in the light of a true successor. I would be in the showroom; I would greet clients and be seen. Eventually, mine would be the face behind Grenfell's name. My appearance would speak for me, and so I stood obstinately before him, a perfect presentation of our standard of excellence.

Aunt Lavinia came down just then, and she started so violently at the sight of me that I regretted I had not forewarned the dear woman. It was positively spectacular, the way her hands flew to her heart then her mouth then her heart again, as though she was not quite certain which part was in more urgent need of resuscitation. She fluttered weak-kneed onto the settee, fanning herself with her handkerchief while Lucy arrived and unbuttoned the neck of her dress to help her breathe. She could not take her gentle cow eyes off me, and I truly did regret shocking her. Papa thought her behavior a little excessive and did not appear the least bit sympathetic, standing there with an eyebrow raised in silent disapproval while Mrs. Scholfield arrived with smelling salts and waved them under her nose. Lucy knew all about my scheme, but she was the soul of discretion and kept her eyes averted.

Finally, Papa said something to Aunt Lavinia—I think it must have been rather harsh, which is quite unlike Papa—but it clearly relieved her attack of nerves, and she became quite calm. Once the servants had left, Papa asked her to wait for us in the dining room. She patted back her hair, struggled to her feet, and tottered out of the room. Then Papa approached me and said, with unusual clarity and emphasis, "When my daughter comes down, we shall proceed into dinner."

"Papa," I began, holding his gaze, "I wish to be present in the showroom tomorrow. And every day thereafter. I shall begin where you wish. Open doors for clients. Hold your chalk and notebook during the fittings."

"Attired like this?"

"Yes."

"Have you gone quite mad?"

"I truly believe it can work. At first, I shall be very discreet. Then, when our clients are comfortable with my presence, you can call me into a fitting to ask my opinion. When they see us working as a team, it won't make any difference. These clothes are not meant to mask my womanhood; they're meant to show the client what I can do for him."

"Our clients will turn tail and run."

"I wager the young fashionable set will flock to us in droves."

"We'll be the brunt of ridicule."

"Not after they see what I can do for them. You know I have more talent than a dozen Balduccis."

"I have never questioned your talents, my dear."

"Then let me put them to work."

"There are wives who will be scandalized."

"It's the gentlemen we clothe. The gentlemen will come, I promise you. And you know that gentlemen are very sensitive to a lady's opinion. I shall be that opinion."

"And what of your own reputation, my dear? Your womanly virtues will be compromised."

"I am deaf, Papa. I don't have the same prospects a hearing woman has, so why should I be confined by the same rules? If I am going to be singular, then I shall be splendidly, gloriously, magnificently singular. And Grenfell's will rise like a phoenix from its ashes!"

The last must have sounded a little too grand— although I believed it with all my heart—because a glimmer of amusement broke across his face, and his harsh resistance melted away.

"My Veda," he mouthed, taking me by the shoulders and tenderly kissing me on the forehead. And then, unable to resist, he turned his attention to the details of my coat. There was unconcealed admiration in his eyes as he examined the collar and the fit of the shoulders and paid special attention to the way I had loosely knotted my cravat.

"What do you think?" I asked.

He wagged his head in disbelief. "This is splendid work, my dear. I confess, you make a very elegant young gentleman."

I thought I might burst with pride.

"Tomorrow Lord Bentley arrives for his fitting," I said.

"Indeed, he does."

"Well, we could start with him. He is quite liberal-minded. Fond of music halls, you know."

"Yes, he is fond of the theater."

"May I assist you in the fitting? I think he will be a good subject."

He took me by the arm and turned me toward the dining room. "You may open the door and greet him, Veda. Let's wait and see his reaction before we press further."

To our surprise, there was little reaction at all. Lord Bentley was a man of good taste and considerable conceit and was much more concerned with his own appearance than my presence. I don't even think he noticed me as I welcomed him at the door. When I appeared in the fitting room with Papa's assistant, he merely fixed me with a curious stare, then lifted his monocle to his eye and gave me the once over, remarking on the striking color of my waistcoat.

"My nephew might like something like that," he conceded. "Too raffish for me."

And so I took my place at my father's side. As I had hoped, the fact that I simply appeared without comment and worked discreetly beside my father set the tone for my acceptance. Papa said there was some discussion on the subject in the lounge, but there always seemed to be great sympathy for Papa and me because of my deafness, and a keen recognition that I was highly respected by everyone in the showroom. Most important, they took notice of how I dressed. Since I was a curiosity, they allowed me the freedom of a certain dash, a discreet but unconventional touch here and there.

I'm sure there were drawing rooms that buzzed with the indecency of it all, but the distinction in appearance and in the garments we delivered were real enough to work to our advantage, and my presence in the showroom in fashionable and immaculate garb began to lend a favorable reputation to our custom. After all, Grenfell's had been established for generations, and few people apart from the lending houses knew of the financial losses we had incurred. Perhaps we had less show of personal wealth, but our firm's reputation was as solid as ever. Now, it gained a new distinction. My appearance in the showroom began to be expected. I became the hallmark for the young and fashionable set who were growing tired of the strict and sober standards set by the Queen and who were looking for something amusing and new.

As important as my new situation was to me—indeed, I saw it as nothing less than a miracle—I revealed none of it to Harry. I knew that Harry had always preferred to turn a blind eye to my connections to trade. From our first meeting when Sir Francis was painting my portrait, he had seen me as a genteel young woman of flawless education and manners—not a tailor's daughter. My hearing may have been faulty, but there was nothing below standard about my upbringing. The person I presented to him through my letters was of my own creation. Thanks to Reggie and Mr. Nicholls, and the fact that I had been forced to turn to books as my companions, I had acquired a facility with the written language that equaled that of any well-bred young lady. Indeed, Esther said I was much better educated than many noble ladies who were content with a few desultory efforts, who considered a little tinkling at the piano and reading pretty passages from pretty books all that was necessary to snare the hearts of suitable gentlemen.

When the Season began and England's aristocracy came to London for the opening of Parliament and the summer's activities, there were a good number of young sporting men who had heard about the new Grenfell's and wished to give us a try. One of those was Lord Stamford's nephew who had been referred to us by Lord Bentley, the admirer of my waistcoat, and who specifically asked for me, to Papa's astonishment. He, in turn, referred to me an extraordinary client, an American civil servant for whom I made a sumptuous Karakul lamb's wool frock coat with velvet cuffs and collar. I greatly regretted that he would not be wearing it in London society.

Word of my budding success made the rounds, and in July I received a short but distressing letter from Harry.

> Tell me this is not you, he wrote. A young woman dressed as a man tailoring for her father? And the firm's name is Grenfell? I confess, I did not see this in you, and you have given me no hint of such proceedings in your letters. How can these two ladies—if they both be ladies—coexist in the same person? I admit I am shocked and wonder that your father—who seems to have raised so well the young lady whom I delighted in knowing—should condone such behavior. I cannot believe that you have been forced into this situation, for I am sufficiently acquainted with your firm character to know you would do nothing against your nature.
>
> Or could it be that the scandal is only in my own mind? For I confess, none of the gossip has been scandalous in tone. On the contrary, you seem to have created quite a stir among Lord Lansderry's set for the excellent new wardrobe your father and you are making for him. I gather your father is the steady beacon, but you are the fresh, new guiding light.

I did not know how to respond to his letter. I disliked the inference that I had been coerced into my roll by some monstrous slave-driving father, but I also knew that my friendship with Harry was predicated on his belief that I was as far removed from trade as a generation would permit, that the only threads my hands touched were those woven into the floral borders of verse samplers. Most frustrating of all was the fact that I so wished he could admire my talents without condemning me, for I still dreamed of dressing Harry.

After days of redrafting letters, I finally wrote:

My dear friend,

So, you have found me out.

Since it seems to be such a fat fly in the ointment of our friendship, then let us go on as before. If you believe these two women cannot coexist in the same person, then the bold one will conceal her face, and the one you know will continue to preside over our friendship.

Let the Amazon, as she is now being called, remain an enigma. I promise, she will never make an appearance in Burford at the home of our mutual friends, nor would I ever bring her along on an excursion in the Cotswolds, nor would she ever be so rude as to appear uninvited in our midst.

Yet, I think you do yourself a grave disservice in condemning her so swiftly without a thorough hearing. She is an impassioned young woman, quite obsessed by dress, and although it is most peculiar that she is a lady particularly keen on gentlemen's fashion, it seems there are many fashionable young men who are willing to submit to her authority and come away the better for it. From my knowledge of her, she seems to be of indomitable spirit and fortitude—for she struggles with the same afflictions as do I—which are difficult enough in familiar surroundings of family and friends, but present even greater obstacles when dealing with that society which can at times show itself to be so contemptuous and unreasonable. Notice I do not include vanity among their faults, as the brave Amazon shares that distinction with them.

I warn you, however, that she may one day decide to step outside the threshold of Grenfell's on Savile Row; she just may decide to carry herself along to the stables in Bayswater and try riding astride First, in her coat and trousers. Now <u>that</u> would be shocking and scandalous, to be sure—but only if her identity were known. Otherwise, she might find the experience quite liberating. I should think it would be quite liberating to walk down the street in the guise of a gentleman. I should think it marvelous fun to stride freely down the street without fear of being accosted, to smoke a cigarette, to buy a newspaper and be called 'sir.'

But she will not do these things. I think they are only in her dreams. Silly dreams of being different from that which God Almighty ordained.

I shall certainly be in Burford toward the end of the season. And as I am now outlawed from venturing into the countryside without a guide, I should be most happy to have your company if you find yourself in the vicinity.

Your devoted friend,
Veda

Harry responded by return post:

I am both intrigued and humbled by your letter. Yet, I am in no haste to meet this Amazon. For the present, I would prefer to keep my memory of you un-blemished by such shenanigans. Indeed, I plan to be at Longmeade in Au-gust. Lady Stamford will certainly have a calendar full of events, and I am sure you will be able to find an entertainment or two to suit your taste. If the Amazon is courageous enough to measure that old codger Lord Doonesbor-ough for a new hunt coat, then surely Miss Grenfell can summon the forti-tude to weather a sunny garden party on the lawn of Longmeade.

Shenanigans! It took me weeks to get over that slur. To think he only took me seriously when I was bobbing around in a dreaded crinoline!

By the time I had arrived in Burford, all the roaring indignation had melted, and my nerves were a swarm of timid butterflies. Esther was wait-ing for me at the Oxford station, waving to me from the back of the crowd as I stepped down, and with one swift glance at her figure, I knew she was in the family way. After hugs and tears and more hugs, with a glance at her slightly thickened waist I indicated that I was eager to hear all about this thrilling news. She only beamed and nodded, and we had to endure an in-terminable ride in a stifling hot coach to Burford where I dashed up to my room, splashed cool water over my face, removed my crinoline, and smoothed down my hair which had gone quite wild from the heat of the train, before tripping back down to the drawing room.

Esther sat there in a pretty chintz chair with a toothy smile stretched so tight I thought she would split open from ear to ear with happiness.

"Here," she said, pulling a folded letter from her pocket and passing it to me. "I wrote it down to make it easier for you."

"Oh, bless you, Tiggy," I said, at once falling back into the relaxed pleasure of her company, thinking how terribly I had missed her companionship this year. I set the candle at my elbow and read:

My dearest Topsy,

First things first: I am in good health—having regained my strength at last, and we estimate the new arrival sometime in January. Ned is delighted; I am at last reconciled. As you know, I was not anxious to possess a family and feel myself thankful to have escaped so long. There is such measureless energy spent on children and I shall have none left for my work, which demands its own labor and constant devotion. I confess I do not look forward to the dulled concentration and melancholy awaiting me, and the nerve-wracking adjustment that will follow the arrival of a little one who will devour all my reserves. Although Ned has promised to engage a nurse, I know I shall be depleted of all my mental and physical resources. I even fear for our friendship, as I know how little uninterrupted time I shall have at my disposal: I will be capable only of hastily written letters of a few pithy sentences and very little contemplative thought.

I looked up, eager to assure her that our friendship would certainly survive the birth of her firstborn, and many more after that, but dear Esther had fallen sound asleep, her head tilted on her shoulder, her jaw slack, and her tea cup slipping down the slope of her skirt. I did not wake her but carefully withdrew the cup from her limp fingers and set it on the table. Then I quietly sipped my tea and let my thoughts turn toward the pleasant weeks of leisure ahead.

I had written Harry in care of Scrimshire—the desk clerk at his London club, and the only man in England who knew where Harry was at any given moment—informing him of the dates of my visit to Burford. Harry was far too unpredictable for me to expect any sort of warning of his arrival, so I took great care in my dress every morning, just in case. This year I came prepared with a stylish new wardrobe for country wear. Packed into my trunk were silk skirts and matching jackets in peacock-blue, crimson, and deep, cerulean blue, all to be worn with a white embroidered chemisette. There was also a stunning little white piqué Garibaldi jacket with black braid to be worn with a skirt of black and scarlet figured silk, and I had ordered new parasols and narrow-brimmed straw hats. I may have had little experience with country living, but I knew precisely how to dress.

To my astonishment, the day after my arrival a letter came by post addressed to Esther. In it Harry wrote of his intended arrival at Longmeade in two days' time, saying that he hoped to keep an unfulfilled promise made last year to escort us on an excursion in the county and thought we might like to make a day journey to see the Iron Bridge, which he boasted was "a feat of modern engineering" and should take precedence over anything in the region. Esther knew Harry and I had exchanged correspondence, but she had always dismissed our attachment as something superficial. She preferred to believe that Harry thought of me as an appendage of his friendship with Ned. I made no effort to contradict that opinion; I would let Harry determine the course of her enlightenment.

"What?" Esther gestured when I looked up from the letter. "Ironbridge is on the other side of Birmingham! It's miles away."

"He proposes the train."

"But how terribly unromantic and unscenic. When there's such delightful countryside to view around here."

"That's just like Harry," I said.

She gave me a quizzical look.

I said, "He takes great pleasure in machines and that sort of thing."

"And how would you know this?"

"From his letters."

"His letters? You mean there were more than one?"

"Yes," I said, with a quiet smugness.

She stared at me thoughtfully, and instead of dismissing it with her usual skepticism, she asked pointedly, "Are you in love with him?"

"Now that would be foolish," I answered, with a playful wag of my finger meant to foil her probe. "That would rank right up there with piano lessons, wouldn't it?"

She seemed quite relieved. "Perhaps we could get him to change it," she suggested hopefully.

"Change it?"

"Our excursion. There's a lovely old priory not far from here. And a Roman fortress."

"But he seems so keen on the bridge."

"I think it's terribly rude to expect me to travel all the way to Birmingham and beyond, in my condition."

"He does not know you're expecting, Tiggy dear."

"Oh, yes," she frowned. "That is true." Then, "Well, do you really want to see this thing?"

"I should think it rather interesting."

"It's quite ugly, Topsy. And it must smell dreadful, all that iron ore, and the heat from the foundries in August must be intolerable. A village full of iron workers, what could be less picturesque?"

"Would you mind so terribly if I did go?"

"By yourself?"

"I should so like to get out, and he *has* offered."

With narrowed eyes, she said, "If I were your mother, I'd say absolutely not."

"But you're not. And I'm nearly twenty-two."

"But you're in my charge."

"We shan't be alone. Servants are coming along."

"Servants are of no good whatsoever. They just look away."

"Oh, bother, Esther. He's not going to do anything indecent with me."

"I should hope not!"

"He thinks of me as a sister," I said, praying in my heart that this was not true. "He's written to me about her, you know. It's something we shared when his mother was alive. His mother thought I resembled her."

"Oh," she said, and again I saw the anxiety melt into relief.

"It will be perfectly respectable," I assured her.

"He can really be quite caddish, you know."

"He's never been anything but kind and decent with me. And very generous."

"Oh, all right then." She affected a puckered look of consternation. "But it's really quite unorthodox for an outing." She rolled her eyes. "Ironbridge."

WE DEPARTED JUST BEFORE DAWN from Burford by a very smart closed carriage to Oxford where we would catch the train to Birmingham; there we would be met by a second carriage that would take us to Ironbridge. Very little communication was exchanged between us during the carriage ride to Oxford, for the sun was only just burning through the morning haze, and the shadows were too dark for me to read his lips. Yet, every time

I glanced across at him, he met my gaze with a warm and eager smile, and I keenly felt his frustration, for he was a voluble man, and I sensed he was eager to share his many thoughts with me.

At the station, a porter loaded a wicker trunk full of provisions onto the train, while Harry and I settled into a first-class compartment he had reserved for us alone. Once we were on the train, the first thing I did was open my traveling case to remove the writing stand and journal he had sent me. The relief that flooded his face touched me deeply, for it revealed how ardent was his desire to communicate with me. I was afraid to write anything myself, for I feared my hand would not be too steady, and so I passed the stand to him, and handed him the pen and said, "Tell me what we shall see today, Harry."

Watching Harry write was one of the great pleasures I took in our moments together. I could not hear his voice, but I had the privilege of watching him closely in these quiet, unguarded moments. I became familiar with the movement and appearance of his hands and the way his fingers clutched the pen. I memorized the way his whiskers widened farther down the side of his cheek, the color of his chin early in the morning after it had been shaved, and late at night when the stubble of his dark beard had begun to appear. I studied his hair in all kinds of light, and I know how thick and dark it is at the roots and exactly where the sun has lightened it to a reddish gold tint. I know the pale red mark his hat leaves across his forehead when it has sat on his head for hours; I know how his hair sweeps back over each ear, and how it falls over his forehead in a soft wave. I know the back of his neck, how his soft loose curls lightly brush the top of his linen collar when his head is bent. I have all these marvels in my sight while he is so earnestly fashioning words for my benefit. And then he would look up at me, with those grey-blue eyes that eclipsed the rest of his countenance, and with eager expectation, pass me the Talking Book.

I think he doubted himself with me. He doubted that his brilliance would shine the way it did in hearing company, for he would occasionally glance up at me as he wrote, wondering if I was patient enough to endure the silence. He could not understand that silence was all I knew.

On the train to Birmingham, when he passed me the journal and I read his first entry, I understood then how important this journey was to him. He had written for me a small history of the Lunar Club of Birmingham and explained his reverence for those men who had once met on the occasion of each new moon to discuss topics of interest in science and industry. I was not familiar with all the names, but I soon learned who they were and how they had contributed to progress, engineers like James Watt and Matthew Boulton, men like Josiah Wedgwood and Charles Darwin.

I took no interest in the scenery from the train window that morning; my only landscape was Harry's countenance.

The journey to Birmingham passed much more quickly than I had anticipated. When we alighted from the train, we were greeted by one of Lord Stamford's private carriages painted with his coat of arms, which Harry had sent on the day before, so that we could travel in comfort to Ironbridge. Never had I ridden in such a fashion. The plush interior of the carriage was padded in a cerulean blue, while the exterior was a deeper, more regal shade of blue; family crests on each door were trimmed in gold, and there was not a scratch anywhere. All the other vehicles were obliged to give way to us, and we flew along the highway at an alarming pace. I saw wagons loaded for market pull to the side and farmers in the fields remove their hats as they watched us go by. One gig found itself in a ditch when, according to Harry, he failed to heed the coachman's cry. I confess to feeling terribly self-important, but it was a matter of course for Harry, who sat there quite coolly as the world cleared a path for him.

Yet, he had chosen me to spend the day with him, when there were many other young women of rank who would have eagerly made themselves available should he have desired it, and he had gone to considerable pains to plan the outing.

After one stop at a coaching inn to refresh the horses, we left the highway that followed the River Severn, taking a much smaller road that wound up into the hills. Finally, we came to a stop, and the footman unfolded the steps and handed me out onto a gentle treeless slope. Below, a few miles downriver, a high iron bridge spanned the gorge. I was so taken by the apparition, this astounding piece of iron stretched high between the wooded banks of the Severn, dwarfing the village and foundries smoking below, that I actually started when Harry touched my arm.

"Oh," I gasped, "it is quite astonishing, sir. What a brilliant accomplishment, to envision such a feat, and then to realize it."

I was quite earnest and sincere in my praise—it came from my heart— and Harry could see as much. He followed my gaze as it returned to admire the sight, and he pressed my elbow warmly in confirmation of the sentiment. How happy I was at that moment, and how relieved that Esther had not come along.

As if he had read my thoughts, he tapped me on the arm and I turned to him and he said, "I regret Mrs. Jones could not accompany us, but I wonder if she would have enjoyed herself."

"Not as much as I am enjoying myself, sir," I said.

Below us, where the slope leveled out just at the edge of a wood, the footman was setting up a picnic lunch in the shade. I opened my parasol and took the arm Harry offered me. As we made our way down the hillside together, I was obliged to lean heavily upon him. I think I could have crossed that iron bridge with my eyes closed had Harry been at my side.

That afternoon, there was not a doubt in my mind that he cared for me. I was a master at reading the clues, not only those that are directed to me, but those unguarded moments when politeness invites us to look away, and I did not. That I scrutinized him so closely unnerved him a little at first, but by afternoon he had grown more comfortable with my mannerisms and with me. We passed the Talking Book back and forth with ease, and soon he began to look over my shoulder as I wrote, and I did the same with him. I urged him to talk to me, so that I might grow accustomed to reading his lips, for every person was different, and I grew more adept with practice. He made a great effort to speak with clarity and willingly repeated himself when necessary for my comprehension, and it did him some good.

It was quite warm that afternoon, even in the shade, and we sprawled on the rug that had been laid down for us, feasting on cold meats and ale, and strawberries and cream. We shrugged off the formality of our previous encounters, quite literally, as I removed my jacket and Harry took off his coat and cravat. That day Harry slowed down to a manageable pace with me. My deafness did that to him. He came up against it like a brick wall and eventually relinquished his struggle. I don't think it's possible for a hearing person ever to understand this affliction, not the way one can imagine blindness by closing one's eyes, but Harry began his journey into my world that afternoon. There I sat in utter silence, amidst the music of the wind and the trees and birds, and the sweet modulation of this man's voice that I had heard so long ago but had since forgotten, all of it lost to me, but never had I felt so intensely in touch with life and living.

After we had eaten, Harry dozed off while I made several sketches of the bridge to capture the intricate ironwork pattern of the arches and supports. Eventually I put the book aside, laid back on the rug, and fell asleep myself. When I awoke, he was no longer beside me, but had risen and walked around the edge of the wood to take in the view of the gorge. When he saw me sitting up, tidying up my hair, he came back and sat down beside me.

"We'll head back now," he said.

"We're not going down into the town?"

"There's not enough time, and it's not a picturesque town."

"I should have liked to cross the bridge."

He paused for a moment while I looked down to fix a comb in the back of my head. When I glanced back up, the expression on his countenance took my breath away.

"I wonder," I said, folding my hands in my lap to quiet them, "why you choose to make such an effort with me, when there are others who are such an easier audience for your brilliance and charm."

"I would rather be in your company than anywhere else," he replied.

"But it requires great exertion."

"Indeed, it does. More for you than for me. You have a calming influence on me, Miss Grenfell."

"Calming?"

He took up the writing stand, moved beside me, and settled it on his knee.

He wrote, *You excite my mind, but my soul is tranquil. I seem to put my normal state aside in favor of something I rarely see in myself.*

"Which is?"

He wrote, *I think it is light-heartedness.*

"I have noticed your usual brilliance seems subdued in my presence, but I have always attributed this to my deafness and the difficulty it poses to any exchange."

And do I shine less brightly in your heart than in the hearts of all those rapturous admirers of mine? he wrote.

"I cannot judge that, sir, for I do not know the magnitude of your star except as it appears in my own eyes."

He smiled as he wrote, "You foil the question like a lady of considerable experience."

"I am a novice in those things, sir."

"Do we speak of the same thing?"

"I believe we do. And I have never played that game. I know it is played quite seriously by some, but I have had no string of lovers in rich and romantic settings."

"I should hope not. You are as fine a woman as ever graced the steps of any great house. I find your qualities extraordinary for one so young and so marked by tragedy."

"I wonder, sometimes, if you should have taken such an interest in me had I not been deaf."

"How cruel of you!" he replied, and I saw that I had offended him deeply, so I took the pen from his hand and moved the stand onto my own lap, for I wanted my reply to be clear.

I wrote: *It has occurred to me that my deafness presents a challenge to you that you have never encountered before. Everything has always come to you so easily, Harry. Every project you undertake has met with success. You jump from breeding race horses, to breeding fox hounds, to building lighthouses, and then you write a few brilliant poems to fill in the time before dinner. And I wonder, is it my deafness that appeals to you? Do you approach it like another invention or exploration? Am I just another world to know and investigate?*

I watched him closely as he read these words, fully expecting him to see insult where there was none, but it was a risk I had to take. I knew my heart was on the verge of plummeting from heights much greater than that bridge in the distance, and if I was only fodder for his curiosity, then I needed to restrain myself.

To my surprise, he seemed to understand my fears. He wagged his head in denial, then took the pen from my hand, dipped it in the inkwell, and wrote:

I have too much talent for too many things. I would wish to narrow my field of interest, but nothing holds my attention.

Gingerly, I touched the back of his hand, and he paused in his writing.

"And people? Do any persons hold your attention for long?"

I think he was as reluctant to answer as I was to read it on his lips, for he hesitated a long while, leveling me with a gaze that kept my heart and breath in abeyance.

"I think you are the best candidate for that honor, Miss Grenfell," he smiled, and in order to make sure I understood, he took the stand and wrote it down. I watched his hand move, and I couldn't resist the smile that crept over my own face. I covered it modestly with my hand, and Harry noticed. I felt ever so awkward and blushed.

I know I would have allowed him to kiss me then and regretted it later, but Harry had not brought me there to take advantage of me, and he was far too aware of the perfection of the day to spoil it at that point. So he blotted the ink on the page and closed the book. Then he stood, extended his hand to me, and drew me to my feet.

That evening, when I returned home and found Esther waiting up for me in the drawing room, all anticipation and bright flashing eyes, she gestured, "How did it go?"

I replied with a bored shrug of the shoulders, "It was a bridge," and yawned. And then I kissed her good night and went up to bed.

Chapter Seventeen

THERE WAS TO BE A GARDEN PARTY AT LONGMEADE TO WHICH WE were invited, along with all of the county notables: the Bishop and archdeacon and other important clergy, the neighboring gentry and wealthy mill owners, and such other distinguished locals as Mr. Rose, a renowned landscape painter and Royal Academician who lived nearby. It was rumored that there was an important American gentleman visiting from Virginia accompanied by his pretty daughter, and an American author whose works were as popular in his native country as Mr. Dickens's novels are in our own, along with his English publisher. It was an odd set, but it was known that Lady Stamford enjoyed provoking the more pious and sober local gentry with an occasional foreigner and an artist or two.

Although the older local families may have looked down their noses at some of the guests and kept to their own tight circles during the festivities, they never turned down an invitation. Lady Stamford's parties were the most entertaining events ever to happen at Longmeade, and the young people adored them. Refusing an invitation to one of her dances or theatrical *soirées* would have caused a riot among the youth, and so the older set went along and did their best to decorously restrain their pleasure. Indeed, the activities particularly appealed to the young and young at heart. This party—touted as a "breakfast"—began at three o'clock, with "breakfast" served at five by servants got up in fancy dress as gardeners. There would be archery, croquet, lawn tennis, even maypole dancing throughout the afternoon, and more dancing in tents until midnight.

I had hoped to view the interior of Longmeade, but when we arrived that afternoon down a long *allée* of tall sculpted yews, our vehicle was diverted around the side of the great house. We entered a broad forecourt enclosed by a stone balustrade, at the foot of which bloomed massive displays of roses and clematis, asters and salvia. I was struck not only by the sumptuous colors but by the evocative fragrance borne across the lawn. Along one side, small round dining tables were arranged under tent tops supported by poles decorated with gaily colored ribbons, and a larger tent stood at the foot of the park where musicians were playing. A game of croquet was already underway, and beyond the iron-grilled entrance, on the vast sweep of green park that had once been the entrance to the house, young sporting men were showing off their skills at archery. It struck me how similar it all felt to the colorful and lively atmosphere of a circus.

As we made our way up the steps to the stone porch on which the Earl was welcoming his guests, I worried that Lord Stamford might remember me as the young deaf woman who interrupted the maharajah's shooting party the previous summer, or even worse, that Lady Stamford would recognize me as the tailor's daughter who clothed her little primate friend. I should not have been worried, for I was introduced only as Miss Grenfell of London, and Lady Stamford passed over my face and my name without the slightest hint of recognition. Once freed from that trial and the requisite effort to conceal my deafness, Esther and I settled onto chairs on the lawn while Ned took off to look for Mr. Rose. I turned my attention to the animated scene before me and searched for Harry.

Mingling with guests was out of the question for me, and Esther gladly kept me company. We enjoyed each other's silent companionship as we so often had in the years since my deafness, sipping the iced mint drinks offered to us by an old servant dressed in a tunic and straw hat and making very discreet signs to each other when we noticed something amusing. The archdeacon kept me company for a time while Esther went off to play a game of croquet, and he was kind enough to walk with me around the perimeter of the lawn to enjoy the profusion of flowers in bloom. He was ever so attentive, attempting to mouth the various names for me, even spelling out the words on the palm of his hand if I failed to understand, for he was an amateur botanist and more interested in the flora than the human species.

My purpose in ambulating was to allow me a better view of a small group of guests beyond the gate where the archers were competing, for I had spied Harry in their midst. There was one young woman who had drawn the admiration of a group of young men, for she was the sole woman who dared to take up bow and arrow and test her skills against those of the opposite sex. I could not see her face; it was too far, and she wore a veiled hat, and a very pretty but ostentatious dress. Harry appeared to be holding himself back from the pack, but his deference was not to be confused with concession, for it was clear that the young woman's preference was for him. She turned to him for approval between each shot as if the other young men were nothing more than a mirage. She was indeed an accomplished archer, for each arrow struck near the bull's eye, eliciting a round of applause and cheers from her admirers—all but Harry, whose expression I could not discern. He stood with his hands clasped behind him, rather stiffly I thought. I wished I were close enough to see his face, for I know I could have read his thoughts.

My own thoughts dwelled on our conversation last year when he had invited me to the dance at Longmeade and had pledged his devoted attention, promising to see me through the evening so that I might never be neglected. Now, here I was, vainly attempting to make out the names of little bell-like purple flowers on stalks and feeling a headache brewing, undoubtedly from the sun and the mild spirits in the punch, and on top of it all my heart was breaking because a young woman was charming Harry. Of course I knew he was constantly being pursued by eligible young ladies and their mothers, and probably by ladies not so eligible as well. He was nearly thirty by now, and I'm sure they were all thinking that he was bound to fall soon. But I had never been subjected to the unpleasant reality of Harry's bachelor life, and it nearly crippled my heart that afternoon, for it brought home, as swiftly and painfully as an arrow drawn from that young woman's quiver, how ephemeral and hopeless my dreams really were. Although I didn't doubt for a moment Harry's attachment to me, I was never foolish enough to imagine it might develop beyond friendship. Harry had no illusion of marrying me, but nevertheless, I could not easily witness the moves between him and a young woman for whom the game held a real chance of winning.

I turned away from the troubling scene and, determined to enjoy myself despite my disappointment, took leave of my elderly companion and walked with my head high across the lawn to the croquet game underway, arriving just in time to take up a mallet and challenge the next round of participants. I fixed my attention on the game and resolved not to glance Harry's way again, but then, at the fifth wicket, when I had just succeeded in knocking the challenger's ball out of range, I looked up to see Harry beside me, leaning on a mallet with an insolent pose and beaming as though believing himself the sun in my heavens. I really had no intention of snubbing him, but my heart was so frittered that I met his gaze with cool disregard, then turned away to watch the next player. Immediately I felt his hand on my elbow, but I refused to look at his face, and he had no choice but to step into my line of sight.

"Veda," he said, drawing my gaze to his troubled eyes. "What ever is the matter?"

At just that moment, there passed on the lawn a short distance behind him the young Diana in the company of an older gentleman. They were engaged in conversation, but it was clear that Harry was the subject of their discussion, for both of them looked our way and fixed us with a steady and scrutinizing gaze. The lady lifted the veil of her pale lemon-colored hat, and I saw her face. The haughty tilt of her chin was not in the least softened by her eyes, a blue so clean as to seem almost transparent, pierced in the center by a bead of jet black, eyes that some might say were too large for her small and exquisitely refined little head, but they were just the kind of eyes artists sought to paint. I thought them vacant and unseeing, like those on the marble heads of Greek statues. Her hair was unreasonably fair and caught up in elaborate, silky swags around the back of her head.

Harry followed my gaze in their direction, and his attention was met with an amiable nod by the gentleman, but the woman demurred, lowering pale lashes before gliding on across the lawn toward the tents.

As soon as they had passed, Harry turned back to me, and I caught the trace of his smile. I suddenly realized that it was a forced smile and nothing at all like the smiles he bestowed on me. He said something to me, and I gathered that this was the American gentleman and his daughter, but I understood little more. I was disinclined to read his lips, for it exacted a concentration and will of which I was at that moment incapable. I tried bravely to smile and hide my melancholy behind a pleasant and cheerful countenance, but I think Harry saw through all that and realized that he had made me suffer. His eyes told me so. When it was my turn to play, I had no strength left in my hands to even clutch the mallet. My next stroke virtually missed the ball. If I had dared to look up, I'm quite sure I would have found myself surrounded by a sea of laughing faces. I thrust the mallet at Harry, pleading heatstroke, and hurried back to the tent where Esther and Ned had gathered with a group around a table, for the meal was about to be served.

I could hardly eat anything, for my eyes were on Harry and the young woman who were seated beside one another at Lord Stamford's table, and my stomach could not tolerate the thought of food. I watched delicious fruits—pineapples, strawberries, mangoes, and oranges piled high on silver dishes—pass before my eyes without the slightest twinge of temptation. Soon afterward, to my great relief, Esther wished to leave. She was feeling rather ill and was out of sorts with Ned, who had been locked in conversation with Mr. Rose all afternoon, virtually ignoring her. After some subtle coercion, Ned was persuaded to leave, but as we waited on the front lawn for our conveyance, Harry came striding around the corner of the house. He was in no happy frame of mind, that I saw quite clearly. He appeared quite crestfallen that we were all leaving so early, but then Ned took him aside. I could only assume he was announcing to him the news he had kept so quiet until now, that Esther was expecting a child, for Harry's face broke into that boyish smile I so loved. He hurried to Esther and lifted her hand to his lips, pressing it in such delightful sincerity that Esther blushed with pleasure.

He stood there while we drove away, and I think I would be right in saying he appeared quite disappointed to see us go.

It was becoming difficult for me to get Harry out of my thoughts, despite our many activities. Esther and I took long leisurely walks together along the River Windrush and often received friends for tea in the small rose garden behind the house. I even gardened a little alongside Esther and tried not to inflict too much damage on the poor roses, for I am not good with green things. We were frequently called on by art collectors or gallery owners, for Ned had begun to achieve considerable success, and it was more or less understood that he would be named to the Royal Academy the following year. There were numerous informal evening affairs with discussions of art and travel, but I could only sit quietly in a corner and fiddle with some needlework. We took the gig for drives around the countryside and went into Oxford one day so that Esther could purchase some supplies for Ned, then we returned another day to visit the university, although it was all very quiet and rather soulless without its black gowned students and professors. The archdeacon whom I had met at Longmeade took a pitiful kind of fancy for me and brought his strange daughter to call. She was quite pale, with dark pouches under her eyes, and sat stiffly with her Bible clutched in her peasant-like hands, never uttering a word. I was exhausted after their visit and went up to my room to rest after they had gone.

I waited for news from Harry. While Esther sat at the breakfast table each morning sorting through the mail, I did my best to feign indifference, but it was difficult for me to sustain an appetite. Esther noticed it; I told her it was the heat.

Around the end of August, just before I was due to depart for London, I finally received a letter from him.

My dear Veda,

I have neglected you quite shamefully, but it was not intentional, and I'm afraid it was unavoidable. I have spent the last two weeks touring England with the lady and gentleman with whom you observed me at Longmeade. I have wanted all along to write to you to put your mind at ease, but every minute of every day has been spent in their company, and my evenings have been spent planning excursions and arranging for lodging at the homes of various friends. The gentleman is Mr. Erskine, an eminent American financier my father met in Paris last spring. He is accompanied by his daughter, Miss Arabella Erskine. They are an old and distinguished family of Scottish origin, and with distant family ties through the Stirlings to our Breadalbane and Campbell clans. They have been renting our house in London, and at my father's request, Lord Stamford was kind enough to invite them to Longmeade, as London is so terribly uncomfortable in August. Unfortunately, the gentleman is a rather dull dog unless he's talking investment schemes and railroad financing—a real detail man, which I can appreciate but find tedious in big doses—and his daughter is childish and prone to bouts of homesickness. Apparently, her mother is an invalid, and she has had little opportunity to travel before now. Her questions and observations are of the naïve kind that try my patience, and it has been a most tiresome situation, but I have done my filial duty and kept my promise to my father. Their company has made me appreciate yours all the more keenly, if that is any consolation to you, for I know I have been terribly remiss. I fully intended to have days of leisure at Longmeade and had hoped to show you around the old hall, as I have been working with the architect to design parts of the restoration. The chapel will be finished soon, and there will certainly be an occasion to celebrate its completion. Since Ned designed the stained-glass windows, he will be one of those honored at the festivities. I do not yet know when this will take place, but I know your name is high on the guest list.

I have given much thought to your theory of our friendship, and I have concluded that you are mistaken as to my motives. If I were shallow, I should find it offensive, but I fully understand your need to question an attachment as unconventional as ours. Pray bear in mind that my lack of patience does not necessarily preclude a lack of judgment of character, and I continue to find it worth my while to persevere in our exchanges, whether in person or by correspondence. Could it be that you underestimate your own charms and accomplishments and hide them beneath a bushel, believing that they have been overshadowed by your affliction?

I am off to Scotland now to enjoy a bit of blood sport in the wilds. I have had enough of the grim and heavy reality of the city, hemmed in by the jumble and mob. In the day time, London fairly seethes with the heat of dingy brick and black soot. I do so detest it at this time of year and should never have been here at all were it not for my father's obligations.

I await news of your own happenings at Burford, and remain,

> Affectionately yours,
> Harry

As usual, the effect was bittersweet. He professed a fondness for me I had thought diminished, but heaven only knew when I would see him again.

What tender hopes I did entertain were dashed to smithereens the night before I departed. I was down on my knees rearranging my trunks, for the housemaid had made a wretched mess of my packing, and I started at a hand on my shoulder and turned to see Esther standing there, holding her sides the way she did when she feared she had exerted herself too much.

"I'm sorry, Topsy," she said, pulling up a chair. "I know I startled you." Generally, one had to stamp on the floor outside my room to gain admittance, for I could feel the vibrations on the wood planks and would open the door, but it was such an uncivil way of announcing oneself, and Esther had long ago decided she was exempt from such antics.

Feeling I had done my best to restore order and minimize damage to my dresses, I closed the lid and sat down on the trunk.

"Are you finished?" she gestured.

"Yes."

"I shall miss you, Topsy," she said, reaching for my hands. Her eyes quickly filled with tears and she looked quite miserable. She was ever so sensitive these days.

"But I'll be back sometime in the autumn," I said. "For the dedication of the chapel. I shan't miss that."

"Oh, yes," she said, dabbing at a tear with the back of her hand, "but that's months away. And then the baby will be born, and I'll be cooped up here until—until forever." She heaved a sigh of melancholy.

"But you'll have your baby, Tiggy," I said, seizing her hand and pressing it with all the warmth I felt. "And you won't want for anything else."

"Yes, I shall. I shall want for the smell of oil paint and canvas and new brushes."

She looked like a little girl. She was nearly thirty, and I not yet twenty-two, but there were times when I felt much older than she.

"I'll come to see you."

She pulled a handkerchief from her sleeve and dabbed at her nose, and then she looked over at me with woeful eyes, and I instantly knew there was something more troubling her.

"What is it?" I asked, suddenly alarmed.

"It's Harry."

"Has something happened?" I started.

"Well, in a way, yes. What I mean—"

She saw my confusion and looked away as though reluctant to speak. She rose, found a slate and chalk on the dressing table, and motioned me to sit beside her on the bed.

She wrote: *That young American woman at Longmeade—*

"Yes—" I nodded.

They are discussing marriage—

"Marriage? To whom?"

"Harry," she said quite solemnly.

I stared blankly back down at the slate. I could feel my brow constrict quite involuntarily, against my will. I did not understand.

"Oh Topsy," she said, leaning into my line of sight so as to gain my attention. "You really are in love with him, aren't you?"

"I am not," I said sharply. Then, attempting to soften my voice, I added, "Harry is my friend. Nothing more."

"Well, then, I'm sure he'll tell you."

"I'm sure he will."

She shook the chalk dust from the cloth, erased the slate, and wrote: *But it's his father's doing. His father wants him married.* Then she said, "They're quite wealthy. The Americans."

"But Harry has his own wealth."

"I think much of it's gone," she said.

"How?"

She shook her head, "I don't know. Horses, perhaps. His father races them, too."

"And this—this girl is the answer?" I asked, incredulous.

"The Earl seems to think so."

"And Harry? Has he no choice in the matter?"

Esther shrugged. "He's the heir to the title. He must obey his father's wishes."

I dismissed this nonsense with a scowl. "Harry is not his father's puppet."

"Are we any different? You were willing to marry Balducci to please your father, were you not?"

"Only at the beginning, when I thought it would please me," I said. "But I was mistaken." Then I thought how dejected I must appear, for Esther's eyes were full of pity, and I was determined to conceal my true feelings. "All right, if he must marry, then why this American when there must be very good marriages to be made here in England?" I asked coolly. "I'm sure there's at least one young woman of excellent breeding among all those chasing after him that he could fancy."

She wrote: *Because of his father—no one wants to live at Blackroak now that Lady Hambledon is gone.*

"Goodness, is his father such a brute of a man?"

She lowered the slate and gave me a solemn stare. "I dislike writing these things."

"What things?"

With the air of one breaking unpleasant news, she said, "I should tell you."

"Tell me what?"

"Ned swore me to secrecy."

"Oh, do be clear, Esther. I do so dislike mysteries."

"But it's only rumor."

"What?"

"Well, Lady Hambledon's riding accident, when she broke her hip—"

"I didn't know—I believed she had been born with her infirmity."

"Oh, goodness gracious, no. They said it was a riding accident. But rumor has it that the Earl pushed her down a flight of stairs."

"Who told you this?" I asked warily.

"Lady Stamford told Ned. It all came out after Lady Hambledon's death, because everyone thought—well, another riding accident—"

"I'm sure it's nothing more than malicious gossip."

"She heard it from Lord Stamford."

"Do you mean to imply the Earl might have murdered his wife?"

She wrote a hasty reply. *Earl cleared of all wrongdoing—but imagine the gossip, after the first "accident"—which indeed was his doing.*

I was suddenly sick at the idea of that noble lady enduring such suffering.

"But surely, if he had hurt her so badly the first time—I cannot see her, of all women, continue—"

"But what could she do?" she said, then added on the slate, *Law affords little protection to us in such cases.*

"Yes. Yes, I am sure of it."

We can only hope our hearts lead us to a safe harbor.

"But Harry would never allow his wife to come to any harm, if that's what you imply," I protested.

These men of rank see themselves as beyond rebuke—you know that—you have witnessed their arrogance—they deem a husband's right so indefeasible, his title so sacred, that even a wronged wife should keep silent. And they are always so slow to admit a wrong has been done.

I suddenly thought of Aurelia. I had always wondered if there was more to her flight than religious zeal.

"So, marrying an American is a solution of sorts," I said.

"It may be," she answered. "If they are ignorant of the rumors. Rather difficult for her family to intervene. They couldn't exactly come rushing up for the weekend, could they?"

She continued in writing. *I've heard there were several flirtations over the past few years that have been nipped in the bud by the girl's parents. The young women are quite ready to take the risk, of course. If it were just Harry that mattered, they would be lined up all the way to the border.*

Then she put down the chalk and said, "But wouldn't you risk it? For Harry?"

I smiled. "So, you admit his charms."

"Of course I do, silly."

"Is it such a forlorn place? Blackroak?"

"More remote than forlorn, I should think."

I reflected and then said, "How odd. I always imagined it to be quite lovely. Wild, but lovely."

IT WAS SO VERY GOOD to get back to Savile Row. Entering the workroom with its peculiar odors of wools and silks fresh off the bolt, and the rows of hard-working tailors bent over their knees at their benches or cross-legged around a coal stove with a measuring tape dangling from their neck and spectacles perched on the end of their nose, their knotty fingers toughened and deformed from years of needlework on heavy garments, I felt as if I had returned to solid shore after months at sea. I had misgivings about how I might feel taking up gentlemen's dress again, but I was not deterred, for I felt more than ever that this was where my destiny lay, and this was my only solace in troubled times. I took up my needle with a bit of a vengeance, knowing how it had offended Harry, and feeling a certain satisfaction in defying his opinion. I was not sure I valued that opinion so highly anymore. I thought a good deal about the words of warning that had been directed at me in this regard by both Mr. Nicholls and Harry, and I was all the more determined to move boldly ahead. No one could accuse me of singularity for its own sake. I had been born to this, just as Harry had been born to rank and privilege, and I refused to allow my sex to deter me. If skirts were the offending culprit, then off with them!

Within Grenfell's, there was no longer any discussion as to my status, and little reaction from the other tailors. Had I returned and confined myself to the back room in my skirts, working away as an anonymous tailoress, I think they would have been disappointed in me. The previous spring, my appearance in the showroom had caused quite a stir within the trade, and a few outraged opinions had been voiced in the trade journals. But then, in late September, an article in the *Tailor and Cutter* mentioned me once again. They seemed to feel it their duty to repeat the alarm of impropriety but muted it with a favorable critique of my talents and bearing. That I conducted myself with such dignified moderation, neither servile nor pretentious, and had left such a favorable impression on those clients who had dared work with me, did not pass unnoticed. My deafness was not mentioned at all, and the omission of this detail led me to believe that the critics had, by virtue of my affliction, allowed me a certain license they never would have allowed another woman.

Early in October, Papa took me along as his assistant to Colonel Hayworth's house in Kensington. I had worked on the alterations of the Colonel's lounging coat in the spring, putting in new hand facings and buttons, and had added a few innovative touches suited to a gentleman's smoking habits. He had been so pleased with my work that he requested me specifically to fit him for another lounge coat and a beaver-trimmed cape of Elysian wool. It was the first time I had assisted at a fitting outside Grenfell's, and it was a defining ritual for me. As a little girl I had watched my father leave with his procession of assistants bearing garments all carefully packed in brown paper, and I had imagined how thrilling it would be to step into the private chambers of great men. It was a great privilege to be entrusted with their defects, both real and imaginary, with corpulence and lopsided shoulders, pigeon-breasts and hunched backs. Now, I had earned that privilege. I would set about wielding my craft like a magician, using chalk and shears like wands to defy the laws of *optiks* and *physiks*. I would take a hollow shell of fabric and fashion it to accommodate an imperfect form—not to give the impression of perfection, but of an improved man.

I WAS BEGINNING TO QUESTION my hasty judgment of Harry, for he was even more faithful in his correspondence than he had been the previous year, and much less reserved. His letters were short but steeped in witty and often scathing observations of the sporting society he kept. His accounts of their shooting and fishing expeditions were full of anecdotes of bullheaded and preposterously arrogant men attempting to be civil to one another, of risible accidents and ludicrous misadventures, but beneath the cleverness was a subtle self-indictment and the eternal restlessness that plagued him. It came across in the postscripts and afterthoughts in which he recounted with enthusiasm how he had spent the afternoon with the gamekeeper in the gunroom at Blackroak Hall discussing his idea for an invention to facilitate the process of loading the shells, or how he sat up at night flytying, using the white tips from a grey squirrel tail and old pieces of lace. Indeed, he had special flies of his own invention for salmon and trout and had given them each names.

Nothing could be further away from my world than these things, but in my letters to him, I always attempted to seize on some detail of his life and spin a web around it so that he would feel comforted, for I sensed Harry was in great need of comfort. In the process, I spun myself into the design, so that he would see me as a part of it. When words failed me, I sent him humorous sketches depicting some of the events he had described or caricatures of himself. It was the closest I ever came to revealing my talents to him, for I never spoke to him of tailoring, although it occupied a good deal of my week. Harry never once referred to Miss Erskine and her father, although he did mention that he had a vague but growing interest in America and thought he might like to travel there when that country was once again united, as he was sure it would be one day.

He stunned me by sending me a birthday present, a small gold mechanical pencil sheathed in red and black porcelain, attached by a gold chain to a pin so that it might be worn as an accessory. It was absolutely beautiful, as lovely as any piece of jewelry, and I'm sure quite costly. I nearly cried. Papa was awestruck. I think for the first time he realized that Lord Ormelie was more than just a fanciful dream of mine, but a real admirer.

Despite Harry's silence on the matter, I did believe that we had not seen the last of this Miss Erskine, but if there were prospects of marriage between Harry and the American, I felt it was anything but certain. And I, too, could be accused of falseness by omission, for I am quite sure the Miss Grenfell he pictured in his thoughts bore no resemblance to the one who stood before a looking glass each morning carefully pinning her cravat.

ONE MORNING IN NOVEMBER, I was upstairs in the workroom checking on the progress of a dress coat for a new client of mine, when Lucy appeared at my side. I turned astonished eyes on her, for she never came into the shop, and watched while she mouthed the words, "It's him, Miss. It's him."

"Who?" I gestured.

She threw a withering glance at a tailor who had looked up to stare at us, and once he had lowered his eyes, she carefully mouthed the words, "Lord Ormelie."

"Are you sure?"

She bobbed her head firmly up and down.

"Where?"

She indicated with a toss of her head and flick of her eyes that he was waiting for me at home.

"Oh, my goodness," I breathed, my eyes widening with shock.

She glanced down at my clothing, my trousers and waistcoat, and winced.

I slipped back home through the kitchen and crept upstairs to my room, hiding behind Lucy's skirt, for I was terrified he might emerge from the drawing room and I would not hear him. Lucy had told him that I was out but was expected to return any moment, and begged him to wait, which he agreed to do. Unfortunately, Aunt Lavinia was at Mortlake and was not there to entertain him or give me the courage I needed, for I was terribly nervous about receiving him in my own home. It took only a few minutes to divest myself of shirt and trousers, but then there were my chemise and stockings to wrest on, and the dreaded crinoline and corset, and all the hooks on my saffron silk dress with its lace-trimmed under-sleeves. My nerves were in such a terrible state—my palms moist and my knees weak—that I had to sit on the bed while Lucy sponged my neck with cool water. While she was brushing my hair, Mrs. Scholfield poked her head in to warn us that Lord Ormelie had started to leave once already, and that she had stalled him, and that we should hurry or he would be gone. Lucy hastily pinned my Medusa-like curls into something that looked like a frittered old mop, and I glanced in the mirror and felt like breaking into tears. At least there was color in my cheeks.

As soon as I entered the drawing room and he rose, all my anxieties were swept away. He seemed so genuinely pleased to see me that my heart virtually swelled in my chest, and I forgot all about my hair.

"Veda," he said, bowing deeply, and I extended both my hands to him. He grasped them warmly while we stood there in the dull November light beaming at each other.

I motioned to the settee and gestured to the slate on the table beside him, then realized with embarrassment we had no chalk and had to ring for Lucy to bring some.

"And where is our Talking Book?" he asked, making the gesture of an open book.

"Oh!" I started. "Yes, of course! That was quite thoughtless of me. I should have remembered. I'll send Lucy to fetch it."

"You must excuse me. Perhaps I should have sent a note."

"A note? Oh, that would have been quite unnecessary. You are very welcome at any time."

"I didn't know which days you received callers."

"Oh," I exclaimed wide-eyed, "we have no set day. Any day is fine. I don't have many callers, you see. Polite conversation is generally wasted on me." With that, a bemused smile broke over Harry's face, and I laughed, which set us both laughing. Within the bat of an eye, we were both instantly at ease again.

"I have missed you, Veda," he said, once he had his mirth under control.

I said nothing, but how could he have missed the sparkle in my eyes.

Lucy came in then, and we sent her off for the Talking Book and chalk. She paused at the door to steal a look at him before hurrying out.

There was another awkward moment, and then we both spoke at the same time, and again we laughed.

"What brings you to London?" I asked.

"My father," he said. He hesitated, and then added, "He has sent me here to see our solicitors on some business related to Blackroak." I gathered from his glum look that this was not pleasant business and refrained from pursuing the subject.

"I'm very pleased you called," I said.

"I wasn't sure what I would find."

Lucy arrived with the book, and we sat ourselves at the table and opened it. We waited while she arranged inkwells and pens for our use. When she had gone, he turned to me and mouthed the words, "I would have liked to have kept this with me, to recall our picnic this summer."

I nodded. "Yes," I said. "It has been a happy reminder."

He glanced through some of the pages. "But many of your replies are missing," he protested.

"*I* don't miss them," I smiled.

He stared at me thoughtfully, then dipped his pen in the ink and wrote, *You have none of the peculiar habits one usually finds in young women of your upbringing.*

"Meaning what, sir?" I asked, when I had read him.

Trades people. They generally lack the genteel manners that come with good breeding.

I took up my own pen, pulled the book toward me, and wrote, *I believe, sir, that politeness can be learned by anyone who has the desire to learn it. And coarseness is not confined to those of humble birth.*

He wrote in turn, *It is not those of humble birth who offend, but those who reek of avarice and dishonesty.*

And do you think all tradesmen carry this unseemly vapor about them?

Many of them do.

Perhaps you will find this doubtful, but it is possible to engage in trade for reasons other than money. And I find this prejudice of yours does not suit a man who believes so strongly in the march of progress and the rational structuring of society, and the greatest good of the greatest number.

Are those my words?

They are. Taken from your letters, sir.

By then, we were shoulder to shoulder, and as our minds sparred, we seemed to grow bolder. As we passed the book back and forth or paused to rock the blotter over the page, our hands frequently touched without embarrassment.

You have a formidable memory, Miss Grenfell. Equaled only by your observation of human nature.

Then may I offer one such observation without offending?

I would find it difficult to be offended by you.

I paused, warning him with a teasing look, and then wrote, *You'd be much happier were you not so titled, I think. Then you might put your brilliant mind to work without shame.*

It is indeed a pity when we are born to a life that stifles our natures. My rank stifles me just as your sex stifles you.

Oh? And how is it you have come to this conclusion about me?

I have had reports.

At this, I put down my pen, and said, "Reports? Or rumors?"

He answered me, speaking slowly, "I disregard rumors. Only reports are of interest to me."

"And may I know the content of these reports?"

"That you are an excellent tailor."

I watched his face for clues, but it was difficult to judge his sentiments, for he knew now how carefully I read his countenance.

"Show me your tongue, Harry," I said.

"My tongue?"

"Yes. To see if those words have burned a hole in it."

He laughed. Even without hearing it, the mirth was so infectious that I too laughed.

He said, "I cannot picture you in my mind. Never in a thousand years could I imagine you like that." He shook his head, appearing a little baffled, but there was such warmth and gentleness there that I forgave him his lack of imagination.

He dipped his pen again and wrote, *I think you allow me to see only that which you want me to see.*

As I read these words, I laid my hand on his and said, "It is to our benefit that I do so."

His gaze softened, and I think with the slightest encouragement he would have kissed me. I saw in his eyes the struggle to control his desire, and it took my own breath away. I withdrew my hand, and there was a long and unsettling pause during which we both sat with our eyes fixed on the book, the thoughts we had put down there, and our hands, only inches apart.

Then he dipped his pen again and wrote, *Indeed, both of us might breathe a little easier were we not so confined by these unwritten laws.*

But do you not believe that these are God's laws?

He hesitated, and then wrote at length: *I believe that certain laws are the result of social experiment and growth—as such they are neither divine nor irrevocable. Perhaps we might be wise to regard certain changes into which we are drifting as things to be accepted rather than resisted, and it might be to our advantage to make the best of them rather than the worst.*

I was waiting, pen in hand, to respond, and I quickly wrote, *But is this not subversive?*

Something is not necessarily unrighteous because it subverts our present arrangements. On the contrary, there may be greater justice in a new manner of living, and a new order in the relations between men—between master and servant, women and men—may be more righteous than anything we have as yet put into practice.

He put down his pen and leaned toward me to seize my attention. "We have grown far too serious." He smiled.

"Why are you not in Parliament?" I asked.

He seemed much more interested in my countenance than in respond-ing to my question, but at last he said, "Because I am a hypocrite."

"A hypocrite?"

He wrote, *I fear I could not shake the hands of my constituents without rushing back home to wash them. It is both haughty and contemptuous, and I am helpless before my own prejudices.*

I protested, "But this is not the man you reveal to me in your letters."

He turned a sharp eye on me and lifted an eyebrow, and I caught the irony of what I had just said.

I smiled, "So, are we both false?"

"Perhaps it is in speaking of our falseness that we can be true." Then he wrote, *I sometimes think I might be able to shed these prejudices were I to go abroad.*

"Do you think it is that easy?"

He replied in writing: *Sometimes our prejudices are branded on our soul, and then they stay with us forever. But there are some men whose prejudices enclose them like the walls of a prison, and were they to escape, they might find themselves acting more freely, guided by common principles of human dignity rather than a set of rigid rules rooted only in tradition and privilege and a false sense of moral superiority.*

Then he laid down his pen, and noticing how I sat watching him with my chin on my hand, he said, "My dear, I have tired you."

I was embarrassed to have let my demeanor slip, and I sat up straight and shook my head. "Not at all."

"Understanding is indeed a strain for you. So much exertion is re-quired. I see that now."

I said with a weary smile, "But you are so worth understanding, Harry."

There was a long, quiet moment when we gazed at each other, and then he said, "I have stayed too long. I must take my leave."

I rose with him, and at the door, he turned and glanced around the drawing room and asked, "Where is your portrait?"

"In my father's study."

"May I see it?"

"Certainly."

He followed me down the hall and into Papa's study. I watched his face as he studied the painting. He said nothing, but as we stood quietly side by side, I felt his hand reach for mine.

Then he turned, and mouthing the words loudly and slowly so that I could not fail to comprehend, he said, "I shall see what I can do, to break us out of this prison."

There must have been a noise in the hall, for he quickly released my hand. It was only Lucy with his hat and gloves. He took them from her, settled his hat on his head, and with no further explanation, he departed.

That night, I turned back to our conversation as recorded in the Talking Book. What I had heard from Esther threw an entirely new light on his situation, and I felt I understood him better than ever before. His enigmatic parting words left me quite unsettled in the weeks ahead. I was fortunate to have my work, and the weather was not too bad, so that I was able to ride nearly every day. When I still had no news by Christmas, I sent him a pretty greeting card—a new custom in fashionable society—wishing him all the best for the holidays. I received a thoughtful but dispassionate note in reply.

Chapter Eighteen

ONE AFTER ANOTHER, EVERY OPPORTUNITY TO MEET HARRY FAILED
to materialize. When the dedication of the chapel at Longmeade was postponed, I consoled myself with hopes of seeing him at the christening of Esther's baby, for both he and I had been named as godparents, along with members of their families. After giving birth, Esther became very ill with a fever, and her aunt from London went to Burford to nurse her. Knowing I would only be a burden, I thought it wise to delay my visit until she was well. Esther, anxious for her baby's health, wished to proceed with the christening without all the incumbent festivities, which could be set for a later date, and so the christening took place at the first of February in a quiet little ceremony organized at the last minute at the Burford church.

Then, several days later, a letter arrived from Harry.

My dear Veda,

How disappointed I was to find you were not in attendance at little Ellen's christening. I was there, holding up my end of the bargain, although I'm sure the true spiritual rock will be the other godfather, Ned's elder brother, a clergyman.

I confess, I am godfather to countless children and seem to be much in demand in that capacity. I do not believe it is because of my particularly righteous living, but rather because the fathers think I'll be of use when the sons are ready to ride and hunt, and the mothers think I'll be invaluable when their daughters come of age and are looking for suitors. It seems there is always room on the ticket for a godless godfather, or at least one with connections in this life as opposed to the hereafter.

Of course I write this in a humorous vein. Ned's baby is a rather ugly little creature who will grow up to be quite lovely, I'm sure, and I deem it an honor to perform such a function.

He is delighted to be a father and seems not at all concerned that it is not a boy. I only hope it does not distract him from his painting.

I understand from Esther that the only reason for your absence was your belief that you would be burdensome to the family at such a trying time. What nonsense.

Esther is improving rapidly, and she asks me to send you her love and hopes to see you soon.

Your friend,
Harry

What an infuriating letter. That he should despair at not having seen me in Burford and then neglect to suggest any plan to see me elsewhere left me in an emotional turmoil. And then there was the salutation—*Your friend*—whereas his previous letters had been signed *Your devoted friend*, or *Your constant friend*, always with some qualifier to distinguish his sentiments from the ordinary. But then, in truth, he had proven himself anything but constant and devoted.

I rewrote my reply countless times over a period of several days, and each time my good sense grappled with my wounded sensibilities, for his silence had indeed grieved me. After a colossal and sustained effort to sweeten my incorrigibly tart pen, I eventually excised every hint of reprimand.

Dear Harry,

I am flattered that my absence was in some way a disappointment to you, but my decision was not made lightly. Esther is always so very solicitous of my well-being, and I know her well enough to believe that she would have been anxious for my safety as well as my comfort. Perhaps she did not tell you that my Aunt Lavinia, who was to drive down to Burford with me and stay at the coaching inn, has been suffering from severe gout and is unable to walk without assistance. Although I was more than willing to lodge alone at The Lamb, Esther would not hear of it. She preferred I visit at a later date when she would be better able to enjoy my company and I may fawn at leisure over her firstborn. I assure you I deeply regret missing the event. I take solace in the knowledge that the responsibilities of a godmother extend beyond the attendance of the ceremony to include lifelong stewardship. It is a duty I intend to fulfill to the best of my abilities.

Your presence surely made up for my absence. That you were able to re-arrange your schedule on such short notice in order to be present speaks highly of your character. I know it meant a great deal to Ned. Your friendship is a source of inspiration to him. And I doubt you need worry about his painting.

As for the nonsense of feeling myself a burden, you might be pleased to know that I have at last accepted an invitation to a ball. It is to be given by the Countess of Alba who is renowned for extravagant parties to which she invites persons of all nations—but I'm sure you know this as I believe she is a distant relation of yours. I have been told there have been assembled under her roof real savages from the wilds of America and the Pacific Islands. On this occasion she is lionizing an adventurer of the literary type, a young French poet whose scandalous verses have alienated even his own publisher in France—making him the perfect candidate for her net. My association to all this comes by way of my faithful tutor, the Reverend Mr. Nicholls, who—in addition to his excellent teaching and inspired preaching—has distin-guished himself by his translations of Racine's religious plays, *Esther* and *Athaliah*. He also enjoys the patronage of the Countess since he now holds the living of Christ's Church in Southwark. Mr. Nicholls finds Mr. Baude-laire's poetry offensive, but he is bound by duty to attend as the poet is famil-iar with Mr. Nicholls's translations and desires to make his acquaintance with the hope that Mr. Nicholls would translate his latest collection of poems. Mr. Nicholls, knowing my fondness for French poetry—an appreciation I owe to him—has secured an invitation for my father and myself. There will be other literary lions there as well, along with a prominent playwright and even a few theatricals, and he assures me that a deaf young lady will pass unnoticed amidst the flurry of wampum and war paint.

I esteem it will be a suitable "coming out" party for me. My French will certainly be put to the test. I have had little opportunity to speak or lip read the language since my deafness—although Mr. Nicholls has re-cently devised some exercises to remedy this weakness. It is to him that I owe what small progress I have made in lip reading. He is a con-scientious man, and I am ever so grateful to him for his constancy and affection.

I send this to your club in London, believing you may have left Burford by now, and may be in America for all I know.

But I remain here, and fondly your

Veda

Satisfied that it was in no way offensive, I folded it, sealed it well, and sent it off to his club. I was glad when it was done. Then I could direct my thoughts toward more pleasurable things—more specifically, what I would wear to the Countess's ball, for I had no intention of passing unnoticed.

Fortunately I had ample time to work with my seamstress, the French woman who had made last summer's wardrobe. Since evening wear was always slow to adopt new styles, we agreed that the dress should reflect traditional taste, but that we would add some subtle yet original touches. As a young unmarried woman, it would have been unseemly for me to dress in extravagant laces and beadwork, but neither would I be happy with the simple and unadorned styles deemed suitable for innocent girls during their first social season. We settled on a skirt of white silk with a delicate pinkish cast, finished at the bottom with bands of pleated silk tulle ruche edged in silk piping and shimmering *blonde* lace; adding volume was an overskirt of delicate embroidered tulle caught up in loops with tiny satin rosettes. The bodice was fitted, with a higher waist reflecting the newer fashion, and a low curved neckline baring my shoulders and arms, trimmed with the same tulle ruche and a narrow band of the *blonde* lace. It would have been a very demure dress were it not for the striking back which dropped in a low V. Knowing how I abhorred bell-shaped crinolines, Madame agreed to have made for me one in the new style, which had less fullness in front so that the skirt flared more gently from the waist and lengthened just slightly toward the back.

As for my hair, we decided to abandon the idea of ringlets, which was an impossible style for my wild curls, and Lucy tamed it into a simple low and loose chignon which we covered in a white chenille net made especially by Madame Le Pince's private milliner in Paris. Nets were very popular for day wear, but Madame had never before seen them worn in the evening. The milliner sent us an exquisite confection that we could not refuse. Pink silk thread was crocheted into the velvety white yarn, which was then beaded with tiny white pearls. Along each side, arranged so that they billowed around my head like a soft coronet, were clusters of downy white feathers. I wore no necklace, only Mama's pearl pendant earrings.

On my feet, over my *cloqued* Lisle stockings, I wore white satin slippers with dusty pink roses painted on the toes. Since it was winter, I had the opportunity to design what was the most splendid part of my wardrobe—a hooded circular mantle of white cashmere woven with silk, lined with dusty pink satin and trimmed in white Karakul lamb.

Papa was his gallant best that evening. Always an elegant man, he was immaculate in his spotless white kid gloves, a perfectly blocked black silk hat, and exquisite white silk embroidered waistcoat. He was not keen on attending, indeed had not been to a dance since before Mama died, but when we paused at the bottom of the wide marble staircase of Melrose House with my dress shimmering in the flickering light of tall candelabra, and I placed my hand on his arm, I thought I had never seen him look so proud. I lifted my fragile tulle skirt, and we followed an ancient and equally fragile-looking retainer up the stairs where we were presented to the Countess—a heavily painted and bejeweled old lady with the shriveled air of a woman who found little in life to amuse her. I wondered how, with a face like that, she had gained a reputation as such a formidable hostess. She fixed me with a sharp, appraising eye, for I believe we had been invited against her better judgment, but that sharpness softened when I executed a graceful and perfectly appropriate curtsey before taking her hand. In dress, manners, and bearing, neither Papa nor I could be faulted. After all, we were quite accustomed to the company of viscounts and Etonians and the sort of men on the alert for the tiniest breach of the social code.

Mr. Nicholls, who had been called into duty as an interpreter, stood next to the poet in the reception line. Upon seeing him, I felt an immediate relief and quite unexpected surge of pleasure. It was the first time I had seen him in formal attire, and he was very handsome indeed. He grew quite flustered when he caught sight of me and nervously tugged at his gloves and fiddled with his collar. I got through my introduction to the poet without any awkward moments, and before I knew it, Papa and I had taken a refreshment and then passed into the ballroom.

It was a grand ballroom with an ornate and immensely high ceiling, so high that the crystal chandeliers hung like distant moons in a gilded and azure sky. On the parquet floor, dozens of blazing bronze candelabra as tall as street lamps illuminated the dancers. Along each wall were placed rows of plush scarlet settees trimmed in heavy gold *bouillon* fringe. The vastness of the room virtually dwarfed the ladies in their sprawling white gowns and reduced the gentlemen to insignificant stick-figures. The effect left one feeling that the room had once been inhabited by giants who had long ago vanished, and it had been taken over by humans who were no match for its mammoth scale.

Early in the evening, I was flattered by a constant stream of suitors. It was terribly awkward for the poor things when they learned I was deaf, but then I'm sure word got around the room. As late arrivals clustered among friends and surveyed the ladies, I noticed how the gentlemen directed their attention toward me and held me in their sights for a long moment while their companions discouraged them from approaching me, although I believe some did so with a flicker of regret.

Mr. Nicholls was kind enough to bring Mr. Baudelaire to meet me in a quiet corner of the conservatory where I confessed that I had obtained a copy of his collection of poems from France and read them in anticipation of meeting him. I told him I had found them most beautiful and melancholy, even *angoissant,* although I did not fully understand them. He understood my French better than I had hoped, although I had a good deal of trouble lip reading him. Nonetheless, he seemed sincerely flattered by the favorable review, even from one as innocent as I. Mr. Nicholls was quite upset after that, because I had read the poems. He grew very stern and would not look at me for the longest while.

It was a long evening for both Papa and me, for I could not dance, and Papa could do so only when Mr. Nicholls found time to keep me company. I had often imagined balls when I was a little girl, but I had never imagined that I would experience them like this: hundreds of mouths moving in laughter and conversation that I could not hear; satin slippers and leather soles gliding soundlessly over a heavily waxed floor. I could no longer recall the rustle of satin and silk and the delicate tinkle of a filigree bracelet at a lady's wrist, but I knew they were there. I watched the dancers—most of them quite accomplished, although there were a few stiff gentlemen and awkward ladies—move through the intricate patterns of a quadrille or gallop through a polka, or spin round and round in a graceful waltz. I loved the waltzes best, for the twirling movements bared the ladies' ankles and shoes, and revealed their lace-trimmed petticoats, and showed off the billowing layers of silk and muslin and tulle of a dress.

Yet, their gaiety seemed to me almost comical as I could not hear the music which inspired it nor the laughter which sustained it, and as the evening wore on, a certain melancholy crept into my heart.

At one point in the evening I felt a terrible longing for Harry. Watching the grand ladies in their jewels and the distinguished lords, I thought how this kind of gathering was so familiar to him. I entertained myself by imagining him in a ballroom like this, and then, all of a sudden, there he was in the corner beside a palm tree, standing stiffly upright and looking unapproachable and terribly bored. He was there for only a moment, and then he disappeared.

I told Mr. Nicholls I needed to retire to the ladies' lounge, and I cautiously made my way along the side of the ballroom past the dancers, into an adjoining drawing room where a set of older ladies and gentlemen were playing cards. They took no notice of me, although a butler came forward and said something which I did not catch. I turned away and caught sight of a door into the hallway and quickly made an exit. I didn't know where he could have gone, but I was determined to find him. There were several more rooms farther down the hall, and as I stood there, fanning myself by a cool glass window, two young men passed by me and knocked at a door, which was opened by a valet. I crept closer, feigning to pass behind them, and peered over their shoulders. Through a thick screen of smoke, I caught a glimpse of men gathered around gaming tables with cards clutched in their hands. If Harry was in there, I certainly could not follow. Suddenly, I was startled by a hand on my shoulder.

It was Harry. He took me by the hand and drew me away, back down the hall to a console lighted by a candelabra.

"I have been looking all over for you," he said. He seemed a little drunk, rather wretched, and very tired.

I fanned at him. "You reek of wine and cigars, Harry."

"No wonder," he said, drawing out his watch. "I've been here more than an hour." He tucked his watch back into his waistcoat pocket and frowned at me.

"And how much of that time did you spend playing cards?" I asked.

"Well, I was winning. Rather heavily. But I left to look for you again. It made me very unpopular. Particularly with Lord Haversham."

"Why didn't you let me know you'd been invited?"

"I invited myself," he said with a rather disinterested air. "The Countess is my father's cousin." He held up a cautionary finger. "Now, you wait here. I left my gloves in the gaming room. I shall return to fetch you. Do not stray."

He slipped into the gaming room and then came out again, tugging on his white gloves.

"Come with me," he said, taking me by the elbow.

I resisted him. "But I can't. I must go back. Mr. Nicholls will be worried about me."

"Mr. Nicholls?"

"Yes." I thought he was being intentionally obtuse. "Mr. Nicholls."

"Oh, bother Mr. Nicholls."

"Harry!"

"All you write about is Mr. Nicholls. Mr. Nicholls this. Mr. Nicholls that. Are you going to marry this Mr. Nicholls?"

I stared at him in astonishment. He was miserable, as miserable as I was, and I had no desire to torture him.

I shook my head gently. "Nothing could be farther from my mind."

This seemed to appease him somewhat, and the angry lines on his face softened.

"I wanted to dance with you," he said.

"Dance with me?"

He nodded.

"But I can't dance, Harry," I said, finding it all rather amusing and very endearing—Harry just a little drunk and urging me to dance.

He frowned. "Did you dance with him?"

"With Mr. Nicholls? Of course not. Besides, he doesn't like dancing. He's very strict."

"Pray, dance with me."

"I can't," I pleaded, leaning in to him and tapping him playfully on the chest with my fan. "How can a deaf girl dance?"

"Well, I am not deaf. I can hear the music. All you need to do is lean on me."

His reply took me by surprise. It made a good deal of sense.

"But I don't know the steps. I should make a fool out of myself."

"Then we shall go outside. On the terrace."

"Outside?"

"No one is there."

He glanced around to make sure no one could overhear, and then he leaned closer so that I might easily read his lips, and he said slowly, "I beseech you, Veda. Allow me this honor. After tonight, I shall ask nothing more of you. I shall leave you alone to your Mr. Nicholls."

All of a sudden, I understood. The realization sank to my stomach like lead, and I thought I might be ill.

He touched my chin with his fingertips and drew my gaze back to his lips.

"Do not look away."

I could have looked into his eyes forever and beyond, but I only had one night.

"Are you to be married?" I asked, not sure if the words were loud enough for him to hear.

"Let's not talk of it."

I took his arm, and he escorted me down the hallway and through the drawing room. Guests were crowded around a refreshment table at which ices and coffee were being served. One by one, faces turned toward us, all of them wearing an air of condescending ease with a hint of boredom. I wanted ever so much to catch a word or two whispered between them, but it would only have demeaned me. As we passed an older gentleman and two ladies of middle age who turned to acknowledge Harry with a few words, I grew suddenly anxious, fearing I might be drawn into a conversation. Sensing my hesitation, Harry laid his other hand over mine, as though afraid I might bolt; we paused for only a second and then went on.

Clearly, he knew the house, for he guided me across the hall to a library in which several guests were admiring a set of prints on a table. We paused at a window overlooking the back of the old Palladian-style house.

"There," he said, pointing to a stone terrace below. "We shall go down there."

"Will you be able to hear the music?" I asked.

He turned to me with the sweetest smile and studied me closely, as though only now taking the time to see me. "Yes," he nodded.

As we turned to leave, the Countess entered the library with Monsieur Baudelaire. My heart jumped, for I feared Mr. Nicholls might be with them, but he was not. Upon seeing us, the Countess halted abruptly and drew herself up in an alert manner as though awakening from an eternal tedium.

"Ah! Lord Ormelie," she began, pausing to allow her presence to be fully felt while her eyes drifted over me and then fixed on Harry, "I see you are acquainted with this young lady."

"Yes, Countess, I am. Well acquainted." I noticed that he replied with his face angled toward me so that I might understand. As soon as he had spoken, my eyes snapped back to her face.

"Well, I can tell you, I have had many a young man inquire about her this evening." Then, turning condescending eyes on me, she added quite slowly and with deliberate emphasis, "What a pity she's deaf."

Immediately, Harry reached for my hand and drew it around his arm. He said something I did not understand, nor did I catch her reply, for my eyes were filling with tears. This old woman had wounded me needlessly, and Harry knew it. I averted my eyes and thereafter understood nothing that was said. I was relieved when he bowed, and I took the cue and curtsied, and we left.

We descended the wide staircase, and in the hall he paused to speak to a wigged and liveried footman who lifted a silver candelabra from a table and lighted our way through a heavy door and across the floor of a darkened drawing room. There the footman drew aside a heavy curtain to reveal a long wall of windows looking onto the back. Following Harry's direction, he removed a plant from a stand and set the candelabra in its place so that the light would shine through the window. The servant opened the door, and we stepped outside onto the broad stone terrace. It was a cold night, and a low fog hung over the city. The mist softened the bright light cast from the ballroom above, wrapping us in an immense golden halo.

Harry turned to me and said, "I beg your pardon. I neglected to get your mantle." He then stepped back and removed his coat. "Here," he said, holding out the coat for me. "You won't have any objections, will you?"

His teasing made me smile. He stepped around behind me, and I slipped my arms through the sleeves. The warmth spread over my bare arms and shoulders, and it felt as though he had embraced me.

Harry took my hand and drew me to the center of the terrace. My heart was beating wildly. I feared I might be terribly clumsy and spoil the moment. I was trying to remember the steps I had danced with Mr. Nicholls, but the last thing I wanted was thoughts of Mr. Nicholls swimming in my mind. Harry slipped his arm around my waist, drawing me closer, and I felt a shiver that was not from the cold. His gloved hand found mine, and I placed my other hand lightly on his shoulder and looked up into his eyes. We had not moved, had not taken one step.

"What music is playing now?" I asked a little nervously. "Is it a waltz? I think I might manage a waltz. I might recall the steps, if you're patient."

I shall never forget his face that night, so still and motionless, set against the absolute stillness in my head. He seemed unreal, as did everything around us. I never noticed when he leaned forward, nor was I aware of straining to reach his lips, but somehow the distance between us vanished. I could feel the warmth of his breath followed by the faintest brush of his warm lips against mine. He drew back and hesitated, his mouth not a finger's breadth from my own, and I thought I could feel his heart pounding in the air between us. I could not move; I had no breath in my lungs, and my heart seemed stunned into silence.

When he kissed me again, I found myself unable to respond. I thought that if I so much as twitched, he might disappear into the fog and fade away, and I would be standing there in the cold night, all alone.

He moved back, and searched my eyes for clues.

"Veda," he whispered.

I didn't know how to show him that I wanted him to kiss me again, and I didn't know what to say. I gave in to the only guide I had, which was my heart. I melted into him and into the next kiss, and I felt my body quicken. I had never been so pleasantly close to a man before, had never known the texture of man's beard nor the scent of his skin. It awakened something in me that felt like a powerful hunger.

It was Harry who drew back, staggering ever so slightly. I opened my eyes but I found it difficult to focus them on his face. When I was able to clear my head and look into his eyes, I saw there the most remarkable gaze: I think it reflected the very thing that I was feeling. I also sensed it was dangerous, and that he was struggling to control it.

He took up my hand again and gently pressed my waist, and before I knew it I was dancing with him. I stumbled a little at first and was rather stiff, but as I followed him, my body recalled the rhythm. Harry's rhythm was perfect.

"Relax," he whispered, smiling and giving my waist a gentle squeeze. "Relax."

I did, and soon I began to anticipate his movements. It was really quite simple, the same step, round and round. My dress swirled with me, and I felt myself lifted up, as though my feet were barely touching the ground. I was laughing, and he was smiling, and it seemed to me I had never seen him so happy.

I don't recall much of the rest of the evening. There was a bit of un-pleasantness when Harry returned me to the ballroom and faced Mr. Nicholls and Papa. I couldn't catch all that was being said, but there was certainly a lot to be read on their faces. Mr. Nicholls was really quite vexed and ready to give me a scolding until he realized who Harry was. Then he grew speechless and looked a little cowed by Harry, although Harry was terribly apologetic for having worried them. Papa was all confusion and trying to be stern but not too stern for fear of offending the heir to an earl-dom. I suffered through supper with Mr. Nicholls being morose and very gloomy. On the way home in the carriage with Papa, it was too dark to converse, and I managed to keep the world at a distance and Harry close to my heart.

The next morning, an enormous bouquet of white roses came with Harry's card attached, on the back of which he had written a note re-questing to see me the following day.

It was terribly awkward, for Papa insisted on speaking to him when he called, but I was vehement in my refusal. Aunt Lavinia would be present during his visit, but I would not tolerate any embarrassing discussions with regards to his intentions. I explained that the roses were to celebrate my long-awaited coming-out and nothing more. I did not want to lie to Papa, but neither could I reveal what was happening between Harry and me. I was not sure of anything except that I loved him and I believed that he loved me. I said as little as possible to Papa over breakfast and stub-bornly refused to look at him when he spoke to me. I fear I was rather hard on him. I think after Balducci he no longer trusted his own judgment and prayed that my own judgment would see me through.

Eventually, Papa acquiesced. Although I'm not sure he believed me. I think I must have looked different after the night of the ball. I certainly felt different. I don't think Papa was astute enough to notice, but Aunt Lavinia noticed. She always tended to surprise one like that. So inconse-quential in so many ways, just a rather dull presence, and then she noticed some secret you kept in your heart, something you thought you had con-cealed from all the world.

She sat in the drawing room throughout his visit, with her gouty feet on a footstool and Ivanhoe on her lap. Ivanhoe had become her dog as she was home all day with him and spoiled him terribly. Harry said later that Aunt Lavinia was the quietest creature he had ever encountered, and that he would not have known she was there were it not for the clicking of her knitting needles and an occasional long, low ruminating hum drawn from the end of a sigh.

Harry was most charming to her when introduced. She was quite used to seeing me converse with friends seated side by side at a writing table, and we were allowed a certain intimacy which might have appeared unseemly under normal circumstances. I think from the first she sensed that he was special. She had put on her best brown morning dress and a fresh lace cap to greet him, and there was something wistfully sweet in the way she smiled at us, so I think she knew.

I could barely look at him. I kept remembering his kiss, and I would blush. I would watch his face as he spoke and recall the touch of his lips and the pressure of his hand around my waist, and then I would feel quite weak, as if my bones had turned to jelly. I had a terrible time understanding what he said. It was miserable and heavenly all at once, and all I wanted was to be near him.

Thank goodness he maintained his composure. He settled himself beside me at the table where I had set out pens and inkwell and our Talking Book, and when I reached to open it with a trembling hand, he laid his hand over mine to calm it. I looked up into his eyes and he smiled at me. Then he dipped his pen and wrote:

I offer you my deepest apologies for my behavior the other night.
You took nothing from me which I did not willingly give.

When he replied, it was after much hesitation. I sensed he was formulating a response that was difficult to write and choosing his words with great care. Several times he put his nib to the paper, withdrew it, and then dipped it again before he finally wrote: *My behavior should have been the prelude to honorable actions, but I find I cannot act as I would have wished. I cannot offer you that which is in my heart. I have duties and obligations which weigh heavily on me and which I wholeheartedly detest.*

I wrote: *Is this why you abandoned me? You left me in utter silence after Longmeade. As if the silence in my head is not enough, you confined my heart to an even deeper silence.*

He replied: *It was never my intent. I had always wished that I could change the shape of things, to make them suit my wishes. I have often been able to do as much, but in this case, I come up against a wall as impenetrable as your silence.*

And does this mean an end to our friendship?

He answered: *No amount of distance nor silence could ever weaken what I feel for you. I am not a callow youth, Veda. I have known attachments, I have believed myself to be in love. But what I feel for you has eclipsed anything I have ever felt for another. It has taken hold of my soul like an Evangelical fervor; indeed, I see myself turning to God more than ever, in order to find peace within myself. I have never even had the courage to inquire as to your own sentiments for me—*

I stopped his hand and impatiently snatched up the slate beside me and scribbled in chalk, *But you must know them.*

He wrote: *Then I am not mistaken to think that you feel at least some small fraction of what I have just confessed to you.*

I couldn't help but smile, and I took up my pen and wrote my own confession below his: *How could you mistake what is in my heart when it sits so defiantly on my face in spite of every effort I make to conceal it?*

I know you have had other suitors.

I have. But none I encouraged.

He laid down his pen, leaned back in his chair, and contemplated me with a visible air of relief. I could only imagine how this man, who all of his life had been given everything he desired, might feel in the face of a debacle so ordinary and so hopeless.

I wrote: *So, it is settled then. You are to be married?*

I turned the book back to him. He replied: *They are plotting as much. Even as we speak, my future is being laid out paragraph by paragraph, penned by some anonymous clerk in our lawyer's office.*

To Miss Erskine.

Still he refused to answer directly, but wrote in reply: *My father wishes me to marry. He wishes to have a mistress for Blackroak, and since he has no desire to burden himself with a new wife, he is imposing it on me. I shall continue to resist their efforts. I have held firm so far. But I fear the worst. I have resisted marriage in the past, but for different reasons. I fear, this time, I shall lose the contest. And the stakes have never been higher.*

Chapter Nineteen

Rarely did Harry speak to me ahead of time of his plans or intentions, and on the few occasions when he did, more often than not he failed to see them through. But he was never absent from my life for long. He exacted a patience from me I was willing to concede to no one else.

During those days I lived in a state of constant turmoil. My moods swung from ecstatic heights to the depths of despair. As always, I found solace in my sewing during the days, and at night I performed silly little rituals that eased the yearning in my heart. I pressed each and every one of his white roses into a book. I lingered over poems long forgotten or never quite understood, poems which now spoke straight to my heart. I sketched numerous portraits of Harry from memory. I was very good at capturing his particular manner of dressing, and the book was full of cameo details: the way he wore his collars and tied his cravat; his tie pins—he had a fondness for topaz and ruby, but his favorite was the one with an emblem of White's Club on the head; or the mother-of-pearl cuff links he wore the day he declared his love for me. My greatest source of consolation was our Talking Book, which was now secured in a small locked chest, the key to which I wore on a gold chain around my neck. I read it over and over again, memorizing the words, and each night I wrapped it in a square of silk the precise color of his eyes and clutched it to my heart as I slept.

His stay in London was brief, for although he had never said so directly, it was clear that I alone had been the reason for his visit. In the weeks that followed, I received small tokens of thoughtfulness, delivered by way of Scrimshire, the clerk at White's Club who received and forwarded Harry's private mail: a generous bouquet of hothouse peonies, a small book of insipid poetry of the kind ladies generally fancy—he said he doubted it was to my taste but feared any book I might find engaging would have been censored by my father—and notes written hastily while a coach waited at the door to whisk him off to his next social obligation. Lucy became quite adept at skimming his letters from the pile before she delivered the mail to Papa each morning, for I feared any sign of sustained attention from Harry would arouse Papa's suspicion.

Then, one morning over breakfast, as Papa sorted through the mail Lucy had just handed over to him, I watched in shock as he turned over a letter closed with Harry's seal.

"What's this?" he asked, throwing me a curious gaze over the rim of his spectacles.

"I'm sure I don't know," I said coolly. I stole a glance at Lucy on her way out. She only flashed me a baffled look meant to protest her innocence and then closed the door. Aunt Lavinia rapped her butter knife on the table, and once I had turned toward her, she said brightly to Papa, "Perhaps he's asking for permission to court your daughter, George." You would have thought Papa the deaf one, for he paid her no heed whatsoever. Seeing he would not respond, Aunt Lavinia only gave me a wistful smile and dove into the jam. She had been ignored all of her life and was resigned to it. I think had she possessed the intuition of the Delphi oracle, he would have continued to dismiss her.

I didn't have the faintest idea why Harry would be writing to him. It was not a brief letter, that much I could see, but I could read nothing from Papa's stony-faced concentration. When he had finished, he folded it up and passed it to me with what could only be called a quizzical glare.

In the letter, Harry wrote of his acquaintance with the Right Honorable Mencken Benchley, a long-standing liberal MP who was himself deaf and who had succeeded quite well in Parliament despite his difficulties. It seemed that Harry had recently come across an article Mr. Benchley had written some time ago for the London *Times* wherein he made a forceful argument for the pursuit of music as pleasure by deaf persons. In his experience, the conductivity of certain materials enabled particular sounds to be passed through the body and perceived in spite of faulty hearing. With the assistance of a pianist friend, he had developed certain rules of musical composition based on these experiments, and the result was a small repertoire of musical pieces intended for enjoyment by the deaf or hard-of-hearing.

I thought Harry showed surprising restraint, for knowing him as I did,

I would not have been surprised had he written an entire monograph on the conductivity of sound.

When I had read the letter, I looked up with a bright and bemused smile and said, "This is quite like Ha—" But I caught myself just in time, for I had to constantly watch myself lest I refer to him as Harry. I began again. "This is quite like him." I folded up the letter, and with the air of one indulging a tedious bore, I said, "He's seemed to latch on to me like one of his projects. But I really can't object. He is very much like his mother. He has my happiness at heart and has been concerned about my reclusiveness."

Papa was writing on his slate as I spoke. He passed it to me, and I read, *You intend to allow him to fiddle with your deafness as though it were some machine that needs fixing?*

"Well, this kind of thing is very much in Lord Ormelie's character. He's an ingenious sort of gentleman and has an engineering sort of mind. If he wishes to knock holes in my wall of silence and build little windows onto the world so that I may enjoy this life more fully, then I am deeply grateful to such a man for his kindness and attention."

Papa only shook his head and sawed away quite savagely at his grilled chops. "I don't like it."

"He is acting out of friendship, because he takes an interest in my well-being."

"But why should he? What are you to him? What am I to him?"

"I am his friend."

"I fear he's trifling with your affections, which is most dishonorable. I won't have you setting your hopes on something so unattainable as this."

"Lord Ormelie is not courting me. He will soon announce his engagement to an American heiress. He has promised me nothing other than a little enjoyment of music. I shall accept his offer. It would be rude to act otherwise."

He was silent while he finished his chops, and I laid the letter down beside my plate and nibbled at my toast. Finally, he laid down his napkin and rose from the table.

Looking down at me, he said, "Your Aunt Lavinia will chaperone you."

"Of course she will," I said, turning a beaming smile on her. She wasn't listening to us anymore. She had risen and was standing at the sideboard, dropping a big dollop of marmalade onto her plate. From the beatific smile on her face, I imagined she was probably humming.

That morning, I rapidly penned a reply to Harry's letter and sent it off directly to the post:

My dearest Harry,
I am hoping Papa will write you to accept your generous offer, but if he does not, then you must be satisfied with this letter as a reply. He is all in a flutter because he does not like me mixing with the upper ranks of society. He's very old-fashioned in that way. But he finally gave his consent. I will wait for you next Wednesday. I am most eager to see what you have planned for my enjoyment.

Fondly,
Veda

Frankly, I didn't care what he had planned. I would have been content to sit on a park bench with him—in the rain or snow, or beneath a sweltering sun, it made no matter. The Right Honorable Mr. Benchley and his wife lived in Bayswater, and Harry came to collect us. On the ride there, he was ever so charming to Aunt Lavinia. Although it was difficult for me to follow their dialogue in the shadows of the coach, I surmised a good deal from the expressions on their faces. It was the first time they had really spoken together, and I was struck by the kind attention he showed her. She became quite animated, even handsome, in the light of his flattery. Again I was able to witness, this time at very close range, that considerable charm of manner and ability to fascinate that Harry possessed in abundance. It seemed neither false, nor learned, nor motivated by a desire to impress, but rather like a pure force springing from his very nature. He exuded an absolute self-confidence typical of the aristocracy, yet this assumption of moral and social superiority did not prevent him from talking naturally with those who were not of his rank.

It was a very relaxed evening, and I was intrigued to see how Mr. and Mrs. Benchley freely used gestures to communicate. Although Lucy and I used signs as often as possible, Papa had always resisted this, and our domestic life was somewhat strained because of it. The event was not a typical musical *soirée* but rather like a lesson in which I was taught how to relate to a musical instrument in a completely new manner.

To my relief, there were no drums, for I find them rather startling and grating on my nerves, nor were there any wind instruments, for I was told by Mr. Tuckner, the pianist, that they were undistinguishable. There was only a trio of violin, cello, and piano. Mr. Tuckner bade me stand behind the piano, a beautiful black lacquered Pleyel from France, and press my nails to the wood inside, near where the hammers strike the strings, while he played a series of scales. To my astonishment, I found that when he played the high notes I was conscious of an agreeable sensation in my fingertips. I was terribly self-conscious at first, but then Mr. Benchley came up and stood beside me and showed me how I might better experience the sound by laying my head on the piano. His easygoing and avuncular manner put me at ease, and I gave up my inhibitions and did as he instructed.

Mr. Tuckner began to play, and I soon forgot the others present in the room. With my eyes closed and my hands and face pressed against the wood, I began to feel the music enter me and take up residence inside my body. There, my imagination took hold of it, dressed it in rich color, and painted it with emotions as well. When Mr. Tuckner had finished his last piece, I lifted my head from the piano and found my cheeks were wet with tears. Mr. Benchley, who had remained beside me throughout the experiment, seemed quite touched to see me so moved, and he artfully shielded me from the view of our little party while I dabbed at my eyes with my handkerchief.

The evening, although extraordinary, was a drain on my nerves, all the more so because every time I glanced at Harry, it seemed that his eyes were either on me or seeking me out, and the reserve imposed upon both of us only heightened the intensity of our emotions. Every time I caught his eye or stood near him or exchanged a few words with him, I felt a current flowing between us. Since I did not have the pleasure of hearing his voice or his laughter from across the room, I relied on my eyes, and I fear they were constantly searching for him. I had no interest in the general exchange of polite conversation. When I could not see Harry, it was as if he had disappeared from my life altogether. On one occasion, when I could not find him, I felt my stomach tie itself in knots, and I tried desperately to avoid showing my panic until he reappeared.

It was not until the ride home, when Aunt Lavinia fell asleep in the corner, that we had a chance for an intimate moment together. Harry sought out my hand and pressed it with all the ardor I felt, but I could not bear to let him drive away with only that brief touch to satisfy my need for him. Before we arrived at my door, I took out the mechanical pencil he had given me and wrote a note on the back of my calling card asking him to return in the carriage to Savile Row in about fifteen minutes' time, and to wait for me, and I would come to him.

After he had delivered us to the door and we had said good night, I went up to my room and shed my low-necked evening dress and dreadful crinoline, changing into a warm skirt and bodice. I waited at the window until I saw his carriage appear. I drew on my cloak and slipped down the dark stairs.

I did not yet feel the desperation of our situation. That we were falling deeply in love was clear to both of us, and there was no room in my thoughts for anything else. For the time being, all that mattered was finding a way to be together.

That night, as I closed the front door behind me and slipped down the stairs to where the footman waited to hand me into the carriage, I was so nervous I feared my knees would buckle beneath me. I slid onto the seat next to him, arranged my skirts, and slid back the hood of my cloak. There was but a moment's hesitation before he took my face between his hands and kissed me. The coach pulled away. I didn't know where we were going and I didn't ask. In the darkness, behind my wall of silence, Harry's touch was my only link with the world. His kisses were my world.

HARRY LEFT FOR NEWMARKET THE next day to see to his horses, after which he would return to Blackroak until racing season began in earnest. I didn't expect to see him again for many weeks, even months, and I threw myself back into my work with a missionary zeal. Grenfell's was always my refuge from any troubling emotion, and as I took up my place behind Old Crawley and whipped out my neat little stitches, all my fears and worries lifted from my shoulders. All the emptiness of Harry's departure was filled with the pleasure of my work. It was rumored that no tailor at Grenfell's could match my speed and artistry, and I felt I had indeed earned my reputation. It was only when I exited those doors and returned home to my domestic life that I began to yearn for something I feared I would never have.

Within a week, Harry was back in London and surprised me by calling one morning when I was next door in the showroom, reviewing a substantial order I had taken the previous day from the Marquis of Harrington—a shooting jacket of green Angola, a peacoat of grey Witney wool bound with black braid and lined with a checked linen, and two fine silk lounging coats. It had been a refreshing morning. I had been thoroughly absorbed by my work, for the Marquis was a man of considerable taste and influence, and this was the second order he had placed with me this year. His repeated custom only confirmed the change in attitude that we were beginning to see. Once gentlemen were in my hands and working with me, they were more concerned with their own appearance and the way I left them feeling about themselves than with my own unconventional circumstances.

When my apprentice slipped Lucy's note into my hand, I felt as if I had been rudely booted out of my peaceful refuge. The last time Harry called, I was determined to turn the heavens upside down to hide my tailoring activities from him, but I was beginning to feel differently now. I couldn't wait to see him, but at the same time I no longer wanted to hide this part of my life from him. I remembered only too clearly the letter I had written him, urging him to see only one side of my nature, the side that would be most agreeable to him and most easily digested. He had come to imagine my life in his absence as that of any young genteel lady, days filled with social calls, shopping, and riding. Nowhere in that mental portrait was the person who spent her days in the showroom of Grenfell's. Perhaps he believed that she had been purged, that she no longer existed. But she did. And I thought it was time they should meet.

Fortunately, I was able to drop what I was doing at that moment and race home through the kitchen area downstairs. Lucy was waiting in my room, a steeled look on her face, with my corset in one hand and my crinoline on the floor ready for me to step into it, but I fell into a chair, looked up at her, and said I would receive him as I was.

She nodded. "Yes, Miss," but I could tell she thought I was mad. "Your hair, Miss? Shall I give you a few curls?" she gestured.

I rose and went to the looking glass in the corner of my room, tilting it to reflect my image. Whenever I wore gentlemen's garb, I wrestled my corkscrew curls into a low chignon. My desire was always to create an illusion of a gentleman. I never *ever* wished to give the impression that I sympathized with those caricatures of women in drab tweeds and spectacles who smoked and live in chambers like a man.

"I shall wear it down, Lucy."

"Down, Miss?"

"Yes," I said, pulling out the pins as I spoke. "I think I shall like the effect."

I studied my reflection while she hurriedly undid my hair and brushed out the mass of curls. The effect was good; it reminded me of the women in the Pre-Raphaelite paintings. If I was going to upset Harry, I wanted to soften the blow the best I could.

"And give me a little salve for my lips," I said, gesturing to my dressing table.

As a final touch, I attached the mechanical pencil with an albert to my waistcoat pocket. Lucy took a clothes brush to the back of my coat, and I was ready.

Even under the close and sometimes rude scrutiny of the men and women of great wealth and rank with whom I was in daily contact, I never faltered in the presentation of my person. Either by nature or observation, I had acquired Papa's languid grace of gesture and carriage. When I began to dress as a gentleman, I was obliged to rethink my gestures and movements, for a gentleman does not have the same mannerisms as a lady. The end result was something of a dandy, but without the affectations, for I wished to give up none of my feminine graces, yet needed to adopt certain postures to suit my attire. In the end, the clothing made the man, for I found it almost natural to mimic certain ways of standing or bearing while wearing a coat and trousers. It was all for the effect, and I had somehow managed to distance my personal self from the image I projected, just as a stage actor might do.

As I descended the stairs to the drawing room, I agonized over Harry's reaction. Would he laugh? Would he be revolted? Would he simply cease loving me on the spot?

If ever I was to be bold and sure of myself, this was the moment. I opened the door and entered the room to find him waiting for me on the hearth rug, hands in his pockets, and when he caught sight of me, the loving smile on his face froze instantly as though hit with a blast of arctic wind. His mouth twitched, and I'm not sure if he spoke or not. If he did, I failed to understand him. He drew his hands out of his pockets and pulled himself up in a rather formal manner, and then said something about arriving in town from Newmarket last night, and an appointment with his solicitor, and returning to Blackroak. He seemed quite embarrassed and ill at ease, as though he had caught me in a state of undress.

And then, shaking his head, he finally blurted out, "I find it very difficult to look at you dressed like that. It's very queer and makes me uneasy."

Without speaking, I crossed the room and pulled the bell rope to call Lucy, for we had no slates, and I had completely forgotten our Talking Book.

I turned and cast a confident smile at him, for I refused to be cowed by his discomfort. "I know this is frightfully awkward, my darling. But had I taken time to change, I fear you might have left, and I would have rather died than miss seeing you again. I always think it's the last time, you see. I never know if I'll have another chance."

He grew quiet, then, and some of the warmth returned to his eyes.

"I'm afraid I don't know how to greet you."

"And how would you have greeted me otherwise?"

"With a kiss."

"Harry, it's only clothes."

"It changes you."

"I'm a fashion plate. That's all."

"It makes me quite uneasy."

Lucy entered then, and I asked her to bring down my Talking Book. When she had gone, I turned back to Harry. He was staring at me with the confused and wounded air of a man who has been the brunt of a terrible hoax.

I said, "Harry, I am a tailor out of passion, not necessity. You must know I would never be content living the life of an ordinary woman. And I am single-minded to a fault."

"But you go too far. This kind of unconventional behavior is a slur on your reputation."

"Oh, I've had quite enough warnings about my behavior from gentlemen who say they have my interests and reputation at heart. Really, I cannot suffer men who preach only penance in this world and terror in the next. I've had enough of it. Really, I have."

He knew very well of whom I spoke. I immediately regretted my sharp reply. I felt the blood rush to my face.

Harry approached and stood near me, and I dared lift my eyes to meet his.

"Veda—"

"That was unkind of me," I interrupted. "I spoke harshly of a dear friend. I did not intend to condemn him so."

"You looked quite like a lady just then," he smiled gently.

"I am the same."

"You must give this up."

"My work?"

"You say you don't need it."

"My spirit needs it."

"I can't have it, Veda. I can't. I cannot continue my friendship with you if you persist in this activity."

"I have been dressing like this in the showroom for a year and working with my father for longer than that. And only now does it offend you?"

"But everything has changed since then."

"Nothing has changed. You have decided that we shall never be husband and wife, nor would I ever consent to any lesser arrangement with a man, so what hold do you pretend to exert over me? You have my heart. What else do you want?"

"You are a mule-headed woman."

"You wish to usurp my sovereignty. And as an unmarried woman, that is all I have. Until I am betrothed, and the ink is dried on the lines, I will submit to no man's authority."

At that moment, Lucy finally arrived with the chest and set it on the table. I pulled the key from beneath my collar, unlocked the chest, and removed the book.

"You see?" I said, as I sat down at the table and brushed my hair back from my face, "what a treasure you are to me? I keep your very words under lock and key." Then I dipped my pen in the ink and wrote on a fresh page, *Harry, I don't court your disapproval. But I cannot relinquish the only thing in my life that offers promise and assurance. You will marry another. And where shall I be?*

He stood over my shoulder, reading the words as I penned them, and then he sat down beside me and replied in writing:

You would have no lack of suitors if you had been properly introduced into society.

I replied: *Into what society? Is there a special society for deaf daughters of tradesmen? Oh, but did I forget to mention, it must be a genteel society, with proper education and suitable wealth, for she has all those things. Surely, there are those who would be tempted to take her for her inheritance alone, with no affection for her, no sentiment whatsoever, but even these dishonorable men would be deterred by the limits such a union would impose on their society, for what gentleman would take a woman as his wife and sit her at the head of his table knowing that even a simple dinner party would be beyond her capabilities?*

That is not true. You exclude yourself more often than others exclude you.

I do so out of courtesy.

Then let <u>others</u> prove themselves courteous or discourteous, and let the cards fall where they will. Let friends prove themselves and their moral courage by the way they face your affliction. Let your husband protect you from false friends. By his authority, let him demand that you be included or suffer exclusion themselves.

He wrote with such passion that ink flew from his pen. Tears welled up in his eyes, and he finally threw down the pen, rose, and stormed the room with his hands clutched behind his back so that you would have thought him a prisoner in handcuffs, which is perhaps just how he felt.

"And where am I to find this husband, Harry?" I said, turning in the chair. "This fine, courageous gentleman with such a generous spirit. Where am I to find him?"

He swung around and stormed back to me with a face full of emotion, jabbing at his chest with a finger, mouthing the words, "*I* would be that man if I could. If I could."

I don't think I completely trusted Harry until that moment. Suddenly, all my reservations were swept away, and I saw straight into his heart. I rose and went to him, and without a second's hesitation I slipped my hands around the back of his neck and drew him into a kiss. He forgot all about what I was wearing.

And from that moment on, somewhere in the back of my mind where thoughts lie waiting to be shaped by words we are not yet ready to utter, I knew we would one day be lovers.

Chapter Twenty

FOR A TIME THAT SUMMER, I WAS FOOLISH ENOUGH TO BELIEVE IN the impossible. I never really understood the difficulties Harry was facing, for he wrote or spoke about his situation only in the broadest of terms. His love for me seemed inextricably entangled with emotions about his father, and there were times when his thwarted will expressed itself in a dark and brooding resentment of patriarchal authority. I don't believe Harry ever told his father about me, and if he did, he must have portrayed me in a most general sense. He always seemed to be trying to protect me, as if there might be some danger in revealing my identity. He thought I was in particular need of protection from myself. He had witnessed the risks I was willing to take ever since the night I had slipped out of the house and stepped into his waiting carriage. It was an incident he did not want repeated. He often reminded me of how strongly he had disapproved of my rash behavior and swore that he had only come back to meet me for fear of leaving me stranded in the lane at midnight. I then reminded him how ardently he had welcomed me and how quickly his protests had faded once I was in his arms.

He was still very vague about the business with Miss Erskine. I never pressed him on the subject, neither in writing nor in person, but I sensed his anxiety and knew the problem had not entirely disappeared, although I felt it was in abeyance. That summer Harry took a bachelor's sitting room in St. James, near his club and near me. I suspect it was done for reasons of economy as well as convenience, for I learned from Captain Naylor while pinning up the shoulder on his court dress uniform that Ellesmere House had been rented out for the Season and might well be sold, as the Earl rarely came down to London since the death of his wife. That summer, Harry and I began to exchange correspondence exclusively through Scrimshire. We had grown too open in the expression of our sentiments to risk my father's intercepting one of our missives. Every Tuesday and Friday I sent Lucy around to White's Club to leave my letters and pick up any addressed to me. There was always at least one, sometimes more. She brought them back and tucked them away in the inside pocket of Dolly's jacket—Adolphus being the code name for the clothed mannequin in my room—where I then retrieved them after dinner.

By all accounts, London was having a brilliant Season. Although the Queen was still deep in mourning—many believed she would remain there until the end of her days—London society was beginning to shed its heavy pall of sobriety. After the young Prince of Wales's wedding to his pretty Danish princess and his settling in at Marlborough House, our fun-loving aristocracy found itself once again in royal favor. Unlike his dowdy parents, who had nothing but harsh words and a cold snub for the fashionable set and their social calendar of glittering events, Bertie was proving to be the patron saint of pleasure pursuits. Now, if the Duchess-of-This or Marchioness-of-That hosted a dinner, you could be assured the Prince would be there.

Royal favor always creates a stir, and the change was immediately apparent in our custom. We noticed it as soon as Easter week had passed. The increase in orders was so significant that Papa even began including Bertie in his thanks every evening at the dinner table. Papa always thought that if the Queen had given her son any real political authority within the realm, he might have turned his prodigious energies toward more sober pursuits. But I am inclined to disagree; I think it was in Bertie's nature to appreciate beautiful things and beautiful people. Grandpa thought it a good and necessary change. He remembered the days before Victoria, when riders on Rotten Row were as pleasing to the eye as the colorful sweets in a confectioner's shop. Then the young Queen married her earnest and hardworking German, and soon the masses were copying Albert. Fashion sank into sobriety and restraint, and no gentleman would be caught dead clothed in anything except browns, blacks, and blues; even a red carnation in the lapel would be scorned as frivolous.

Well, that Season we were still in browns, blacks, and blues, but there was good reason to refurbish one's wardrobe, even if the palette remained the same. Everyone knew how the Prince appreciated fine things.

Papa said he could not recall a Season as busy as that one. Our custom nearly doubled in June, and the number of new clients referred to me personally did the same. I found myself frequently called to London residences for fittings, taking with me my own staff, along with our books of swatches, samples, and trimmings. It was an unwritten rule that I never traveled beyond London. When I received a letter from Sir Herbert Nibbetson, Bisham Park, Greenwich, requesting my services to measure and make a number of garments for him at his country house, Papa wrote back that my services were reserved exclusively for London clients, but that Papa himself could attend to the gentleman. Instead, Sir Herbert replied that he would be in London in a fortnight and requested an appointment for a fitting at that time, with me. Papa never let on, but I know it must have wounded his pride.

When at work, I had little time to pine over Harry. I was frequently so exhausted at the end of the day that I could do no more than scribble a few short lines to him before falling into bed. At least now he was aware of my activities, although I rarely spoke of my work and did so with restraint and in a general vein. I knew Harry did not want to think of me spending my day hunched over my knee, whipping stitches into the coral silk lining of Lord Roeberry's waistcoat. Besides, it was a rule of trade never to discuss a living client—although we certainly liked to boast about the deceased ones.

Even as near as he was, it was terribly difficult for us to find a clandestine arrangement that suited Harry's strict ideas of propriety and fit into my working day. I did whatever I could to see him; I would reschedule a client or work all night in order to finish a baste before a fitting. When we did meet, it seemed like the encounter was always too brief, and inevitably something or someone barged in to shatter the intimacy for which we so desperately yearned. I found myself attending flower shows and gallery events, even lectures given by some authority on something I knew nothing about beforehand—nor after. To stand in a sweltering hot hall amidst a throng of rapt listeners from the London Literary Society, walled in behind my silence, and pretend to be ever so keen on what was being said by some portly old codger up on a dais was an exercise in tedium. Watching a bobbing grey mustache was as exciting as watching an egg boil.

The most excruciating part was waiting for Harry. Harry seemed to change the very nature of time; either he weighted it down like stones, or gave it wings and set it in flight. I would search the crowd for Harry's face, then, having found it, I would will him to find me. From the moment he would see me to the time it took for him to wend his way through the crowd to my side seemed an eternity to my pounding heart. Sometimes, knowing he was approaching, I would grow faint, and I would close my eyes and fan myself violently. I would be conscious only of a black silence and the quivering of my bosom and the insufferable heat. Lucy would step back, and I would know he was there. He would surreptitiously slip his hand into mine, and my heart, once faint, would beat wild with joy. One time, I felt him fumbling with the button at my wrist. As he peeled the white glove from my hand and pressed his own bare hand against mine, it was as if he was undressing me there in a crowded hall. My entire awareness seemed to be centered in the bare, moist palm of my hand.

We were able to ride in the Park together that summer, very early in the morning when there was little risk of running into any of his fashionable friends. These were not Harry's best moments. He was not accustomed to early hours, and he often came directly from his club after a night of cards, having had no more sleep than what he was able to catch during the carriage ride. While the groom was saddling Fellow and First, I would lure him back to an empty stall for a kiss. He made a pretense of disapproval, but he was generally too tired to resist. I rather liked him in the mornings—disheveled and rough around the edges, with a night's growth of beard on his chin. He was terribly virile and always very gentle. The night had dulled his brilliance and energy, and there was a mellow quality to his tenderness. Despite these distractions, we still made it onto the trails just after dawn, when the mist still hung in the air and there was the sweet scent of dew on the green. It was heavenly. We bothered little with conversation on those mornings and rejoiced in each other's company without thought for the morrow.

It was an inevitable result of working with gentlemen that I should become more at ease around them. This and the necessity of always observing and meeting a man's gaze directly taught me habits I never would have learned had I led the normal, conventional life of a young hearing woman. Harry told me that in this respect I resembled the American women he had met, that I had seemed to acquire a rather refreshing boldness, although he knew quite well that I behaved as such out of necessity and not out of coarseness. I took this as a compliment, although it pained me to think that he was comparing me, however favorably, to Miss Erskine and her lot.

As July drew to a finish, a sense of foreboding closed in on me. I shared this sentiment with Harry in a letter.

My darling,
It is late at night, and I cannot sleep unless I pen my thoughts to you.

I am dreading the end of the Season. I fear it will be the last of our time together. You have spoken little of your dilemma, and yet I know it has not been resolved to your satisfaction. I notice everything, Harry, and the human countenance often reveals more than words. In the infinitesimal subtleties of your gestures and expressions, I read perhaps more than you intend for me to know.

We must find a way to meet in August. I shall be in Burford around the eighth and remain at least a fortnight, if not more. Surely you can manage a few days at Longmeade.

During that time, I should like for you to make arrangements for us to travel together. I have traveled very little since my deafness, and I should like to see the sea again, with you. I beg you to indulge me just this once.

Your Veda

Lucy took the letter around to his club just after breakfast, and that evening I found a reply in Dolly's coat pocket. My hands trembled as I tore open the seal.

My dearest,
How your letter troubled me. I think sometimes I must be the guardian of your virtue, since you take such little care for it.

I cannot possibly obey your wishes, as much as my heart is inclined to do so. Fortunately for both of us, my head still rules in these matters. I shall see you at Burford, but we shall meet in circumstances that will not cast doubt on your reputation.

I have not time to write more, but my thoughts are ever with you.

Harry

All throughout the day, I thought about his reply. My moods swung dramatically, from pain and disappointment to anger at his refusal. Only occasionally did sentiments plod along the rather dull plains of reason, and they never remained there for long. I toyed with the idea of calling on him, and by the time we had finished dinner and everyone was in bed, I had made the decision to do so. I refused to remain locked away, denied the freedom to walk out the door and call on whom I wished simply for the sake of womanly virtue. Woman be damned. I'd go as a man.

Unfortunately, there was my hair to contend with. It has always been a bane to me, tamed with enormous difficulty. Poor Lucy has slaved for hours ironing out my corkscrew curls only to see them spring up as soon as I walk out into the damp air. Even a hat did not conceal the full chignon at the nape of my neck, but it would have to do. I slipped next door to the showroom and borrowed one from a display case.

I took a cab from Regent Street directly to his lodgings in Pickering Place, a small courtyard of eighteenth-century houses accessed through a tiny alleyway from St. James Street, and sent the footman around to White's Club with a note that his friend Adolphus was waiting for him at his lodgings.

I waited on the pavement beneath a streetlamp, and when I caught a glimpse of him crossing the square, I could tell by his angry stride that he was vexed. He greeted me coolly and invited me into his sitting room. While the parlor maid lighted the candles, Harry poured two glasses of brandy and offered one to me. I shook my head, but he insisted, so I took it anyway. He did not go so far as to offer me a cigarette, although he lit one for himself. I could see he was trying to teach me a lesson. After he had dismissed the maid, he stood staring into the cold fireplace, twirling his brandy and puffing on his cigarette. I was too wounded by his cold reception to speak up on my behalf, to explain that I was tired of the deception, of waiting for him to announce his intentions, of the duplicity of our lives. The longer I stood there, holding his wretched brandy, the less inclined I was to stay. Soon the room began to fill with smoke.

"Please," I coughed, setting down my glass and fanning my face. "You've made your point."

With the manner of a man disgusted with himself, he tossed the cigarette onto the cold ashes in the fireplace, then snatched the glass he had poured for me and dashed the brandy onto the smoldering cigarette. He filled the glass with water from a tumbler and offered it to me, mumbling his apologies.

I drank the water and set the glass on the table beside me. I dared not raise my eyes to him for fear of breaking into angry tears. How could I possibly explain to him all the confusion and fear in my heart, and how this had brought me to his doorstep at one o'clock at night?

With as much pride and dignity as I could muster, I said, "You will oblige me by seeing me to a cab. I should not like to venture alone through the club district at night."

I turned away to search for my hat. The parlor maid had taken it from me upon my arrival, and I had not paid attention. I found it on a chair near the door. As I reached for it, I felt his hand on my arm. He gently turned me by the shoulders to face him. He removed my hat from my hand, set it on the chair, and tilted my face to read his lips.

"It is very difficult to quarrel with you if you won't look at me."

"I did not come to quarrel. I cannot bear to quarrel with you. But you have treated me with disrespect, and I did not deserve as much."

"You have every right to scold me. I beg your pardon. I have no wish to cause you pain."

Slowly, as though it were beyond his powers to resist, he lowered his face to mine and kissed me.

"This is all I came for," I whispered. "Only a kiss. I only wanted a kiss."

"I know."

After a moment, he said, "There, is that better?"

"Much," I murmured.

"I confess, your note arrived at an awkward moment."

"You were playing cards."

"Indeed. I was losing."

"I don't trust you, Harry. I'm afraid that one day you will disappear, and it will all be over. Just like that. Your letter was so short. And I always fear each letter will be the last."

He released me and turned toward his desk. Opening a drawer, he drew out a letter and presented it to me. He said, "I began this after lunch, but I'd not yet finished. I would have sent it tomorrow."

I stood by the mantle and read it by candlelight:

My darling,
I was too abrupt in my reply, but I was pressed for time. Perhaps I should have left you in silence another day rather than send such a curt and censorious letter.
    If there were only ourselves to consider, I would disregard every rule that

keeps us apart. But your reputation affects others as well as yourself, and we cannot do anything that would embarrass your father or your family and ruin all that you have built. It may come as a surprise to you, but I do have a good deal of respect for honorable men of trade, and I know your father to be such a man. There are swindlers and cads in every profession, but it is men like your father, a man of sterling character, who lifts his profession to a superior level and sets a standard for all others to meet.

My darling, I am not without my spies, and I know you have succeeded, quite miraculously, to establish a professional reputation without damage to your personal one. If you knew how much talk comes to my ears! If I have led you to believe that I am ignorant of this gossip, it is because I do not wish the matter to come between us. With the passage of time, I have gained a better understanding of this unquestionably eccentric side to your nature, and my patience and silence have proven justified. Although there are always a few cads who will cast a salacious eye on every situation that appears just slightly amiss, those exceptions apart, you are spoken of in near reverential terms. How many times have I listened to an account of a client's first glimpse of you in your showroom and struggled to silence my pride. They say that the impression one has of your person is always stunning, that you are acclaimed as one of the most exquisitely dressed "gentlemen" they have ever seen. There was a time when I avoided all mention of you so as not to hear your name slandered, but now there is little said about you which elicits anything other than fierce pride in my stubborn heart. Were I not in love with you, I would have come to you long ago to clothe me.

It is time to speak of that which has hovered over our heads all summer long, and that is my pending engagement to Miss Erskine. If I had known that I would feel as I do now about you, my darling, I never would have allowed the marriage negotiations to progress as far as they have. But there is hope. There are legitimate concerns that still need to be addressed, and it appears I may have legal grounds upon which to retract my proposal.

It is my father who is overseeing the entire matter. He takes an unseemly interest in it all. He has always been in his own world at Blackroak and spent as little time as possible in London, coming down only for the opening of Parliament or an important vote in the House of Lords, and then returning to Yorkshire. He is very much a country gentleman and dislikes the city intensely. Blackroak is in a remote corner of England, and one is inclined to pay little heed to what goes on outside the county. But it is more than just an ancestral home to him. The walls themselves seem to have something of his spirit in them, and he in turn carries its essence in his blood. How a man of flesh and a house of stone can resemble each other in substance is a mystery to me, but it's a mystery acknowledged by everyone who has set foot there.

I turned over the page, but there was no more. I could hardly believe what I had just read. It was the first time Harry had ever spoken so openly about my family and our connections to trade, and I had never dreamed he felt the way he did. I began to think that he understood me far better than I had imagined.

I looked up and asked, "You didn't finish it."

"No."

"What more did you wish to say?"

He was silent for a long while, searching my eyes, and I could not read him. Finally, he took the letter from my hand, laid it on the mantle, and took me in his arms. Gently, he kissed my forehead and my cheeks. Then he said, "I will do as you wish. I will take you away, to the sea. We shall go to Whitby. Far up on the coast. You are not likely to meet anyone there you know. But I shall set one condition, and you must agree to it."

"What is that?" I asked.

"Do you promise?"

"Whatever it is, I promise."

"I wish you to go there as my wife."

I feared I had misunderstood him. The words catching in my throat, I asked, "You wish me to pretend to be your wife?"

"No, Veda. I do not wish to pretend. I want you to be my wife, in this world, and forever." He smiled at my puzzled face and kissed my cheek again. "We cannot live outside the rules, and you are far too heedless of your reputation. You once told me that I had no authority over you, as I was neither husband nor brother nor father. For your own sake, my dear, someone must take you on."

Chapter Twenty-one

As Harry stated in a letter he wrote to me later that week, *What we are doing, we do to save our souls, although it may well wreck our lives.* That resolve never faltered, despite the cares and fears that at times nearly overwhelmed us.

It had to be done in secret if it were to be done at all. To announce our intentions would literally bring down the temple—not only Harry's but mine as well. Balducci had never threatened the structure of work and family that gave my life its stability. A union with Harry would take me away from the only life I had ever known as both a hearing child and a deaf woman, and there was no challenge so great as the one that lay before me.

I lay in bed at night contemplating the wreckage that would ensue: There were my clients upon whose custom Grenfell's now so heavily depended, and my departure might very well lose them for the firm altogether; there was the specter of idle hands longing to cut and sew and fashion beautiful garments; there was the loss of my family of tailors, the men who had relinquished their prejudices to make a place for me in their world. And then there was Papa. My imagination had never painted a picture without Papa in it. I think he had grown to believe I would be forever beside him at the breakfast table in the morning and the dinner table at night, scribbling on my slate and making my gestures and strange sounds to which he had never quite grown accustomed.

During those last weeks in July, I learned a great deal about Harry's circumstances. He made it a point to be forthcoming about everything concerning his financial situation and the business with the American. It was finally established by his lawyer that there were legal grounds to justify withdrawing his marriage proposal, but Harry's father was reluctant to have him do so. Apart from the complexities of ridding himself of an unwanted fiancée, I knew that Harry was taking enormous risks in marrying me. Although he doubted he would be disinherited, there was always that risk. Harry assured me that even then, we would not be penniless. He had a separate income from his mother's estate, which would allow us to live quite comfortably. Once all had quieted down, I knew Papa would settle a generous sum on me.

Harry and I had both lost our mothers, and I had lost Reggie and Harry had lost Aurelia, and I believe Harry felt much the same kind of obligation toward his father as I did mine; it translated into a powerful sentiment that went beyond mere filial duty and respect. That we shared these tragic circumstances helped us understand each other and respect the difficulties each of us faced leading up to our marriage.

During those weeks, I think I may have shed more tears of sadness than joy. Secrecy meant that I must forego all the traditional announcements and parties. There would be no festive dinners at which the young lovers were toasted with champagne and cheers; there were no gifts for a new home, and not even time to have a wedding dress made. Instead, I reworked the lovely white tulle I had worn to the only ball I had ever attended, when Harry had danced with me and kissed me for the first time. I was determined that Harry have a new waistcoat for the ceremony, and I sat up at night working on it by candlelight, an exquisite thing of cream satin embroidered with forget-me-nots and ferns in single strands of very fine colored silk. Stitched all throughout the lining in fine gold thread were our initials, intertwined.

The end of the Season was always terribly busy for us, as all the clients wanted their orders filled before they left for their spa retreats or their country homes. I had little time to plan for what lay ahead. Harry had decided to leave for Whitby to establish residence there in order to apply for a license. We were to be married in the parish of St. Mary's by a trustworthy clergyman who had been a devoted advisor to Lady Hambledon. As our plans unfolded, the secrecy began to weigh on me quite heavily, for I had never imagined a wedding that could not be shared with my closest friends and family. I thought of all that I was giving up, and as the days passed I began to feel quite lost and alone, as if I were already cut off and set adrift with nothing to anchor me anywhere anymore. I wrote long, tearful letters to Harry. I think a lesser man might have grown quite impatient with my incertitude, but Harry was my wellspring of hope, and I drew my strength from him. Before he left, we met one more time at his lodgings to make our plans. He told me that evening that he would have married me long ago had his mother been alive. I held that thought to my heart all through the weeks of his absence. I felt her blessing to be upon us. Indeed, I felt she knew about it and was on her feet applauding with all the souls in heaven.

When Papa finally put me on the train to Oxford and kissed me good-bye, I broke down in tears and made an awful scene, which he found rather baffling as he knew how I thoroughly enjoyed my visits to Esther. I waved at him for the longest time, flapping my canary silk handkerchief from the window long after the train had left the station. Then I pulled out a book of Southey's poetry and hid behind it for most of the journey, for I was helpless to stop the tears.

Once in Burford, released from the driving pace of the sweltering workshop and the foul smells that always overwhelmed the city during the summer months, I began to breathe more easily, and my mind wandered along more pleasant shores. Sometimes I would wake in the morning, pull back the lace curtains, look out onto a scene of rustic tranquility, and remind myself that a few days hence I would be the wife of a viscount.

I had visited Esther earlier that year, just before Easter, and taken her all the new undergarments I had made for her, and the pretty blankets I had trimmed in ribbon for baby Ellen. It had been a brief and rewarding visit but difficult for me. Esther had eyes only for her baby. I thought Ned looked more glum than happy, and I wondered if it was always like this.

Little had changed since that visit, except that now she was having a good deal of trouble managing her maidservants. The nurse had given her notice, so Esther had taken to sleeping upstairs in the nursery with the baby, which had upset Ned. The chill between them was particularly noticeable to my intuitive eye. Conversing with me is always a difficult task, even for those closest to me, and Esther had patience for little more than exchanges of the most practical sort. Although I was happy to be away from London, I felt lonely in Burford. I spent a good deal of time walking along the riverbank and writing to Harry.

Harry and I had agreed that Esther and Ned should be informed only by letter after my departure, but I longed to confide in someone. There were many questions and fears weighing on me, things of an intimate nature about men and women that I needed to understand. Not only had I been denied the education a mother passes down to her daughter, I had not even the opportunity of overhearing conversations between Cook and the housekeeper, or the gossip of maids, as most young women do. I was going into marriage without the foggiest notion of what was expected of a young wife. I did recall pronouncements by Aunt Lavinia about "enduring" the marital obligations and submitting to the husband's baser needs, but I never thought of it in those terms. My trust in Harry was irrevocable and absolute. I knew him to be the most tender and caring of men, and I suspected that love-making might hold delicious surprises that Aunt Lavinia had never imagined. My greatest fear was that I would not know how to please him. If anyone were going to teach me that, it would have to be Harry himself.

The morning I left for Oxford, I felt I had endured a demanding trial of secrecy. I had been forced to rely upon my own will and determination to see me through and felt myself stronger for it. I already belonged to Harry, in the most absolute and definitive way.

The coach passed through Burford very early. Knowing Esther's nights were disturbed by the baby, I had insisted we say good-bye the night before. Ned came down to see me off, and while we stood in front of the coaching inn watching the groom load my trunks, I pressed my letter into his hand.

"What's this?" he asked with a worried frown.

"My dear Ned, there are things written there that I longed to share with you, but could not do so until now. I do wish circumstances had been different."

He turned it over to break the seal, but I stopped him.

"Wait until Esther can read it with you. I hope you will both be happy for us."

I kissed him warmly on the cheek and stepped up into the coach. When I had settled in with the other passengers and smoothed down my skirts, I turned to the window. He was standing there wearing a confused look, glancing at the sealed envelope and back at me, and all of a sudden he seemed to understand. His eyes lightened and his face split wide with a grin.

Pointing to the letter, he mouthed, "Harry and you?"

I nodded, beaming through the window. He looked ever so pleased, and I thought he might jump for joy right there in the middle of the dusty street. As the coach pulled away, he mouthed the words, "Good luck," and jubilantly waved the letter in the air. I nearly broke into tears, so relieved was I to think that someone, ever so briefly, shared my joy.

On the long, sweltering ride to Oxford, I was seated opposite a tooth-less old farmer's wife in a tattered bonnet, with two young farm laborers beside me. Someone had brought the smell of farmyard dung along with them, although it wasn't quite clear who. I was quite miserable. I was ter-rified that Harry would not be at Oxford to meet me, having convinced myself that something had happened to thwart our wedding, that his wicked father had discovered our plans and locked his son away in some dark tower in Blackroak. I didn't know my imagination was capable of such silliness. I was so weakened from the heat and nerves that when we arrived at the Oxford station I could barely stand. My trunks were un-loaded onto the platform and placed at my feet. I sat down on one of them, loosened the ribbons of my bonnet, and rested there fanning my-self, praying for Harry to find me before I fainted.

And he did. I looked up to see him coming toward me along the plat-form, and the sight of his familiar figure striding confidently through the crowd, so elegantly attired, with his well-blocked hat and gold-knobbed walking stick, and the cravat tied just a little carelessly as if to say that per-fection was beneath him, all this swept me out of my cares and into the or-bit of his world. I was but a pale moon beside his brilliance, compelled into sweet submission by love.

My anxieties must have been written on my countenance, for his smile faded to alarm.

"Come, my dear," he said and bade me to lean on him while he gave in-structions to a porter to handle my bags. He escorted me into the tea room to a quiet table in the corner and ordered tea and sandwiches. I pressed a handkerchief to my throat and neck, and he watched me with eyes full of tender concern.

"I was very worried," he said, reaching for my hand. "I don't like you to travel alone."

"I am quite all right now," I said. I knew he had come from Whitby by train the previous day and spent the night in Oxford in order to accom-pany me back. "You must be tired, my darling. You've had such a long journey yourself. And now you must endure another."

"It makes no difference, now that I'm with you."

"I am in such a state."

"I knew you would be."

"I was afraid something would keep you away."

"Nothing could keep me away from you."

"How long is the journey to Whitby?"

"Almost five hours to York. Then we change trains. We change again at Pickering. We won't arrive until this evening."

The waitress brought our tea, and I tried to pour, but my hand was trembling so that I could not. He bade me set the pot down.

"All is arranged," he said as he poured my tea. "We have separate rooms for tonight, and we shall be wed in the parish church of St. Mary's in the morning."

"Early, I hope."

"You will need time to dress. I can't imagine you dressing hastily on your wedding day, my dear."

"I have always been an early riser. Tomorrow will be no exception."

He appeared to be restraining a smile, as though he were fighting to hold back certain pleasant but unmentionable thoughts. Finally, he said, "Well, I hope there will be many exceptions after tomorrow."

"Harry!" I scolded. I could feel a blush rising to my ears, but his naughty humor put me at ease and made me smile. I took a deep breath and sipped my tea.

"I've engaged a maidservant for you. I hope she'll be suitable."

"I'm sure she'll be perfectly acceptable."

"I shall take care of you, Veda. From this moment on. You need never worry about your welfare again."

His words so overwhelmed me that I had to lower my eyes, something I am always reluctant to do because it draws an immediate barrier between me and the other, but I set down my tea and slid my hand over the table to his. When I dared raise my head, the look in Harry's eyes was so intense it caused me to look away again, down at his hand caressing mine.

"If I should faint," I said, hoping it was a whisper, "it will not be from the heat."

He tapped my hand, and I looked back up.

"Eat something, my dear," he ordered. "You need to eat. The train will be here soon."

I obeyed him and nibbled on a dry sandwich, although it was not in the least appetizing.

As before, Harry had reserved an entire first-class compartment all to ourselves. While we waited for the train to depart there was a good deal of banging on the door and heads popping in and eyeing our empty seats, for it was August and the train was full. Harry said something to the porter, and a coin or two exchanged hands. After that we were left in peace.

In the privacy of our compartment, I felt at liberty to remove my bonnet and gloves. Harry laid his coat on the rack overhead, and we settled in comfortably for the journey. Harry opened a newspaper he had purchased from a newsboy as we had boarded the train, and I took out my book of poetry. When he noticed what I was reading, he commented, "Ah, Mr. Southey. He is the one who convinced me I must marry you."

"Whatever do you mean?" I laughed. "He's been dead for years."

Harry took the book from my lap and flipped through the pages until he found what he was searching for, then returned it to me.

"There. Read that."

I looked to where his finger pointed:

> "What will not woman, gentle woman dare,
> When strong affection stirs her spirit up?"

"Well," I replied coyly, "it seems I'm not the first woman emboldened by love."

I closed the book and laid my head on his shoulder, and within minutes I was fast asleep.

FROM THE MOMENT WE STEPPED from the train and were greeted by the sharp sting of salt air, I was struck by the wildness and strangeness of the Yorkshire coast. I had known only the gentler regions of England and the mild climates of the spa towns in Germany where we had spent holidays before Mama's death. In my innocence, I had imagined Whitby to be like the resort town of Scarborough, only smaller and less fashionable. As our cab passed along the harbor and crossed over the River Esk, with the gloom of dusk settling onto the rabble of cottages on the cliffside, with the dark bay and wide maw of sea beyond, and ashen clouds bloated with rain churning the distant grey horizon, I felt I had been thrown into a chillingly foreign and inhospitable land. This was not England. This place belonged to the sea and to destinations beyond. The brigantines and luggers anchored in the harbor appeared like a web of masts and rigging caught in the grips of a spasm, each vessel swaying and bobbing in turn as the swells rocked their wooden hulls while they waited sullenly for dawn. Climbing the East Cliff, we passed a tavern where fishermen sat on a row of lobster pots smoking their pipes. They watched us drive by with a sort of quiet resentment, not even curiosity. Very few persons were out and about—a peasant woman with a loaf of bread under each arm jumped out of our path, a barefoot little boy with a bandaged ankle stared blankly at us from an open doorway. I thought it a miserable place in which to be married and spend my honeymoon.

The White Horse and Griffin was warm and inviting, and I saw that Harry had indeed arranged for everything. The staff, along with Harry's valet, were waiting for us in the dining room downstairs, and it seemed they had gone to great trouble to put on a respectable appearance. From the narrow cobble lane the establishment appeared insignificant, but my room on the third floor—which I would later share with Harry—was quite spacious and comfortable, with an adjoining sitting room overlooking the courtyard. Only later, when I noted that we never seemed to cross any guests, did I learn that Harry had taken the entire inn for the two weeks of our stay.

Weary as we were, Harry insisted we dine, and he ordered a light meal of cold meats and ale sent up. Harry had said I mustn't bother to change gowns, so I merely brushed out my hair and washed, and passed into the sitting room. During my brief absence, the room had been transformed. The candlelit table was adorned with flowers and set with fine china plate and silver chalices Harry's valet had brought from Blackroak Hall. Beside my plate rested a small silk pouch inside which I found a ruby ring set in diamonds that had belonged to his mother. I had been determined not to cry again, even from joy, but this gesture touched me more deeply than I could say. Harry was quite impressed with the waistcoat I had made. He was eager to try it on and astounded at the fit. When I slipped it off his shoulders and showed him our initials stitched into the lining, he became very quiet and stood for the longest time examining the delicate embroidery and exquisite finishing.

"I do hope you will not regret giving this up," he said, turning toward me.

"Do you mean tailoring?"

"Yes."

"But I shall still make for you."

"That you will do. But for no other."

"Unless it be our sons."

He grew very sober at this, and he hung the vest on the back of his chair and turned to face me. Taking both my hands in his, he kissed me chastely on the forehead and asked, "Do you wish to have children right away?"

It was a question I had never dreamed he would ask me. "I didn't know I had a choice," I answered.

"There are things I can do."

I blushed so deeply that I felt compelled to lower my gaze. He waited patiently, still holding my hands.

"I would like to have you to myself for a while, if possible," I said, looking back up for his reply.

"Good," he said with relief.

"I have seen what a strain babies can place on a young couple, and it seems sometimes they divide husband and wife. Is that true?"

"It can happen."

"I should not like anything to come between us. Not yet."

He seemed very pleased with my answer.

"Then I shall take care," he said.

I asked hesitantly, "What does that mean?"

"You'll see." He smiled, kissing me again on the forehead and then the cheek.

"I'm afraid I'm quite ignorant in these matters, Harry," I said timidly, wondering if my voice were even loud enough to hear.

"I shall teach you everything you need to know," he answered.

"There is one thing—" I began, and then hesitated.

"Yes?"

I looked down, still blushing. He lifted my chin with his finger.

"Ask me. Don't be afraid."

"It's ever so delicate. I've never discussed these things with anyone. Not even Esther."

"Not even Aunt Lavinia?" he teased.

"No." I laughed. "Not even dear Aunt Lavinia."

There was a long pause, and when he saw I was struggling, he said, "You're wondering what it's like?"

"I've been told it's very painful."

"Not always. Not if the husband is gentle."

"Tell me, are there things a wife should not do?"

"What do you mean?"

"Well, are there things that mistresses can do that wives mustn't do?"

This he found very amusing. "I can't think of anything you might wish to do that would not be permitted within the sanctity of marriage."

"Good. That's good. Because I wonder about myself sometimes. I wonder if it's sinful to feel what I feel."

"Not if we're married."

"Then I think I shall be all right," I said. "Well, I am a little nervous, but I'm not frightened. When I'm with you, I only want more of you. I want more of your touch, more of your kisses—"

"I shall feed them to you like sweets to a spoiled child."

"Yes, do spoil me like that," I said, pressing my hands to his chest and looking into his eyes.

"You must not tempt me," he said, catching my hands and kissing them. He kissed me good night and sent me off to bed.

St. Mary's stood on a clifftop overlooking the sea. I remember the carriage ride up the steep cobbled street and entering the churchyard clutching my tulle skirts with the maid fluttering around me trying to catch my veil. It was in many ways a most unmemorable occasion set in a darkly cavernous church, attended by faces I shall not remember, reciting vows I could not hear. The absence of all these external artifices turned my inner ear toward Harry standing next to me. I had never seen him so quiet and confident. Never were priestly words and sacred ritual so useless as they were that morning. They merely closed the door on the life behind us. We had long ago passed into a state of grace.

After the ceremony, we stood for a long while on the cliff overlooking the sea, with the windswept cemetery at our back, and Harry held me close to him. He was overcome by emotion. He pressed my hand to his lips in a manner of deep gratitude, and his eyes were moist with tears.

We returned to the inn, and when the maid arrived to attend to me, I dismissed her and sent for Harry. When he opened the door to find me standing there in my wedding gown, removing my earrings, he thought I had dismissed her out of dissatisfaction. But then I smiled, and he understood and closed the door behind him.

As he crossed the room toward me, I said, "Undress me, Harry."

I AM ALWAYS OBLIVIOUS TO thunder, and I cannot hear the savage sounds that wind can make coming off the sea. Harry claims there were terrible storms in the days that followed, but my sleep was never so sound as it was with him beside me. Our bond of flesh became so compelling that it seemed not only a bodily necessity, but a spiritual one as well. It swept away all my careful training and silenced even the most rigorous and stern voices in my head. To be dragged away from him, even for a moment, invited the very death of me. Nothing existed for us outside each other. The world beyond our door receded, and the loss of my hearing seemed less of a loss in those days.

I AWOKE TO THE LIGHT of a candle across the room. It was sometime in the middle of the night, long before dawn, and Harry was bent over the desk writing a letter. He heard me rise and turned toward me as I slipped on my dressing gown and crossed the room to him. He laid down the pen and smiled at me in the manner of a man welcoming a warrior-in-arms come to his flagging defense, for that's indeed what I was.

"Good," I said as I stood behind him and encircled him with my arms. "You're writing to him."

For days I had watched him wrestle with the unpleasant task of informing his father of our elopement. I had wisely written a letter to my father while in Burford, when I was still inclined to spend hours at my desk agonizing over how best to reveal what we had done, and had sent it off from Whitby the day after our wedding. Harry's task was infinitely more difficult, and the longer he delayed, the more it weighed on his moods. That very night before we went to bed, I had laid out pen and paper and urged him to set about the task. He had fallen asleep in my arms, and I had no inclination to disturb him.

I nestled down in his lap, and his eyes changed the way they always did when I drew close to him.

"You mustn't fret so," I said, kissing the deep furrows between his brows to soften them.

"I do fret."

"Have you finished?"

He turned the letter so that I might read what he had written.

I was surprised by the tone. I knew quite well that it was a troubled relationship, and yet the language was deeply respectful. For the first time, I caught a glimpse of how Harry saw me, or at least how he wished to portray me to his father.

"My goodness, darling." I smiled. "You do flatter me. But you didn't tell him I'm deaf," I added.

"My father despises weakness, and he will see your deafness as a weakness." He kissed the tip of my nose and said, "He will not take this lightly. The issue is not only that I have married the deaf daughter of a tradesman, it is that I've defied him on a matter of utmost importance."

"We shall turn him around, my dear, the two of us together. It may take years, but we shall do it. He'll change his mind."

I had never dared ask him about the American, and even now, in a moment of conjugal intimacy, I hesitated before prying into his heart.

"Harry, were you very fond of Miss Erskine?"

He studied me with a tender gaze, as though fearful of wounding me. "I found her company to be pleasant."

"That's not what you wrote to me in your letter."

"I don't recall what I wrote."

"You said she was childish."

"She could be. At times."

"And you would have married her?"

"Yes, because her father was not put off by our situation. In short, she would have me."

He said this with a bemused and slightly cynical smile, but I knew he was making light of a serious matter.

Even before he had left London in July, Harry had informed me fully on all matters concerning his estate. I considered his openness yet another testimony to his integrity. Confirming the rumors of insolvency that had come to me over the years, he explained that Blackroak was in a terrible state of disrepair, that it was hardly livable, and that there were barely enough servants employed to keep it up. When he confessed what I already knew—that the only two women he had ever pursued in marriage had been dissuaded by their families because of his father's neglect of the estate—he never mentioned his father's character and what role this might have played in their decision. I did not dare question him on the matter.

"I'm not convinced that Miss Erskine ever really understood what she was getting," he said, brushing a thick lock of hair back from my face. "But her father was well informed," he continued. "I am quite sure of that. Father first made their acquaintance in Paris, you know, at the races at Longchamps."

"Paris—where?"

He drew up a blank sheet of paper and wrote down the word.

"Oh, yes. The racetrack."

"Her father had purchased a stable, and my father kept his horses there. It's really quite an illustrious line."

"Quite what?"

He dipped his pen and wrote, *Illustrious line. The Erskines, I mean. Held in high esteem by the crown at one time. Her father 6th in line to Earldom of Mar & Kellie. 6th or 7th. Father was quite impressed.*

I gathered that Harry, too, was impressed. Aristocratic genealogy was something in which he occasionally indulged, and he savored it quite thoroughly. His natural charm seemed to slip just slightly, replaced by a chiseled arrogance. The transformation on his countenance reminded me of the way his mother used to swing back and forth between familiarity and haughtiness.

"And I suppose she's wealthy?" I asked.

"Exceedingly so," he said. Then, with a bat of an eye, he was warm and familiar once again, as if he had only momentarily lost me amidst all those tombstones of the past. He kissed me on the lips and said, "Why do you pain yourself, Veda? I never think of her. I can think of nothing but you. From the moment I saw you on the platform at Oxford station, sitting on your trunk and looking so frightfully lost and alone, I have thought of nothing but your happiness."

His gaze fell to my neck, and he slipped my silk dressing gown off my shoulder and kissed me there.

"Harry, look up," I said, pausing to kiss the top of his head and breathe in the now familiar scent of his hair and skin. "Do tell me about her. I should so like to know."

He lifted his head. "What else is there to say? You have seen her."

"Yes. She's very pretty," I conceded. "Why would she want to come to England? Why doesn't she find a husband in her own country?"

"She was engaged before. A confederate captain. He was killed at the start of the war."

"How dreadful."

"Yes. Very nasty business, that war of theirs. They came abroad for her health."

"Did they visit Blackroak?"

"Good Lord, no. Father made all manner of excuses. Told them it was under construction. He had paintings of course. It looks quite stately in paintings."

After a moment's reflection, I said, "But surely, when their solicitors were negotiating the marriage settlement, they must have made inquiries."

"Indeed they did, but Mr. Erskine was quite undeterred." He tried to kiss me again, but I pressed his face between my hands.

"Harry—"

He grinned. "Oh, all right." He settled me more comfortably on his lap and withdrew our Talking Book from a small stack of books at the back of the desk.

He wrote: *Erskine quite willing to sink money into renovation of estate his grandchild would inherit. As for debts, I do not believe he would begrudge my father the pleasure of his horses when a good deal of his own fortune is squandered in the same way. Only thing to which daughter might have objected was remoteness of our estate—she would be quite isolated.*

Returning the pen to its holder, he added, "I don't think she has any idea how bleak it can be up there in the winter. I doubt anyone told her."

"Perhaps they did. Perhaps she was in love with you."

It took him by surprise, so that he had no time to affect a guise of denial.

"Ah," I said, "so it's true."

"She was rather fond of me."

"I'm sure she wasn't the first one," I said, feeling the sting of jealousy. "I remember, when I was just fifteen, I was at Ellesmere House taking tea with your mother, and I met a Miss Wotton who was ever so smitten with you."

He threw back his head and laughed. "Miss Wotton! My goodness, you do have a memory."

I took advantage of the moment to kiss his neck, and I felt his arms tighten around me.

"My dear, all this is of no concern, I assure you," he said, pulling away from my kiss and withdrawing his arm so that he might pick up the pen again. I read along as he wrote: *I have seen what happens to a marriage when there is very little compatibility & no real love & little respect for the woman—I was determined not to make that mistake myself.*

He paused to blot the ink and turn the page. I could only presume he was referring to his own parents. It was the first indication he had ever given that there might be some truth behind the rumors of his father's brutish treatment of his mother.

Mother understood my unwillingness to marry. Told me I should wait until my heart spoke more loudly than my head & once that had happened, I should allow a full season to pass away from the woman I loved. That I should endeavor to sustain that love through friendship & if I succeeded, then I would have found the woman I should marry. That is exactly what I did. Every day we are together, I am more and more convinced of how right we are for each other. You may be limited in your understanding of the words I speak, but there is absolute understanding of me as a man. You see through my eyes— feel through my heart—you make me think I am not so alone in the world.

I was overcome by his words and lost all interest in interrogating him on the matter of Miss Erskine. I kissed him deeply, urged him to finish his letter quickly and come back to bed.

WORD OF OUR WEDDING QUICKLY spread throughout the town. When we ventured outdoors on quiet little expeditions, on walks along a rocky beach where girls gathered limpets for bait, or to a jet warehouse where we observed the deep, black stones being cut and polished and where Harry bought me an exquisite pair of earrings, or to the end of the pier to watch the gulls drift lazily on the wind, we were greeted with smiles and curtseys. I was called Lady Ormelie by the man in the sweetshop, and it put a tremulous smile on my face. It was the first time I had read my title on anyone's lips.

By far, my favorite excursion was the one to Robin Hood's Bay where we stood high on a clifftop overlooking the North Sea with Ravenscar in the distance and the wind so strong it nearly swept us off the edge. Afterward we continued down the coast to Hayburn Wyke and proceeded on foot along a heavily wooded path to an oasis where Thorny Beck cascades down a rocky promontory into a clear pool of green water. A rainbow hung in the cool mist rising from the waterfall, and the air was warm and close. I discarded my crinoline, shoes, and stockings, and tied up my skirt so that I might wade into the pool with Harry.

Every evening after dinner we strolled along the pier, for there was nothing so eventful for me as the turbulence of seagulls flocking overhead and waves crashing at the breakwater and storm clouds marching out to sea. The movement of all these things had their own kind of sound in my silent world, and I often thought how right Harry had been to choose this place, with the pungent odors and vivid sights of its rough sailors and rowdy children, its fish markets and the fishing fleets heading seawards down the harbor.

At the inn, we spent hours huddled over Harry's drawings of Blackroak and the estate. He showed me the rooms where we would live, and together we spoke of how we might be able to afford the renovations he was planning, for he was determined to make the house as comfortable as possible for me. We anticipated a good deal of hand-wringing and wailing when the news of our wedding surfaced, and we looked forward only to calling on a few faithful friends. We had decided we would not brave Blackroak that winter but would travel to the continent, to Paris and Monte Carlo, perhaps Rome. We would return to Blackroak in the spring when the snows had melted. Harry wanted my first impression to be that of the yellow daffodils in bloom along the banks of the River Dove.

A FULL SIX DAYS PASSED before I received a reply from Papa. There were stern words for both of us. He went on at great length about "beautiful propriety," the kind of which makes for elegance and good taste in dress and manners, and he compared our union to a young gentleman who, in his enthusiasm and love of fashion, "gets it all wrong," opening himself up for ridicule by those whose acceptance he craves. It was a subtly crafted letter and bore witness to Papa's long experience of striking just the right note of deference and dignity when addressing aristocratic society, for he managed to censure our union without maligning Harry.

As tradesmen, he wrote, we cannot join Society, my dear. At best, we can shadow it and lead our lives within our own social set with dignity and self-respect. Remember, the familiarity that transpires in my clubby little lounge behind the showroom is not transferable to the drawing room, and I would not have my daughter groveling for acceptance among those who are unwilling to appreciate her inestimable and shining qualities. If the Earl had no objection, of course I would be honored by such a match, but you say that he does, and that this is the reason for your subterfuge. How can you think that your elopement will make your case any easier to win? On the contrary, had you openly lobbied for his approval and rallied around you all your friends and family, I'm sure you could have obtained his consent. But now, having acted so rashly in defiance of his wishes, you stand every chance of being cut off, and I cannot bear to see you excluded from society when you have struggled so hard to make your way back into the world. You deserve a family who embraces you, not one that rejects you. You are too precious a treasure to suffer the disgrace of social contempt.

To my relief, there was no mention of my work, nor how my absence might affect our business. Papa knew better than to speak of such base things in light of my elopement with the heir to an earldom. Nor was there even the slightest hint of coarseness, not a shade of pompous pride or self-satisfied gloating of the type one might expect from a tailor whose daughter has just married a peer. He ended the letter with an assurance that he would, as I had requested, honor the secrecy of our marriage until advised to the contrary, adding that we would be warmly welcomed at home. He assured me that a proper financial settlement would be worked out with all due haste.

When Harry finished reading, he turned to me with the astonished air of a man whose prejudices had been dashed to smithereens and said, "Why, what a tempered reply. Very reasonable. Of course, he doesn't know my father, so he has no way of knowing how wrong he is. But it's quite the thing one would expect from a gentleman. Yes, he strikes me as very much a gentleman. Very much a gentleman, indeed."

Harry could not have paid him a higher compliment.

BY THE FIRST OF SEPTEMBER we still had no reply from Lord Hambledon. Harry concluded that his father had decided to keep to his traditional calendar of sporting pleasures and had gone up to Scotland to shoot grouse. His silence was the first in a long series of snubs we would be expected to endure.

The afternoon before we were to depart, I had gone out to shop for jet jewelry to take home as gifts. I had seen delicately carved brooches I thought might please Aunt Lavinia and Aunt Mary, and cuff links for Papa and Grandpa. When I returned, I found Harry closed in our sitting room and his valet standing guard at the door.

"What is it?" I asked as I untied my bonnet and left it with the parlor-maid.

"Mr. Collingwood, Lord Ormelie's lawyer," he said, repeating it several times before I had understood, for the old man's mouth barely moved when he spoke.

"From London?"

"Yes, my lady."

"My goodness, he's come all the way up here to meet with Lord Ormelie?"

"Yes, my lady."

Immediately, my heart began thumping. It could not be good news. I set my purchases on the table in the hall, for I had wished to show them to Harry, and I stepped into our bedroom to tidy up my hair. When I returned, I caught only a glimpse of Mr. Collingwood's back as he hurried out the door.

Harry stood staring down at the fireplace grate, hands braced against the mantel. He did not turn when I closed the door, and so I settled quietly onto a chair with my small parcel in my lap and waited. He was struggling to compose himself, and I knew better than to disturb him. It was a long while before he acknowledged my presence. Finally, without turning, he extended his hand to me, and I rose and went to him. He gestured for me to pour him a glass of claret, which I did. While he drank it down, I lighted the candles in the room, for dusk had fallen.

"Preposterous," he said. He repeated it several times and muttered some things I could not understand. When at last he had mastered his violent feelings, he turned to gaze at me. The monster in him softened, and he shook his head with a look of disbelief.

"What has he threatened?" I asked.

He told me to bring him a slate and chalk, and we sat at the table and he wrote it out for me.

A lawsuit. Against me.

"What charges?"

Breach of promise.

"But you had grounds to withdraw your offer."

Our action blocked by my father's lawyer—settlement agreed upon without my consent. My father threatens me with suit if I don't marry her.

"Can he do that?"

Early on, I allowed him to proceed on my behalf. When I was first introduced to her.

He was too impatient to continue writing, and he threw down the chalk and turned to me, taking me by the hands, speaking loudly and slowly mouthing the words. "My father does not wish to marry again, and so I must produce an heir. If not, the title and lands will pass to his cousin. He loathes his cousin. He loathes him so much that he would never disinherit me even if I were the most vile and ungrateful son on the face of this earth. I told you this, do you remember?"

I nodded.

"That's why I know he'll never use the threat of disinheritance with me. So he's looking for other means."

"But this lawsuit—might your solicitor do something?"

"I must speak to my father. I shall not be intimidated by lawyers and suits brought against me in court."

I laid a soothing hand on his. "It would be best, perhaps, that you go to see him alone." Harry began to object, but I stopped him. "We must give him time. We've kept our marriage quiet thus far, we can do so for another few weeks. To announce it publicly while he is still so vehemently opposed would only make matters worse. I shall return to London and wait for you there. With time, he'll come around. And we are married now. He can't change that."

"Ha! Indeed! He is trying to do just that!"

"I beg your pardon?"

"He insists on an annulment."

"What?"

As he wrote the word down on the slate, I felt suddenly quite ill. It was not the kind of faintness that comes from a shock to the senses; it was more complete than that. My entire life, the way I envisioned it with Harry, collapsed beneath the weight of that solitary word.

I rose and walked to the window. Night had fallen, and there was only a tinge of light left in the sky to the west. In the street below, a hunch-backed old man led a donkey slowly up the steep cobbled incline. The world seemed suddenly bleak and hopeless. I felt Harry's hand on my shoulder, and I knew he wished to speak to me but I could not look at him. The happiness we had known for those scant weeks of our marriage now seemed fragile and fleeting, and I wondered that love could be so easily poisoned by the smallest doubt.

"Is that what you want?" I asked, wondering if my voice sounded as cold as I felt.

He took me by the shoulders and turned me toward him.

"How can you say such a thing? How can you doubt me?" he said. His countenance was full of such brutal emotion that I was overcome with shame at my own inconstancy. He crushed me to him and held me close. Again I felt the sheltering strength of his body and will, and believed in the impossible.

With separation now imminent, our last night in Whitby seemed more like an ending than a beginning, and the incertitude of our future only drove us deeper into an intimacy tinged with sadness.

Chapter Twenty-two

IT WAS STRANGE BEING BACK AT HOME WHERE NOTHING HAD changed when I felt myself to be profoundly altered. There was Aunt Lavinia in her lace morning cap, wearing her sweet vacant smile at the breakfast table, and Papa, preening in front of hall mirrors on his way out the door, and Lucy, zealously tickling the dust off the railings whenever one passed by. But I was no longer the same. I felt the change most acutely. I saw it when I slipped out of my chemise each night or when I leaned over to wash in the basin and caught a glimpse of myself in the standing mirror. To think that he had seen me like this sent a rush of heat through my being. I had never dreamed a covenant of the flesh could be so binding, that it could affect the way in which I perceived my very person. My body carried within it the memory of every sensation I had experienced with him, and through the days and nights of our separation I had only to close my eyes to summon his presence.

The night of my return, while Lucy was unpacking my trunks, I went downstairs to greet my father who was waiting up for me in his study. I had traveled by train from Whitby that morning and wanted nothing more than to drop into my familiar bed, but it was imperative that I speak to him and explain my predicament. Always, ever since I had been a child, Papa had been my champion. He had championed my education and my talent, and as unconventional as it was, he had taken enormous pride in my ambition. He could also scent danger whenever his way of life was threatened, and when that was the case, as it was with Mr. Nicholls, he could behave without pity. I had hoped the champion would win out over his more selfish instincts, but I was painfully disappointed.

He must have been stewing a long while, nursing his claret and cigars. He burst out at me as soon as I entered the room and closed the door.

"You deceived me!" he said, waving the cigar clenched in his fist. "You deceived me most treacherously! He must have been courting you all along, right beneath my eyes. He was, wasn't he? That time you snubbed Balducci in the Park, you were with him, weren't you? You both made a fool out of me. I find this quite vexing, Veda. Quite vexing indeed. A man who shows such little respect—"

He bit down fiercely on his cigar.

I drew a chair over from the table, placed it squarely in front of him, and sat down.

"Aren't you the least bit happy for me?" I asked.

He whipped one leg over the other and turned away from me like a petulant child. He was acting very badly, I thought.

Folding my hands in my lap, I addressed him as calmly as I could. "I admit you've been wrongfully denied the opportunity to judge Harry's suitability, but he is a fine and honorable man and truly loves me. Now that it's done, must you still be so angry?"

He flicked an ash off the lapel of his silk dressing gown, still avoiding my gaze.

"Your only objection seems to be his rank, that he is so far superior to us socially, but I did not marry for a title, Papa. I married for love."

This provoked a stinging reply. "Ah, yes, love!" he exclaimed, his nostrils flaring in a sneer. "Love! We must accommodate love, mustn't we?"

"You would have preferred I marry a man I did not love in order to accommodate *you*," I said, in marked reference to Balducci.

"If you had not treated Balducci so scornfully, all that nasty business could have been avoided. And he was just the kind of man suited to our situation."

"*Our* situation, Papa? Is my personal happiness worth nothing? Tell me, what strange morality dictates a daughter should refuse a chance to better her situation when it lies within her power? Should I not consider my own pleasure? And what of Harry's worth as a man? Might you not wish to weigh his qualities and devotion to me against the obstacles and disadvantages?"

But he could not.

"I'm confused, Papa. Your letter was so—"

He cut me off. "Did you think I would air my grievances in a letter for your husband to read? Most certainly not!" He stewed a bit longer and then added, "And what of your clients? What am I to tell them? I have accommodated you here, believing that this was to be your life, our life. Does Grenfell's mean nothing to you anymore? Do I mean nothing to you anymore?"

I calmly explained that the marriage must be kept secret for a little longer. I chose not to elaborate, stating only that Harry had gone to meet with the Earl in Scotland to smooth things over and would be returning to London when everything was in order. At that time, we would make our marriage public.

With a deep sigh of fatigue, I concluded, "Until then, I believe it's best I return to the shop. In the meantime, we must plan for my departure. As soon as all of this is settled, I'll be leaving for the Continent. Harry is taking me abroad, for our honeymoon."

He looked up at me with a chilling glare, and the veins of his temples rose like whipcord beneath his skin. "You have abandoned me. In the worst possible way, you have abandoned me."

He stamped out his cigar and rose stiffly from his armchair. With his hands thrust deep in the pockets of his dressing gown, he strode past me out of the room without another word.

I penned only one line to Harry that night and sent it off in the morning:

> My darling, come quickly. All is falling apart here. I feel like a stranger in my own home.

Within days I had returned to my life as a tailor, huddling over black worsted with a thimble on my finger and my wedding ring strung on a gold chain around my neck, concealed beneath my bodice. I only dressed as a gentleman if I was expecting a client for a fitting. The rest of the time I took my old seat back in the workroom. There was solace in the familiarity, but I no longer felt to be one of them. Sometimes, lost in my thoughts, I marveled at the intricacies of deception. I was always pretending to be that which I was not, whether out of choice or necessity. I dreamed of the day when I would simply be Harry's wife.

I began to avoid dinner with Papa. On the nights he dined at his club, I kept Aunt Lavinia company, but when he was home, I would ride First in the Park until dusk and return to a quiet dinner in my room. When I felt in particular need of comfort, I would abduct Ivanhoe from Aunt

Lavinia's lap and steal away with him to bed. What helped the most was making for Harry. I had returned from Whitby with a pattern cut to his figure, and once again my bedroom became my workshop. I set about sewing a new smoking jacket and frock coat from the finest cloth I could find. It helped bring him to life in my mind.

It took much longer to sort it all out than I had thought it would, and when at last he came back to London, we were still very secretive. I went to his lodgings in St. James, and we agreed to put aside all the business with fathers and lawyers. We were together again and nothing mattered but this. I removed my ring from the chain around my neck and slipped it on my finger. At midnight he surprised me with oysters and champagne, and then I fitted him in the garments I had been making for him. I worked barefoot in my chemise, my hair tied up with his cravat, basting up the shoulders of an elegant dahlia-colored beaver frock coat with velvet cuffs and lapels. Making for Harry was one of my greatest joys, and he was quite taken with his figure in my clothes.

"I do say, you've got me looking very smart."

"You can be a little ramshackly at times, dear," I told him. He laughed and tugged on the cravat so that my hair came tumbling down over my eyes.

The following evenings, while I sewed, he sat at his desk and took up the deluge of correspondence that awaited him, or we would sit and read, he with his Gazette and me with my Ruskin, immersing myself in visions of Venice and places I would soon be seeing with Harry. It felt as if we were properly together and married, not as the inn at Whitby had felt, but more homely and honest. I brought little things from Savile Row, a few knickknacks that mother had left me, and arranged them in his sitting room. I even brought some of Aunt Lavinia's crocheted antimacassars, which we had piled up in the linen closet, and smoothed them over the backs of the armchairs. Harry didn't mind. He had lost all taste for bachelorhood, he said.

He must have hidden a good deal from me. There were times when I caught the worry in his eyes. He became ever so tender with me when I tried to draw him out, but he always resisted. I know he didn't want to burden me, which only made it much worse, because the blow was so completely unexpected. Harry knew how much I believed in him, how I trusted he would work it all out.

That afternoon I had stopped at the bakery for scones and bought flowers from a street urchin in the square, and on the way upstairs as I was shaking the rain off my bonnet, I passed the housekeeper and ordered tea to be brought up. Harry had told her I was his wife, but I know she didn't believe him. She always followed me with sharp, insolent eyes.

Harry shot to his feet when I entered. "My poor darling, you were caught in the rain!"

"Look! Scones from that delightful baker in Piccadilly Street. They're still warm," I exclaimed, handing the parcel to him. "And I've ordered tea."

He had already started a fire in the grate, and the room was cozy and glowing. We had only the housekeeper, but we managed with just the two of us. Harry minded it more than I. He was accustomed to having servants for every little thing, but I didn't like having to be on the watch for them when we were together. I could never hear them coming and going.

I was arranging the flowers in a vase when I felt his hands on my shoulders. With my eyes closed, I pressed my cheek against the back of his hand. I wished for nothing more than this. Harry's touch was the world to me.

He withdrew, and I turned to find him lighting a candle on the table. He motioned me to sit next to him, and as I picked up my skirts and settled myself in a chair, I noticed the dark look on his countenance.

"My goodness, what is the matter?" I asked.

He was busy getting out some chalk and wiping clean a slate. It meant there was something important to discuss. Even seated, I felt my strength ebb and a strange tightening in my throat.

"Oh, Harry, do not tell me it's bad news. I couldn't bear it."

I laid my hand along the side of his face and the touch softened his expression. He pressed his lips into my hand and murmured something.

"I despise all of them for doing this to you," I said, smoothing back his hair with my free hand.

He picked up the chalk and wrote, *Gone further than I had ever expected.*

"Your father?"

His lawyer. Heaton. Must have been his idea. <u>Monster</u> of a man, he wrote, underscoring the word with a heavy chalk line.

"My goodness, what has he threatened?"

He could not look at me.

Your father's trade.

"What about it?"

He says he can destroy it.

"But how?"

Call in the loans.

I sat there in stunned silence, feeling the faintest chill at the back of my neck.

"He's made inquiries into our finances?"

Harry nodded and scribbled, *Your loans are held by Solomon.*

"But Solomon wouldn't call in the loans. He's carried our debt for years. Papa's always dealt with him."

Father has influence to sway Solomon if he wishes.

"But that's impossible," I cried. "Our trade is dependent on this money. Every tailor is dependent on credit. If Solomon calls in his loans, we can't stay in business."

Harry answered on the slate and passed it to me. *There are other lenders. We'll work something out.*

"Has he already taken action?"

"He says he has, but it may just be a threat."

"But what if he has? He must be stopped!"

"It will not happen overnight. I will see to that. In the meantime, we shall find other lenders."

"But Harry, if your father is ready to destroy my family to have his way, if he is willing to do something as—as despicable and utterly ruinous as this—and still we resist him, what will he do next?"

Harry's attention was drawn away by a noise. The housekeeper had knocked.

After she had laid out tea and gone, we sat opposite each other in arm-chairs beside the grate with our cups on our laps, staring at the fire. The scones remained untouched on the table behind me.

The question I had asked remained unanswered, but it hung over our heads like a dark cloud. Even knowing what I did about the Earl, I had never imagined he would exert his authority in such a loathsome way.

After a long while, Harry set aside his cup and turned to me, taking my hands in his.

"Veda, my father is not an evil man. He is—he can be—"

He faltered. I thought how difficult it must be for him to defend a tyrant he could not help but love.

He released my hands, sat down at his desk, and wrote me this:

I regret that you have only seen the worst in him. In the right company, he can be a very affable, jovial man, but those who challenge his authority provoke him to the extreme. He is right-minded & will not have his opinions changed. Yet, he loves me in his own way. It is difficult to be loved by one who expects in return that you see the world through his eyes & judge it as he does. It is a terrible prison, which treats its prisoners with grave injustice. Should the prisoner break out, he is sure to suffer scathing disapproval and bitter scorn. My sister chose to abandon our family. I could not. When my mother was alive, it was easier for me. She always urged me to be my own man, to live without his love if need be, rather than sell my soul to him. But now, with only the two of us, the bond of father & son has grown deeper. He needs me now more than ever, but the only son he will have is one who conforms to his will in all things.

When I had read this, I fixed him with a tender gaze and asked the question I had been longing to ask for months. "Why did Aurelia run off? Did it have something to do with your father?"

He sat staring leagues away for a long while. I waited patiently while he took up a slate and wrote: *Aurelia was devout—even more so than my mother. But she was not always sane—she had rages—angry rages—& said fiendish things. Wished to convert to Catholicism & would not be dissuaded. You can imagine Father's reaction. She locked herself in her room & rejected all food & sustenance for 6 days. Came out on the 7th day. The maid found her in the hall. She was so weak she was crawling on hands and knees & could not stand. Mother took her away to the Continent & her health improved. When it was time to return, Aurelia disappeared. Months later, we learned that she had been taken in by nuns at a chapel in St. Germaine en Laye. It broke my mother's heart.*

When he had finished writing, he cleaned the slate quite thoroughly so that not a word of that shocking story remained.

"I have told no one of this," he said.

Thinking of his shame, I stroked his hand and said, "I am not your judge, Harry. All families have their trials."

Later that evening I watched him as he sat at his desk writing more letters to lawyers and bankers, anyone who might exert some influence on our behalf. He refused to give up the fight, but I knew it was futile. As I lay in his arms that night, I felt nothing but an immense emptiness. All the passion had been drained from me.

Within a month, my once shining world was in ruins.

PAPA NEVER KNEW ABOUT THE Earl's threats to ruin us, nor was he aware of Harry's efforts to stall Heaton's actions—the letters written and discreet visits to the money lenders who held our loans. During that time, Papa needled me. "Well, my dear, when are you going to announce this marriage? Very suspicious to hide it from our family. Very suspicious indeed. Are you or are you not the wife of a viscount?" Whenever he questioned me, I pretended not to understand and looked away.

I think Papa must have skillfully coerced some gossip out of one of his clients, because he caged me in his study one evening before dinner and told me he had heard rumors that Lord Ormelie was to be married—to an American.

"Confound it, daughter! What is going on? Will you tell me or must I hear it in the fitting room?"

"It's true. Our marriage is being annulled."

"What the deuce does that mean?"

"That I shall no longer be married to him."

"I know what an annulment is, daughter! but by my soul, how did this happen?"

"The Earl was resolutely opposed. He made threats."

"So, a little resistance and he discards you like soiled linen, is that it? Well, it sounds to me like you have been abused. Abused most dreadfully. We can take action, you know."

"We shall do nothing of the sort."

"Oh, but we shall! Oh, yes we shall! This is scandalous!"

"May I remind you that you, too, were sternly opposed to our marriage?"

"Am I on trial here? Are you criticizing my judgment? Listen here, Veda, your husband is a cad! A spineless coward!"

I turned away from him, but he stamped on the floor.

"Come here, daughter! You will know what I have to say on this matter!" He motioned me to approach his desk.

It was all I could do to keep up with his rambling rampage. He would write a few lines, then shout something at me, and then write more. I understood more than I cared to.

This is what happens when you behave so recklessly. What a disaster! What a mockery, this marriage of yours! Thank God we kept it secret. Why, think

*what fools we would be if it got out! Of course, we should deny it. Yes, you see,
I was right all along. You are a tailor's daughter. We are trade. We are the servants of society. We do not mingle with lords on equal terms & I will not have
us sneered at and held up to ridicule—have you treated with hardness and
contempt. No, no, it is all for the better. I'd say there's a touch of the desperate
in it. A viscount and a tailor's daughter. Nonsense. You're better off without
him. What kind of husband is he that he would give you up so easily? First sign
of trouble and he walks out on you—*

I rose and left the room. For weeks I did not come down for dinner.

Harry sent me a copy of the legal documents dissolving our marriage,
but I burned them without ever reading a word.

I still continued to meet him in his rooms in Pickering Place whenever
he came to London. It was the only home we ever shared together, and we
kept it our own until the end. Each night before I returned to Savile Row,
he would present me with a small parcel containing something old and familiar that belonged to him and that I might wear after he was gone—a
linen shirt or braces, his favorite string cravat, a pair of pearl cufflinks or
studs. It became a ritual that eased the parting. We agreed that once he was
married, all communication between us would cease. Harry had argued
this point with me, but he understood as well as I did that further contact
would only prolong our heartbreak. The night before his wedding was the
last night we were together. It was December, only a week before Christmas. A heavy snow fell, and we awoke in the morning to find the square
covered in a blanket of white. I helped him dress as though it were a perfectly ordinary day, and he was dressing for lunch at his club.

PAPA DIDN'T CARE A FARTHING that my heart was broken and noticed
my misery with little sympathy and much indirect sarcasm. My constitution was much shattered, and I lost a good deal of weight, which worried
Aunt Lavinia no end. I disliked Papa very much during those days. My
love for him felt heavy and cold, like something dredged up from the bottom of a primal sea.

I unburdened myself to Esther and suffered her honest reply.

For all your dear Papa's merits, which are many, he is a selfish man who puts
his own interests before your own. There is no one left but you, and he
would be intolerably lonely without you. He would suffer your loss to the

firm as well. You have become a bit of a celebrity in the trade—you know it quite well. It was your own ambition and you succeeded beyond your wildest dreams. Your marriage to Harry would have deprived him of a partner as well as a daughter. I think, if he had the choice, your father would prefer you remain a spinster, abandoning all hope of conjugal bliss to accommodate him.

The annulment must have been a terrible blow to his pride. Even if he opposed it in theory, what status he would have gained! After all, marriage to a lord, really! You quite outdid yourself. Then you undid it all again. Ah, Topsy, you did put him through quite a bit, you know.

I, too, discouraged your hopes for a match with Harry—I remember all too well our arguments. I thought you were being very silly and childish. Could it be I was jealous? Perhaps. I adore Ned, but Harry is—well, in Rossetti's words, he is "a stunner." From the moment Ned showed me your letter that day you eloped, I have had nothing in my heart but hope and joy for you. Harry must have loved you desperately to challenge his ogre of a father. Really, when the father had such ambitions for his son, to see him elope with a mysterious commoner with connections to trade—

I would come to see you, but our wet nurse has taken ill and I am frantic to find a new one before Christmas. My sisters are coming up and the house will be full. Ellen will be a year old in January. You must come to her birthday party. You need not worry about running into Harry—even after his honeymoon. Ned is furious with him and regrets naming him a godfather. He declares he will not have him in our house. You must allow your friends the indignation that is your due. I know you are too forlorn to feel it yourself.

Know that Harry loved you and surely loves you still—if that is any consolation.

THEN, THERE WAS AN INKLING of something new, a vague insinuation that my body had a secret. I was inexperienced and there was no one to tell me what that secret was. I was often ill, too ill to travel to Ellen's birthday party in January. I floundered on in ignorance until it was ridiculously obvious.

I wrote to Harry at his club, in care of Scrimshire, as I had always done.

My darling,
Only weeks since our parting, and already I am breaking the vow we made, but it is with good reason.

I am with child. It has been confirmed by two physicians.

For the moment, no one knows. Not even Papa or Esther.

How shall I proceed? What am I to do? I give myself up to your superior judgment. I am in no state to think clearly. The fact that our marriage was kept a secret makes my situation all the more delicate.

I beg of you, write quickly. I need your guidance.

Your loving Veda

I waited three long weeks before I had a reply.

Miss Grenfell:

Viscount Ormelie is at present touring the Continent with his bride.

He has instructed me to inform you that circumstances dictate there be no more contact with you, nor with your child. The generous sum he settled on you following the annulment of your marriage should be sufficient to cover any incidental expenses.

Sincerely yours,
Sir Douglas Heaton
Lawyer to Henry Breadalbane,
Viscount Ormelie

Heaton. Harry's lawyer was Mr. Collingwood. Somehow, my letter had fallen into the hands of the Earl's lawyer. I dreaded to think what this meant.

The next day I went around to White's Club and waited in the carriage while my note was delivered. After a moment, the boy returned with this message:

Madame,

I regret to inform you that I can no longer forward your correspondence directly to Viscount Ormelie. I have been instructed to deliver all his messages to Sir Douglas Heaton.

I regret that I cannot be of further assistance to you.

Sincerely yours,
Jonathan Scrimshire

That afternoon, I penned a frantic note to Esther, and she sent an immediate reply.

You can be sure they never sent him the letter. He would never have responded so cruelly. Ned does not know where he is, but he might find out from Lady Stamford—if Lord Stamford knows. At the very least, we might send inquiries to the hotels where he usually stays. They are quite good about forwarding letters if they are given an address.

We cannot know if Heaton has informed the Earl about the contents of your letter, nor can we know what his response would be. Perhaps it's best that you refrain from any more attempts to reach Harry through his club or his friends. There is your reputation to consider for the time being. No one knows you have ever been married. Oh my dear, you have been so wickedly wronged.

Most important, you should put your health and the health of your unborn child above all other concerns for now. You must not worry about your clients nor your father. You need to leave London and distance yourself from all that business as quickly as possible. I agree with you that France would be a good idea. I shall write some letters on your behalf—I know a woman who might help. Take heart, Vevey. We shall find a safe refuge for you.

Papa suggested I give up my baby—that I turn him over to cousin Grace to raise. I had only to stiffen my shoulders and that was sufficient. He never brought it up again. I took courage in the knowledge that Harry's child was growing inside me. This was not something that could be annulled. No one would ever take this away.

Chapter Twenty-three

THE CHATEAU DU GUÉ DU SASSETÔT WAS THE FAMILY SEAT OF THE Vicomte du Baffy. From our trips abroad when I was very young, I had retained some romantic notions of elegant hotels on the continent, but in this instance I had been duped. The chateau was an old Renaissance manor house of crumbling red brick with gothic arched windows, all of it drowned in ivy. The minute we arrived, I set the little boy Renaud to cutting it back so we might have some light. Inside there was a lot of gilded nonsense, carved mirrors as tall as the ceilings and musty tapestries and mildewed chaises. And everywhere there were vases of dried flowers. I had them all thrown out. It was much farther from the sea than we had been led to believe. In truth, very little was as we had been promised. The neighboring village of Orbec was barely even that—just an inn, the Auberge des Trois Chats, a bakery, and a blacksmith. The bakery did a little business as a greengrocer, most of whose produce came from our farm.

I gathered the du Baffys were crumbling much like their ancestral home. For years the estate had been left in the hands of an estate agent who was to greet us but never appeared. In short, it came down to the farmer and his two married sons to work the fields and tend the livestock, while their wives tended to the domestic duties and to the many children whose number I never did quantify as I never saw them all together at once. They seemed to be merely different sizes of the same creature, with a slight variation in length of hair and style of clothing—all ruddy little things with brilliant berry-colored cheeks and dark lank mops of hair. Jeanne, the older unmarried daughter, kept house for us, and the farmer's wife, Madame Tessier, cooked for us. It was Madame Tessier's reputation as a midwife that had brought me here. I prayed her skills were not as fraudulently represented as the rest of the situation seemed to be. They knew only that I was the wife of an English lord who had married against

the wishes of his family. I doubt they believed it.

I brought with me Nelly, a super-stitious farm girl from Suffolk I had engaged as a lady's maid. We met for the first time at the inn in Dover at which I had arranged for us to spend several days together prior to the crossing to France. She was raised with an older brother who was born deaf and was very close to him, which is why I preferred her over the much more experienced and mannered girls Papa proposed. I found Nelly to be ex-ceedingly clever for one from such a humble home. She could read and write in a pleasant and legible script, and she was quick to show me she had no scruples about using finger language. Nelly's family had devised their own finger language, and during the crossing—which was quite an ordeal as I was still suffering from morning discomfort—she began teaching me their signs. The only thing I held against Nelly was her slovenliness—a bane for someone as professedly fastidious as I. I warned her even before we left Dover that she would need to change her habits, that she must bathe more often were she to wait on me, but it was always a battle with her. I did coerce her into wearing a tiny phial of perfume pinned to her bodice, but even that could not always mask undesirable odors.

Nelly was the only familiar face in all that strangeness. Familiar and English to the bone. Even though I spoke French and she did not, I relied on her. She was solid. It was so much easier since she had lived with deaf-ness in her family. She became fiercely loyal to me. The isolation drew us together, but I think it was also her nature, for she was tenderhearted to a fault. She believed wholeheartedly in my capability, more so than Papa. Papa didn't think I would be up to the task of mothering on my own. He warned me that I would not hear the baby cry if he needed me, and should he fall or put himself in danger, I would not know unless I kept constant watch over him. Nelly reassured me that a mother must keep a constant eye on a child in any event, and I would be all the more attentive and a better mother for it.

I had singled out Renaud from the moment we arrived; he was the only child I did distinguish from the horde. The eldest of the children and a terribly shy boy, he was a very willing little messenger when needed. From my window one afternoon, I watched him race into the village with a letter for the post. He sprinted so quickly down the muddy rutted drive that the dogs couldn't keep up with him. I think he knew I would be watching and wanted to show off for me. I never knew if he was speaking to me, because his face was always cast down, although I continually urged him to look me in the eye when he spoke. On the occasions when we needed a carriage, I would send Renaud in to the village blacksmith for an old brougham and a pair of seasoned horses.

Apparently I was not the first lady to take refuge there. An Austrian empress had briefly lived at Sassetôt more than a century ago during some political scandal. I don't know what became of her.

I still thought of myself as married to Harry. I wore my ring and kept all his fine things in a beautiful red Moroccan leather case—the cuff links with his family crest, the gold shirt studs, watch fobs, and tie pins he had given me to wear. It seemed as if he had died and yet our union had gone on living. I could not think of it any other way.

I wrote lengthy, thoughtful letters to Esther:

> A moral burden has been lifted from my shoulders. My situation is of no importance to the Tessiers nor the villagers. I may be homesick, yet I feel much more comfortable here than I did at home. I am quite sure I would have been miserable had I remained in London. How the opinions of others damage our spirits!

My correspondence with Papa was of a different nature. I wrote only to reassure him that I was bearing up and being well cared for. His letters were full of complaints with regards to my clients, and I drew some satisfaction from his concession that I had managed brilliantly with some exceedingly difficult gentlemen, most notably Mr. Percy Naylor, a very disturbed gentleman who rejected absolutely everything he ordered. Papa also had to deal with the wife of Sir Henry Pennyman, a nitpicking and crabby old woman who attended every fitting and dictated fashion and fit to both her husband and me. After each fitting, Sir Henry would quietly drop in to the shop and beg me to make small concessions in his favor, hoping that his wife would not notice at the next visit. He was a man losing his youth and wished only to enhance his aging figure, and she only wished him to go quickly to the grave.

Papa had promoted Mr. Shaw to fill my position, but he was very cautious and dared not trust him blindly, as he had Balducci. Mr. Shaw was a fine tailor and would serve Papa loyally, but Papa complained a good deal about Mr. Shaw, too. Sometimes his letters were so morose that I would put them aside to read another day.

I had practical needs to be considered, and I threw my energies into dressmaking for Nelly and myself. We transformed one of the downstairs *salons* into an *atelier*. It was the brightest room in the house and the most suitable, with two high windows on the west wall and a French door that opened onto the south terrace. Nelly and Jeanne scrubbed down a worktable from the shed and moved it into the *salon*. The floors had to be scrubbed as well as I would tolerate no filth.

The day my first shipment of cloth arrived, they all crowded around me as I untied the bundles one by one. When I unrolled a few feet of amethyst silk from the bolt and draped it over a chair, their eyes grew wide as saucers. I am quite sure none of them had ever seen such fine fabrics.

Nelly surprised me with her quick little hands and sharp eye. I certainly had not intended to train her as an apprentice, but the needlework she turned out was clean and even—not one knot or twisted thread. It was comforting having her company as we worked.

One day, I received a very kind letter from the village priest, Père Hérault, explaining that he had received an unexpected visit from his old friend, the Abbé Oddos, who was on his way back to Caen with a young man who was to teach at a new school for the deaf in that town. The young teacher, himself a deaf man, was most eager to make my acquaintance and enquire as to the manners and methods of teaching the deaf in England. The Abbé and the deaf instructor, a Monsieur Leclerc, would be guests in his home until the following week, and if I were so inclined to accept his humble hospitality, he would be honored to receive me any afternoon at my convenience.

The messenger waited while I penned a reply suggesting that the Abbé, Monsieur Leclerc, and he be my guests at dinner, which would give us an opportunity to communicate at our leisure. The Abbé was an important man in the region, and Madame Tessier dropped everything to prepare for his arrival. For the next twenty-four hours, Sassetôt was a frenzy of cleaning. Around late-morning, a bevy of village women descended on us—faces I had never seen before. Silver plate was unlocked and polished to a white-hot gleam; floors were scrubbed, stairways swept, wall tapestries removed and beaten to within an inch of their faded lives. Elegant gilt-edged porcelain dinner service with the du Baffy family crest appeared on the sideboard, and the chipped dinner plates on which Nelly and I were served were stashed away out of sight.

I must say the chateau took on another life that evening. The windows had been left open all day to the May breeze, scenting the air with sweet perfume from lilacs growing in heavy-headed clusters at the corners of the house. The *salon* and dining room were drenched in candlelight, and wood fires burned in both rooms. In England we would never waste wood or coal on such a mild evening, but the heat did indeed take the dampness out of the air, and the fire was very agreeable. Fresh flowers stood in the *salon* and on the dinner table. Even a wobbly Louis XIV chair had been repaired.

I had no idea what to expect from Monsieur Leclerc, and I certainly had little to say for the education of the deaf in England, but I was eager to meet him. I invited Nelly to join us at dinner as my interpreter, but I warned that she must subdue her antipapist sentiment. I was anxious about entertaining perfect strangers, even deaf ones like myself, and I needed her comfort and familiarity. I was rather poor at lip reading French, and my spoken French seemed to baffle the Tessiers, so I assumed I would be communicating most of the evening with chalk and slate. With this in mind, I had thoughtfully placed several slates around the room in convenient locations.

From the minute they were shown into the *salon*, I saw that these gentlemen had no need of slates nor chalk. Within moments of greeting me and taking a seat, Monsieur Leclerc and the Abbé let fly between themselves a volley of signs of such complexity and speed that Nelly and I turned to each other in utter astonishment. The sign language they shared was nothing at all like the rather comical miming we used. These were quick, small, intricate movements, very close to the body, the fingers seeming to move in an acrobatic display of dexterity. Their faces played along with their hands, but there seemed to be an order, a continuity and logic that told me this was a highly structured finger language they were using. Not once did they resort to chalk and slate when they spoke to one another. When they had proper names to communicate, they used a system of finger letters: They had an alphabet. The words fairly flew off their fingers.

Even before we went into dinner, Monsieur Leclerc had me signing the first letters of the alphabet. What a remarkable teacher he was. He never displayed the least sign of impatience. He was not much older than I, but he was born deaf and had been to the Abbé de l'Epée's celebrated school for the deaf in Paris where this finger language was taught. I explained that in London, if a deaf child tried to gesture, his hands were struck with a wooden paddle.

Madame Tessier was not at all pleased with us that evening. Our hands were so busy we took forever to finish our soup, and by that time the lamb and roasted potatoes and asparagus had gone stone cold. I think she could have set Sassetôt on fire that evening and I would have soared out of the flames on celestial wings. I was elated to discover there was a language the deaf could use among themselves.

It was decided that Monsieur Leclerc would return the next day to begin teaching this language to Nelly and me, and that we would continue on a daily basis until his departure for Caen—which he kindly agreed to delay for several days in order to immerse us in the system. He would then return to us on a weekly basis to continue our lessons.

I became passionate about learning the language, which was not nearly as simple as I would have thought. I felt the same inhibitions I had felt when I first struggled with the sounds of French and Monsieur's pure vowels. My hands were stiff and awkward compared to Monsieur Leclerc's nimble fingers. I never thought of eloquence in terms of a gesture, but Monsieur was indeed eloquent, his language beautiful and expressive. The hand language Nelly and I had invented was grotesque compared to this, like the difference between a ballerina and a clown.

Nelly and I would walk around the house signing the words of things and spelling them out. Nelly's spelling was faulty, but I could usually grasp the word if she got enough letters right. One morning while we were walking through the farmyard—Nelly's favorite arena—signing the names of the animals, I became so convinced of our progress with our new language that I took my slate from around my neck, flung it into the air, and watched it sail over the fence onto the top of a haystack. Nelly had to climb up a ladder to retrieve it, which vexed her terribly.

Monsieur Leclerc assured me that with hand and facial expression there would emerge an individual personality, much as our voices become a part of our character. Most important, I realized that this would give me a bridge to converse with my child. My heart thrilled at the idea that he would not be a silent stranger to me.

As we became more fluent, Nelly and I conversed with striking ease and simplicity. To our amusement, Renaud began following us around making signs that were absolute gibberish, so we decided to teach him as well. He would steal away from his chores whenever he could and dally by the open windows, staring at us as we worked in the *salon*. We would make signs to him and he would sign back. Each of us had a finger sign name, a simple, easy-to-remember gesture drawn from some peculiarity or a behavior or physical appearance. Mine was a quick dip of the hand with the thumb and forefinger pressed together as if holding a needle; Nelly, with her dimpled grin, was signed with a finger to the cheek; Renaud, who was always twirling his hair around his finger, would be signed by a twist of the thumb and finger to the forehead.

"I have decided to open a dress shop, Nelly," I said one morning as she was pouring water into my bath. "In London. I should like you to come and be my assistant."

She emptied the bucket, set it down, and signed a reply as she spoke, *You mean a sewing assistant, my lady?* she asked.

"Yes. A sewing assistant."

"But I can't afford an apprenticeship."

"I shall pay for your apprenticeship. And you'll be paid a salary on top of that, so you can't refuse me." I slipped out of my robe and stepped into the tub, and Nelly helped ease me down into the warm water. "You're too good to lose," I said, looking up at her. Without looking me in the eye, she bustled around the bathroom, picking up my undergarments and tossing them over her arm.

"So? What do you say? Turn and face me, Nelly, so I might read your lips."

She said shyly, "I should like that very much, my lady."

"So, it's settled?"

"You can count on me, my lady," she said, with just a hint of smug satisfaction spreading across her moon-like face.

"Or perhaps Paris. Paris might be a good place to start. What do you think?" I asked, reaching for the sponge floating in the water.

I'd like London better, she signed, now struggling to repress a grin.

"I suppose you're right," I answered, thinking about my suppliers and finding a location. I would know exactly how to proceed in London. "But I like the idea of Paris. We must not eliminate it altogether."

"Is your water warm enough?"

"Bring up just one more bucket of hot."

"Yes, my lady," she replied. She curtsied and left the room, leaving me to stare at my figure rising out of the water, a splendid and pale mound, firm and ripened almost to bursting. I closed my eyes and thought of Harry.

Esther's efforts to locate him had proven unsuccessful. I deeply regretted that he had been excluded from the birth of his first child, but I had resigned myself to my situation. There would be time enough later to share the joyous news. I was terribly proud of my figure as it expanded and I wished that Harry could see me like this. I would not have felt so in London. In Sassetôt I felt neither shame nor embarrassment. I loved the sensual pleasure of my weight as I took my daily walks with Nelly, nosing around barns and traipsing across fields. Here, there was room for my spirit and my body to swell sweetly and innocently away from stern and rigorous gazes.

Perhaps the house depressed me, but nothing lifted my spirits as much as the *Basse Normandie* countryside. It was splendid in the spring and summer months: white apple blossoms blanketing the hills; a leafy willow drooping lazily on the banks of the stream where Nelly and I brought a picnic lunch; magnolia trees in dusty pink, mauve, and white; bluebells dotting the meadows. We had arrived too late to see the daffodils. They had bloomed in March, but I was glad of that. They would have reminded me of Harry's promise, that we would return to Blackroak in the spring when daffodils covered the banks of the River Dove.

Late in May, cottonwoods on the riverbanks began to release their cotton. It was most abundant midmorning when the sun was out, when the warmth opened up the pods. The air was full of wisps of cottonseed; it floated through the open windows and doors, and in the afternoon the grass seemed to be covered in a bed of soft, delicate snow.

By June the dogwood was in bloom, and scarlet poppies appeared overnight, dropped from the heavens into a sea of green swells.

I HAD HOPED TO FIND a kindred soul in Madame Tessier or her daughter, but they remained aloof to me and treated Nelly with cruel disregard. Papa and I had negotiated a generous fixed fee that included all our meals, and which I paid promptly at the first of each month. After several months, I began to notice the quality declining. One week we were served nothing but weak broth with bread, butter, and radishes on Wednesday, beef tongue accopanied by a single boiled potato the following day, and a slightly thicker broth on Friday. I picked up my skirts and tramped through the mud with my slate in hand and had it out with her. She always managed to wheedle more money out of me, and the meals would improve for a short time, and then it would begin all over again. In July her currant jelly and bottled cherries never found their way to our table unless Renaud stole a jar or two for us, and there were times when roasted lamb wafted up from their cottage while we dined on a watery shepherd's pie. Nelly called her a thief, but we were her captives and could do little more than complain. It worried me. I sensed she was derelict in her duties and would take every opportunity to put an extra penny in her pocket. Yet, she was called from all over the province to midwifery, and I took some reassurance from this fact.

MY WATERS BROKE IN THE first week of August, and Madame Tessier immediately sent one of her daughters with Nelly into Caen for a physician. When I asked why this was necessary, she informed me that, because I was English, she required an English physician present for the birth. I had never heard this discussed before, and Nelly understood no more than I did. I didn't want Nelly to go, but they hurried her away. I endured a day and night of excruciating labor with Madame Tessier or her daughter-in-law at my bedside. They were very harsh with me and called me foolish when I cried. Without Nelly there to sign to me, I could not know what was happening, and I was terribly frightened. I suspected from the beginning that something was wrong. I knew it from the looks on their faces,

and the way they turned away when they spoke to each other so I wouldn't
be able to read their lips.

I had not imagined I would feel so lost and alone. I had hoped to be in
the comforting community of women who had shared my lot and could
ease me through my suffering with encouragement. I was resigned to pain,
to the inevitable physical agony of labor which I had accepted as a
woman's lot in life, but not this. I could not lose Harry and then lose his
child. It was not possible. Fate could not be so refined in its cruelty as to
rip open a wound so raw and fresh.

The second day, I noticed the presence of a stranger. I thought he was
the English doctor, but he never came forth to speak to me, and Nelly had
still not returned. He remained in the hallway or hung in the shadows at
the back of the room, vague features I retained only as an impression, for
I was exhausted and weakened by my trial. Madame Tessier said he was a
priest. He was there to purify my baby boy and send his spirit to heaven.

I never saw my little boy. Not a glimpse. They swaddled him and
whisked him away. He was unsightly, a monstrosity, not something I
should see. I should think only of his soul, which was perfect and beautiful, and had gone up to God. I was furious at her for taking him away. No
sound came to my ears, you see. No crying, no gurgling or suckling, none
of the glorious sounds of birth. And I was deprived of the sight of him,
too. I would have rather looked upon his twisted limbs than have nothing
to hold in my memory. When Nelly finally returned, it was too late. It was
all over.

The Tessiers were a good deal kinder to me after the ordeal was over.
They had remedies to alleviate the hardness in my breasts and to prevent
hemorrhaging. They took great care to feed me well. They served me five
times a day with delicious soups and herbal teas, and they brought delica-
cies we had never seen before—breads with cream filling and raisins, and
fresh peach tarts. Nelly fed me whatever I could manage, which was very
little, and then ate the rest herself. Bless her heart, she never left my side.
She slept with me in the four-poster bed, and when my weeping woke her
in the middle of the night, she would console me tenderly as a mother
would do. There had been no one but her to share my joy, and now there
was no one but Nelly to share my grief.

I wrote Esther at her parents' home in Wessex, where she and Ned were
spending the summer.

What am I now? Am I mother? Am I wife? Widow? Why is there no word in our language for a woman who has lost her child? I have had nothing yet lost everything. Papa calls upon me to exert myself against grief, but grief and I are one. I have no substance but that anguish which lives fully in me every moment of my wakeful hours, so that wakefulness is like a frightful dream that makes me long for a death-like sleep. What is there for me to hope for? To live for? Where is that enduring consolation for which I must bear up? Where is family? Husband? Child? I am so worn out by grief.

As soon as I had regained my strength, I went to the cemetery in the nearby village of Orbec where my infant had been buried and ordered a marble marker for his grave. I remained long enough to see it in place, and then we packed up and left Sassetôt. I wished never to see that vile house again. I took Nelly and we went to Caen, where we were welcomed warmly by Monsieur Leclerc at the Abbé's school for the deaf. The children's liveliness and expressiveness touched me deeply. As Nelly and I grew more proficient in signing, I felt less and less inclined to leave their community. My dulled senses left me incapable of doing much more than stumbling through the simplest daily routine. Returning to London was out of the question. I abhorred the very idea. I felt as though my past life had been severed by the death of my infant, and yet I had no clear path to the future. Esther would have come to see me if Ned had not made such a fuss. She was expecting their second child, and a long voyage would have been both reckless and foolish.

After a month, I gave in to Nelly's gentle prodding, and we left Caen, traveling south to Cannes and on to Rome, hoping that the warmer climate might restore my spirits. I took little pleasure in our excursions, but behind the numbness, I recognized the necessity of getting on. Nelly was delighted by the opportunity to travel. She had never been outside her village until she came to work for me, and it pleased me to think I might repay her loyalty in some small measure. There was never a problem with money. Papa immediately cabled any sum I requested.

Chapter Twenty-four

IN THE WINTER, WE RETURNED TO NICE WHERE I TOOK A LEASE ON a shop in the *vieille ville,* advertising myself as a widowed seamstress. I took only a few clients, enough to keep my hands busy. We made for several English ladies, but we preferred the Italians and the French. They minded less that Nelly and I communicated in signs. My pleasures were simple and few. In the summer, I walked the promenade with my parasol and a small book of poetry under my arm, looking for a place on the pebbly beach to sit and read. In the winter, when it rained, I spent a good deal of time at the window with my mind wrapped in ashen silence. Even in the splashing southern light with the sea sparkling at our feet, I was always cold.

Papa was relieved when we ceased our wandering and settled in Nice. He took extraordinary pains with his letters, but he annoyed me with his eager talk of my return. Sometimes I wouldn't even bother to finish a letter. I would leave it to Nelly to read, and she would write a reply. She was quite clever at reassuring him.

I wanted only to endure the first year, to get past the awful milestones—the first anniversary of our wedding and the birth. Only by distancing myself, by throwing up miles of plains and mountains between me and those events, would I be able to go on. I had lost all desire to see Harry again. Esther and Ned had not heard from him since his marriage to Miss Erskine. He cut ties with many of his old friends and no longer frequented the same social set. Drawing on scant gossip from a washer woman in Burford with a daughter in service at Longmeade, Esther learned that Viscount Ormelie had visited only once with his bride before withdrawing to Blackroak. It was rumored that he had given himself up to domesticity, that a child might be on the way. He spent most of his time in Yorkshire now. Each bit of news always twisted my heart, and I eventually asked Esther to refrain from any mention of him.

It was Esther who informed me of Mr. Nicholls's marriage to a wealthy widow in his parish, and who forwarded the following letter to me:

My Dear Friend,

It is a great relief to my heavy spirit to at last obtain a means by which our frail lines of communication might be reestablished. For nearly two years now, you have kept me at a distance, for reasons I knew not but which I respected. When you fled to the Continent, and when my inquiries met with firm resistance from your father, I feared some tragic decline in body or soul. That I was helpless to offer you spiritual guidance caused me great anxiety. Had I not happened upon Esther by chance at an exhibit in London, I dare say we might have lost contact altogether, for I shall be leaving London and Christ's Church to take the post of archdeacon with the bishopry of York, accompanied by my new bride, Mrs. Charlotte Iceton, the widow of Captain William Lacey Iceton, previously of York.

I am blessed to have secured the affections of such a virtuous woman of superior understanding and unimpaired self-possession and see in the fidelity of such a union a solid and tangible good. Having persevered in my attentions toward you for so many years, even in the face of hostile and unjust opposition, I have finally come to believe that you were right in withholding your love from me. Rather than vainly pursuing an empty shadow, it was my duty to seek a marriage that would glorify Him. I feel my marriage to the former Mrs. Iceton will accomplish that lofty goal and relieve a loneliness which has become too great to bear.

I could not pretend to have fulfilled my long-standing duty as both friend and advisor were I not to admonish you to seek a full and penitent reconciliation with the church and with Christ our Savior Who sees all our Suffering and forgives all our Sins. Scripture warns us that all lots do not fall in pleasant places, and only by moderating our expectations with patience and resignation may we cultivate a fruitful and virtuous life.

I remain yours sincerely,
Edgar Nicholls

After years of taking his affections for granted, upon reading this I was struck with how deeply he had loved me, and behind his overbearing righteousness I sensed a melancholy filled with regret for that which could not be. I had tinkered with his heart for as long as I could remember, and now that he had taken it away from me, I felt strangely deserted, as though a ghost that had haunted me for years had finally removed itself from my premises, and I felt an emptiness I had no right to feel. His honesty moved me more than he could know. It was a call to action, and I felt a feeble stirring of my old willful self. It was time to go home.

We began our journey back in August. When we arrived in Normandy, we stopped in Caen to visit Monsieur Leclerc and his pupils. Monsieur and I had corresponded regularly, and Nelly and I had taken it upon ourselves to sew for the children, sending trousers and jackets through the post every month, as the school had little money for much of anything except food. Even the books were so worn that the print on some of the pages had faded from excessive use.

Conversing with Monsieur Leclerc and the other teachers was extremely satisfying, for I now used signs almost exclusively with Nelly, and expressing myself was as effortless as taking a breath. On our second evening there, as we sat down to dinner at Monsieur's modest table, he informed me that I should expect a visitor in a few days' time.

Who?

A young friend who has waited a long while to see you again.

How do I know this young friend?

The boy, Renaud—he signed the name—*from Sassetôt. You do remember him?*

Certainly, I remember Renaud. He is coming here? To see me?

Yes. He came to see me after you departed. Very anxious to speak to you— very sad to learn that you had gone.

What did he want?

To tell you something. Something very important.

What?

He would not say. He went away, but asked that I send for him immediately should you ever come by again.

Curious. Strange.

He would not divulge his secret. He said only that you should know it.

I often wonder what would have happened had it not been for Renaud. Sometimes I think he was an angel steeped in earthly grime.

He stood in the courtyard, wringing his cap, with his ruddy face scrubbed so clean it looked like a polished pink apple. I leaned out the window and motioned him inside.

He was too timid to sit. He had grown much taller, and his natural shyness was compounded by the awkwardness of his age. I told him to leave off wringing his cap and offered him a cool drink, but he refused. I was astonished that he still remembered some of the signs we had learned from Monsieur Leclerc.

It's about the baby. He used the sign we had learned, the fingers slashing the crook of the elbow, where a mother cradles her infant.

A sudden shiver ran down my spine.

"You mean my baby?" I asked.

He nodded. "I was there, Madame," he said. "They sent me out, but I was listening and watching at the window. Madame, it was not as they told you. He cried, Madame. He made a good deal of noise." He repeated himself, making sure I understood his French.

"What are you saying, Renaud?"

"There was a man who took your baby away."

"The priest took him away. To bury him."

"No. The man was not a priest."

I recalled the face hiding in the shadows of my room.

"I don't understand."

"I didn't see your baby, but I know he was not dead. He cried very loudly when they took him away."

"That can't be," I said, wondering if I had completely misunderstood him. "You say my baby did not die? Is that right? That he was taken away by a stranger?"

"An Englishman."

"An Englishman?"

He nodded.

"How do you know?"

He drew up his shoulders in typical Gallic indignation. "Madame, I know an Englishman when I see one."

I shook my head in astonishment. "But Renaud, are you saying that—that this—this terrible tragedy—it was all a farce?"

"Yes, Madame."

"So—your mother, your aunts—everyone—they all lied to me?"

He dropped his head in shame and went back to wringing the cap.

"But why? Why would they all lie?"

He shook his head, denying any knowledge, but I felt he knew.

"Why did they do this?" I cried, feeling my voice swell in my throat. "Look up at me, Renaud. Why did they lie to me?"

He shrugged.

"But you do know. Tell me."

He rubbed his fingers together, the sign for money.

"They were paid? Someone paid your family?"

He nodded.

"They were paid to trick me into believing my child was born dead?"

He nodded again and shuffled his feet on the rug.

"But how?"

And then I remembered. Nelly had been sent away and had returned after it was all over.

"Did they send Nelly away on purpose?"

His nod was heavy with remorse.

"Why did you not tell me this? Why did you allow me to leave thinking my baby had died?"

He lifted such stricken eyes to me that I could not, for all my indignation, condemn the boy.

More memories came pouring back—the glances between the women, the faces turned away. I had interpreted Madame Tessier's anxious looks as concern for me and my baby—but it wasn't that at all. She was afraid that I might read on their lips or on their faces what was happening. They had taken advantage of my affliction and duped me in the basest, most despicable manner.

They had sold me and my child.

No. It couldn't be.

My heart pounded so hard against my chest that I felt it might burst. I sat back, pressing my hands to my chest to try to calm myself.

Renaud seemed frightened.

"Who was this man?" I said, softening my expression so as not to intimidate the boy.

He didn't know.

"English."

"Yes."

"Do you recall his name?"

No. The family had been very secretive about it.

"But surely, someone saw him pass through the village. Someone would have noticed him."

He wrung his hat some more and worried his brow in concentration. "He arrived in the blacksmith's carriage."

"The carriage for hire?"

He nodded.

"Then he must have stayed at the Auberge."

An idea struck Renaud. "The blacksmith's son," he said. "He's my friend. I can ask him."

"Yes," I said, removing the cap from his hands and planting it firmly on his head. "Go. Now. Hurry back to Orbec. And if he knows anything— anything at all, bring him to me. You and your friend shall both have a handsome reward. And there will be more, if you help me find the man who took my child."

But I already knew who took my child. There was no doubt in my mind.

He brushed back a lock of the lank hair and watched while I withdrew a small purse from my pocket.

"Thank you, my dear boy. Thank you from the bottom of my heart."

I put some coins into his hand.

"How did you get here?" I asked him.

"I walked to St. Pierre and took a van from there."

It was more than fifteen miles. "Here," I said, pressing another coin into his open hand. "Go to the tavern down the road. They have gigs for hire. And eat something before you go."

He closed his fist around the coins. With the fiery look of a zealot, he touched his cap and flew down the stairs.

I WAS AWAKENED BY THE light of a candle and opened my eyes to find Nelly leaning over me in her nightgown, shaking me gently.

The boy, she said, spelling Renaud's name with her fingers.

"He's here?"

She nodded.

I wrapped myself in my tartan shawl and followed Nelly's figure down the stairs. He had returned that very night, in the rain, with Pierrot in tow. The pair of them stood in the hallway in their mud-caked boots, drenched from head to toe, looking every bit like the spies they were. Nelly instructed them to remove their boots and then ushered them into the sitting room.

As soon as Nelly had lighted some candles, Pierrot began his story.

"There were two gentlemen. I think one was a nobleman."

"How do you know?"

"Because of the way they treated him."

"How old was he?"

He shrugged. "He was not young."

"The other man with him. A servant?"

"No. They called him *maître*. They arrived together with a woman. An English nursemaid. The nobleman stayed behind at the inn, and the *maître* took our gig and hurried off to Sassetôt. While he was gone, the nobleman took all his meals in his room. He did not want to be seen. Then the other man came back with the infant and took him upstairs to the nursemaid. Immediately after that, they paid for the gig and left by carriage."

"Do you know where they went?"

"To Lisieux. I recognized the driver. He has come through Orbec before."

"If I paid you, could you find this driver?"

"But of course."

"And if you come back with the name of the inn where they stayed in Lisieux, I will pay you even more."

"I can find this out, Madame."

After a long hesitation, I allowed my gaze to drift from the boys to Nelly and back.

"So, this little grave in Orbec. There is nothing there but—what? An empty wooden box?"

The boys looked down in embarrassment, but a smile broke over Nelly's countenance.

She signed to me, *He's alive.*

Yes, I nodded, returning her smile. *Yes, Nelly. He's alive.*

THE FOLLOWING WEEK, ABBÉ ODDOS accompanied me in his private carriage to Lisieux. He was an influential man, and we easily obtained the information we needed from the innkeeper at the *Cheval Blanc*. We learned that the gentleman, whom I believed to be Heaton, the Earl's lawyer, had remained in the town for a month, apparently biding his time until I gave birth. The second gentleman had arrived much later. I could not believe that the Earl of Hambledon had personally traveled all the way to France to abduct my child, but there was no doubt in my mind that he was behind the plot.

The Abbé suggested we inquire at the bank, thinking that perhaps the scoundrels had received funds from England during their stay. He was right. Money had been cabled to one of the gentlemen in Lisieux from a London bank.

The clerk wrote the name on a sheet of paper for me.

I stared at the writing in stunned silence.

"Are you sure about this?" I finally asked.

"*Très sûr, madame.*"

"Do you have any transactions in the name of Douglas Heaton?"

"*Non, madame.*"

"You are absolutely certain."

"*Oui, madame.*"

It was stifling hot in the carriage on the way back to Caen.

"This heat is really unbearable," I said as I untied my bonnet. "Do you mind?"

Je vous en prie, madame, he signed.

I removed my bonnet and laid it on the seat, then loosened my collar. I must have appeared quite pale, despite the heat, for my friend signed, *Are you ill?*

"I fear I am not well," I replied.

Shall I stop the coach?

"Yes, if you please."

We spread a blanket in the shade of a chestnut tree and rested while the sun gradually sank lower in the sky. The driver stretched out beneath a tree near the road, and the horses dozed. No one passed us. It was much too hot to travel.

"It was not the person I suspected," I said finally.

Yes. I noticed. It gave you quite a shock.

"It wasn't the Earl's lawyer at all. It was Mr. Collingwood. Mr. Collingwood was my husband's lawyer. If he was here, it means—it means that my husband was somehow involved."

Your husband?

"Yes."

You believe your husband took your child?

I could not answer.

I reflected a long while and then said, "Do you think—?" I faltered.

What, my dear?

"Is it because I'm deaf?"

I do not know your husband, my dear. I cannot answer that.

"But I would have been a good mother, I'm convinced of it."

I am sure of it.

I recalled my conversation with Harry on our wedding night, and the steps he had taken to prevent a pregnancy. Perhaps he had never believed I was fit to be a mother. Perhaps he had never intended to have children at all.

I said, "Maybe, he thought, without a hearing father, I would not be capable on my own."

Many people think the deaf are not capable of leading normal lives.

He signed something else, but my vision was blurred, and I could not read his hands.

I dabbed at my eyes with the back of my hand.

"I beg your pardon, sir," I said. "It's only the heat."

MY HOMECOMING WAS OVERSHADOWED BY an unfortunate turn of events. Two thousand tailors were threatening to go on strike, and Papa, as chairman of the Master Tailors' Association, was negotiating around the clock with the workers' union. He was at a meeting when Nelly and I arrived home, and despite the urgency of the situation, he hurried home to greet me. I found him in his library, striking a pose on the hearth rug with a cold cigar clutched between his fingers, still every bit the man of style. He was perhaps a little heavier, and haggard from anxiety and sleepless nights, but his cravat was a perfect knot, his carriage full of grace, his entire self exquisitely neat. My impression of him was rendered more vivid from long absence, and it softened my heart and reminded me of my old obsessions and passions, now faded.

He greeted me with a firm kiss on the forehead, affecting a sternness I know he did not feel. I would not release his hands, and I pressed them a long while. Finally I gave in to my emotion and threw myself on him, hugging him quite savagely. He patted my head roughly and tenderly peeled my arms off his neck.

"You look exceedingly well, daughter," he said.

"Do I?"

"Quite well."

"I am in good spirits. Perhaps it shows."

"Indeed, it does."

"I know it's late, and we're both weary, but there is something very important I must tell you. Really, it cannot wait until morning," I said. I handed him a letter I had written while still in Caen, in which I explained all that I had discovered.

"What is this?"

"Astonishing news. Quite astonishing. Go on, read it."

He settled into his armchair and adjusted the spectacles on his nose. When he had finished reading, he appeared troubled rather than elated.

"My dear, dear daughter," he said, shaking his head sadly. He removed his spectacles and gazed up at me with eyes full of tenderness. "My dear child, you have suffered so much. I cannot allow you to go chasing off on some hopeless pursuit."

"Is it because you don't believe it?" I asked, seating myself in a chair opposite him.

"It is madness to think this family lied to you. That they could even feign such a thing."

"But they did. I know it for a fact."

"My dear," he said, leaning forward to take my hand and patting it, "you must put these melancholy thoughts out of your mind. It will only lead to more misery."

"Why? Why do you urge me to ignore such a thing? Read my letter again, I beg of you. Look at the evidence. How can you not believe it?"

"This Renaud, this village idiot, he put these ideas in your head."

"No. That's not true."

"You must come back to your senses."

"I believe it was Harry in Lisieux. Not his father. It was he. I am sure of it."

"Perhaps. Perhaps it is true. Then you must let it be. He has done the right thing."

"What?" I started. "Whatever do you mean?"

I looked around for a slate, but there was none. Of course. I had been gone well over a year.

Reluctantly, Papa tossed his cold cigar into the grate and settled himself at his desk.

You are better off without the child & the child is better off without you. Would you spend the rest of your life hiding behind lies, suffering insult & contempt, shunned by genteel society? Even if you would be willing to live with such censure, think what degradation would await your child!

I was looking over his shoulder as he wrote. "No," I said even before he had finished. "This is nonsense."

He jammed the pen back in the stand and turned to me. "Nonsense? Nonsense?"

"I shall go on with my plans."

"What plans?"

"I shall find him. I shall get him back."

"I will not allow it."

"Not allow it? What do you mean? I am nearly twenty-five. I have been married and given birth to a child. What do you mean, you will not allow it?"

"I only want you to see reason. You are such a willful girl. You must listen to reason."

"What reason counsels a mother to give up her child?"

"Leave him where he is. If he is with his father, he will be well cared for."

I smoothed down my skirts and clasped my hands before me. "I regret that my homecoming has only brought discord back to our family. We are both too tired to discuss this further. Good night."

Back in my room, I went immediately to my desk and penned my thoughts in a note I would show him the morrow:

I know what I must do, and I shall allow no one to stand in my way. All my life I have suffered doubts about my character. I have been criticized harshly for my indiscretion and imprudence, for my contempt of decorum, for defying scruple and trampling on it like a broken-down hedge, but the losses I have borne have left me more convinced than ever of the necessity of self-reliance, of judging matters for myself. No longer do I regret not having those feminine elements which society prizes—the coy restraint, the dependent reason, the submissive spirit. I am determined to reclaim my son. I shall be a mother again, for this was God's will, and Man has stolen it from me.

I HAD MISSED ESTHER TERRIBLY during my long ordeal on the Continent, but now she and Ned were living in London, and frequent visits were once again possible. Ned's admission to the Academy had eased their financial worries, permitting them to take a large house and studio in Holland Park. An upstairs bedroom had been converted to a smaller studio for Esther, and she often received me there that winter after my return. She had grown into motherhood, helped along by the additional staff they could now afford, and she had been able to return to painting. Her fondness for great mythological subjects had faded, and her passions had been redirected by the changes in her life, for she saw the world quite differently now. She painted those very things she had often scorned. There were many charcoal sketches of her two children, Frederick and Ellie, and oil paintings of quiet, domestic scenes. She wholeheartedly supported me in my quest to reclaim my son.

I was sitting by the fire, nibbling on some sandwiches with my tea while she sketched my portrait.

"Come, talk with me, Tiggy," I said, setting down my cup. "I need your good cheer."

She finished a few strokes, then peeled off her tunic and came to sit with me.

"When are you leaving?" she asked.

"Next month. When the roads have thawed."

"Have you decided on a plan?"

"I have several, none of which is appealing."

"Have you had a reply from Mr. Nicholls?"

"I have. He struck a rather grand tone with me."

"Well, I shouldn't be surprised." She picked up a slate and scribbled, *Wife's influence.* I had shown Esther the letter he had written me, and she thought I should have taken offense. *How did he describe her? A lady of "unimpaired self-possession"? What does he imply by that? That you are not?*

"I was not insulted. On the contrary. But he is in a high position of authority as archdeacon, and I was hoping he might help. He would have parish records, of births and christenings throughout Yorkshire. I'm sure Harry would have had the baby christened."

"And then?"

"Well—" I smoothed out my skirt with a nervous gesture.

"What? What shall you do?"

"You won't approve."

She laughed. "I rarely do. But that has never stopped you." She set down the slate and took my hand. "Nor has it ever weakened my love for you."

"I have given it much thought."

"Tell me."

"I have one skill at my disposal. I'm a tailor. And in the country, it's common practice for a certain class of tailors to travel around working in private houses. We would be given room and board while we made clothes for families and their servants. I would find out all I need to know."

"Not alone!"

"I shall have Nelly. She's a great comfort to me, and I've trained her well. I shall hire an apprentice in York, a young man to take on all the manly tasks."

"This is folly. It's dangerous! It would be dangerous—and compromising—for any young woman—but for a deaf woman who can't even hear a coach barreling down the street? And to reduce yourself to such a low rank—and live among common laborers and farmers! What a disgrace!"

"My ancestors did as much. My ancestors were journeymen tailors."

"Oh, Vevey!" she cried, and her eyes grew moist. She picked up a fan from the tea table and fanned herself vigorously, then turned to me with eyes full of sympathy. "Dear God, why did Harry do such a thing? Why?"

"I think I know. But I can't be sure."

"But he married you. You would have been mother to his children."

"But now I'm nothing but the deaf daughter of a tradesman. He is a nobleman. Noblemen have their rights."

I was loathe to leave for York. Although Papa frequently dined at his club now, leaving me to quiet teas and dinners with Aunt Lavinia and her set of spinster and widower friends, I had nonetheless found my heart warmed by the sight of our tailors busy at their workbenches, and the apprentices blowing in off the wind-chilled streets from their errands, and the smells of new spun cashmeres and wools.

When Nelly returned from a well-earned visit to her family, we set off for York where I had rented a small house near the center.

I HAD HOPED MR. NICHOLLS might invite me to his home and that I might have the privilege of meeting his wife, for I truly wished for his happiness. However, there was no invitation forthcoming, and he received me in his study at the Bishop's palace. His letter had led me to believe that he had a dim understanding of the reason for which I left England, but he was not at all prepared for what I was about to tell him. He sat behind an impressive desk, surrounded by ecclesiastical volumes, with pastel-hued light from a stained-glass window tinting the air above his head, listening to my story with the air of a man whose sanctity had just been desecrated. I thought he might have run from my presence had he been able to do so with dignity. If I had hoped for compassion, I had been gravely mistaken. I had never forgotten his sympathy for Reggie and how, despite Reggie's misplaced passions, he had never judged my brother harshly. But I was a woman, and different rules of tolerance applied to me. There was no room for missteps in his ideology, and it occurred to me then, sitting opposite him, that to be vehemently in love with a woman of whom he disapproved so fiercely must have been a heavy cross to bear. I had hoped that marriage might have softened his stern and bigoted views, but it seemed he had finally found a woman as high-principled as himself. Perhaps he did not feel the same passion for her as he had felt for me, but he esteemed her most highly, and this would endure.

When at last I came to explaining how I hoped to find my son, he folded his hands beneath his chin and replied, "This is most imprudent. This is madness."

"What kind of madness is it that tears a newborn infant away from its mother?"

"I do not condone what has been done to you, but you must seek legal means."

"He would have every advantage by law. And I would have nothing but a protracted struggle and public scandal."

"You have no clues as to where the child might be?"

"Only reason—and intuition. Working together, I think they may turn up something. Some clues."

"How do you intend to go about this?"

"There are records in each parish. I thought you might use your influence to obtain them. There must have been a christening."

"So you would chase down every boy child two years of age?"

"It's a beginning."

He hesitated a long while, his knuckles pressed to his forehead. Then, rising and extending his hand to me, he replied, "I shall pray on it."

Apparently, the Almighty was silent on the issue, for I never heard from him again.

Chapter Twenty-five

THEY SAY THE WIND UP HERE IS PIERCING AND KEEN, THAT IT ARticulates a sound so piteous that even the sternest old souls of ancient lineage, that race of taciturn men who inhabit this desolate place, look up from the fireside on a March night and take note of it. Nelly often pauses in her needlework and glances over her shoulder in wide-eyed terror, but I know it is only the wind inciting her imagination. The people themselves are scarcely less fearsome. I was warned that they were particularly inhospitable to outsiders, but I have found that their ill humor is shared equally among themselves and their families as well. Indeed, only the wild marshes and moors command their respect, for humanity certainly does not.

Their foul ways must not be confused with that coarseness which is a natural consequence of ill treatment, poverty, and hardship, for in the vales that extend beyond the domain of Blackroak there are plenty of small-landed proprietors who have made themselves rich. Yet, sitting on thousands of pounds, they will part with not even a penny's worth of education for their sons, preferring instead to breed offspring of an equally misanthropic disposition, who pass their years sniffing cur-like at the air, waiting for the scent of decay that signals the time when they shall inherit the miser's legacy.

There were a few genteel persons in the market town of Swidden who should be excluded from my wide-sweeping reproach—most notably a wealthy draper whose fortune had been made on wool but whose pride kept him firmly rooted in his native county; a doctor of questionable skill and his Evangelical mother; a rich tanner of some standing; and finally, a drunken vicar whose influence was rarely felt beyond the soot-blackened walls of the Royal Oak Pub where we had taken rooms, unless it was by one of his common-looking daughters on whom he frequently let loose his crop as well as his tongue.

Over all of these gradations and various ranks loomed the iron-clad preeminence of Blackroak Hall, ancient seat of the Earls of Hambledon, a domain so old and rich in legend that it had escaped the transformations sweeping the nation. It had never repented its excesses nor its arrogance and had made scant changes to ameliorate the plight of its laboring poor scattered throughout the high moorlands and slopes of the dales on what remained of its once-vast estate. But this intransigence was not only accepted, it was all but revered by the locals, for if the Earls of Hambledon had resisted adopting a more virtuous, humane, and beneficent face before the example of a virtuous and high-minded court, neither had they fallen into the silliness of the previous century.

The Earls of Hambledon were descendants of the great Scottish Earls of Breadalbane of the Clan Campbell through a disinherited son passed over in favor of his younger sibling. Seething with vengeance, the elder son had crossed the border with his loyal followers and joined forces with the powerful Dukes of Cumbria and Northumberland. For services rendered to the crown, he was settled with monastic lands and forests in the vast moorland just north of the vale of Swidden. Marriages to daughters of powerful English lords and the acquisition of even more monastic lands as far as Holmsley to the south and Bramsdale to the west resulted in yet more titles and baronies. Harry had at least four titles that I recall: Viscount Ormelie, Lord Derwent, and Lord Holmsley from his father, Robert Breadalbane, the Earl of Hambledon; as well as Lord Cleves from his mother—also possibly heir to title of Lord Holburton and the barony of Toquedale, but these were all titles without land. Of all that great wealth, only Blackroak remained.

Blackroak itself might well have fallen into decay had it not been for the vagaries of fate. Over the years there had been many attempts to shift the family seat to another estate, but circumstances inevitably drove them to return to Blackroak or to remain there. Blackroak Hall always seemed to reclaim the hapless Breadalbanes, whether they wished it or not. The women in particular dreaded Blackroak, for despite the efforts of generations to accommodate the great hall with increasingly modern comforts, and several necessary additions undertaken by Harry's grandfather, it retained a hostile and warlike face of feudal grandeur.

For years now, all across England, there had been a flurry of building, of remodeling and renovation. Gothic wonders with crenellated towers, conservatories, billiard and smoking rooms were being built with both old and new wealth. There had been little attempt at Blackroak to cultivate a false image of domesticity, no effort to become more serious or religious. No chapels had been built, no new servants' quarters added to permit a separation of men and women. This place was too wild, too ancient, too remote to feel more than just a feeble swell from that mighty wave of change.

BY JUNE, AFTER THREE MONTHS of slogging from farm to farm and house to house with Nelly—who was being rewarded handsomely for her pluck and venturesome spirit—and Jack, the apprentice I had taken on in York, I had come to know the temperament of both the land and people. I often marveled at how Harry, having hailed from a place as wild as this, had cultivated such progressive interests. I already surmised that much of it had to do with his mother and her influence, and I wondered what it must have been like for her, closed away in such a desolate region for months on end, awaiting the visits of family and friends to lighten the moroseness of her life. And I wondered about the woman Harry had married and how she had adapted to the barrenness and isolation.

Even among the most taciturn of races, gossip has its place, and after several months word got about that the Tailor's Widow made as good as you could get in the finest shops in London. A neighboring farmer would send a boy four or five miles across the moors to ask me to come next to the Outhwaites to make a wedding suit for a cabinet-maker's son, or to Sir William's manor house up on Booze Moor to make his coachman's new livery. It was how my ancestors had made their living, and the difficulty of their way of life was brought keenly home to me. Journeying tailors generally turned out work of an inferior quality—the best tailors had shops in town and served the gentry or rich tradesmen—but it never occurred to me to make a jacket for a wheelwright with any less care than if I were making it for the Duke of Manchester. Perhaps the cloth was homespun and the man a crude and impatient sort with weathered hands and hardened gums where his teeth should be, but I would have been ashamed to turn out clumsy work, whatever the garment and whoever the client might be. Sometimes they appreciated the quality; more often they did not. The women cared more than the men. Some of them recognized how rare it was to find a tailoress who could cut, sew, and whip the finest buttonholes

they'd ever seen. The farmers only wanted their garments cheap and serviceable; as long as it held together well, little else mattered.

There was a good deal of very dull work, repairing or altering old clothes to fit younger sons. Nelly did much of this and groused a good deal about it. Jack made trousers, which were the least difficult of the garments to make. He was not particularly quick, but he was good-natured and never groused at all. I had hired him away from a master tailor in York who had often beat him for his laziness and suspected him of theft, although it had never been proven. Jack despised his master and was eager to get out of his contract, even if it meant clambering over the moors with two "kippers" looking for seasonal work. He knew only that I was a master tailor's widow fallen on hard times and driven to journeymen's work to bring in extra money. For all his faults, he was a clever boy and suspected there was much he was not being told. He was indeed lazy, but he never lacked in respect. He took on much of the men's work in our queer little threesome, drove the wagon and tended our horse, and tolerated a much harsher life than he would have in York, often sleeping on the hard settle beside a cold fireplace or bedding down in the barn while Nelly and I were generally offered a cupboard bed or shared a mattress with one of the women of the houses where we lodged. I think he was a little in awe of me and smitten with Nelly, who liked to make fun of him just to watch his big ears turn bright red.

The farmhouses were crude and cold, all harsh stone and floors strewn with straw or sawdust, and low ceilings blackened from years of soot. Everything about them was elemental, even the smell of things: oatcakes on a smoking bakestone, goose feathers and blood, animal dung, men returning from the fields bathed in salty sweat. There was rarely anything beautiful to look at except the moors, with which I fell in love. I often wondered what it would have been like to live here as Harry's wife. Sometimes I made myself believe he was not behind this deception at all, but then I would remember, and the betrayal would rack me all over again. It was like waking from a nightmare and finding the waking more wretched than sleep.

My life was measured in stitches and miles, and when we had finished at one farm and were moving on to the next, I would begin to hope again, wondering if perhaps this next house would yield secrets I so desperately needed to know. I had resolved to find my son through a methodical acquaintance with every family in the domain, for I had convinced myself the boy was hidden somewhere not far from Blackroak Hall. Knowing that Harry rarely visited London or Lord Stamford's estate anymore, I felt confident my search would not be in vain. As soon as we pulled up in a farmyard, I began looking for the children and judging their ages. Whenever I came across a toddling little boy my hopes would soar. Inevitably, there would be factors to rule him out as my son, and yet I would persist in my acquaintance with the family, believing that somewhere, under one of these roofs, someone knew of his existence.

At every house we visited, there was always gossip about Blackroak Hall and its inhabitants. Most of the farmers I visited were tenants on that estate, and their master's business was their business as well. Even the occasional gentry I called on would yield snippets of information. I struggled with reading their dialect and their quaint way of speaking, but I watched closely and observed, and I understood a good deal from the women's mannerisms. Nelly was not much more successful at following their conversations than I at first, but she learned to listen for certain names and expressions. Even if much of their prattle passed over her head, she was sure to catch anything they said about the master or his son, or the son's new wife.

I would sit there in quiet thrall, trying to read their lips and piece together the stories that Nelly would recount in full later in the evening when we would sit together at the fireside, speaking freely with our hands. What I learned was disturbing. Although I knew that the portrait being painted of the family was filtered through the eyes of a people inclined to violent and intractable opinions, people who fed on rumor and conjecture, I knew there must be some truth in what they said.

Most of the rumors centered on Lady Ormelie. Each family seemed to have a different story to tell about her. Some said that she was deceitful and without scruples, that she had been caught spying through keyholes and nosing through the Earl's papers and mail in his study. Others said that the servants were openly defiant and that she had no authority over them. Some saw it as a war of wills between the Earl and his daughter-in-law, that if she sacked a servant for impertinence, the Earl would rehire her; that if she gave an order, he would be sure to overturn it.

Lord Ormelie had been sympathetic and caring at first, but she had driven him away. Each time he departed, even for a few days, she would make scenes, pleading with him to stay. After he had gone, she would lock herself in her room and write him letters, sending as many as three in one day. When he returned, she punished him with long torturous silences. She would lock him out of her room at night.

She had worn him ragged, the poor man, just beat him down.

No wonder he didn't have the stomach for her.

Pretty as she was, he never went near her room anymore.

I was not a reluctant convert to unflattering opinions of Harry's wife. I had disliked Arabella Erskine from the first moment I had laid eyes on her on the green lawn of Lord Stamford's estate, dressed in her pert little straw hat and maize-yellow dress and her archer's gloves, showing off her accomplishments to admiring young gentlemen and following Harry with her eyes like a hawk follows a titmouse in the field. She was pretty and spoiled and well-born. I had judged her to be shallow and silly as well. A perfect Rowena.

No one ever spoke ill of the Earl. Nelly said the children seemed to fear him. A kind of superstitious thrall hung over their heads, as if the slightest suggestion of impertinence toward the lord might bring down the wrath of God on their houses.

I WAS AT THE RICHMONDS' farm when I got word that farmer Platt of Rushcross Grange had been struck by lightning while bringing the sheep from the fells to the beck, and his wife sent her boy to beg me come to make her a decent mourning dress. I had been at Rushcross Grange just the previous week and had made a new suit for Mr. Platt—his first new suit since their wedding. I had found Hannah Platt to be an unusually refined woman, with a charitable heart. She had shown me an eager sympathy and taken an interest in my affliction and the unique manner in which Nelly and I communicated.

I left Nelly and Jack to finish our work for the Richmonds and returned to Rushcross by foot the following day. The sober industry that marks the occasion of death was all too familiar to me, and the household took little notice of my arrival. That very night I set to work by candlelight in an upstairs room, down on my knees on the clean scrubbed floor cutting a black superfine wool I had brought with me. By the next morning, after a short nap at dawn, I had the bodice basted and ready to fit. Mrs. Platt stood quietly in her shift and petticoat while I worked on a sleeve. I think it was because she was alone and away from the others that she broke down and wept.

She was drying her eyes on a handkerchief I had proffered when she glanced over at the window with a look of alarm. I gathered she had heard a commotion outside. Then her sister came upstairs and told her something that threw Mrs. Platt into a terrible state of agitation. I tried to help her out of the bodice, but she fell to weeping again. Her sister went away and returned. Mrs. Platt said yes, all right, and her sister went away again. After that, Mrs. Platt made a hurried attempt to compose herself.

The door was opened by the sister, and Arabella swept in. The contrast between her elegant figure and the dreary barrenness of the attic room struck us all with a momentary sense of awe. As critical as I was inclined to be, I found nothing to reproach in her dress—the Napoleon blue moiré and Genoa velvet mantle, the feather-trimmed hat, the earrings. She was as pretty as I remembered and every bit as haughty, but she seemed surprisingly at ease in such a humble setting. I felt sure she had called here before. She looked my way, and for the briefest moment I feared there might be some recognition from that day years ago when she had found Harry talking to me on the croquet lawn at Longmeade. But there was none. She glanced quickly back at Mrs. Platt.

"Where is everyone, Hannah? The house is fairly empty."

"They're all down at Beech Beck, m'lady. It's sheep washing."

"But how inconvenient. They should be here with you."

"Couldn't be helped, m'lady." I knew that just before the accident, Mr. Platt had sent word to the neighbors to help with the sheep washing, and the beck had already been dammed. He would be mourned after the work was done.

"There will be no festivities," Hannah said. "They'll be back come nightfall."

"I'm so very sorry, Hannah."

"You are very kind, m'lady."

"When is the funeral to be held?"

"On Thursday, m'lady."

"At the church in Swidden?"

"Yes, m'lady."

As she pulled out a small purse of coins and pressed it into Mrs. Platt's trembling hand, it occurred to me that Arabella was paying Hannah a condolence call, and a very prompt one at that.

"Here. For a good headstone. And some mourning clothes for the family."

"That's very generous of you. Thank you."

"Fate is not kind, Hannah."

The older woman nodded heavily.

There was a brief moment when neither of them spoke, but there seemed to be no awkwardness. Suddenly, to my astonishment, she gathered Mrs. Platt in her arms and held her tightly. Words were murmured that I could not understand, but I felt sure they were words of kindness and solace.

Lady Ormelie stepped back and said, "I see you've found someone to make you a mourning dress."

Mrs. Platt dabbed at her eyes and attempted a weak smile. "Mrs. True-lock here is very skilled. She had a dress shop in Nice, m'lady."

"In Nice?"

I nodded, and she held out her hand to me as a way of introduction. I took it and curtseyed demurely. Her fingers gripped mine quite firmly, and when I glanced back up, her sharp blue eyes were still resting on me.

She turned to examine the wool I had cut out for the skirt and draped over the bed.

"Hannah, you should have crape for mourning. I shall order it for you."

"Oh, this is quite good enough," Hannah replied. "Crape wears badly, m'lady. It's not suitable for life out here."

"But you should have at least one crape dress. For Sundays and feast days." She looked up at me, and I knew there was a clever intellect operating behind those sharp blue eyes. "If this woman can't work with crape, then I'll have the seamstress in Swidden make it."

"I can work with crape," I said with a flash of pride and immediately bit my tongue.

I could tell from the look in her eyes that I had hidden nothing from her. She appraised me coolly and then turned back to Hannah.

"It's as you wish," she said.

"Mrs. Truelock does very good work, m'lady. Never had a seamstress like her around these parts. She's a master tailor's widow, and made Mr. Platt the nicest coat he's ever had." Her eyes grew moist, and she said, "He's wearing it now. He'll wear it in his grave."

"There, there, Hannah. I didn't come to make you cry. We've shed enough tears together, you and I."

She turned back to me with eyes kindled with new interest.

"If you had a shop in Nice, then you must know French fashion."

"Yes. Of course."

"Are you the one who made the coachman's livery for Sir William?"

"Yes, ma'am."

"He was very pleased. Apparently it's quite spectacular."

I merely nodded, my eyes fixed on her countenance, praying I would not misunderstand.

"I should like some new everyday livery for our steward and footmen." Here she directed her glance toward Hannah and added with a flash of wryness, "Provided his lordship will agree."

Then, to me she said, "You would oblige me by coming to Blackroak."

When I failed to reply, she asked, "Did you understand what I just said?"

"Yes."

She motioned with a gloved hand to her ear. "You're hard of hearing, aren't you?"

"Just a little," I lied.

She seemed to reflect on this, but her countenance was cool and passive, and I could not divine her thoughts. She asked me when I would be finished with Mrs. Platt's dress.

"I'll be done today, ma'am."

"Goodness, you are quick," she said with an air of disbelief. "So, come to me tomorrow," she concluded.

Then she pressed Hannah's hand and was gone.

That night, by flickering candlelight and in an unsteady hand, I wrote an anguished letter to Esther.

God help me, Esther dear, what have I done? I am marching straight into the Lion's Den—and yet this is the road Providence has led me down, and I must not shrink from it. Our search has proven futile so far—as many predicted it would. It may be that my son is far from here on another estate, or even in another country. My conviction is that he is nearby, but perhaps I have only deluded myself with fanciful hopes and wishes. I have grown so accustomed to conjecture, to finding meaning in only a few scant clues, that it is quite possible I have seen something that never existed. I was indeed mad to do this, to pretend to poverty and take up such a wretched way of life in this remote and harsh land when Nelly and I could be sitting comfortably in some fashionable little dress shop in Oxford Street. I have been weakening in my resolve these past few weeks, thinking I have made a colossal error and subjected myself and my faithful Nelly to countless physical dangers and moral debasement, but this encounter with Arabella Erskine seems providential—does it not?

I am resolved to go. If you were here I know you would dissuade me, and you would be right to do so. I am quite alone to decipher the world around me from behind my barrier of silence, and it's a confusing, baffling world indeed, replete with misunderstandings and erroneous perceptions. Yet, I wonder if I am any worse off than the man who puts his faith in pure diction and polished elegant phrases, for language can be sorely manipulated, and we are all wont to find truth where we want it to be.

Mrs. Platt says she believes Harry is not presently at Blackroak, but she cannot be sure. She does believe the Earl is there. I shudder at the thought of an encounter with the horrid man, and yet I think I would risk a good deal to set eyes on him just once. The hall is vast, and I shall be quartered with servants; therefore, it is unlikely that I cross paths with either Harry or the Earl. I shall do my best to learn what I can from the servants, but I am at a terrible disadvantage without Nelly. I shall send for her and Jack as soon as they finish at the Richmonds.

Now, Arabella Erskine is not at all as I had imagined her to be. She strikes me as quite confident and at ease in her role as châtelaine, very poised with a proud head, and more sympathetic than I would wish to admit. Clearly she has a friend and loyal servant in Mrs. Platt, and a discreet one at that as Mrs. Platt was quite reluctant to discuss the lady after her departure. I was able to understand a good deal of their exchange, and I feel there has been some trauma to which Hannah has been privy. The lady is not as plump as I remembered, but rather delicate in appearance, with fine porcelain skin and haze-blue eyes, and yet there is nothing meek about her demeanor. Her face is quite expressive, and I find I can readily read her countenance. I wonder if this is an American trait. I found myself wondering about her voice; I imagine it to be rather high pitched. She was exquisitely dressed, a very decorative woman, and yet I sense she is not content to exist solely as an adornment. I remember Harry had thought her childish, but that was more than two years ago, and I am sure much has changed since then.

I wonder how much of my rashness is fueled by my own wretched pride. It's all I can do to defer to her without appearing impertinent or disrespectful, but good gracious, Esther, I was once Lady Ormelie myself, and I can't forget it for a second.

There is so much conjecture, I cannot know how it will all unfold. I am quite mad to proceed with this.

Chapter Twenty-six

I LEFT RUSHCROSS GRANGE JUST AFTER DAWN, CROSSING THROUGH a quilt-work of pastures before turning north into the rise of fells beyond which lay Blackroak Hall. There, I left the ridge and struck straight into the heath, wading knee-deep through the scrubby grey growth down to the narrow hollow which I held as far as New Mill, after which I turned away from the beck into high moorland heath. All morning the sky was dark, and ominous clouds threatened rain that never fell, although the wind smelled strongly of it. I passed a farm at which I had lodged only the previous month and caught sight of the Kertons and their children on the slopes above Moor Close cutting peats. Farther up the vale, a row of men moved along the hillside scything bracken at a languid rhythm that belied the tremendous power behind each stroke. Their old bearded sheep-dog froze and kept me fixed in his sights until I passed by on the path below. In the shaded vales, black-faced sheep grazed in folds cut out by low drystone walls, but farther up in the open moorland they seemed but isolated fixtures on the vast treeless landscape. Even in the early summer, with the bleak fells fleshed out in soft hues of greys and greens, and the hay meadows rich with wild flowers and grasses, it seemed an unlikely place for human habitation.

I had never grown accustomed to the bleakness of my new life. There were still many nights when I pined for my comforts, for clean shoes and clean skirts, for my books and my down-feathered mattress, for servants to wash my clothes and put food on my table. I did all these chores for myself now. It seemed my back was always aching and my head nodding over my supper. Yet I felt I had entered into this strange land more completely than any place I had ever known before. When the clouds marched across the sky casting upon the hills a rolling swell of shadows, when the wind whipped the sea of grasses into ever-changing patterns, when the lightning split the heavens and you could see the rain in the distance descending to the earth like an ashen wall, these things thundered with sound in my imagination and evoked profound and inexplicable emotion. Sometimes I was certain I had heard sound, but I knew it was only the power of what my eyes saw and my heart felt.

Despite my determination to resist any tender thoughts of Harry, the knowledge that these were his ancestral lands weighed heavily on my mind—nor could I ignore the fact that through my son, I, too, was linked to this place.

I arrived at Blackroak Hall just before dusk. As I came up over a knoll from the west, a grove of trees and the crumbling abbey wall obscured the house. My first sight was of the park framed by the remains of the abbey's entrance. A single vaulted arch supported on each side by skeletal arched windows beckoned the traveler to look through the portal and beyond to the black hills and moody skies. The arch stood in spite of itself, in spite of its own massive weight and the eroding years and man's determination to bring it down, as though proclaiming this vast and bleak land worthy of its grace.

As I came up over the rise and the great hall came into view, a few weak rays of evening sun pierced the clouds, bathing the walls in golden light. The lichen-covered stones and dark mullioned glass fairly throbbed with luminosity. I could go no farther without pausing to set down my traveling bag and gaze upon these walls that had loomed so great in my mind for so many years.

In the Talking Book, Harry had written:

Blackroak is a magnificent old-fashioned muddle, a sprawling Tudor hall with parts of a medieval abbey still embedded in it. It is really quite charming. All that rigorous symmetry breaks down into a squadron of towers along the west wing where it rambles away into the landscape. Poor old thing—it has never been able to sever itself from its crumbling past.

It had been rebuilt in several brief bursts of activity when one earl or another had reconciled himself to his lot, but then interest or funds failed, and each addition was merely absorbed into an incongruous whole.

There was little sign of activity save a few men on stools milking cows in the pasture, and a boy leading a donkey loaded with back-cans in the direction of the house. I followed him down a path toward a low barn hidden by a hedge of old yews, passing stables and a coach house. A young man with a wheelbarrow paused to stare at me from a vegetable garden. I came at last to a small outer courtyard and startled a scullery maid nearly out of her wits. She fled inside, and within a heartbeat I was surrounded by a motley pack of snarling curs. All I could do was freeze in terror until a white-capped woman appeared in the arched doorway drying her hands on her apron. She was too far away to allow me to read her lips, and I dared not tread one foot toward her, so I called out my name and business, adding that I had come specifically at Lady Ormelie's request. Finally, the housekeeper appeared and the hounds slunk away.

I followed the woman through a laundry into the kitchen courtyard, past a well and a larder, down a dim and twisting corridor of stone where my nose, sharpened by hunger, detected a joint roasting on a spit; then it was up a few steps, past a steamy kitchen and a blur of white aprons, through a massive iron-studded door into a hall, and finally, after pausing to light a candle, up a cramped, dark tower stair, four flights to the very top. We came out into a small chamber with a sharply pitched ceiling buttressed by blackened arches and beams. It was an old Tudor closet, once used as a private place of retreat from the public throng. The housekeeper paused to light a candle on the ledge, and when she turned to me, I shrank with panic, realizing that this was to be my lodging. Only a faint half-light of dusk passed through a narrow double window choked in spiderwebs and dust, and the plain stone fireplace, unadorned by so much as a mantel, was cold and dank. There was a bed at the end of the room, an ancient worm-eaten wardrobe, and a small nightstand. No table nor even a chair.

The woman was attempting to tell me something, but in the wan light I could not read her lips. My eyes kept darting around the close, dark confines, thinking that I was to be imprisoned here. When she turned to go, I seized her arm. She fairly threw me off, turning on me a countenance full of contempt. Her features were regular, perhaps at one time handsome, but now drawn and soured by age and ill temper, and her iron-grey hair pulled taut around her temples did nothing to soften the severity of her face. I beseeched her to show me where the candles and matches were kept. At the sound of my strange voice, she held her candle to my face, examining me curiously in the manner of one examining a two-headed calf.

"You're deaf!" she shouted.

"I am indeed a little hard of hearing. Now, am I to understand that this is where I am to be lodged?"

I couldn't make any sense out of her reply. When I knelt down to remove my slate from my bag and begged her to write upon it, she pushed it away with an impatient air. Clearly, I could not expect a woman of mean understanding and questionable temper to deal with my shortcomings. She grabbed me by the elbow and wheeled me around the room, opening the wardrobe to show me candles, bedding, and an old-fashioned chamber pot. I understood that I would need to fetch my own water in the morning. Finally, yielding to expedience, she set down her candle, picked up the slate and scribbled, *breakfast 6:30.* I was to have nothing to eat until then.

When I asked her name, she printed slowly and ceremoniously, *Mrs. Brumfit.*

Then she retrieved her candle and swooped out.

NOT ONCE SINCE MY DEAFNESS had I slept isolated from other humans, and suddenly, here I was confined to a chamber somewhere in the deep gloom of a crumbling tower, listening to the stone cold heart of a darkness more palpable than anything I had ever known. Quickly, I set about lighting more candles, then, realizing how few had been allotted to me, I snuffed them out and relied on only the one. It's meager light barely penetrated the low rafters, and I sat on my bed for a long while, struggling to calm my thumping heart. Finally, I mustered up the courage to explore my surroundings. Apart from the door to the stairwell through which we had entered, there was a second door, which I presumed led to an antechamber and the rest of the house, but this was locked. Nor could I pry open the large carved trunk at the foot of my bed. After I had poked around the shadows and convinced myself there were no ogres, I undressed and crawled into my damp and chilly bed, telling myself all would be right with the light of day. I took from my bag the one sole book I had carried with me into this hinterland; it was that remarkable collection of poetry by the Frenchman Baudelaire whom I had met in London on the occasion of my one and only ball, the night Harry had kissed me. I told myself I did not keep the book for sentimental reasons, but out of appreciation of the rebellious nature of the poetry. Certainly the poems' decadence would have been better understood by one more worldly than I, and their lyrical quality was lost on my deafness, but the texture and density of the meaning appealed to me all the more so because I could not hear its music. His poetry quickened my soul. It took a tremendous effort of concentration, but eventually I gave myself over to the poet's voice. The darkness around me faded, and I fell into a deep sleep.

Upon awakening, the room was glowing with light and I thought it was morning. Then I saw Arabella sitting on the trunk at the foot of my bed, bent over something in her lap, a gas lantern burning brightly on the floor at her feet. I sat up and pulled my shawl over my shoulders. I realized with a start that she was reading my book of poetry.

"Pray, what are you doing?" I asked.

She looked up. Her blond hair was fashioned into a mass of stylish coils behind her head, and she wore a low-cut gown and jewels.

"I am reading your book," she replied matter-of-factly.

"I can see as much. Pray give it to me," I said, holding out my hand. "You have no right to nose about my things. I am not a servant."

"But it's French," she replied, ignoring my outstretched hand. "What's a seamstress doing reading French poetry?"

"I lived in France. I told you, I had a shop there."

I believe she said something about seamstresses being dim-witted little creatures.

"I beg of you, give it back," I repeated.

"I have heard of this poet. Monsieur Baudelaire. He's quite shocking. He caused a terrible stir in France."

My hand remained extended. "If you please."

"Well, I suppose, since you were married, you can read what you wish." She stared at me in silence for a moment, her eyes betraying that same piercing intelligence I had sensed earlier. "You're not at all what you pretend to be," she said.

Baffled, I shook my head.

Leaning closer, she repeated, "You're not at all what you pretend to be," then asked, "where were you educated?"

"By tutors, at home. I was not born deaf."

"But your speech is queer."

"It's difficult to make a sound if you can't hear it," I said rather crossly, for I was still quite groggy.

"I suppose so." She studied me deliberately. "I've never met a deaf person." She looked down thoughtfully at the book in her lap, closed it, and passed it back to me. There was something strikingly original about her, an independence of spirit in her reaction to situations.

"And your dress is very fine," she said, gesturing to the black silk that hung on the door of the wardrobe.

"I was not always poor."

"How old are you?" she asked.

"I'm twenty-five."

"You're not much older than I." She stared at me thoughtfully and said, "How very sad." Then, noticing the slate and chalk I had left on the trunk where she sat, she picked it up.

"Why do you need this? You seem to understand what I say well enough."

"I only pretend," I said as I shivered and pulled my shawl more tightly around my shoulders. She seemed to find this quite amusing, not knowing how true it was.

She examined the slate as if it were just another toy for her amusement, and after reflecting a moment, she wrote, *I think I would prefer you as a companion over these brainless and jealous creatures I have to tolerate at our dull little dinner parties. Clearly, you are clever and know something of misfortune.* Then, having passed it to me to read, she extended her hand and said, "Come, take a walk with me."

I was quite put out by her manner, but I felt compelled to follow her out of sheer curiosity if nothing else. She gave me the lantern to carry and herself took up a candle; I snatched up my slate and followed her. The door I had found locked earlier that evening now stood open, leading to an antechamber not much larger than my closet. This room was more comfortably furnished, with window curtains and a rug, and a mirror hung on the stucco wall. I could not catch all she said, but I gathered that this was to have been my room, not the bleak little closet where she had found me sleeping. The housekeeper—"that Brumfit witch" I believe were her words—had intentionally disobeyed her orders. I suspect it was the challenge to her authority which vexed her more than any inconvenience to me.

After making it clear to me that I should move into this room the following day, we passed into a second chamber clearly intended for noble use, with dark oak paneling and a plasterwork ceiling of geometrical design. This room she had made her own, she explained. I had the impression that we were far from the reach of the main house. The room might have been a library were it not for the absence of bookcases and a certain feminine quality to the furnishings—there was a large round table covered with a fringed Indian shawl where newspapers and books were arranged in neat little stacks, a comfortable chaise and pillows, a writing desk equipped with writing paper and silver ink pots in a tidy row, a painted screen, a book stand, as well as a number of colorful Oriental vases and a tall leafy palm near the window. Large gilded mirrors hung on every wall reflecting the light from my lantern. It was all very orderly. She paused, and I watched as she pinched a dead leaf from a potted azalea.

"They never water my plants. They always forget," she pouted prettily.

Then, turning to me she added brightly, "He promised me a conservatory and I shall have it. I insist on that point. I must have green things indoors in the winter. The winters here are so dreary."

I wasn't sure if she had spoken of Harry or the Earl, but I dared not ask. I did not think she had the patience to deal with my faulty comprehension. I let her chatter away and turned my gaze to the long dark gallery that stretched before us. At the far end, moonlight filtered through an oriel window. As we advanced with the lantern, portraits of past earls, their wives, and offspring, emerged from the shadowy walls. Even in death, they faced the outside world as one unbreachable phalanx, shoulder to shoulder and ruff to ruff. One unbroken chain of succession. Individual happiness meant nothing to them.

"Is His Lordship's portrait here?" I asked.

She turned a wicked eye on me and said, "I wish it were." Then she laughed. "You have to be dead to hang up here. The living ones go downstairs where everyone can see them."

I had been referring to the Earl; I only hoped she was doing the same.

Farther along the gallery I caught a glimpse of a full suit of armor on display, a remnant from that vast armorial collection that had once lined the walls. Suddenly, she swept off down the hall shading the candle with her hand, glancing at me over her shoulder and calling out what I assumed was an invitation to follow. Wheeling to a stop before the solitary knight, she motioned me to hurry along. As I approached, she dripped a pool of wax onto the helmet and wedged her candle on his head. Standing eye-to-eye with the squat iron-clad figure, she saluted him in mock military fashion. Then she stood back and laughed. I mustered up a grim smile in return. I was not being taken on this tour for my own benefit; I was here to keep Her Ladyship company. She was oblivious to my discomfort. The hardwood floor was cold and bare, and I had no slippers, only a shawl, which I clutched awkwardly to my chest while I gripped the slate under my arm. Yet, I was touched by this strange effort to hold my attention. She had the charm of an innocent but spoiled child who expects to be worshiped and adored, and desires instant friendship. Arabella's loneliness was palpable, and I found myself moved with pity.

Crossing the hall to an alcove where a billiards table stood, she passed her hand along the smooth green felt and glanced up at me with a languid smile, expecting a reply to a question I had not understood. An impatient look flashed across her face, and she hiked up her skirts and swept past me muttering cross words I could only imagine. I could take no more. I set down the lantern on a gilt French table, dug the chalk from the pocket of my nightdress, and stalked after her, thrusting the slate into her hands.

"Your Ladyship, I cannot read your lips through the back of your head, nor can I see in the dark, so if your musings require a response, you might wish to write them down."

Her eyes widened. "Don't be impertinent with me," she replied. Then, snatching up the slate, she scribbled, *Everyone here is rude to me. If you're rude to me, I shall send you away.*

I looked up from the words she had written, thinking how sadly childish they were, and I tried to temper my reply. "It was not my intention to be rude, Your Ladyship. But you must be aware of my shortcomings if you wish me to understand what you say."

She seemed to be considering this, perhaps weighing her desire for confidence against the frustration of dealing with me. That was the first time she seemed to take note of me as a human being with my own feelings. I sensed she was not in the habit of seeing others in this light.

She erased the slate, bent over the billiards table, and wrote, *Looking at you, one cannot know you are afflicted so—not like with a blind person, or a cripple.*

"That is true," I replied. "And it leads to a good deal of misunderstanding."

Her gaze softened, and she wiped clean the slate and wrote, *There are many of us like that, we have some vital piece missing in us but no one knows it by looking at us, now do they?*

Her words stunned me, and while I was reflecting on the implications of her statement, again she erased the slate and wrote, *He's quite fond of billiards—taken to it rather late in life. Two more tables—another in his tower—heavy spectacular Moorish things inlaid in ivory and pearl.*

Once again, she was referring to the Earl. It struck me that her reference in nearly every comment concerning Blackroak and its business was not Harry but his father.

"I play with him sometimes. He's teaching me," she said, dusting a smudge of chalk powder from her skirt.

Suddenly, her head shot up, her attention drawn to the end of the hall; someone had spoken to her from the darkness. My heart nearly leaped out of my chest. Fearful that it might be the Earl, I stepped back into the shadows. A flame pierced the blackness, and a middle-aged woman in a white cap approached with a candle; it was her maid.

Arabella turned toward me, exaggerating her words slowly in what I imagined was a whisper, "They always find me." She tugged on a diamond earring. "They want to lock up the jewels."

Then, as an afterthought, she bent over the billiard table and wrote, *This is fine! We shall write things down and then erase them—no one will overhear us—no traces of our conversations!*

As she snatched the lantern from the table and hurried away, I was seized with sudden panic, for the candle on the knight's helmet had nearly burned down.

"Please," I cried, running after her, "Your Ladyship, leave me the lantern."

She turned to stare at me in the manner of one who had just been asked for a small fortune, but then a softness fell across her face, and she smiled kindly.

"Why, certainly," she said, passing it to me, and then she hurried away, her pale silk taffeta slicing through the darkness until it swallowed her up.

AFTER BREAKFAST THE NEXT MORNING, the entire household assembled in the hall for devotions. Being unfamiliar with the customs and rituals of a noble house, I did not know what awaited me until the Earl appeared at the balcony of the gallery above and greeted the staff. It was a terrible shock to suddenly find myself in the presence of that evil man who had been so diligent in destroying my happiness. He settled his spectacles on his nose and turned to Mrs. Brumfit who carefully placed a massive Bible in his hands. Even without my hearing, I knew the room had gone dead silent. No one moved. Casting a furtive glance at the under-butler in front of me and the scullery maid next to him, I saw that their faces were fixed in stony attention on the figure above. In body as well as spirit, he was a colossal man—a good six-feet six-inches tall, with a breadth of shoulders and chest in proportion, down to the massive hands cradling the Bible. He adjusted his spectacles once more and began to read. I did not expect to be able to follow the service, but all those years of memorizing biblical passages with Mr. Nicholls proved quite useful. Shortly into the scripture, I recognized the passage as from the First Book of the Chronicles:

> "Thine, O Lord, is the greatness, and the power, and the glory, and the victory, and the majesty: for all that is in the heaven and in the earth is thine; thine is the kingdom, O Lord, and thou art exalted as head above all."

He spoke with such authority that even without hearing the sound of his voice, my heart was cowed. Again, I darted a glance at the faces around me. I sensed a silent yet troubled allegiance, a loyalty founded on fear. As I watched him, I felt a fist tightening around my chest and my heart, and I found I could not breathe. To be forced to submit to his pretense of godliness was more than I could bear. Yet, bear it I would—every morning that I remained under his roof. When he had finished the scripture and concluded the prayer, the servants fairly fled from the hall. I stole a last glance at his face as he closed the Bible and returned it to the housekeeper. Then I, too, hurried away.

Days passed before I heard from Arabella again, days spent in the confines of my room mending the Earl's riding coats—a loathsome task—and watching from my window whatever activity I could glimpse in the courtyard below. One morning when the Earl was absent, I bribed a young groom with a promise of a new waistcoat if he would show me the house, for I had already been lost countless times in its labyrinthine corridors on my way to and from the kitchen. The symmetry of the main block was deceptive, for the west wing had embraced a circuit of old medieval towers, and the rectangular park was addled by the abbey remains. Whether inside or out, one was never quite sure which way it all turned, and what faced where. The sun was an unreliable guide, breaking through black, swiftly moving clouds just long enough to lift my spirits out of the sodden gloom, but never long enough to establish a sense of direction.

There was a bleak arrogance about Blackroak Hall, in the manner of a destitute nobleman convinced of a superiority founded on a crumbling myth—an observation that led me to recall what Harry had said about the inexpressible likeness between the Earl and the domain. Only a few public rooms were furnished for use—the great chamber, the library, a drawing room, and the dining room on the ground floor, which could only be reached by crossing the great medieval hall or along an equally dreary and drafty back corridor built in a later century. The very scale and magnificence of the rooms dwarfed the small comforts arranged within—the worn settees and padded armchairs, the side tables and newspaper racks.

Everywhere I turned, glassy-eyed stags and boars glared down at me from over a doorway or a fireplace. On the library floor lay the skin of a huge tawny tiger, a trophy from the Earl's visit to India. Stuffed foxes flourished, frozen on their lean little legs with a curled lip. Trout retained their delicate blush. There was even a parrot entombed in a glass cage, but he had flown there on his own around the turn of the century and died of old age—at least that is what I understood. Absent was any concession to delicacy or refinement of sentiment. What should have been confined to a gentleman's smoking room now infested all the living quarters. Arabella must have found it as gloomy and disconcerting as I did. It was a dreadful place in which to entertain friends with musical *soirées* and balls, all those things a young woman would want to do. Only the Earl's men came with their guns and fishing rods, pounding through copse and wading through streams on a weekend. The groom told me the only time since Lady Hambledon's death that there had been music and dancing in the hall was on the occasion of Lord Ormelie's wedding to the American heiress; there had been no more festivities since.

The Earl's portrait hung downstairs on the carved mahogany screen at the entrance to the hall. It had been painted when he had first come into his title, as a clean-shaven young man exuding an air of fiery conceit. The artist had portrayed him in Court attire, in his robes, with the Earl's coronet resting on a table at his side. Clearly, there had been a time when he was handsome, but the proud, noble features seemed set with a callous glaze. Whether the artist had intended this or whether it was my own clouded perception, I did not know.

There were as many portraits of dogs and racehorses as family. Harry's portrait hung at the opposite end of the wall next to his mother's. I nearly broke down when I saw it. Harry loomed so large, so invincible, so real. I was terribly upset after that, and I cut short the tour and returned to my room.

I searched for a portrait of Aurelia, Harry's lost sister, but there was none.

ON THE FOURTH DAY, I wrote to Nelly at the Richmonds' giving her instructions. I walked the letter into Lowendale to post at the coach-house, for I did not believe the servants trustworthy.

At last I have been given a task equal to my talents, but it is not livery. I am to make dresses for Her Ladyship. You might be surprised to learn that she is nothing like the small-minded and peevish creature the villagers painted for us. I have seen a different side to her, a side I do not entirely dislike. She does seem to be at war with the housekeeper—a perfectly horrid woman—but I sense no real animosity toward her father-in-law; on the contrary, she seems in thrall to the odious man. I'm still not sure what I think of her. In the meantime, I shall sew for her. She is curiously against your coming to assist me. She says she doesn't want a troupe of journeymen tailors under her roof. I think it may have something to do with the Earl and his mistrust of outsiders, or it may stem from her desire to maintain absolute authority wherever she can—for clearly, I am one of the few persons she feels she can order around at will. When I told her how I rely on you for comprehension, and how we speak our own private sign language, she wrote on the slate, "But then you would talk in front of me & I wouldn't know what you're saying. I should not like that at all."

It was a terrible blow to me to think I shall have to do without you, for the constant effort required to understand what is said drains my energy, and my spirits are low. This place can be terrifying at times. I am sure I would hear ghosts if I could hear.

You and Jack must return to Swidden and take rooms at the Royal Oak and wait for me there. Tell the ostler he will be paid as before. I trust you to keep Jack busy and out of trouble as he may still be useful to us. I may be in the robber's den, but there is no sign of the treasure I seek.

Arabella had informed me that they would be going to London for the rest of the Season as soon as Harry returned from Scotland. It would be too late to have anything made in town, and it was imperative that she arrive with some new and fashionable dresses. We spent hours thumbing through *La Mode Illustrée,* which she received through the post directly from Paris, and she had hoards of cloth and trimming purchased indiscriminately through drapers in York and London stored neatly in chests. She took meticulous note of the placement and volume of every little flounce and fold in the fashion plates we studied. However, I quickly discovered that she was wrought with indecision. No sooner had we agreed on a day dress with looped-up skirt to be cut from the light blue poplin over a white petticoat than she would throw up her arms in despair, crying that it was all terribly wrong, that she would be mortified to be seen in such a rag. We would then return the blue poplin to the trunk and roll out the striped grey chiné silk and begin all over again. It took days before she could decide upon what I would make. I have never cut into a cloth with more trepidation than I did the brown moiré antique silk she finally settled upon for a walking dress. I felt great sympathy for all those dressmakers of lesser skill who had suffered her critical eye. She was an extremely tidy woman, to the point of fanaticism. For five minutes I stood by watching her upbraid the maid for a stain on her lace cap. She felt it her prerogative to inspect my room daily to make sure my bed slippers were not in sight and that I had left no hair combs lying about. When she noticed a tiny crack in her sandalwood fan, she threw it into the fire. When I asked why she didn't give it to one of the maids, she rejoined, "But it was spoiled. No one wants anything spoiled."

Her upstairs sitting room was transformed into my workshop during the day, and the door to the antechamber in which I slept now remained unlocked, allowing me the liberty to move about the upper floors of the main building. I never feared running into the family as no one ever came up to the gallery except the parlor maid and an old retainer who would spit and rub a mirror or two and then disappear. The view from those lofty gables was breathtaking. I could sit by the window for hours, at times sewing, at times trying to make sense of the bustling activity in the courtyard and stableyard below, at other times merely gazing at the distant moors, entranced by a wilderness of livid sky and heath just coming into purple bloom. I was beginning to wonder at the strange turnings of my heart, for I was growing sadly fond of Blackroak's bleak and crumbling beauty. The thought that Harry might appear any day kept me in a state of suspended excitement. I didn't know what I would do if he should find me here. I had come to find my son, but I seemed to have lost my sense of direction.

My peculiar status at Blackroak made it difficult for me to enter into the confidence of the household staff. They were jealous of me and resented the favors conferred on me by Lady Ormelie. I was neither upstairs nor downstairs. I took my breakfast in Mrs. Brumfit's room with the upper servants, and dinner in the servants' hall, but I was given the privilege of taking tea in my own room, although it was generally brought up by the odd-man and not a maid, and it was always cold. My deafness made it all the easier for them to exclude me from conversation, although I understood much more than they thought I did.

I observed the Earl carefully during those weeks. From my window, I studied his habits and learned when he would be in the stable yard inspecting his racehorses or taking his hunter out for an early morning ride. I watched him during morning devotions in the hall and Sunday after chapel in Lowendale when we all trailed out to greet the vicar on the steps. His eyes were always concealed or too far away to scrutinize. Even when he was only at arm's length, I was distracted by his stature, how everything about him seemed so huge and expansive and irrefutable—the bushy red beard and whiskers and prowlike chest, the way he seemed to take up more than his share of earth and sky. He was all stature, all physique, and would have seemed brutish were it not for his noble bearing and a certain affable air. When he laughed, he threw back his head, and everyone laughed with him, but it was dishonest laughter. Once I saw him take up a pitchfork and go after a stable boy who had displeased him. When the boy stumbled, the Earl stepped back and shook with laughter. Everyone else laughed, too, except the boy who lay there in the dung cowering in fear. He was obsessed with his horses, and his dogs fawned about him in that perverse way dogs have of worshiping a master who mistreats them. I grew to despise him those first weeks before he ever once took notice of me.

IT WAS BITTERLY IRONIC THAT I, a deaf woman, became Arabella's confidante. In the mornings if there were no callers, she would come upstairs and sit with her needlework or write in her journal while I sewed. Sometimes she would leave without saying a word. At other times she would talk at great length, and I would be required to put down my ribbon and bodkin and strain to read her moving lips. Although I entreated her to write on my slate, she was often too impatient to do so and thought I understood her well enough without. Sometimes she went on chattering even when I had turned my eyes back to my work. Perhaps she simply needed the purge of talking. That I was neither a servant loyal to the Earl's family, nor the meddlesome wife of a neighboring squire worked to my advantage. She was deeply mistrustful of those people. Although my education and manners made her more at ease with me than she might have been with another woman of an inferior position, I think she trusted me simply because I was her dressmaker, because ours was a trade known for its tight-lipped service, for receiving confidences and taking them to the grave.

She took only a perfunctory interest in managing her household and its attendant correspondence. When the maid brought the mail, she would glance up impatiently and inquire if there was news from her family or from Harry. There were occasional letters from Virginia, which she opened immediately. I never saw her receive a letter from Harry. Sometimes she simply dismissed her duties with a wave of the hand.

"Oh, take it away. Let His Lordship send a reply. I really cannot be bothered."

There was an air of secrecy about her writing, and I suspect she preferred the upstairs drawing room not only for my company, but because she could avoid the staff's prying eyes. She lost herself for long periods of time in her journals and kept them locked away in the trunk at the foot of the bed in which I had slept my first night. One day, after abruptly seizing my attention by dropping a paperweight on the floor, she laid down her pen and announced, "Mrs. Truelock, perhaps some day I shall have you read some of my poems."

"I would very much like to read them," I replied, rubbing my finger where I had pricked it with the needle, for she had startled me.

"You know, my sentiments about you have been justified. It was that book of Monsieur Baudelaire's poetry. He is a poet of unusual sensibilities."

"Indeed, he is."

"If I were a man, I should like to be a Baudelaire."

"But society holds him in contempt," I replied.

"Perhaps, but I am quite sure he has no contempt for himself."

She observed me in silence for a moment, and I returned to my work. The paperweight dropped again, and I raised my eyes.

"It's a pity you are reduced to living like this."

"I do not complain."

"No, no, of course not. You have no choice. But you are quite sure of yourself. For this you can be thankful."

She put down her pen and sat staring leagues away. Again, I returned to my stitches. Then, a few minutes later, I was startled by her presence at my side.

"Put down your work and come with me."

I followed her across the drawing room, through my bedroom, and into the adjacent closet where her trunk was stored. Producing a key from her pocket, she knelt and opened the lid. Inside, arranged in tidy stacks, were dozens of small leather-bound journals.

"Do you see?" she said with a smile. "All of this is my poetry." She withdrew a journal and opened it. The pages were filled with minute, indecipherable script. I marveled that a hand could write so compactly. Judging by her countenance, it was clear that these efforts meant a good deal to her. She flashed me a smile of complicity and then locked the trunk.

In the drawing room, she returned to her writing desk and bade me pull up a chair beside her. She took up her pen and wrote:

So! You have seen them. They are quite small. It is rather odd—that my soul is bursting with sentiments—some of them quite savage—& then they are reduced to this. I cannot seem to do much else with them.

I began to speak, and she pressed her finger to her lips to silence me. I took up her pen and wrote, *Them?*

My sentiments. Such a small space for such powerful emotions.

And the writing is so small, I added.

A reflection of my soul's confinement. If I conceal my thoughts from the world, it is because I know the world will condemn me. Or worse yet, the world will not believe me.

She paused to observe my face, and she must have been satisfied with what she could read there, because she continued:

Anger is most unbecoming in a lady, is it not? I am quite angry with them, and I am at a loss as to understand why. I can only conclude that I am wicked and sinful. You see, I am drawn to darkness. I fear I am not suited for Heaven at all.

Suddenly, she snatched the paper from me, took it to the grate, and set fire to it. She looked on while the sheets burned, then she stirred the ashes with a poker. When she had finished, she dusted off her hands and left the room without a word.

I HAD SPENT DAYS WORKING on the brown moiré to the exclusion of all else, and we were ready for a close fitting. She came into the sitting room that morning in a dressing gown followed by her maid with an armful of petticoats, but she soon grew impatient with the older woman's clumsiness and sent her away. The walking dress I had made was the latest in fashion. We had moved away from the ugly bell-shaped crinolines toward a line more appealing to the eye—although it required tighter lacing of the corset. The upper part of the crinoline had been reduced to make the figure appear as slim as possible below the waist, allowing a flatter skirt in front and moving the bulk of the dress to the rear, thereby creating an undulating shape. The overskirts were hitched up behind into a bulging mass of silk. Arabella seemed enraptured. She could barely stand still. Even before I had finished marking my final adjustments, she pulled away from me to parade about the room, moving from mirror to mirror to catch a reflection of herself in motion, in this attitude or that, from the back, the side, and front. She was particularly enchanted by the slightly shorter skirt, which allowed a pretty display of foot and ankle.

I had persuaded her to come back and stand still long enough for me to finish the hem. I was on my knees when I looked up and started at the sight of the Earl's massive reflection in the standing mirror. He stood behind us in his riding habit, tapping his mud-caked boots with his crop and fixing her with a narrow gaze. Although she greeted him with a pretty smile, there was a suggestion of fear in the way she stiffened her shoulders and clasped her hands tightly at the front of her skirt. She seemed to shrink from him. It was only barely perceptible, but I had grown accustomed to interpreting such mannerisms in people who believed they were hiding their feelings.

I did not know that he had spoken to me. When I failed to respond, he stepped forward and jabbed me rudely with his crop, gesturing to me to leave the room. I rose quickly to my feet, my heart thumping in my chest, and I would have unleashed an indignant cry had Arabella not stopped me with a hand on my arm.

"No, it's quite all right. Please stay, Mrs. Truelock," she said. Then, begging his indulgence with a winning smile, she asked his opinion of her gown. With a turn of the shoulder, she drew his eyes toward her arched back and the curve of her narrow waist. My eyes were not on the gown, they were on him. Never had I felt so powerfully the impact of a coarse gaze from a man, and it troubled me deeply. I understood full well that certain styles of dress were intended to excite the admiration of the beholder, but in good society there were rules by which the beholder must abide, and these rules had been broken. A line had been crossed. I was not sure what it meant, but his gaze had elicited a disturbing and repulsive response in my chest.

I watched the Earl prowl around her. He seemed amused, and pleased, by the allure of the dress's exaggerated curves. With the tip of his crop, he explored the bustle as though it were some curious growth; he flicked the bows and tickled the rosettes along the braided trim of the skirt. I stood aghast, watching this vulgar behavior, thinking she might at least brush away that rude instrument, even playfully, but she submitted to his inspection almost like a favored slave would have done, with the understanding that there would be rewards for submission and punishment for rebellion.

He gazed curiously around the room. I gathered that he rarely came up here and was looking upon the place with the air of a man making a discovery. Again, using his crop, he flipped over a few pages from *La Mode Illustrée* and leaned over to squint at a fashion plate. He studied it for a moment.

"I like this," he said, jabbing at the page with the tip of his crop. "This one. I should like to see you in this one."

He tilted his head back and scratched his bearded chin, then turned to Arabella. "Harry will be home Tuesday next," he said. "Good occasion to look your best, don't you agree?"

Then his glance fell on the pile of petticoats. He strode across the room to where they lay in a heap, a jumble of scarlet flannel and white muslin frills. He lifted one on the tip of his crop, and turning to us with a bemused grin, said something I failed to understand. Then he tossed the petticoat over a chair and marched out of the room.

After his departure, Arabella lost all interest in the fitting. She seemed distracted and plucked nervously at the velvet trim on her cuffs, and would not look at herself in the mirror.

Chapter Twenty-seven

I COULD NOT FORGET WHAT I HAD SEEN. THAT BRIEF GLIMPSE OF the dark side of his nature had disturbed me more than I could ever say. I sat at my workbench, sewing Arabella's dress, thinking about the things that are unseen and how they make up the fabric of our lives.

I have always tried to see more good than evil in even the most wrong-headed men. That innocence has served me well, for it has been the cornerstone of my hope and fight against despair, and I have stubbornly held on to it through all my trials. Were I to stay any longer in Blackroak Hall, I feared that innocence would be destroyed. And yet I stayed. I sat by the window with the warm July sun filtering through thick leaded panes, whipping thousands of fine stitches into the silk lining of the satin bodice as if it were a suit of armor, with the belief that I could render her invulnerable to his seduction by the sheer perfection of my skill. It was the mother's job, but our mothers had forsaken us. Harry was away. He was always away. There was no one to protect her but me.

The dress would be exquisite, a sateen of rich reddish Grenat, half-trained for dinner rather than a ball, with the bodice cut low off the shoulders, trimmed in black velvet braid and ruched in black lace. She came up briefly every morning for a fitting, but she was not pleased with what she saw. She was not fond of the braided trim on the skirt, and we had only enough lace to trim the bodice.

"I wanted rosettes," she said, pouting at the mirror.

"There's some silk Hungarian cord in the trunk. We could use that instead of the braid, and I might just have time to make a scalloped under-skirt."

"I hate it. It's horrid. Monstrous."

"I'm sure Lord Ormelie will find you most enchanting."

"I shan't wear it. I refuse. I don't like it. We don't have any pretty trimmings. I shall wait and have a dress made in London. My husband won't care what I'm wearing. He won't even notice. He hates me. He wants me dead."

Once again she had talked herself into a state of extreme agitation, and tears swelled in her eyes.

"Take it off me," she ordered, stamping her foot. "Now."

She had tried my patience that morning, and I could no longer hold my tongue. I stepped back, hands on my hips, my measuring tape slung around my neck, and declared most forcefully, "There is nothing wrong with the dress, Your Ladyship."

She swung around to me, her eyes reddened and swimming with tears. "Of course there's nothing wrong with the dress, you stupid woman. It's me! It's me!" she shouted. With the countenance of a woman dispossessed of all reason, she strode past me toward my workbench, snatched up my shears, and began slashing away at the skirt of her dress. I could not stop her for fear she might turn on me, and I was forced to stand by, watching helplessly, while I beseeched her to stop. Finally, she hurled the shears across the room and collapsed onto the chaise, cradling her head in her hands. I quickly retrieved the weapon and hid it in my room, locking the door as I came out. She had grown calm and was inspecting the horrific damage she had done to her skirt. She looked up at me with eyes full of remorse and dabbed at her tear-stained face with the back of her hand.

"It can be repaired," I said, hoping my voice was not trembling, for I was certainly trembling inside.

She rose, gathered up her tattered skirts, and went to the standing mirror.

"Make me look like an angel, Mrs. Truelock," she pleaded, turning toward me. "An angel. I must look angelic."

No amount of reason nor common sense could be brought to bear on her. She could not see the pretty girl without, the blond wispy curls tumbling over her forehead, the dimpled cheeks, the porcelain skin; she saw something else, something powerfully disruptive, something she did not wish to be.

After she had gone, I sat at my workbench with the shredded skirt spread across my lap and gave in to my own tears. It seemed she had robbed me of my self-possession. I had become so preoccupied with her life that I had lost touch with my own. My tragedy had been dwarfed by hers, and I boiled with resentment. And yet, once I touched the silk and put my imagination to work to find a way to conceal the damage, I became calm and in control again.

That night she startled me out of my sleep. She was standing at my bedside in her nightdress, holding a candle and talking to me. When I failed to understand, she set down the candle on my nightstand, peeled back the counterpane, and crawled into bed next to me. I was far too tired to resist. For all her tantrums, I was not afraid of her. She was a small thing and seemed even slighter without her armor of ruches, flounces, and crinoline. I found her warm presence comforting, and I knew she was safe with me. I slept soundly for the first night in a very long time.

On Sunday morning on the way back from the church in Lowendale, I caught sight of a lone figure moving along the path at the top of Beeching Rigg. I slowed my step, falling back from the rest of the household staff, and when no one was looking, I turned away from the road and struck off through the heath with the intention of following the escarpment to where the path descended from Beeching Rigg down to Blackroak Hall. I had recognized the woman's mantle, even from a distance; it was Hannah Platt. After three weeks entombed in Blackroak, I was elated at the thought of encountering a kind soul like Mrs. Platt. I gave her quite a turn, for I fairly raced up the path and threw myself on her. She was pleased to see me but appeared reluctant to reveal her business to me. The path led down toward the abbey remains behind Blackroak Hall, and there she paused to bid farewell. Perhaps my wounded sentiments were too evident on my countenance, for as I started up toward the hall, she stopped me with a gentle hand on my arm.

"I have come to pay my respects to my Lady," she said.

I was confused, believing I had misunderstood, for I knew Arabella would be out for the day. She lifted her basket, gesturing to the wildflowers she had picked, and said, "For her grave."

"Do you mean Lady Hambledon?"

She nodded.

"Is she buried nearby?"

She motioned to the abbey. "There is a large family plot where a few of the Breadalbanes are buried. It's where the Earl will be laid to rest."

"Would you take me there?"

She nodded, and I followed her through the portal and down to a wooded area beside the lower abbey wall. There stood a cluster of massive marble crypts carved with heraldry and topped with stone angels. I followed Mrs. Platt through an iron gate to a grey tomb, grey as the sky itself, and the shock of finding that noble lady interred in the rude wilderness brought sudden tears to my eyes.

"She is buried here?" I asked. I suspect the surprise came out in my queer voice, for Mrs. Platt turned to me with a curious gaze.

"Did you know her?"

I gazed into her eyes, trying to gauge her trustworthiness, and answered, "Yes, I did."

"Did you sew for her?"

I hesitated and then shook my head. "No. She was my friend. I had lost a mother, and she had lost a daughter." I looked away again, but I could feel her eyes on me. "When I became ill with the fever that brought on my deafness, she wrote me very kind letters. Her death touched me deeply."

I dusted off a corner of a lichen-covered tomb, sat myself down, and folded my hands in prayer. I prayed for her soul and mine; I prayed for her daughter's soul and that of the frightened young woman now mistress of Blackroak Hall. It was only at that moment, as I prayed, that I realized, in some manner, we had all been cruelly damaged by the same man.

When at last I had finished my prayers and looked up, I had expected her to be gone, but she was still there. She had placed the flowers in a vase at the foot of the tomb and then taken a seat beside me.

There was something about the moment that emboldened me, and I felt compelled to take a chance.

"Do you know anything about a child?" I asked.

A look of alarm flashed across her face. "A child? What child?"

"A child that would have been brought here nearly two years ago as an infant."

The alarm faded to relief. She hesitated, fixing me with a puzzled eye. "What business is this of yours?"

I feigned misunderstanding. "It was a boy. A little boy."

"Whose child would it be?"

Looking her squarely in the eye, I replied, "Lord Ormelie would have been his father."

"A bastard?"

It was a horrid question, one I refused to answer. "Would you know where he might be?"

She studied me intently. "I think you must be mistaken."

I watched her face closely, and I believed she was telling me the truth. Her alarm at my query made me think there might have been another infant, another secret, but it was not mine. A deep sadness rolled through me, as cold and dense as fog.

"Do you have your slate?" she asked suddenly. I pulled it from the small pouch I always carried over my shoulder. She took it from me and wrote: *I made herbal remedies for the Countess, Lady Hambledon.*

She smiled and nodded in the manner of a woman proud of her superior knowledge. I returned the smile, hoping to encourage her trust.

She erased the slate with the corner of her shawl, jabbed a finger at herself and added, *Midwife.*

I laid a hand on her arm. "Mrs. Platt," I said, "is Lady Ormelie in any danger?"

She eyed me with mistrust from beneath the rim of her faded bonnet. "Danger? How?"

"I don't know. But I know she is frightened of something."

Suddenly, her countenance clouded. She took back the slate and wrote, *Her Ladyship suffers from melancholy. She is fond of telling false stories. You must not believe everything she says.*

She seemed suddenly eager to be away from me, as if I had probed too far into their business. She rose and slung the basket over her arm. Then, after a brief and fretful hesitation, she said something about her son, and I was given to understand that he was a stable boy at Blackroak. When I could not make out his name, she picked up the slate and wrote, *William. Very tall. You need anything, find William.*

Then she hugged her shawl around her shoulders and hurried off.

THAT EVENING, AS I WORKED on the dress, I decided to reveal my presence to Harry upon his return. Somehow, I would find a way to see him alone and demand he account for his actions. After my encounter with Mrs. Platt, I had come to accept the fact that my son was nowhere near Blackroak Hall. Harry had hidden him well. I could understand why.

On Tuesday morning at breakfast when I inquired about Lord

Ormelie's arrival, I learned that he had been delayed and would be home in two days' time. I was enormously relieved; I had been so nervous at the thought of seeing him again that I had lost my appetite. And the dress was not yet finished.

Upon returning from breakfast, I found Arabella in my room. Like a child, she was heedless of the boundaries between us, presuming all that a child presumes and believing it her right to appropriate anything that was mine. She came into my room whenever it pleased her and took an interest in any little thing I possessed. On this morning I found her curled on my bed with her back to me, still in her nightdress and wrapped in my shawl. I thought she might be sleeping, but at the sound of my footsteps she sat up, turning to me a face reddened and swollen from weeping.

"Where have you been all this time?" she said, her face drawn in a pout. "I've been waiting ever so long for you."

"At breakfast," I rejoined with a touch of exasperation. "What ever is the matter?"

"He's not coming."

"Yes, I know. He's been delayed."

"No," she said, hugging her knees to her chest. "He's never coming back."

"Of course he is."

You would have thought that she was the deaf one, for she would have none of my reassurances. She gazed down at the tartan shawl, picking distractedly at a loose thread in the weave, mumbling words I could not see. Glancing up, she pronounced suddenly, "He has a mistress."

I wished I could have turned away just then, but I was forced to follow every odious word on her lips.

"He has a mistress in Scotland," she said, expressing this revelation with an arch of her eyebrows. "That's why he goes there. I know it is."

I faced her with a frozen countenance, my hands folded tightly at my waist.

"He never loved me, you know." Looking me straight in the eye, she pronounced most solemnly, as if it were an oath, "But I have never wavered in my affections for him. Never. Not once. I have been constant and pure. You must believe me. You do believe me, do you not?"

I tried to appease her with an unconvincing nod.

Then, with the mysterious air of a schoolgirl sharing a dark secret, she swung her bare feet over the side of the bed and motioned me to follow her into the dim little closet where I had lodged my first night. Fishing the key from the pocket of her nightdress, she knelt and unlocked the trunk at the foot of the bed and withdrew one of the calf-skin journals. Clutching it to her bosom, she rose and led me back to my room. I watched while she lighted several candles and set them on the nightstand, then motioned me down beside her on the bed.

She fixed me with an intense gaze, and then, like a priestess administering a solemn ritual, she opened the book and passed it to me. As in the other journal I had glimpsed, each page was filled from top to bottom in a hand so finely executed and on such a miniature scale that it would have been difficult to read without the aid of a magnifying glass. The heavily inked pages might have been ancient writings from a long-dead civilization.

"They would all think these are just demented stories from a demented mind, but they are true," she said, angling her earnest face up at me so that I might catch every word on her lips. "It's all true. You must believe me. They would never believe me. They would say it's only a madwoman ranting. But do I look mad to you, Mrs. Truelock? Do you think I'm mad?"

She had been abandoned, isolated, and tempted, and it seemed to me that every effort had been made to bring about her moral disintegration. She was impulsive and irrational at times, and she was deeply unhappy, but she was not mad.

"No, Arabella, you're not mad."

It was the first time I had dared use her Christian name, and that I had addressed her in such familiar terms seemed to move her deeply.

She took my hand and squeezed it, and said, "Oh, thank you, my dear friend. Thank you."

She took up the slate at my bedside table and wrote, *I have been here two years. I have listened & overheard things they wanted no one to hear. I have read things that were not intended for my eyes. I know a good many secrets that he does not want told. But I told them here, on these pages. I needed a story to tell. I have no story of my own. My poems are worthless. I bear nothing worthwhile. Nothing good comes of me. I am like Spanish moss on a tree.*

She closed the book and laid it in my hands.

"You must keep this," she said. "Keep it with you at all times, so he won't find it. And take it with you when you go."

"Why? Why give it to me?"

Her look was quite thoughtful, and I remember how calm and resolute she seemed.

"Because you will understand. And you will need it to defend the truth."

I HAD SUFFERED TERRIBLY FROM a headache all day long, and it was only my stubborn insistence on perfection that drove me to stay at my task. Knowing how much it would please her, I had scavenged enough material for two small rosettes to be attached at each shoulder. I was diligently working on these that evening by candlelight when I caught a fleeting shadow out of the corner of my eye, nearly startling me out of my wits. I looked up to find the Earl's valet shuffling toward me. He was fairly simpering with glee at having taken me unawares. He was a taciturn old man with rotted teeth and a face disfigured with purple blotches. Always reeking of ale, he followed the Earl everywhere.

He mumbled something quite incomprehensible while he jabbed his gnarly finger in my direction and pointed to the dress.

"It will be finished tomorrow," I declared, recoiling from his unpleasant breath.

Frustrated by my failure to understand him, he lunged for the dress, but I snatched it out of his grasp.

"Pray explain yourself!" I cried, gathering the heavy folds of silk under my arm and rising from my workbench. "If you have orders from your master, pray bring them to me in writing, but do not lunge at me as if I were some dumb beast!"

The valet withered, but it was not my rebuke that had stung him. I followed his gaze directed over my shoulder. There stood the Earl, immaculately attired in evening dress and leaning on a silver-knobbed cane with both hands. Never before had he acknowledged either my presence or my affliction, and now he did so with a haughty air of condescension.

"Can you understand me, missy?" he asked, with a forced smile that never reached his eyes.

I was aware of my heart pounding madly as I clutched the dress to my bosom. This was no mere man, but an enemy whose cruelty was deeply rooted in the evils of an unjust code—a code that declared me inferior and unworthy of a voice; it was the code by which the most powerful among us lived, prospered, and ruled. This man had brought his power to bear most unjustly on myself and his son, and was willfully preying on the ill-balanced mind of an innocent girl. It was not fear that seized my heart, but indignation, a fierce, boiling indignation.

I forced a civil reply. "If Your Lordship speaks slowly and directs his words toward me, I understand a good deal."

He drew his spectacles out of his waistcoat pocket and settled them on his nose, then stepped forward to squint down at my handiwork. He had just come from dinner and his hot cloying breath smelled of sweet wine. Flecks of crumbs clung to his red beard. He straightened and tucked his spectacles back into his pocket.

"Hold it up," he ordered, waving the knob of his stick at the skirt. "Hold it up so I might see it."

"It's quite wrinkled, Your Lordship," I protested as I shook out the skirt and spread the flounces of lace and silk over the workbench for him to examine. "It must be pressed before it is worn."

"Yes, very fine. Very fine. That will do nicely."

He waved to his valet, and the old man sprang into action.

But I resisted. With one quick step I blocked his path.

"It is not yet finished," I said.

I stood there, facing the two of them with my heart in my throat, wondering what folly had compelled me to act in such a manner. Truly, what was a rosette or two? Or a wrinkle here and there? It was nothing more than a garment, a hollow shell, and yet I could not let him have it. Every nerve in my body rose up in defiance. I think I must have intuitively known, even then, that his intentions were evil, for why else would I have acted so impulsively? If I did not resist, who would?

In his eyes I saw it coming, and my arm shot up to deflect the blow. I deftly tore the stick out of his grasp and flung it aside.

Red-faced and outraged, he drew himself up to his full height, spitting insults at me. I dared not look away for fear he might strike me again, and there was no one to restrain him. He could very well murder me then and there, and I was sure his valet would look on in silent complicity. But I would not withdraw. When I saw him pause for breath, I spoke up.

"I am not a brute animal to be whipped into compliance, Your Lordship, nor am I your property," I said, struggling to regain my composure. Then, gathering up the dress, I laid it in the arms of the slack-jawed valet. "You may do with this dress as you like. It is out of my hands."

Shaking his stick at me, he shouted, "You will pack up your belongings and leave my house! Do you understand me? Answer me! Do you understand me? You will leave this house at once!"

"I shall leave in the morning."

I picked up my skirts and turned toward my room, then paused and swung back to face him one last time. He still seemed stunned by such impertinence from one so insignificant as myself, and his scarlet face seemed ready to burst.

I gave one last reply, speaking as distinctly as I possibly could.

"Sir, I have met your son, Lord Ormelie. When I first knew him, he was ardent and idealistic, a true gentleman and a man of character. I fear you have crushed the spirit in him, just as you have crushed so many others. It is a heavy price to pay for righteousness. Good day."

I retired to my room, turned the key in the lock, and sank, trembling, onto my bed. I had behaved in a foolhardy manner. I should have been mortally ashamed, but I was not. Once my blood had cooled, I began to feel an enormous sense of elation, as if I had freed myself from an oppressive tyrant.

When I went downstairs for dinner, I was snubbed coldly. There was no place set for me at the table, and not a word was spoken to me. Throughout the meal, Mrs. Brumfit made a point of turning her face so that I could not read her lips. I sat quietly and defiantly, hoping I might scavenge a plate when they had finished and serve myself whatever was left, but clearly the household had been instructed to starve me out. Once they had eaten, the joint and pudding were whisked away. I went back to my room with a few crusts of bread.

I spent the evening returning Arabella's fabrics and trimmings to the trunks in my room and trying to think of a plan to communicate with Harry now that I had been ordered to leave Blackroak. Mrs. Platt's son, the stable boy, seemed to be my only hope. I would write a brief note to Harry, explaining that I would be waiting in Swidden at the Royal Oak Pub, and leave it with William.

I knew there was a way to reach the stables over the rooftops. At the far end of the gallery, a corridor wound away toward the west wing, and along this was a door onto the roof. I could follow the low-walled lead over the rooftop, past the banqueting tower, and from there make my way down a staircase to the rooms directly above the stables where the grooms slept.

This way I could avoid the household staff. Darkness was my worst enemy. Without sound to lend a sense of realness to my movements, going down dark stone stairs and along shadowed paths felt like stepping off into a black void. I would have to tread cautiously.

It was a clear night. Although there was enough moonlight to guide my path, I lost my way in the circuitous confusion of leads along the roof and found myself following the lead to the one tower I had wished to avoid. In the time of Queen Elizabeth, it had been used as a banquet room, but now it was the Earl's private summer retreat. The billiards room on the tower's ground level was approached through the main rooms of the house, but the smoking room above could be accessed only from stairs inside the tower or by the leads across the jumble of rooftops.

From a distance, I had noticed a light flickering behind the carved oriental screens of the moorish windows, lending it the appearance of a fantastic exotic jewel set against the night sky. I prayed my steps were quiet as I approached, for I intended only to pass around the tower. The shuttered windows, while affording privacy to the gentlemen in their after-dinner pursuits of pleasure, also concealed my presence. I recalled something Arabella had said about her fortune being spent on refurbishing this tower and how richly luxurious it was. Driven by reckless curiosity, and undoubtedly a good dose of defiance, I paused and leaned down to peer through the latticework.

Inside was the strangest, most fantastic chamber I had ever seen. It stood like a secret enclosure set far apart from the rest of the sprawling house, a place one entered to escape from everyday life into a rich medieval fantasy. There was not a single surface untouched by pattern or modeled decoration. Knights in armor crawled over jointed timber; mermaids and monkeys sprouted out of stone lintels; winged dragons broke out of a great frieze of glazed tiles. A massive cupid with muscular legs haunted the hooded chimneypiece. There were deep fringed armchairs and plush settees in dark red and gold; even the legs of a small, circular table were carved with mythical dogs. The atmosphere was ponderous and yet wonderful.

The Earl stepped into sight, attired in an elaborate smoking jacket and a tasseled smoking cap. I felt myself strangely empowered, watching him in a private moment when there was no one about. Only his valet was in attendance. The old man had been summoned to light the candles of a heavy crystal chandelier. As each candle caught fire, the flame was re-flected a thousandfold by countless glittering crystal drops and the crystal star-spangled ceiling, so that the room shimmered with light.

The Earl's attention was suddenly drawn to someone entering the room. His countenance took on a rapturous delight, and he drew himself up in all his hubris and spread his arms in a welcoming gesture. Arabella appeared, dressed in the sateen gown I had made. She advanced hesitantly and paused. At a gesture from him, she set off circling the room at a lan-guid pace so that he might appreciate her charms all the more fully. The valet, having finished lighting the chandelier, was now arranging glasses and a decanter of wine on the table. He bowed to the Earl and then with-drew. I held my breath as Arabella passed near my window. I had never seen her so radiant and lovely, and my heart sank at the thought of Harry returning to her. She had an air of timidity and dependence most agree-able to a gentleman, and when she gazed over at the Earl from beneath lowered lashes, she seemed all innocence and eagerness to please.

The Earl sat cross-legged in his armchair with his glass of port at his side, swinging his foot nervously. He seemed to be directing her move-ments from afar. At his command, she would strike a certain pose, arching her back to draw attention to the high curve of her bustled hips, or lifting her skirt, or even adjusting the shoulder straps to emphasize the décolleté of the low-necked bodice. Having circled the room, she came to a stop be-fore him. There appeared to be some exchange between them. He offered her a glass of port, which she refused, and then she set off on another tour around the room. She had taken only a few measured steps when he stum-bled up out of his chair and rushed at her from behind, slipping his thick hands around her waist. His massive size overwhelmed her delicate figure, and she froze at his touch. Again, there was an exchange of words. His twisted features were bloated with ardor. One hand tightened around her waist; with the other, he brushed back a ringlet of pale hair. Then, nearly crushing her with a bear-like grasp, he pressed his lips against her shoulder.

I sank to the foot of the wall, my hands cupped over my mouth to throttle my cries. What I had intuitively known all along, what had been suggested to me in glances, attitudes, and gestures, had now been played out before my eyes. I was too frightened to run; if I made any noise what-soever, I would surely be caught. I would have to wait until they had gone. I remained there for what seemed like an eternity, crouched against the wall in the narrow open passageway, until a shaft of light broke across the battlements and Arabella stepped outside. At the sight of her, a sick feeling swept over me. She had undressed down to her scarlet petticoat; her corset had been loosened, and the strings trailed at her waist. She advanced along the battlement, then stopped to withdraw a small bundle wrapped in cloth hidden behind a loose stone. When she turned back, she caught sight of me. She started only briefly. With a furtive glance over her shoulder, she approached and knelt before me. She must have known what I had witnessed, but she seemed not the slightest bit unnerved. With her face in shadow, I could barely read her lips, but she seemed to be reassuring me. She unfolded the cloth to reveal a ring of keys, and I understood only that this was a part of some important scheme. Then she pulled me to my feet and motioned me to hurry away. To my astonishment, she leaned forward and pressed a parting kiss on my cheek. I did as she had instructed. When I had cleared the rooftops and reached the door, I turned back and she was gone.

I was in a state of panic as I gathered up my traveling bag and threw on my mantle. My hands were trembling too badly to tie my bonnet, and I stuffed it into my bag. I fled from my room with a candle to light my way, leaving through the closet and down the narrow stair tower, through the heavy oak door into the servants' hall, across the kitchen courtyard and outside. If I had heard the dogs, I might have been frightened into retreat, but I was oblivious to their snarling and growling as they trailed me over the gravel path. I was saved from harm by the gamekeeper, who came stumbling out of his cottage in his nightshirt just in time to call off the curs. I am sure he suspected me of some theft or dishonest act, for why else would I be stealing off like this at a mad gallop in the middle of the night? I was able to get my wits about me enough to ask for William, and when they had dragged the poor boy out of his bed, I drew him aside and begged his help.

"Pray, I must get to Rushcross Grange to see your mother. It is most urgent." I stumbled over my words, and I know he could barely understand me. "I am ill, you see. I have taken ill, and your mother said I could come to you if I needed help. Will you take me there tonight? I can pay you. I have money with me."

My panic must have aroused his suspicion, but he seemed willing to help. He led me across the stable yard to the path beside the yew hedge and pointed me in the direction of the abbey ruins. I was to wait for him there.

I had been too sickened by what I had witnessed to try to make any sense out of it. Why it was happening and who was to blame were questions my mind could not fathom. I was still in a state of shock as I waited on a pile of stone ruins, hugging my mantle around my shoulders with my traveling bag clutched to my chest, wishing I had never set foot in this wicked place. I was terrified of the night, knowing I could not hear the tread of a wild animal, a human foe, and I kept glancing over my shoulder while I waited, imagining danger everywhere. The flight of a bat or an owl through the stone arches overhead, a dark flicker against the moonlit sky, was all it took to send my heart racing again. I prayed William would not forget me, for there was no way I could make it across the moors safely in the darkness.

I first perceived the fire as a glow just above the treetops, and I rose and climbed through the ruins, up the crumbling stone steps to where I could see the house. The tower was engulfed in flames, and with it the Earl's summer retreat. My skin prickled, and I felt a terrible gnawing pain in my chest. I fell to my knees and prayed with all my heart that she might save herself. I pleaded, and begged, and did not quit my entreaties until I felt a hand grasp my shoulder. It was William leading a horse. He appeared distraught and motioned to the fire with frantic gestures. He could not accompany me. He was needed to fight the fire, but I was to take the horse and go by road to Rushcross Grange. He would send someone for the horse in the morning.

I did not head for Rushcross Grange, but followed the path along Beeching Rigg to where it met the road to Swidden. I arrived in the town not long after dawn and plowed my way through the sheep market to the Royal Oak. The chambermaid led me to Nelly's room. The look of relief on her familiar countenance when she opened the door was enough to send me into a fit of tears. She was just up and still in her nightdress, and she hugged me so tightly it hurt. Even using our signs, she could make little sense out the nightmarish story I was telling her. She poured water into a basin and bathed my face and hands. Then she put me to bed and sat beside me. She held my hand until I fell asleep.

The next thing I knew, Nelly was shaking me gently and talking to me urgently in finger language. I sat up and saw a strange man in a uniform lurking just outside the door. The ostler stood beside him, watching us with a queer look on his countenance. I understood that the man was there to take me away. It was about the fire last night at Blackroak Hall. I had been seen fleeing the house. The Earl and his daughter-in-law had both died in the flames. Someone had locked them inside the tower.

Chapter Twenty-eight

FOR TWO DAYS I WAS KEPT IN A VILLAINOUS CELL FURNISHED WITH nothing but a wooden bench chained to the wall and a cot so filthy I refused to sleep on it. Instead, I slept on the hard bench, wrapped in my shawl. The jailer brought his two young sons to see me—they had never seen a deaf woman before—and they amused themselves by playing all sorts of miserable tricks on me. On the second evening, when they came to my cell with my evening meal—a basket of coarse dark bread and sour drink—and found me asleep, the smaller child crawled under my bench and hid while his older brother woke me. When I sat up to eat, believing I was alone in my cell, the child grabbed my ankles, giving me such a terrible fright that I pulled him out by the wrist, turned him over my knee, and gave him a good spanking. The jailer's wife came running, followed by the jailer, and there was a dreadful scene between husband and wife. After that the boys left me alone. I tried to think clearly during those terrible days, but my mind was fogged by fear, and there was no one to counsel me. If only I had kept my wits about me and delivered my letter to William, Harry would know the woman in jail was me and not some wretched seamstress by the name of Truelock. Yet, if my true identity were revealed, it would seem I had a motive for murder. If anyone had seen me on the rooftop that night, there would be more than enough evidence to convict me.

I had been allowed a few personal toiletries in my cell, and I had managed to slip Arabella's journal in among them. I turned to it the first day of my imprisonment, hoping to find some answers. The only light in this gloomy place was received through a high iron-grated window that looked out onto a staircase, and by situating myself beneath it in the early afternoon, I was afforded enough light by which to read.

There was something obsessively secretive about the cramped script. It was not child's play; it had been fashioned to conceal the content of those pages. Exactly when she had begun the journal was difficult to determine, but I suspect it was not long after her arrival at Blackroak Hall. Her earlier efforts at poetry were soon eclipsed by observations and reflections on her new home and family. There was much to complain about—finding the hall in a barbaric state—chipped cups, blunt knives, dirty damp linen, chimneys dangerous and inefficient, the servants old and disobedient— and then, a growing sense of things falling out of order as her mind became increasingly unstable. The frequent references to her past revealed a different story from the one I had been told; there had been no heroic fiancé killed in battle, but a tragic affair involving an older married man. The scandal, as well as Arabella's attempted suicide, had apparently been well publicized. It was clear that she still bore an ardent and impossible love for the man, and I began to believe that her decision to marry and isolate herself in this wilderness may have been a self-imposed exile, a self-inflicted punishment for her own transgressions. She seemed to find something in the Earl that reminded her of her lover, and from the start, the Earl's powerful charisma overwhelmed whatever tender affections she may have felt for Harry. I feel sure Harry was unaware of her true sentiments.

I was spared any account of their honeymoon. At the time the journal opened, it appeared that they no longer shared a bed. Her opinions of Harry and their marriage seemed to vary with her mood—sometimes resentful, sometimes dismissive. As months went by, Harry spent more and more time away from Blackroak Hall.

From the beginning, the Earl exercised his authority over her in a most perverse fashion. At a certain point in the journal, rational observation gave way to disturbing thoughts and images. Sometimes I could not know if the subject of her writing was herself or an invention—but I believe the incident I witnessed between them in the banquet tower had been preceded by other, similar incidents. The Earl had seduced her long before the night of the fire.

He is in love with me. He is smitten with me, she wrote. *I despise him. I shudder at his approach. How can I escape him? He is everywhere and in everything, in my most wicked thoughts and my sinful delights. What part of my being must I rip out to rid myself of him?*

Her friendship with Hannah Platt developed around this time. She wrote of a visit to Hannah to obtain a remedy for a condition, and how Hannah had helped her through troubling times. I recalled my encounter with Hannah on the moors and her response when I queried her about a child. I could not stop myself from wondering if Arabella had indeed been with child, and had gone to Hannah for help. If that was true, I felt certain the child had not been Harry's.

By the second day, I had read as much as I could bear. If I stood accused of murder, I could not possibly make these writings public without utterly destroying Harry. I prayed such a defense would not be necessary.

ON THE MORNING OF THE third day, I looked up to see the jailer swing back the door, and Nelly entered. I jumped to my feet and flew to her. I'd not seen a mirror or a comb in more than two days, and Nelly whipped out a handkerchief and with some urgency tried to clean my face. Then she began tidying up my hair. It was all too much for me, and I began to weep. After a moment, she was able to calm me. Then, with her gaze, she drew my attention to the entrance of the cell.

There stood Harry, his countenance frozen in a stunned look of disbelief. He turned to a thickset, swarthy gentleman at his side, and the two conversed for a long moment. Then the stranger stepped forward to address Nelly.

In finger language, Nelly explained to me that an inquiry was necessary, but that His Lordship was willing to dismiss with a formal hearing and take care of the matter, here and now, if I would agree.

He says he believes in your innocence. Will you answer his questions?

"I will."

What brought you to Blackroak Hall?

"I installed myself at Her Ladyship's request. She wished me to make some dresses for her for the London Season."

Why did you run away?

"I was afraid."

Of what?

"I was afraid of His Lordship, the Earl."

Why were you afraid of him?

"I resisted him over the matter of a dress I was making. He raised his hand to strike me, and I defended myself. I knew him to be a man of violent temper, and I feared for my own safety. That is why I left the house."

The earl's valet said you had stated you would leave in the morning.

"After the incident, I went directly to my room and packed my bags. I went down to have my dinner with the staff, but I was refused anything to eat. I was distraught by the way I had been treated, and I was afraid. I returned to my room and took my belongings and left."

He turned to Harry, and asked him, "Is this sufficient?"

Harry replied that it was.

"You wish her to be released?"

Nelly signed to me his reply. *The fire was an accident. No one is to blame. Least of all this woman. Let her go.*

Then he turned and was gone, without so much as a glance at me.

No sooner had we returned to the Royal Oak than the chambermaid brought up a sealed note. It was from Harry, announcing he would call upon me that evening.

THAT AFTERNOON I BATHED AND changed into a fresh dress. Since I had assumed the identity of a widow, I had nothing but sober black gowns to wear. But Nelly did her best; she scrubbed me raw in the bath, and dusted me with scented powder. She spent an hour plaiting my thick hair, then decided it looked too frivolous so she took it all out, wound it into a soft chignon, and covered it with a net. We had dinner sent up to the room, but I was too nervous to eat anything, and Nelly and Jack shared my portion. Though it was a warm summer evening, we had lighted a few coals in the grate to bring cheer and a warm glow to the otherwise dismal little space. I made sure there was a slate and chalk within reach, then I began to pace the room. After a while I set my watch on the mantelpiece so I would stop looking at it.

Harry arrived under cover of darkness and came unannounced up the back stairs of the inn to my sitting room. He stared at us a little oddly when Jack stepped up to take his hat and gloves. I am quite sure he didn't know what to make of us, a motley band of errant tailors putting on our best face for a great lord.

When Nelly interpreted his first remarks, Harry turned to me with a frown.

"What is this?" he asked with a dismissive gesture toward Nelly.

"You mean the signs we're making?"

"Yes."

"This is a language deaf people speak to one another. I learned it in France. Nelly is my interpreter."

Is it necessary?

"It's much less tiring for me than reading lips."

I had never seen him so aloof and cold in his bearing. Without looking anything like his father, he resembled him in manner. My heart sank at the thought.

You are traveling under a false name.

"Not entirely, Your Lordship. My Christian name is Mary Ann. My mother's name was Truelock."

He dismissed this with a facetious twist of the mouth.

You do realize that if they knew your true identity, they would think you had a reason to set the fire.

"I am guilty of no crime," I said quite forcefully.

His expression softened. *I never once thought you were. But, you must understand, it came as quite a shock—*

"Yes, of course." I added contritely, "I'm so terribly sorry for your loss, Your Lordship."

He nodded stiffly, acknowledging my condolences.

I was appalled to see you so degraded. Were you mistreated in any way?

I shook my head.

He rested an arm on the mantelpiece and stared for a moment into the fire. A cold wave of despair swept over me, and I thought how far we had drifted apart. The only sentiments of which we were capable were these small gestures of civility.

He looked up at me with sad eyes and said, "Why didn't you answer my letters?"

I glanced at Nelly, who repeated his question. Surely I had misunderstood.

"What letters?" I asked, stunned.

"I wrote you four letters while you were in France. I had not one reply."

I answered, "Would those letters perhaps explain why you stole my son from me and led me to believe he had died?"

Color rose swiftly to his face. With his hands clasped tightly behind his back, he drew himself up in a posture of a deeply offended man.

If you never received my letters, then you could not know what I had done, nor why I had done it. I was ignorant of any pain caused to you.

"Ignorant of my pain? Did you think losing my son would cause me no pain?"

I wished only to protect you and our child. I know your character, Veda. You are strong-willed and foolhardy. I see now I was quite right to take the action I did. Good God! Look at what has happened with this ridiculous ruse of yours. What folly!

As Nelly signed his stinging reply, I realized there was a good deal of truth in his reprimand. I was overcome with exhaustion from my ordeal, and more than anything, I needed a sign of reconciliation.

"I was desperate, Harry. I had lost all confidence in you."

And I had lost confidence in you, he retorted sharply. Then he checked himself, and his expression grew quite gentle. *I thought you had cut me off. I had no way of knowing what you were thinking—what you intended. What you felt.*

"Nor did I."

Gradually, as we spoke, as the misunderstandings between us came to light and the anger and confusion melted away, the man I had loved and married slowly emerged. A certain tenderness crept into his eyes, and I cannot deny that it twisted my heart. We trod carefully throughout the next moments, aware that we had both suffered too deeply to abandon our defenses without further understanding, but my sympathy, once encouraged, sought signs of mutual sentiment, and I was not disappointed.

Throughout the exchange, my eyes danced back and forth between Harry's lips and Nelly's hands while I attempted to piece it all together. It seemed that my letter to Harry had made its way into the hands of Lord Hambledon's ruthless lawyer, who had been appointed by the Earl to follow our affairs, the same gentleman who had devised the scheme that forced our annulment. The Earl had little tolerance for this unfortunate episode in his son's life and wished only to be rid of the vain and presumptuous merchant's daughter who had seduced his son. He left the affair in the hands of his lawyer, who kept him only vaguely informed of the proceedings. As I suspected, the heartless reply to my letter announcing that I was expecting a child had been written to me by the lawyer without Harry's knowledge while Harry was on the Continent. One night after Harry's return, when the Earl had won a good deal of money on a race and was bloated with hubris and drunk with wine, he began raving to Harry about his management of the sordid business, going on at great length about his lawyer's clever interception of the letter, and how they had foiled my attempt to create a public scandal. For good measure, he threatened to give his lawyer complete license to do whatever it took to prevent Harry from having anything to do with me or his child.

Harry then wrote to me at my address in Savile Row, proposing a scheme to fool them.

Hearing all this, I was too shaken to remain standing, and I sat myself down on a chair. I raised my eyes to him and said, "So, my father said he had forwarded these letters to me in France?"

"Yes."

"Did he expressly say I had received them?"

"Yes." He nodded. "He did."

"And the reason why I had not replied?"

"Because you did not wish to do so."

I lowered my eyes in confusion and shame.

I turned to Jack who hovered near the door, picking at his nails. "Jack," I said, "I think I'd like a stiff brandy. And I'm sure His Lordship would like one as well."

I drank mine down like medicinal spirits, all the while feeling Harry's eyes on me.

"And my son?" I asked, as I set my empty glass on the tray. "May I see him?"

"Whenever you wish."

I think my voice may have trembled when I next spoke. I said, "Pray, give him back to me, Harry."

My emotions overcame me then. On this occasion, I was not ashamed by my loss of restraint, and I held his gaze firmly so he might understand from my countenance how much I had lost, and how much I hoped to regain.

"I never meant to cause you any suffering," he answered with a look both earnest and tender. "I meant to protect him—and you."

"Then you will tell me where I can find him?"

"I shall take you there."

"Where is he?"

"In Kent."

"Where?" I asked, turning to Nelly to read the spelling. "Kent?"

"Yes. With a cousin of my mother's family."

"I thought, perhaps he was in Edinburgh."

"Edinburgh?"

"I had understood," I said, averting my eyes for a brief moment, knowing he would surmise the source of this rumor, "I had understood you were often in Edinburgh."

"I have had it in my mind for some time to open a school for the deaf in York, and I should like to pattern it off the school in Edinburgh."

"A school for the deaf?"

He nodded.

"A noble pursuit," I replied, with a timid smile.

"I have been inspired by a lady of great virtue and noble character."

I blushed deeply, feeling all the embarrassment of my situation, how I had demeaned myself in his eyes by falling to such trickery.

I said, "It seems to me it would be a great tragedy if, due to a grave misunderstanding, this lady may have conducted herself in a manner which might make you change your opinion of her."

"I am not so cruel."

"And this lady, do you still find her worthy of your esteem?"

"More than ever." He held my eyes with a firm and heartfelt gaze. "More than ever."

I think, had Nelly not been present, our reconciliation might have progressed more quickly that evening, but it was perhaps better that we had time to accustom ourselves to the new situation in which we suddenly found ourselves.

It was foremost in my mind to return to London and to confront my father. Harry had the dolorous task of burying both his father and his wife. That there was hope in our hearts and promises on our lips was enough for now.

When he was taking his leave, Nelly discreetly withdrew, and I offered my hand to him.

"Where shall I write to you?" I asked.

"I shall be at Blackroak for a long time to come. There's a good deal to do. Many changes to make. Many positive changes." He leaned forward and pressed a kiss on my cheek. "There is no one to fear anymore."

He settled his hat on his head and was gone.

HAD IT NOT BEEN FOR Aunt Lavinia, I never would have seen the letters. She herself had lost a good deal of her hearing, and when she wished to follow a conversation, she generally resorted to an ear trumpet. Most of the time I felt she simply ignored what went on around her as she had never been paid much attention, but she had fully comprehended the conversation between Papa and me that morning. When Papa acknowledged that there had been letters from Harry, one or two, he said, and claimed he had sent them on, Aunt Lavinia rose from her chair and left the room without a word. When she returned and offered the small bundle to me, I think she intended it as some small victory of sorts.

"Are these the letters you're looking for, my dear?" she said, gazing up at me with her innocent cow-like eyes.

They were in Harry's handwriting. I turned them over to find the seals had never been broken. When I looked back at her for some explanation, she stated, "He's kept them from you all this time. Hidden in his dressing table." She turned to Papa with a sharp look and wagged a finger at him. "Shame on you, George. It was shameful. You did it out of pure selfishness. You think only of your own happiness. Shame. Shame." Then, as if she had done nothing more remarkable than admonish Cook for too much salt, she sat back down, picked up her needlework, and lost herself in yet another antimacassar.

I stood frozen in shocked silence, my gaze fixed on the letters. I could not bear to see my father humiliated by his own deceit.

"I can't believe this of you," I said without raising my eyes. Then I hurried out of the room.

Harry's letters:

8th July 1865

My darling,

I pray this will find you well and without bitterness and rancor toward me, for only yesterday did I learn that you are expecting our child. It seems you have written to me—how often I do not know, for I have received nothing from you at my club. Apparently Scrimshire can no longer be trusted, and I blame myself for this.

How tragic that such sweet and wonderful news can be twisted into such a weapon. It was my father who revealed it to me, and in the same breath he blamed you for the failure of my own marriage to produce a son and heir. He threatens that should I attempt to see you or the child, his man in the City, Heaton, will trump up some charges with the authorities to make it impossible for you to return to England. You would be banished to foreign soil forever. He is quite capable of taking extraordinary measures, and I believe it wise not to challenge him.

You cannot spend the rest of your life hiding from my father. I have been awake the entire night thinking up a scheme. I am convinced that if my father believes the child did not survive, then he would believe you have no more claims on my heart. My darling, you must not return to London with the child. We must find a way to hide him, and you must agree to separate yourself from him for a while. I am not yet sure how to proceed, but I shall apply all my energies to it, for I fret constantly for your safety. Write to me soon, in care of Collingwood, whose address I note below.

You must know that in relinquishing you, I relinquished my very soul. When I consented to bind myself to another in a loveless and difficult marriage, I was doing so to appease my father's monstrous pride. If you only knew how long I hesitated in declaring my love for you, because I feared drawing you into this difficult family of mine. I had hoped that by keeping you at a distance, I might protect you and still keep you. What an impossible dream it was.

I have struggled to be a dutiful husband, but I know I have failed her miserably. I turn to you often in my thoughts. At what point does an innocent and tender thought turn to betrayal?

I am sending this off to London to your father's address with a plea that he forward it as quickly as possible to you. I cannot leave here at present. By separate letter, I have asked your father to reveal your whereabouts to my lawyer in London so that I may immediately put my plan into action.

16th July 1865

My dearest Veda,

I called on your father yesterday—a most awkward and unpleasant visit. He has assured me he forwarded my last letter and will forward this one as well, but he refuses to reveal your address. Subsequently, I have spent the entire day shouting at Collingwood, who annoys me with his ineptitude. He has suggested a private detective, which seems absurd, but I understand that the situation is delicate, and your privacy must be respected. Esther is the only one I dared to approach, but they are away for the summer. This is a terrible time to try to find anyone as the Season is drawing to an end and offices are closing.

When I told your father I had not received a reply to your letter, he led me to believe that you might not wish to correspond with me. Finally, I revealed that I knew about the child and that I only wished to be reassured that he would be well cared for. I asked what your plans were, thinking perhaps you had decided to settle somewhere under a false identity and raise the child on your own. Your father explained that he had been in touch with a wealthy miller's family in Caen—that they were childless and had agreed to take the baby if you should decide to give it up.

That thought spread terror in my heart. I beg of you, my darling, do not give up our child to a stranger. If you see this child as a blight rather than a blessing, then you must reserve the right to give him up. But you must give him up to his father. I have made arrangements on my own side; he would be taken in by my mother's family and I would be able to see him frequently. I have no intention of concealing my identity from him. He would know I was his father. Moreover, I would, upon my father's death, be able to recognize him as my son.

I must return to Blackroak; there is urgent business I cannot avoid. I would leave this very day for Dover and make the crossing myself if I were at leisure to do so. I cannot escape his damnable shadow. God have mercy on us.

I am putting all my hope in Collingwood, who has promised immediate action.

Again, I send this to your father and pray it makes it into your hands.

Your devoted Harry

12th August 1865

My dear Veda,

I think I have never lived more anxious days in my life than I have these past weeks, waiting for news from Collingwood, or you. I dare not receive any personal correspondence here at Blackroak, and matters concerning the estate have kept me traveling a good deal of the time, so I am constantly out of touch with events.

Collingwood and his team have been quite diligent in their research. He has gone off to Caen with what he believes to be sufficient information to find you. I don't know what to make of your silence. I know you to be strong-willed, but I can't imagine you would intentionally refuse me a father's rights.

As always,

Harry

The next letter was sent to the address at Sassetôt. It must have arrived within days after I had departed. It was then forwarded back to Papa.

9th September 1865

My darling,

I am sitting here at my desk, watching our son sleep in a little cot I had brought into the room so that I may gaze upon him at every pause of the pen. He is robust and healthy and made the journey back home with little fussing, I am told.

I am continually perplexed by your silence. Should I receive no reply to this, I can only assume that you wish to decline all further association with me and relinquish your son to my safekeeping. If that is what you wish, I shall honor it.

Yours,
Harry

I had hoped and prayed that these letters would clear Harry of any misconduct, but they did not. It seemed that he had remained willfully ignorant of how his scheme had played out and how it had driven me to the point of utter despair. Once Collingwood had found me, I could have been warned. I could have been persuaded. Instead, Harry had seen fit to protect his own rights at the expense of mine. It was an arrogant act, and I could not bear to see Harry in this light.

Nor could I forget how they had cruelly taken advantage of my deafness. They had fooled me because I had not been able to hear my infant's cries.

The letter I wrote to him that evening was tempered with reserve and a strong dose of my own family pride.

12th July 1867

My dearest Harry,

I arrived home safely yesterday evening, and I write you this having just read the letters you wrote to me. My father had kept them, as we had surmised.

Curiously, the seals had never been broken. His sense of decency would not allow him to pry into my personal affairs in such a coarse manner. I am sure that if he had dared to read what you had written, had he been aware of the drama unfolding, he would have behaved in a manner befitting a gentleman. He felt it was his fatherly duty to protect me from any more pain and wished only to keep you out of my life and his. It is quite sad, is it not, the damage we do to the ones we love, believing we have their interests at heart?

I still suffer from a deep sense of having been betrayed. Even knowing what I know, the pain sits like a dull sediment at the bottom of my heart.

I pray you are able to endure your own loss with courage and fortitude.

After tomorrow, I shall be at Esther and Ned's home in Holland Park. I leave it in your hands to advise me as to my next steps. I should like to see my son as soon as your situation permits. He will be two years old on 19th of August. I should like him to celebrate his birthday with his mother.

Affectionately yours,
Veda

I defended my father's actions to Harry because I was too proud to admit how deeply he had wounded me. I knew my father loved me more than he could ever say, and I knew the reasons for his deception, but it was not in his nature to admit to wrongdoing, and I could not forgive him without some sign of remorse. I had Lucy bring my dinner to my room, and I sent him a note saying that I would depart the next day for Esther's. I did not say how long I would be gone.

Esther proved to be my rock that summer. Her home in Holland Park was a sanctuary of light and beauty, with its pretty flowered wallpaper and daisies in blue and white vases. Mornings were pleasantly humdrum, Ned drinking coffee behind his newspaper, the children toddling around, Esther chatting away about I don't know what. Everything was refreshingly chaotic, and everyone seemed quite content to live that way. I spent a good deal of time looking over Esther's new paintings and thought her portraits of her children her best work ever. Ned, too, was in fine form, and I was much impressed by a deliciously graceful odalisque he had nearly completed.

It was a great relief to be able to dress in colorful gowns once again and assume my own identity. I had lived for too long within dark walls and seen too many dark things.

I revealed to Esther everything that had happened that awful night of the fire. I had sent Nelly back home to Suffolk for a much-needed holiday, and Esther was reduced to writing on slates and me to reading lips. But she proved to be my ever loyal friend and counselor, and listened and tried to understand.

She was as intrigued as I was with Arabella's journal. One morning as she sat at the table in her drawing room studying the heavily inked pages through a magnifying glass, she picked up the slate and wrote: *It is a stunted piece of work, a failed creation. As if all the energy of her imagination had been confined to this minuscule volume.*

Then she looked up at me and said, "Your letters sounded as if you had grown fond of her."

I hesitated before replying. "Indeed, as one is fond of a reflection of oneself. But the reflection is in every way an opposite of the self, is it not? Perhaps I saw what I might have become without my craft to give direction to my life. What would you be without your art? As much as you adore your children, would you be content to be defined only by your domestic role? For some women, it is sufficient. I don't think it was sufficient for her. She had a sense of a calling, but she did not believe her talents equal to it. I look at this book, these cramped words on these pages, and I think that if she been able to break out beyond these confines, perhaps she would have borne something worthwhile."

Esther nodded vigorously. "Yes. Quite. All her anxieties condensed into this."

"She suffered from weak nerves, but she was not shallow-minded, Esther."

"But to take her own life like that! Oh, Vevey, imagine!"

"I think she was exacting justice for all of them. For Harry's mother and his sister, as well as herself." There flashed before my eyes memories of what I had seen, and my own brief encounter with the Earl. "He was a horrid man," I said, shaking my head. "Oh, such a horrid man."

"Will you tell Harry?"

"Who would believe such things of his own father? Unless he saw it with his very eyes. And what if he did believe me? Could such a proud man accept that I knew these things about his family?" I shook my head. "I fear the knowledge would destroy us."

"So you will keep silent?"

After a long pause, I said, "Oh, Tiggy, what do we do when there is no one to save us?"

"We save ourselves."

"And if we are denied even that?"

Suddenly, with a decisive gesture, Esther closed the journal and took me by the hand.

"Enough. We need to get out. We shall take a drive on Rotten Row. When is the last time you took a drive on Rotten Row? Go and change into something magnificent. Hurry!"

And so we did. We dressed in smart summer dresses and went for a drive in the Park. It was a splendid summer day at the end of the Season, the time when romance is at its peak. All of society was out, and the lanes were crowded with stylish carriages full of eligible young ladies up from the country to see and be seen. They peeked out demurely from behind their lace-fringed parasols at the gentlemen mounted on sleek hunters, their eyes as bright as the colored ribbons tied under their chins. At last, I had come home.

The next afternoon Esther and I shopped for the children, and I enjoyed the pleasure of buying for my little boy. We took the carriage around to Regent Street where a new draper with enormous footage stocked every cloth under the sun. I had never made for children, and I was giddy with excitement as I browsed through the patterns and fashion plates. My son would still be in little dresses, still very much a baby. He would still have his soft baby curls and cherub's mouth. I had lost two years of his life, but I would make it up.

I came home that day with all sorts of delights; there were shoes and caps and bonnets, there was flannel for his layette, and nainsook and piqué and muslin, and yards and yards of lace and ribbon for trimming. I set to work that very afternoon making for my boy.

Harry had been faithful in his correspondence, but his letters were restrained; he no longer opened his heart to me as he had in the past. We exchanged news of a practical nature. We had agreed to ride together by carriage to Kent, where Harry had taken our son to be raised by his mother's cousin, Mrs. Constance Mulhouse, a retiring woman of good breeding. I was unsure as to how I should conduct myself toward Harry or my son. On the night before we were to leave, I was in a terrible state of nerves.

"I still can't forgive him, Esther," I said. We sat together on my bed, both of us in our nightdresses. "It was despicable."

"Vevey, it seems his intentions were honorable. And your father is every bit as much to blame."

"But I don't understand. That man Collingwood—once he found where I was living, why did he not call on me? Why did he not come to the door and explain Harry's plan?"

"Would you have believed him? This man you had never seen before, who comes and tells you he has to take your baby away for its own safety—when you haven't heard from Harry in a year—are you likely to put your faith in this man? With all the terrible things his father did, do you think you wouldn't have been just a little suspicious? Would you have honestly turned your child over to him?"

She was right. I could not deny it. I sighed heavily and pulled my knees up under my chin. Esther brushed a lock of hair back out of my face.

"Yes," she said, "it was cruel, but not unreasonable under the circumstances. Given what he knew, and the very real danger to your child, he was doing what he thought best."

"It was his arrogance."

"Do you still love him?"

I hesitated, and then nodded.

"Knowing how he loved you and fought for your marriage in the face of such awful opposition, how can you doubt his devotion to you?"

I had to struggle to read the words on her lips, for my eyes were filling with tears. I thrust the slate under her nose.

"Please, Tiggy, I can't read you anymore. I'm too tired."

She scrawled on the slate: *This poor wretched woman, Miss Erskine—has unwittingly restored your hope—only real obstacle to your happiness is gone— gone up in flames. Don't throw up more obstacles. Give him the forgiveness he needs. Strive for complicity.*

I WORE A ROBIN'S EGG blue pelisse with low-waisted fitted jacket and a black casquette with a single delicate aigrette. I saw at once that Harry approved. Even while he exchanged greetings with Ned, he kept glancing back at me, as if he couldn't quite believe his eyes. Cranleigh House was but a few hours south of London, and it was a fine day for a drive. I had my slate in my lap, as usual, ready to hand to him should he wish to speak to me, but silence worked to our advantage that morning. I think, had we attempted to explain ourselves, we might have fallen into a muddle of words and meaning, when all we needed was the opportunity to be together freely and openly. I don't know what went through his thoughts that morning, but after we had been on the road for a while, he pulled the book I was reading out of my hands and unbuttoned my gloves. The touch of his skin as he pressed his warm hand into mine brought back intimate memories that had been sealed off for years. I knew then, that whatever pain he had caused me, however faulty had been his judgment, my heart was as open now as it had ever been. Perhaps it was too soon to speak of his intentions, but he was declaring them in a way I understood.

I shall never forget how he wrapped my hand around his arm as he walked me up the steps of Cranleigh House and into the front hall where Mrs. Mulhouse waited to greet us. He gave me the courage I needed to make it through this difficult moment when I was so unsure of myself. She was a reserved woman, and much older than Harry's mother would have been, but she must have known all about us, because she treated me with enormous courtesy. I followed very little of their conversation; I was looking around for Charles Albert.

I was expecting him to appear at some moment, led in by a nanny, but I spied him peering out from behind the trailing leaves of a fern on a plant stand near a window. I couldn't help smiling. I was ignorant of the conversation around me. I could not know if they were urging him to show himself or not, but eventually, still gripping a fern leaf, he toddled forward. He was a beautiful little boy, with pale curls and wide eyes, and he truly took my breath away. Finally, I approached him, and looked down into his face.

Hoping my voice was clear, and that I was not speaking too loudly, I said, "Hello there. You must be Charles."

With a sly glance at his father, he raised his little hand and saluted me, then pressed his little thumb to his chin and splayed his fingers.

He had just signed to me. He had said, *Hello, mother.*

I signed back, *Hello, son,* and he burst into a smile.

Beaming with delight at this secret and magical language, he patted his chest, then made a sweeping gesture from his eyes toward me.

I am glad to see you.

I am glad to see you, I signed back.

That was enough. He ran to his father, and Harry swooped him up in his arms, and any last clinging doubts about Harry faded forever with that gesture.

To my relief, Mrs. Mulhouse went off to see Cook about lunch plans, and we took a walk around the grounds. Just Harry and I and our son. I could not take my eyes off my little boy. He would grin and hide his face in Harry's shoulder, then peek around at me again. Nelly had taught him the signs, I learned. Harry had secretly brought her down to Cranleigh two weeks ago to teach him.

I found Cranleigh to be a charming and comfortable home. While we were walking around the gardens, admiring the profusion of roses in full bloom and the gentle rolling fields of green, Harry asked me if I might be inclined to live nearby.

I said I would.

⚙

HARRY VOWED HE WOULD MAKE sweeping changes in Blackroak's staff, and he was true to his word, but I could never bring myself to return there. The charred tower was demolished, and Harry commissioned a chapel to be built with the stones, fulfilling at long last his mother's fervent wish. Even when the chapel was completed and the Bishop of York came to bless it, I could not bring myself to attend the services. I always found excuses, but I never told him the truth. I never told him what I had witnessed that night. It was my burden, solely, to bear.

Harry has never asked me what I experienced during my weeks in Blackroak Hall, nor do we ever speak of the tragic events that took place that horrible night. He may have his suspicions, but he seems quite content to live with the unknown. We all learn to be deaf to certain things; we live within walls of silence, and rely upon conjecture, and guess at the truth.

Charles Albert has inherited his father's grace and charm, his bright confidence and effervescent wit. And he now has a sister, a raven-haired little beauty named Alice, who has captivated her father's heart.

We built a country house not far from Cranleigh where Harry's maternal family resides; they have received me warmly, as his mother once did. London society has recovered from the scandal of our marriage, and our social calendar is fuller than we should like. Harry says our acceptability is due in good part to my immense dignity and grand bearing, that I have a natural condescension that equals that of any highborn lady. I believe it is because of the tremendous respect Harry commands. He is able at last to focus his energies on worthy causes and has become a formidable MP at the service of justice and equality.

Harry insisted on a speedy reconciliation with my father, and he was instrumental in healing the breach in our little family. He took it upon himself to meet with Papa on several occasions without me and coaxed from him a sincere apology—a letter that brought tears to my eyes. My father and Harry get along quite well. Indeed, Harry enjoys dropping by Grenfell's on an afternoon for a little hock and one of my father's fine cigars. Papa would never presume to gain socially from my marriage, but Grenfell's has certainly profitted from it. My father is now tailor to the Prince of Wales.

On the second floor of our house in Kent, a spacious corner room overlooking the park has been set aside for my private use. Out of politeness, we never call it my workshop; we refer to it merely as my dressing room. My son, Charles, is allowed to play up here while I sew, much to Nanny's horror. And Harry comes up here for his fittings. Of course, he would never reveal the name of his tailor to anyone, although on occasion, over brandy and cigars, attempts have been made to loosen his tongue. Everyone assumes it is my father. That's perfectly all right by me.